# DEGENERATIVE REALISM

LITERATURE NOW

LITERATURE NOW

Matthew Hart, David James, and Rebecca L. Walkowitz, Series Editors

Literature Now offers a distinct vision of late-twentieth- and early-twenty-first-century literary culture. Addressing contemporary literature and the ways we understand its meaning, the series includes books that are comparative and transnational in scope as well as those that focus on national and regional literary cultures.

# Degenerative Realism

## NOVEL AND NATION IN
## TWENTY-FIRST-CENTURY FRANCE

### Christy Wampole

Columbia University Press
*New York*

Columbia University Press
*Publishers Since 1893*
New York    Chichester, West Sussex
cup.columbia.edu
Copyright © 2020 Columbia University Press
All rights reserved

Library of Congress Cataloging-in-Publication Data
Names: Wampole, Christy, 1977– author.
Title: Degenerative realism : novel and nation in
twenty-first-century France / Christy Wampole.
Description: New York : Columbia University Press, 2020. |
Series: Literature now | Includes bibliographical references and index.
Identifiers: LCCN 2019058751 (print) | LCCN 2019058752 (ebook) |
ISBN 9780231185165 (hardcover) | ISBN 9780231185172 (paperback) |
ISBN 9780231546034 (ebook)
Subjects: LCSH: French fiction—21st century—History and criticism. |
Literature and society—France—History—21st century. | Realism in literature. |
Dystopias in literature. | Despair in literature.
Classification: LCC PQ683 .W36 2020 (print) | LCC PQ683 (ebook) |
DDC 843/.9209355—dc23
LC record available at https://lccn.loc.gov/2019058751
LC ebook record available at https://lccn.loc.gov/2019058752

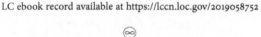

Columbia University Press books are printed on permanent and durable acid-free paper.
Printed in the United States of America

Cover image: Peter Lippmann, *Nobel Rot 8*. © Peter Lippmann
Cover design: Chang Jae Lee

*For Corey*

A civilization begins to decline the moment Life becomes its sole obsession.

—E. M. CIORAN, *A SHORT HISTORY OF DECAY*

# CONTENTS

# ACKNOWLEDGMENTS

I'd like to thank everyone in the Department of French and Italian at Princeton for their boundless support as I wrote this book, particularly Tom Trezise, Effie Rentzou, Göran Blix, André Benhaïm, and Florent Masse. It is a rare gift to be surrounded by such supportive colleagues, and for that, I'd like to thank David Bellos, Anna Cellinese, Flora Champy, Katie Chenoweth, Daniele De Feo, Elisa Dossena, Pietro Frassica, Johnny Laforêt, Simone Marchesi, Gaetana Marrone-Puglia, Nick Nesbitt, Murielle Perrier, Raphaël Piguet, Fanny Raineau, Christine Sagnier, Volker Schröder, Sara Teardo, and Carole Trévise. Our friends on the administrative staff create the conditions for our success at writing and teaching and make the office an exceedingly pleasant place to work. For that, a heartfelt thanks to Kelly Eggers, Sena Hill, Charles Leonardi, Leslie Savadge, and Kathy Varra. I also wanted to thank Kathleen Allen and wish her luck and happiness in her retirement, despite my selfishness in wanting her to stay. My gratitude also goes to the undergraduate and graduate students in our department and to my advisees from our department and other departments and institutions as well. There is too little space here to thank all of my friends at Princeton who've supported me since my arrival in 2011, but I wanted to express my appreciation to Jill Dolan, Eric Gregory, Kathy Crown, Tom Hare, Eileen Reeves, Brigid Doherty, Joe Stephens, Jeff Dolven, Brooke Holmes, and Mary Harper and to the Humanities Council, the Program in Journalism, the Program in European Cultural Studies, the Behrman Undergraduate Society of Fellows, the Interdisciplinary Doctoral Program in the Humanities, and the Department of Comparative Literature for placing their trust in me toward our shared project of promoting the humanities at the university and beyond.

I wanted to thank Alison James (University of Chicago) and Zakir Paul (NYU) for sharing their fascinating research on our "Senses of Realism" panel at the Twentieth- and Twenty-First-Century French and Francophone Studies conference at Indiana University, Bloomington, in 2017. And a special thanks to Laure Astourian (Bentley University), Michael Marder (University of the Basque Country), Bruno Perreau (MIT), Stephanie Posthumus (McGill), and Annabel Kim (Harvard) for accepting my invitation to present their work to our students and colleagues. Also, a special thanks to the many colleagues I've gotten to know well at other universities, particularly Penn, NYU, Duke, Brandeis, the University of Minnesota, and Yale, and to everyone in the Division of Literatures, Cultures, and Languages at my alma mater, Stanford, for the lasting influence they've had on my thinking. I want to thank all of my teachers from the University of North Texas and Middlebury College as well. Without their inspiration and wisdom, I never would have pursued a career as a humanities professor.

I am particularly grateful to the students in two seminars I taught on different aspects of my book project. In the first seminar, taught in fall 2017 and titled Realism and (Post-)Truth, the students brought energy and insight to all of our discussions. A warm thanks to Zehra Ahmed, Elisabeth Bloom, Kate Clairmont, Alex Dantzlerward, Saadia El Karfi, Sarah Kislingbury, Jenna Liuzzi, Jason Molesky, Ingrid Norton, Molly O'Brien, Marie Sanazaro, and Jackson Smith. I also wanted to thank my colleagues Peter Brooks and Hal Foster for agreeing to visit and share their research on realism with our class.

The second seminar, taught in fall 2018, was titled Fear and France, and I appreciated our lively exchanges and fascinating presentations and final projects from the students in the course. Thank you to Akrish Adhikari, Kaveh Badrei, Cole Campbell, Matthieu Dutil, Luke Johnson, Anna Jurew, Ananya Malhotra, Matt Miller, Jake Millman, Jacqueline Pan, Gabriela Pitten, Maddie Pollack, Camille Price, Jillian Quigley, Christopher Ratsimbazafy–Da Silva, Charlotte Reynders, Adnan Sachee, Andrew

Scott, Annabelle Tseng, and Caleb Visser. I would also like to thank Lauren Johnston and Princeton's Small Unmanned Aircraft Systems Management Team for the drone demonstration at Sexton Field, which was organized for us after we read Grégoire Chamayou's *Théorie du drone* (2013) and discussed comparative drone ethics in France, the European Union, and the United States. This experience helped shape my thinking about technological anxiety and its many manifestations in the contemporary French novel.

This book would not exist without Philip Leventhal at Columbia University Press, who enthusiastically took on my project and was extremely encouraging through the entire process, from proposal to copyediting. Thank you, Philip, for your responsiveness, thoroughness, and the many forms of support you offered as the book took shape. I'd also like to express my gratitude to the editors of the Literature Now series, Rebecca Walkowitz, Matthew Hart, and David James, for the keen attention and care with which they handled my manuscript, and to the anonymous readers who backed the project from the beginning and offered indispensable feedback to help sharpen the book's claims. When I had doubts, my mentor Robert Pogue Harrison muted them and convinced me of the relevance of the project, always at the moment when I most needed reassurance. He has never given me one bad piece of advice. A warm thanks also goes to Saadia El Karfi for her skillful translations of the French to English.

My friends and family provided the necessary moral support to help me trudge through the grim subject matter out of which this book emerged. I am grateful to all of them: my family in Texas, Germany, and France and my dear friends strewn across the country, especially those I cherish most, Beth and Karen. The biggest token of gratitude and love goes naturally to Flo, who has stayed with me through it all and who brightens everything he touches.

And a final thanks to the thousands of strangers who have taken the time to reach out from across the world to say that something I've written resonated with them. These conversations with people I'll probably never meet give me the energy and will to keep writing and renew my sometimes weakened faith in humanity. The fact that common ground can be found between people of such different backgrounds, geographies, ages, and political sympathies suggests that narratives of civilizational decay are mostly fiction.

DEGENERATIVE REALISM

# WHAT IS DEGENERATIVE REALISM?

Something in this country was rotting little by little. A slow decomposition.

—OLIVIER ADAM, *LES LISIÈRES*

Realism has, at various times and in various guises, functioned as a tool for describing and diagnosing the social ills of an era, all the while veiling its status as representation. With its focus on the now, realism has often sought to pinpoint what is contemptuous in the contemporary. Because realism shows in great detail the unsightly blemishes and banalities of everyday life, it has been called "the cult of the ugly"[1] and came to be associated with a heightened societal consciousness that privileged truth over beauty. Since the nineteenth century, the realist has been a revelationist whose task was to exhibit what some would rather not see. Despite the crudeness of the realities it presents, realism has nonetheless comforted readers through its mimetic promise, on which they have come to rely.

But what happens to the realist novel in a post-truth age marked by the crumbling of certain practices and institutions that had held up over centuries? What happens when realism loses its ability to reassure? And what is the connection between a wilting sense of reality and a wilting nation?

Some contemporary novelists in France have begun to ask the question: What is real? They want to understand the correlation between a loss of the real and the fears that have seized the collective consciousness: cultural entropy, genetic depletion, national suicide. The social body is ailing, they tell us, and the means used historically for taking account of its health—the novel is one—are in a state of deterioration as well. Perhaps for the first time in the history of French literature, a certain variety of realism has become the key mode through which anxieties about social and political discontent take shape primarily as a questioning of the nature of the real. I call this *degenerative realism.*

Degenerative realism is a type of literary realism marked in both content and form by a poetics of cultural and biological degradation. Its themes are clear: Relying on a logic of decline, the novels I analyze tell of a *collective worsening of life in the contemporary moment.* In formal terms, as I will show, the mimetic techniques used historically by realist writers to create verisimilar worlds begin to break down in the hands of practitioners of degenerative realism. The narrative neatness of earlier realist novels is supplanted by ambivalent deviations from these formulaic conventions. Finally, the novels are suffused with a kind of nineteenth-century ectoplasm, having failed to exorcise the sociologism, Darwinism, Decadence, and positivism of that period. They are also maximalist, like earlier realist novels, in this case like decaying mansions onto which the architect helplessly adds wing after anarchic wing. In the twenty-first century, this important strand of French literary realism has become simultaneously more global and more biopolitical, and many of its characters voice the kinds of reactionary opinions ascendant in contemporary European politics. Degenerative realism has renewed the earlier interest among France's first realist writers in the social sciences and has, on a formal level, embraced once more the *roman à thèse* in its conservative iteration, whose most famous French proponents include Paul Bourget, Maurice Barrès, and Drieu La Rochelle, authors of what Susan Suleiman has called "authoritarian fictions." However, whereas the characters or narrators of the new degenerative fictions make polemical assertions throughout the narratives, the underlying theses of the novels are impossible to discern. The rhetorical certainty and the force of conviction present in earlier *romans à thèse* have vanished. From a formal perspective, these new novels seek to create an *effet d'immédiat,* an immediacy effect, in lieu of the Barthesian reality effect (*effet de réel*). This is achieved by adopting the nervous urgency and hyperbolism of online journalism and social media, to constitute what I call real-time realism. And from a thematic perspective, in many of the most-read contemporary realist novels, a new vitalism and, at times, survivalism manifests itself in the insistence on the struggle of France to survive against forces that threaten it. The protagonists of these fictions are often symbolic proxies for France, under cultural, economic, and demographic assault.

In my last book, *Rootedness: The Ramifications of a Metaphor* (2016), I explored instances in which the metaphor of rootedness was taken literally and used to justify social behavior and political action. To believe oneself to be literally rooted to a plot of land has had sweeping implications, particularly in the modern era, when place and identity have become increasingly troubled by globalization. In a sense, *Degenerative Realism* continues the work I began there, exploring the ways that literature and rhetorical figures like the metaphor respond to political realities but also shape them. But because *Rootedness* featured the theme of metaphor literalization so prominently, I will not repeat those claims here, opting instead for a more subtle analysis of the metaphor of degeneration. I suspect the authors rely so heavily on this metaphor in part for its organicity and its charged history in late-nineteenth- and early-twentieth-century Europe, a history that, as I will argue, has an intimate connection with the novel. Our authors take culture and its yield as biotic objects: in order for something to die, it must have first been alive. In his book *Body and Will* (1884), Henry Maudsley defines degeneration this way:

[Degeneration] means literally an *unkinding*, the undoing of a *kind*, and in this sense was first used to express the change of kind without regard to whether the change was to perfect or to degrade; but it is now used exclusively to denote a change from a higher to a lower kind, that is to say, from a more complex to a less complex organisation; it is a process of *dissolution*, the opposite of that process of *involution* which is pre-essential to evolution.[2]

The earlier Latin root *degenerare* meant "to depart from one's kind, to fall from ancestral quality,"[3] originally in a physical sense but later in a moral sense as well. In the novels I describe throughout this book, the processes of biological degradation are projected onto nonbiological phenomena like cultural artifacts, relationships, economies, nations, and even reality. As I will show, several mutually reinforcing metaphors are used interchangeably with degeneration: decay, decline, decadence, disintegration, *déchéance*.

Degenerative realism is not a literary school or movement but rather a set of patterns that connect disparate authors and seem to offer an outlet for the anxieties of the times. There are three primary tendencies in the novels that I focus on in this book. First, their subject matter is the disintegration of contemporary France, Europe, or the West, what Aristide Leucate has called "*le grand épuisement* [exhaustion] *français et européen*."[4] Though many may know Oswald Spengler's *The Decline of the West* (*Der Untergang des Abendlandes*), whose first volume appeared in 1918, as the definitive companion to European decay,[5] the practice of *déclinologie* has an earlier, perhaps richer history in France, which seems particularly skilled at aestheticizing its own demise. The perceived threats described in these books are the same ones that have fueled reactionaries in France: demographic eschatology; encroaching forces such as American capitalism, radical Islam, and feminism; and the country's loss of a national identity as it is passively absorbed into the European Union. Second, the novels tend to thematize the loss of the real as they explore a "reality" contaminated by conspiracy theories, fake news, bad information, and new or renewed mysticisms that seek to undo the legacy of the Enlightenment. Finally, the novels seem at first glance to be written in the realist mode—that is, they use mimetic techniques to replicate the actual world within a fictional framework—but this realism degenerates in a variety of ways throughout the course of the narrative, with sudden departures into the mode of science fiction or dystopian horror, or with an abrupt introduction of implausible or hyperbolic elements into the story. These departures disrupt readerly expectations by breaking the implied mimetic contract between realist author and reader. The contemporary French novel has reinforced its status as an expressive platform for collective cultural exhaustion, a role not unfamiliar to it throughout the centuries. What distinguishes this latest iteration is that it arrives in an age in which reality and truth have become negotiable. These novelists seem to have lost faith in the power of realism to register the world.

In *Degenerative Realism*, I argue that these patterns are symptomatic of a double disillusionment with both the novel and the nation. Before the turn of the millennium, novelists whose work came to be called postmodern were equally disillusioned, but they responded with irony and self-reflexivity, iconoclastically dismantling literary conventions and toying with established forms. Now, with postmodernism's amusements having lost their luster, realism has reasserted itself as the default literary mode—safe, sure, time-tested, and endorsed by the forefathers. However, to respond to the anxieties particular to this new millennium, its advocates have made a few necessary adjustments. These authors are acutely aware of how fiction and truth now coexist uneasily and have recognized the aesthetic potential in this circumstance. The paradox inherent in realism— that this kind of fiction yearns toward reality but can never achieve it given its status as fiction[6]—makes it an ideal mode through which to represent our current moment, marked by new forms of high-velocity deception: wildfire-quick falsehoods spread via social media, the web of lies that is the internet, and more sophisticated types of capitalist duplicity and political trickery whose transmission has been accelerated by new media possibilities. The realism I'll describe here is so fast, it sometimes gets ahead of itself.

While *Degenerative Realism* offers extensive examples of the turn I've described, it is by no means the dominant literary mode in readerly and scholarly circles. On the contrary, this type of literature seems to recognize the vulnerability and minority of its ideas. When all is said and done, one account of French literature at the dawn of the twenty-first century will have narrated various attempts at an opening-up of once-inaccessible literary institutions; a widening of the canon; an effort at identity-based inclusivity; a persistent focus in scholarly studies on both sides of the Atlantic on *Francophonie*, postcoloniality, and righting the wrongs of France's imperial tentacularity; and an expansion of what counts as relevant and legitimate in the field of literature. For example, the Académie française has tried to increase the number of women and people of color in its ranks,[7] and the juries of prestigious literary prizes have made their decisions more and more frequently in the same spirit.[8] Much contemporary scholarship in postwar French studies tends to focus on postcoloniality, identity politics, marginal writers, women writers, queerness, Francophone literatures, and various forms of alterity, topics that appeal especially to academic audiences.[9] This pattern evinces an acknowledgment and even a welcoming of permanent global connectivity and various forms of social leveling and recalibration that characterize the new millennium so far. The story of this process will be, I believe, the dominant appraisal of French literary history in the first two decades of this century. However, this is not the story I will tell in this book. Instead, I will tell a concurrent but bleaker tale, no less true than the one just described. It is a story of the discontents of this new age.

By and large, the protagonists in these novels are not among the aforementioned beneficiaries of a politics of inclusion, and their cynicism regarding what they see as a spurious flipping of values is palpable throughout the narratives.[10] The reader will notice that the novels presented in *Degenerative Realism* are written almost exclusively by white men.[11] I acknowledge this fact without extrapolating anything from it, a task I will leave to readers if they see something meaningful in this pattern. I will also refrain from commenting on the political orientations of the authors at hand, who, when considered as an aggregate, do not fit neatly into any political camp. Some have shown allegiance to the Right, to the Left, or to no side in particular. In my view, the more interesting question is how contemporary political life in France is portrayed through their fictions. To put it plainly, the reactionary spirit governs these worlds, where pluralism is an abomination, identity politics abhorrent, and political correctness a blow to freedom. These are not feel-good books.[12] France cannot be made great again, they seem to conclude. In fact, they oblige us to suffer along with those who perceive themselves as losers in the twenty-first century. The authors' request that empathy be granted to their ignoble characters feels something like a dare. It is admittedly difficult to respond empathically and accept "reality" as it is presented to us in its degenerated form, but I hope readers will share my conviction that despite the sheer ugliness these novels deliver, their patterns are too conspicuous and consistent to ignore. Understanding what motivates degenerative realism will help us decipher some of the anxieties that beleaguer France in the first decades of this new millennium. Furthermore, I hope that in reading along, other novels marked by degenerative realist features will come to readers' minds, even if I was not able to include all of them here. Because degenerative realism is a mode and not a school or movement, I refer to the authors here as practitioners of degenerative realism, not as degenerative realists. It is a subtle difference meant to discourage a reductive singling out of a list of writers who neatly fit under the rubric. As I will show, writers move in and out of this mode, from book to book or even within one novel. To tack an inflexible label on literary works of great complexity would be an oversimplification.

Regarding periodization, the emergence of degenerative realism coincides roughly with two reality-shaking occurrences: the arrival of the internet and the 9/11 attacks. As I will show, France's Minitel played an early role in reconfiguring the public's assumptions about identity, space, communication, and reality, but the internet's arrival permanently reshaped them. And in reading degenerative realist texts, it is evident that the millennium did not begin on January 1, 2000; it began on September 11, 2001, in an era of already heightened *catastrophisme*.[13] While perceptions of Islam in France were quite different from those common in the United States before the attacks—largely because of France's colonial and immigration history, its strong secular tradition, the Franco-Algerian War and its fallout, and the fierce conflicts that erupted in the space of the *banlieue* throughout the 1990s and into the 2000s—the attacks on U.S. soil permanently altered the image of Islam worldwide and reshaped reality. The role of 9/11 and the rise of radical Islam cannot be overstated in the emergence of the new patterns in French realism I describe throughout this book. The *unreality* of that event is worked through in contemporary French fiction, for example, in Beigbeder's "hyperrealist novel" *Windows on the World* (2003), which shows how the fall of the Twin Towers shook the world's "confidence in the supremacy of reality over fiction."[14] Antoine Bello's *Les Éclaireurs* (2009), the second in a trilogy of novels about a clandestine network called le Consortium de falsification du réel (CFR), which uses its vast resources to disseminate fabricated facts beginning before the internet, focuses on 9/11 and how this event was used to justify an unjust war with Iraq. Faked dossiers— one might say fictionalized dossiers—played a role in the rise of al-Qaeda and in the selling of the war to the American public and to allies of the United States. The inevitable faceoff between Islam and the West rests at the heart of this narrative, and the protagonist even mentions Gilles Kepel, one of the primary French theorists of this clash. As the looped images of the Twin Towers' collapse repeat on the television, the narrator remains "hypnotized by these silent images of unprecedented force, thinking despite [himself] that no scriptwriter could have imagined them."[15] Other novels, such as Michel Houellebecq's *Submission* (2015) or Yann Moix's *Partouz* (2004), focus on the consequences of Islam's ascent. The world is being overrun by Muslims, and the West has become too weak, yielding, and feminine: this is the logic of the new complicated reactionism framed by the novels. It would be reductive to say that these realist fictions are simple manifestations of white, Western, male anxiety, although one must acknowledge that the history of realism in France was always made and marked by such anxiety, from the class-based apprehensions of Zola and Hugo to Barrès's fear of intellectuals, city dwellers, and Jews, among countless other examples. The pathological masculinity that forms the core of many of these new narratives sets itself up as the inverted image of another form of pathological masculinity, namely, Islamist terror.[16]

If the preceding set of concerns contains obvious American signifiers—9/11, alternative facts, fake news, political correctness[17]—it is because what happens in the United States doesn't stay in the United States. Neoliberal ventures, the war on terror, and digital living may be of complicated American provenance but are by no means contained strictly within its national borders. These and other recent global developments have transfigured French literature in remarkable ways, fraying the fabric of the real. The novels I analyze seem to share the conviction that the degeneration of reality began in the United States.[18] The long history of anti-American sentiment in France is well documented,[19] and the authors presented here carry on this tradition, pointing out (oftentimes rightly) the role of America in the collapse of the real.

Degenerative realism is an anxious and helpless mode. Such literature is sensitive to a society whose changes outpace one's ability to make sense of them. In such circumstances, one can less easily discern the difference between fact and fiction, which places the novel in a curious epistemological position.

## SOMETHING IN THE AIR

La vérité, c'est qu'en France, il n'y a pas de vérité.

—EMMANUEL BERL, *LA FRANCE IRRÉELLE*

As I was writing this book, two literary events took place, both of which vindicated my project and highlighted the relevance of my claims. The first occurred in 2017, on an early October night in the council chamber of the Hôtel de Ville in Paris, when the membrane that separates fiction from reality was put on trial. As part of the annual Nuit Blanche night of philosophy, the event titled "Le Procès de la fiction" and organized by Aliocha Imhoff and Kantuta Quirós consisted of a mock trial during which participants litigated the boundaries between fiction and fact as they relate to the novel. The usual juridical dramatis personae were present: plaintiff, defendant, lawyers, witnesses, judges, and several well-known writers participated in the litigation, including Laurent Binet, Maylis de Kerangal, and Yannick Haenel,[20] along with a large troupe of literary scholars, philosophers, sociologists, and historians. The trial lasted seven hours, with each side forcefully making its case from seven o'clock in the evening until two in the morning. In "closed" chambers, with cameras and microphones capturing the conversation, the judges deliberated five charges and delivered the following verdicts:

1) The blurring or erasure of the border between fact and fiction leads to the elision of the difference between truth and alternative facts with grave consequences for democracy. [VALIDATED]

2) Erasing the border between facts and fiction leads to historical confusions causing serious epistemological and ethical harm. [VALIDATED]

3) Noting an increasing reliance on law to litigate literary matters, the increase in writers on trial emphasized that erasing the difference between fact and fiction could lead to the injury of people identified as characters in fictional works and that the increase of these trials attested to the necessity of an upholding of this border. [REJECTED]

4) Emphasizing the difference between fact and fiction is the condition that allows for a real ontological plurality, a plurality of the registers of reality, not just to learn about the world as it is but to derive pleasure from works of fiction by truly distinguishing them from reality as our senses and information present it to us. [REJECTED]

5) Emphasizing that mixing or confusing two cognitive regimes, one oriented toward the real, the other toward fiction, constituted an error that is at the same time a philosophical one with heavy political consequences and a scientific one, in light of advancements in the neurosciences. [HALF VALIDATED, HALF REJECTED].[21]

After deliberation, a final, overarching verdict was delivered: "We find fiction responsible but not guilty" ("La fiction est déclarée responsable mais pas coupable"). Obviously, the fallout from the 2016 American presidential election—when a vocabulary of "alternative facts" and "fake news" had begun to coalesce—added new urgency to the question whether the interpenetration of fact and fiction is good or bad in what has come to be called the "post-truth age." That the organizers of the trial were able to generate such an impassioned discussion among literary scholars and practitioners on the loss of clear boundaries between fact and fiction illustrates the significance of the topic in a moment marked by a creeping loss of the ability to distinguish between what is real and what is not.

Literary scholars such as Françoise Lavocat, Alison James, Christophe Reig, Alexandre Gefen, René Audet, Lionel Ruffel, and others had already been grappling with these questions, focusing on the delicate membrane separating fact and fiction and on the documentary impulse in contemporary fiction.[22] For example, in *Fait et fiction: Pour une frontière* (2016), Lavocat shows "the existence and the cognitive, conceptual, and political necessity of frontiers"[23] between fact and fiction. In an article on *narrations documentaires*, Lionel Ruffel describes a pattern in contemporary literature that emerges from the integration of forms like the travel account, the sociological survey, the political essay, the biography and autobiography, the ethnographic account, the nonfiction novel, New Journalism, and "grand reportage" into realist texts.[24] He notes the tendency of these new narrations in French—he specifically mentions François Bon, Jean Hatzfeld, and Jean Rolin—to borrow the methods and forms of journalism and the social sciences, all the while contesting the power of these fields to offer an exhaustive picture of contemporary reality. Above all, these fictions rely on the document, a literary strategy to which Marie-Jeanne Zenetti dedicated an entire book, *Factographies: L'Enregistrement littéraire à l'époque contemporaine* (2014).[25] Regarding contemporary French fiction, Dominique Viart has evoked a "retour au réel";[26] Philippe Forest, an "appel inouï du réel";[27] Cécile Narjoux and Claire Stolz, a "fictionalisation du réel";[28] and Éric Trudel, a "precarious real."[29] And Joshua Armstrong has coined the term "empiritext," which he defines as "any literary work that is highly dependent upon empirical observation for its content and form; whose content is gleaned by its author in the course of an often ludic, constraint-bound investigation into real everyday spaces; and whose form reflects the nature of those spaces, as they reveal themselves within the parameters of the project."[30] In his book *La Déréalisation du monde: Réalité et fiction en conflit* (2010), Jacinto Lageira uses 9/11 as a starting point for his call to action: "Il faut entièrement repenser les notions de réalisme et de fictionnel."[31] Finally, Philippe Vilain has argued that "le post-réalisme [est] le courant dominant de la littérature française de ce début de XXIe siècle."[32] He describes it as a "véritable culte au réel" (43) and describes its features as follows:

Post-realism takes as its task the exploration of a new dimension of the real, its third, not in the style of Balzac, or even by sublimating it as Breton did, but rather by subjectively investing in the real in order to reinvent it, by rewriting its personal mythology (autofiction), collective mythologies (biofiction), by making literature the space of an immense *reportage* of current events, by supplying a fictional documentation of the world (docufiction).[33]

In Vilain's view, this postrealist literature does not objectify the real; it subjectifies it. He claims that postrealism exalts "le réel à travers une religion de l'événement et du fait, ou, si l'on veut, à travers une sorte de *factualisme subjectif*" (48). This interest in scholarly circles regarding the dissolution of the boundary between fact and fiction and the strategies fashionable among contemporary writers for producing a reality effect shows a distinct preoccupation with *verification*, the process by which the true and untrue are triaged. The works I analyze in this book attempt to capture the essence of the contemporary world—often incorporating well-known public figures, current events, or snippets of pop culture or contemporary political discourse into their narratives—but call into question the stability of these as orientation points in a world of cultural confusion, weaponized disinformation, and bad faith.

The second literary event of significance to my project occurred in October 2018, when an argument over the so-called *Zemmourisation* of French literature began among a handful of academics in France. Johan Faerber, a literary critic and author of *Après la littérature: Écrire le contemporain* (2018), wrote an opinion piece titled "Contre la Zemmourisation de la critique littéraire," in which he accused the scholars Alexandre Gefen (CNRS), Oana Panaïté (Indiana University, Bloomington), and Cornelia Ruhe (Universität Mannheim) of introducing and legitimizing far-right ideas in their "appalling and dangerous" call for papers for the journal *Revue critique de fixxion française contemporaine*.[34] Éric Zemmour's *Le Suicide français*, a controversial 2014 book that attempted to diagnose France's sociopolitical ills since the 1970s, argued against political correctness, identity politics, feminism, and a host of other progressive ideas that he claims are responsible for France's decline. Faerber argues—in an oddly hyperbolic register, perhaps to generate clicks—that the aforementioned call for papers borrows tropes from Charles Maurras (a far-right ideologue and organizer of the Action française) and Zemmour, takes for granted the existence of a French identity, and tacitly operates according to the discursive logic of nationalism. The BibliObs section of the *Nouvel Observateur* picked up the story,[35] and the original CFP authors quickly responded with a spirited rebuttal.[36] The exchange shows a creeping politicization of

literature and an apprehension that the identity-based debates that characterize contemporary politics could contaminate the sacred space of the
literary. This is certainly not the only instance of anxiety about the relationship between literature and far-right ideas in French literary circles.
Think, for example, of then prime minister Manuel Valls's comment in
2015 that "La France, ce n'est pas la soumission, ce n'est pas Michel Houellebecq. Ce n'est pas l'intolérance, la haine, la peur, jouer sur les peurs, en
permanence."[37] Furthermore, in the 2017 manifesto of the *Nouveau Magazine Littéraire*, a reboot of the *Magazine Littéraire* of yore (founded in
1966), the new director, Raphaël Glucksmann, urges readers to reject a
reactionary genealogy inherited from Charles Maurras, Joseph de Maistre, Maurice Barrès, and Pierre Drieu La Rochelle, one that embodies
"*déclinisme* and the temptation to withdraw" and involves "spinelessness
and xenophobia that have dominated the French media and cultural
scene."[38] To be sure, *déclinologie* has become a veritable pastime in France
in recent years, leading the journalist Agnès Poirier to ask, "Is There No
End to Books on the 'End of France'?"[39] With its will to eliminate the enemies of France, the reactionary impulse reaches beyond politics, touching
every aspect of cultural production, including literature.

In his important book *Théories de la dégénerescence: D'un mythe psychiatrique au déclinisme contemporain* (2018), the psychiatrist and psychoan-
alyst Jacques Hochmann locates the roots of civilizational degeneration
theories and contemporary *déclinologie*, also dubbed *collapsologie* within
the framework of the Anthropocene,[40] primarily in nineteenth-century
psychiatry, and argues that their underlying political spirit is reactionary.[41] While my book is not strictly about the reactionary imaginary, it is
important to bear in mind that the emergence of degenerative realism
coincides with—and feeds upon—a resurgence in far-right political fervor,
which has a long and dark history in France. Throughout the long twentieth century into the twenty-first, right-wing ideology in France has taken
many guises. Types of great diversity fall under the rubric of reactionary
or conservative,[42] including Catholic traditionalists, fiscal conservatives,
monarchy nostalgists, antiglobalists, certain Gaullists (in the eyes of *soixante-
huitards*), far-right nativists, anti-Semites, and opponents of immigration,
multiculturalism, feminism, political correctness, affirmative action (*discrimination positive*),[43] and left-wing *bien-pensance*. In an article titled
"Our Reactionary Age," Mark Lilla argued:

Reactionary stories always begin with a happy, well-ordered state where people willingly shared a common destiny. Then alien ideas promoted by intellectuals and outsiders—writers, journalists, professors, foreigners—undermined that harmony. (The betrayal of elites is central to every reactionary myth.) Soon the entire society, even the common people, were taken in. Only those who have preserved memories of the old ways—the reactionaries themselves—see what happened. Whether the society reverses direction or rushes to its ultimate doom depends entirely on their resistance.[44]

What fuels reactionaries of complex and countless varieties is "a sense of historical betrayal" in a world in which "economic globalization and the paralysis of democratic institutions" are the key features. A few of the more famous reactionary figures who've stippled France's history include Maurice Barrès (1862–1923), who envisioned a country emptied of the uprooting forces—Jews, intellectuals, and foreigners—that lured young people away from their villages to the city with money, entertainments, and soul-sapping distractions;[45] Charles Maurras (1868–1952), whose Action française movement demonized the enemies of the nation, what came to be known as "Anti-France," that is, Jews, Protestants, Freemasons, and foreigners (métèques); or staunch neo-Catholics like Paul Claudel (1868–1955) or Vichy officials such as Maréchal Pétain (1856–1951), Pierre Laval (1883–1945), or Maurice Papon (1910–2007).[46] Right-wing thought in France was particularly prosperous in the 1930s and 1940s just before and during the Vichy regime. The history of anti-Semitism in France far predates Vichy or the earlier Dreyfus affair, and its new face—embodied in Dieudonné M'bala M'bala, Amedy Coulibaly, or the Kouachi brothers and in the countless perpetrators of anti-Semitic crimes in recent years— shows an ever-mutating ideology. On the Far Right, there is plenty of hate and fear to go around: in addition to animosity toward Jews, one finds in reactionary circles a whole list of targets, including nonwhites, Muslims, and foreigners. Demographic alarmism has taken many forms throughout the twentieth century, for example, as the dystopian horror presented in *The Camp of the Saints* (1973), by Jean Raspail—a favorite novel of the American white nationalists Steve Bannon, Richard Spencer, Stephen Miller, and Steve King—or as the so-called *Grand Remplacement* population theory articulated by Renaud Camus. A direct genealogy can be traced between Pierre Poujade, the populist purveyor of books and racist tropes who rose to prominence in the 1950s with his founding of the party Union de défense des commerçants et artisans, and Jean-Marie Le Pen, founder of the Front national, mentored in his early days in politics by Poujade, and one clearly perceives the echoes of Poujadist discourse in the tweets and speeches of Marine Le Pen or Marion Maréchal-Le Pen. The Front national's recent rebranding effort—the party's name was changed to Rassemblement national in June 2018—was almost entirely cosmetic. The party's platform and symbolic capital have remained largely untouched. The Manif pour tous, organized in part by Frigide Barjot in response to the gay marriage law passed in May 2013, was a significant moment of solidarity for the Right, as anxieties about gender, the structure of the family, and, implicitly, the detrimental effects of these changes on the nation were vented publicly on the streets of Paris and across France.[47] In the realm of contemporary literature, Michel Houellebecq's literary provocations and Richard Millet's neoreactionary fiction, as Étienne Achille has dubbed it,[48] have gained them reputations as apologists of far-right thought, placing them in a genealogy that would include, say, Céline or Brasillach.[49] Houellebecq has pushed back against the label, arguing:

A reactionary is someone who favors some previously existing social configuration—something it is possible to return to—and someone who militates in favor of such a return. Whereas, if there is an idea, a single idea that runs through all of my novels, which goes so far as to haunt them, it is the *absolute irreversibility of all processes of decay* once they have begun. . . . It is more than organic, it is like a universal law that applies also to inert objects; it is literally entropic.[50]

In his view, right-wing ideas have been stigmatized to an absurd degree. He quipped, "Admire a rural landscape these days and you can find yourself being accused of *neo-Pétainisme*" (116). In a chapter section titled "La nouvelle droite littéraire: Contre l'antiracisme, le multiculturalisme et le féminisme," Gisèle Sapiro compiles a laundry list of reactionary literati, a mixture of writers and public intellectuals including Michel Déon, Alain Finkielkraut, Pascal Bruckner, Éric Zemmour, Philippe Muray, Michel Houellebecq, Renaud Camus, and Richard Millet[51] and argues that their apocalyptic visions originate in a perceived loss of social capital as cultivated white men who once embodied French identity but who have lost this symbolic privilege.[52] If they cannot continue to run the world, it must be destroyed. The derogatory term *réac'* has, in recent years, become perhaps too widespread to hold the power of insult it once had,[53] and in the twenty-first century, we are witnesses to the mainstreamization of reactionary thought, the rise of *"rap identitaire,"*[54] and the coalescence of a *fachosphère*, the far-right underbelly of the internet where Breitbart- or 4chan-like sites such as Fdesouche thrive.[55] Harold Bernat offered this definition of the term "réaction" in its political sense: "préservation oppositionnelle d'une réalité menacée de disparition."[56] The existential battle of reactionaries involves, in their minds, the preservation or restoration of reality.

Which reactionary fears have made their way into the contemporary French novel? The list is lengthy.[57] One feature of the living reactionaries is their shared disdain toward the legacy of May '68, with its push for a variety of social recalibrations. A certain contempt toward human-rights-oriented thinking, affirmative action, or efforts to increase racial equality is manifest in many novels I'll discuss here. Another fear—sometimes shared by the Left, albeit on different grounds—is that of the ineluctable Americanization of French society in the economic, political, and cultural spheres. Other preoccupations include the defense of French identity, the preservation of laïcité as a tool to resist the encroachment of Islam, a recovery of the ideals of the Republic through the classroom or other institutions of cultural transmission, and an attachment to the vertical hierarchy of yore in contrast to democratic horizontalization. Implicit in all of these concerns, what Durand and Sindaco have called "thèmes crépusculaires,"[58] is a fear of decline and a darker future. With overwhelming nostalgia as a motivating factor, the stewards of Frenchness seek to recover what the fatherland has lost: *patriarchie, patriotisme, patrimoine*. The father, as I will show, occupies a conspicuous place within degenerative realism.

There is clearly something in the air. So what accounts for the breakdown in realist representation I describe throughout this book? Why does it happen now? And what is the relation between this foundering and the aforementioned fears discernible in certain contemporary French fictions? The internet is, of course, one causal factor. What percentage of its information is "true"? Impossible to say. Not only has the web opened a space for the free flow of bad information and given every anonymous village idiot a bullhorn, its amplificatory mediation has intensified the most far-flung horrors of the world and delivered them to our doorstep. Insecurity and fear make people receptive to disinformation. Furthermore, the internet has facilitated the blurring of lines between news and opinion, between speculation and confirmed fact. Each person constructs a different world through the internet, customizing their experience and seeking out sites and information that confirm what they already believe. On top of this, the vast space of the web is shared by advertisers and others who benefit monetarily or politically from deception. The natural duplicitousness of capitalism manifests itself in every aspect of internet culture, from the cover-ups of tech companies to paid fake product reviews and other forms of promotional subterfuge.

Ours is an age of communicative paradox. For example, we know intuitively that reality television has little to do with reality, yet a hunger for this *réalité confectionnée* produces revenue surges and the replication and expansion of such programming, which in turn tampers with perceptions of reality. Ruth Cruickshank has noted the crisis-oriented nature of some French fiction at the turn of the millennium, which she attributes in part to a crumbling sense of reality brought by these new media forms. She argues that "as a reflection of and contributor to the *fin de millénaire* aesthetics of crisis, reality television challenges and changes conceptions of reality, authenticity, and communication."[59] The self-fashioning and artifice brought about through social media toys with the public's sense of reality as well. The classification of various platforms such as Twitter and Facebook, where the categories of news, opinion, and entertainment blend seamlessly, poses a special challenge.[60] As Mona Chollet wrote of Twitter in 2011:

The twittosphere brews a singular mix of information, gossip, and commentary, once quite distinct activities, which often breeds mistrust and contempt for those unfamiliar with it. . . . Mystifications and false rumors are indeed quickly identified: the work of fishing and verifying facts, which in the past would only be done by journalists, has now become the responsibility of all internet users and is taking place out in the open.[61]

Another cause of the shifting modalities of the real is the alleged limitations on *how* one is allowed to communicate one's judgments of the world.
If many of the characters in the novels analyzed here inveigh against political correctness, it is because they imagine it as a fracturing force, splitting
the self in two.[62] The opinions developed through observation and experience are curbed by unstable expressive constraints imposed socially, often
by unseen actors. This cleaves the self into public and private halves, fracturing the individual and his or her reality. If each citizen, bisected in this
fashion, must navigate a social and political sphere populated by other
such bisected individuals, which shared orientation points can guide them
toward meaningful and forthright association?

These factors, however, are not specifically French. That a degenerative
realist strain has developed in the contemporary French novel can be
attributed to several more specific factors. In his book *Les Peurs françaises*
(1993), a kind of pep talk addressed to the French people to rouse them
from their cynicism, Alain Duhamel argues that France suffers from a
"collective depression," the result of centuries of accumulated trauma.[63]
He uses the book's nearly three hundred pages to enumerate the anxieties
specific to France and to question whether these fears have any basis in
reality. Among them are increasing crime and social unrest in the *banlieue*; urbanization and the attendant uprootedness experienced by *agriculteurs* and villagers as the country rapidly retreated from its mainly agrar-
ian economy; the dueling realities of Paris and *la France profonde*; the fallout
from decolonization; the looming specter of immigration and demographic
change; rising unemployment and increasing competition with countries
like the United States, whose 1990s tech boom and general entrepreneurial
spirit made the slow and swollen French state seem anachronistic; and the
inevitability that France would be subsumed by Europe, which he
describes as "unstable, indecisive, and sometimes convulsive" (273).
Although 1968 was a turbulent year across the globe, May '68 has left a
particularly indelible mark on French public consciousness and was a
watershed moment for the political polarization that characterizes contemporary French politics. Furthermore, France's colonial history and its
immigrational consequences are forcing the French to rethink identity,
citizenship, and the universalist ideal. Since the end of economic flourishing brought by the Trente Glorieuses, which faltered in 1975, France has

experienced its own crisis of confidence, distinct in its features from the American one Jimmy Carter described in his gloomy 1979 speech. Most importantly, the legacies of the Enlightenment and the Revolution, to which French identity is so stiffly tethered, have been aggressively challenged in the twenty-first century by rising inequalities, irrational populism and right-wing zeal, renewed forms of religious fervor, and a host of other threats. When serious aspersions are cast on two of the defining events that shaped a nation's history, its novelists attentive to sociopolitical turbulence necessarily feel called to use their fictions to respond to it.

Regarding France's own literary and intellectual history, it makes sense that contemporary French realism would again turn toward the social sciences—the set of scientific fields perhaps best suited to help decipher collective angst—since it did so in the past so enthusiastically. We might think of it as a kind of muscle memory. The rich history of social scientific thought in France—from its inception under the Lumières, through its positivist Comtean legacy and Durkheim's articulation of a new sociological field constructed upon "social facts," to Foucault's institutional archaeologies and beyond—has nursed realism in French literature through its contextualization of the individual within the social body. Another factor is the unique history of public intellectualism in France, where controversial *affaires* or *débats* elicit endless series of confrontational responses by well-known figures on television, on the radio, and in print media including opinion pieces or *pamphlets*. We could describe these often fabricated controversies as a form of incitainment—a portmanteau of incitement and entertainment—meant to generate viewership, stir public sentiment, and provide a pressure valve for pent-up political anxiety. A number of the authors included in this study are veritable *machines à controverse*, ruffling the feathers of the reading public and landing themselves in the middle of debates about Islamophobia, misogyny, multiculturalism, and other sensitive matters.[64] France's unique cultural scene, in which writers still occupy an outsize role in shaping public conversations, allows for a blurring of lines that separate academia, politics, journalism, and entertainment. Degenerative realist fiction picks up all of these threads and braids them in sometimes unexpected and compelling ways. While I would not be surprised if a similar degenerative realist tendency has begun to express itself in other Western literatures, the French instantiation is a particularly interesting development, given the country's rich realist tradition.

## SOME NOTES ON REALISM

Nous avançons vers le désastre, guidés par une image fausse du monde; et personne ne le sait.

—MICHEL HOUELLEBECQ

While I won't rehearse in its entirety the long and complicated history of realism as an aesthetic concept—particularly in the realms of literature and the visual arts—and as a philosophical and political term, it is important to highlight a few important elements of this history in order to lay the groundwork for the claims I will make. In France, realism as a literary movement began in the mid-nineteenth century and stretched into the early twentieth, with key figures such as Stendhal, Balzac, Flaubert, and Zola (of the naturalist school) leading the charge. In his famed study *Mimesis* (1946), Erich Auerbach offers the following features of what he calls the "foundations of modern realism":

The serious treatment of everyday reality, the rise of more extensive and socially inferior human groups to the position of subject matter for problematic-existential representation, on the one hand; on the other, the embedding of random persons and events in the general course of contemporary history, the fluid historical background—these, we believe, are the foundations of modern realism.[65]

In addition to these thematic features of modern realism—a focus on the everyday existence of people whose lives, until that moment, had not been deemed worthy of representation and on the conjugation of individual and collective destiny—there were also a number of stylistic innovations that characterized it. Consider the realist advocate and theorist Champfleury's recommendations regarding the appropriate style and subject matter of realist fiction:

1. The realist text proceeds by the observation of minute details, not by "invention" or "imagination."
2. Because it limits itself to reality and to truth, it is absolutely sincere.
3. It must be contemporary, giving *peintures de moeurs* and *scènes de la vie habituelle*.
4. But this does not mean photography, for the author's personality everywhere prevents him from giving a mechanical reproduction.

5. Choice is necessary and the artist must arrange and distribute his materials to make of them a work of art.

6. The style of the novel should be simple.[66]

Ideally, the realist's process is one of selection, not invention, as minute details from everyday life are hand-picked, arranged, and articulated in a direct and neutral style. Despite its popularity in some circles, realism was perceived by its nineteenth-century critics as vulgar, brutal, lacking in artistry, and the result of a purely mechanical reproductive process. Realists were mere *daguerréotypeurs*, photographers of life. Their representations were immoral because they showed the lives of sinners and lowlifes and implicitly asked for an empathic *prise en compte* of these vice-mongers who hadn't yet earned the right to be represented. In the hands of the realists, the ugly is routinely favored over the beautiful, transgressing the prevailing rule that art should strive for beauty. The realists' trompe-l'oeil aesthetic was seen by many as a form of trickery and a plagiarism of nature. Too clinical and too informed by medicine, positivism, and the natural and social sciences, realism was imagined as a rejection of art in favor of laboratorial experimentation. Indeed, Zola's *Le Roman expérimental* (1880) called for an application of Claude Bernard's experimental method in medicine to the novel, which provoked the bracketing-off of naturalism as a subcategory of realism despite the reliance of all realisms on principles of empirical observation and the treatment of humans as a species whose behaviors and physiognomies could be recorded and analyzed through fiction.[67] Realism's lack of idealism—what distinguishes it in part from romanticism—was for some a surrender to the Enlightenment value of reason, detached from higher metaphysical aspirations. Imagined as a stark rejection of the ideals and aesthetic of the romantics, realism asked its consumers to trust the brain and the eye over the heart and spirit. It sought to shake awake the wistful dreamers of the generation before. Stylistically, the pared-down simplicity of realist texts was seen as painfully lacking in ornament and distinctive flair. The style of realism was no style at all. Suddenly, the flowery periphrasis of romanticism was replaced by a more direct French, a fact celebrated by Maupassant, who believed the nature of the French language to be "clear, logical, and vigorous." The "mannered writers" he critiques "never succeeded in muddying it and never will."[68]

In his 1842 preface to La Comédie humaine, Balzac famously announced his intention to offer a history of manners *of* the French *to* the French, using Walter Scott as a model but improving on his ambitious historical project by thinking in terms of coherent wholes rather than disparate stories. Balzac sought unity, systematicity. He invited the novelist to multitask, to become secretary of French society, "[drawing] up an inventory of vices and virtues," collecting, choosing, framing, depicting. He is a painter, narrator, archaeologist, cataloguer, and "registrar of good and evil."[69] But not just these. He must go further, think etiologically, "[investigating] the reasons and causes of these social effects, detecting the hidden sense of this vast assembly of figures, passions, and incidents" (15–16). This forensic spirit is a key feature of realism. Indeed, prefaces to novels or novel series of the nineteenth century like this one are the best places to look for evidence of novelists' purposeful appropriations of the sciences. After outlining his comparative study of humanity and animality, Balzac announces in his preface plans to pursue future scientifically inflected projects, including "The Pathology of Social Life" and "An Anatomy of Educational Bodies." In his preface to *Les Misérables*, Victor Hugo evokes "social asphyxia,"[70] medicalizing the suffering of his compatriots of lesser fortune and stressing the necessity of novels like the one he presents to the reader to address very real hardships. In their preface to *Germinie Lacerteux* (1864), the Goncourt brothers describe their "true" novel as "a clinical picture of Love."[71] Finally, in his introduction to the Rougon-Macquart series (1871), Zola famously asserted that "Heredity, like gravity, has its laws,"[72] claiming that the first book in the series, *The Fortune of the Rougons*, "could bear the scientific title *Origins*" (4). George Becker describes realism's enlistment of the sciences in this way:

[The cult of the little man] has been a powerful spur to human sympathy because it is automatically on the side of the downtrodden and forgotten, and the industrial society has been lavish in its provision of such outcasts and victims. This attitude was soon reinforced and corrected by another kind of interest in human nature, an interest in man as specimen to be examined as part of the great deterministic scheme of things revealed by the physical sciences. We move here from an interest in the pathetic to the brutal, from empathy to objectivity.[73]

As the social sciences developed, realism attached itself to them in an almost parasitic way, even more than to the physical sciences. Contemporary French realists eagerly pursue the social science parasitism of their forebears. From population theory to personal psychology, from economic theory to ethnography, the human is subject to the application of a wide range of social science discourses in the twenty-first-century novels of interest in this book.

Literary realism is often imagined as a ripping away of the veils of illusion from readers' eyes, a feature it shares with other kinds of more politically inflected realisms I'll get to in a moment. The realist novel is tasked to provide a reality check, however brutal. In his obituary for Zola, Henry Thurston Peck writes:

Realism ... was not a creation or a rediscovery by any one particular man. Its germ was in the air. It was and is essentially consistent with the whole tone of modern thought, which limits the scope of the imagination, rejects illusions and demands in a spirit of hardy scepticism to view the thing that is, rather than the thing that seems to be. Democracy in politics, rationalism in theology, materialism in philosophy and realism in literature, are very closely linked together. They are, one and all, simply different phases of the same mood and the same mental attitude toward life. The centuries of dreaminess have gone by perhaps forever, and today man looks with keen unclouded vision into the verities of his existence, asking no one to prophesy smooth things, but banishing illusions, uncovering nakedness, and facing with a certain hard composure born of cynicism, the ghastly facts that render human life so terrible.[74]

Bleakness on every page: this is what degenerative realism has in store for us as well. It is important to note Peck's mention of democracy as the political correlative to realism in literature. In discourses throughout the nineteenth century, realism and democracy were often linked, mainly because of the horizontalizing imperative of each. Given the political turbulence of that century in France, with the tugs-of-war between (constitutional) monarchy, empire, and republic, it makes sense that the new republican ideal would need a corresponding literary movement to accompany it and to mirror its aspirations. "Representation for all" is one of the not-so-hidden demands of the realist school, as was "comprehensibility by all." As Luc Herman wrote regarding realism's simple style, "The realist's only goal is to be understood by everyone."[75] It is significant that degenerative realism arrives at a moment when democracy, particularly in the West, is facing unexpected challenges and steadfast adversaries. If we agree with Matthieu Baumier's claim that in the twenty-first century we've entered a postdemocratic era, an inevitability since "la démocratie travaille toujours contre elle-même,"[76] we must wonder then: Has democracy's correlative literature, the realist novel, also begun to work against itself, breaking down the very representational system it tried to sustain?

Realism, which never really goes away as a novelistic technique, is necessarily affected by the other movements that have punctuated its existence. For realism, there will always be an after. The title of my colleague Devin Fore's book *Realism After Modernism: The Rehumanization of Art and Literature* underscores this fact. Realism was necessarily inflected by the arrival and departure of modernism. Fore writes: "Simply put: Realism after modernism cannot be the same phenomenon as realism before modernism."[77] The same holds true for realism after postmodernism, as I will show throughout this book, which presents a corpus of realist texts that respond with fervency to postmodern metatextuality, combinatoric spasms, and conceptual play. Given realism's fascinating trajectory in France since the nineteenth century, it is fair to say that each notable moment in its development—each before and after—has nudged it in new directions. Here are just a few of those moments:

- The unclean break between romanticism and realism
- The development of the psychological novel—Stendhal's *The Red and the Black* (1830) is an important template—which emphasized the characters' interiority
- Champfleury's early theorizations on realism and the short-lived periodical *Le Réalisme* (1856–57), whose editors, Edmond Duranty, Jules Assézat, and Henri Thulié, fiercely defended the merits of realist literature
- The trial of Flaubert's *Madame Bovary* (1857), which solidified the negative connotations of realism by associating it with obscenity, immorality, and baseness
- The publication of Zola's *The Experimental Novel* (1880), which articulated the naturalist agenda and its connection to the sciences
- The unclean break between realism and modernism, including the arrival of surrealism and its challenges to the old guard
- The 1929 publication of the *Manifeste du roman populiste* by Léon Lemonnier and André Thérive, who rejected the principles of bourgeois realism

- The influence of phenomenology on subjective realism
- The publication of Robbe-Grillet's theoretical articles from the mid-1950s to the mid-1960s and the development of the *nouveau roman*, with its curious object-oriented subjectivity and subordination of character and plot
- The new prominence of *littérature engagée* as practiced and promoted by writers like Sartre and Camus, which encouraged the politicization of the novel
- Serge Doubrovsky's theorizations of *autofiction* in the late 1970s, which conjugates lived experience and fiction, in the spirit of Truman Capote's so-called nonfiction novel
- The fragmentation of the French novel during the postmodern period and the development of the notion of the *extrême contemporain* in the late 1980s, which provided a better framework for understanding and writing about the contemporary novel

While the list is by no means comprehensive, I highlight these shifts in order to remind the reader that the mimetic representation of the real is not a static and perfected art, something that was "solved" definitively in a handbook passed to the next generation. How the real is represented changes constantly, with the arrival of each new technological development, conceptual shift, and collective change in taste and mood. Frederic Jameson writes of this inheritance in decidedly negative terms, claiming that realism "leaves an odd assortment of random tools and techniques to its shrivelled posterity, who still carry its name on into an era of mass culture and rival media."[78] Jean-Louis Hippolyte has also noted that realism is still the default mode in fiction, writing that "most of today's novelists still pander to the well-known fictional recipes of Stendhal and the traditional nineteenth-century novel; a quick glimpse around the shelves of today's libraries would unquestionably show that many a marquise still goes out at five."[79] In his book *The Poetics of Early Russian Literature*, D. S. Likhachev presents a more positive account of realism's recurrence: "Realism is eternally new. It is new because it finds itself in a state of constant search for an expression of reality approaching reality. Insofar as reality moves, so does realism. . . . Realism cannot become outmoded, by its very nature. This is a constantly self-renewing movement, a movement which cannot repeat its stylistic methods, formulas, constructions of subjects, etc."[80] To use a visual example, certain techniques—like the art of perspective and the convincing rendering of three-dimensional space on a two-dimensional plane in the visual arts or the arrival of hyperrealist painting after the advent of high-definition photography—developed over time and have fallen in and out of favor after their first appearance. Historically, authors have turned to a number of strategies in order to inject their narratives with more realness. This book will catalogue some of the strategies used by contemporary realist novelists in order to achieve this effect.

In the period leading up to the turn of the millennium, realism was influenced by the same forces that led to postmodernism. Robert Dion has succinctly noted the features of post-1980 literary realism, in which the real is fragmented, incompatible with the *grands récits* of yore, and composed of antithetical materials: "It is a mixture of facts and rumors, mainstream and subcultures, representations and affects, technical knowledge and beliefs, nonstop information and rampant disinformation, etc."[81] The potpourri of experiences incorporated into the post-1980 realist novel remains in consonance with the general tendency of realism to validate phenomena once imagined as unworthy of representation. In an analysis of visual art from the same period, specifically of Warhol's compulsive repetitions, Hal Foster has proposed the useful term "traumatic realism" to describe how the harrowing event is processed and reactivated through mimetic redundance. He explains: "The Warhol repetitions not only *reproduce* traumatic effects; they also *produce* them. Somehow in these repetitions, then, several contradictory things occur at the same time: a warding away of traumatic significance *and* an opening out to it, a defending against traumatic affect *and* a producing of it."[82] The multiple traumas that unfold in the pages of degenerative realist fiction are of a different nature. While Warhol's traumatic event—a car crash, for example—was excised from the past and forced into the present as what seems something like a self-replicating psychic lesion, the novels I'll describe evince an anticipatory trauma: they rehearse not the traumas of the past but those expected to arrive shortly. These are necessarily inflected by traumatic events of the past—the 2005 Paris riots, for example, or the Charlie Hebdo massacre—but the protagonists mourn the future more than the past or present.[83]

That said, the novels use the harsh, lived realities in contemporary France as fodder for the grieving they perform for the future. Many of the novels presented in this study could fit under the category of what Marc

Augé has called *ethnofiction* and has modeled in his books *La Guerre des rêves: Exercices d'ethno-fiction* (1997) and *Journal d'un SDF: Ethnofiction* (2011). At the beginning of the latter, he defines ethnofiction, which is "neither an academic study nor a novel,"[84] in this way: "A narrative that evokes a social fact through the subjectivity of a particular individual. However, since it is neither autobiography nor confession, that fictional individual must be created 'from scratch' or, in other words, out of the thousand and one details observed in everyday life" (vii). Moving from the particular to the larger social reality, Augé describes "an individual situation and a particular subjectivity" through fiction and "[leaves] it to the readers to imagine the social totality it expresses in its way" (viii). The objective of the writer of ethnofiction differs from that of the novelist: "He does not want his readers to identify with or 'believe in' his 'protagonist' but, rather, to discover in him something of their times" (ix). This is certainly true of every book in this study.

As I was putting the finishing touches on this manuscript, Houellebecq's *Sérotonine*—what Nelly Kapriélian calls a "beau roman crépusculaire"[85]— was published, leading some to ask whether his novel had predicted the uprising of the *gilets jaunes* against the Macron administration.[86] What strikes me most about public conversations surrounding the yellow-vest movement is the pervasiveness of a vocabulary of reality and realism attached to it. The common refrain among the *gilets jaunes* that "the country's leaders are disconnected from reality"[87] has been met by Macron and his allies with calls for a sober realism in the face of the economic and political constraints the country faces. Each side believes itself to be the most in touch with reality, suggesting that the other side is living inside a fiction.[88] A new or renewed interest in philosophical realism,[89] capitalist realism,[90] speculative realism,[91] compassionate moral realism,[92] postapocalyptic realism,[93] and other varieties of realism across disciplines is symptomatic of an increasing sense of the contestability of what is real. The proliferation of these and other recent appeals to political realism led the linguists Stéphane Bikialo and Julien Rault to publish *Au nom du réalisme: Usage(s) politique(s) d'un mot d'ordre* (2018), which surveys the disparate meanings of the word *"réalisme"* and explores its complex uses at the height of calls for a new political realism. Claiming that the term was historically associated with right-wing political discourse, reliant on a logic of pragmatism, lucidity, efficiency, austerity, and "la force des choses,"

Bikialo and Rault write: "Une rapide recherche d'occurrences, dans la littérature française, tend à confirmer cette idée puisque les œuvres où le mot apparaît le plus fréquemment permettraient de constituer une singulière bibliothèque: Barrès, Maurras, Péguy, Bernanos, Mauriac."[94] As Jean-François Kahn put it, "Le réalisme est un pétainisme."[95] Bikialo and Rault argue that in political discourse, calls for realism are inherently paternalistic (20). The authors make a distinction between the real (*le réel*), things as they really are, and reality (*la réalité*), the social construction of what is real. The force that has always pushed back against realism was idealism, a spirit historically embodied in left-wing politics, but Bikialo and Rault note the increasing tendency among French centrists and left-wing politicians to appropriate the realist language of the right-wingers in order to persuade the public. Each side claims ownership of the real.

All of these remarkable occurrences led me to write *Degenerative Realism*, which takes stock of the twenty-first-century literary landscape in France and situates the aforementioned iterations of realism as a political response to a culture perceived to be in decline. An idealist by nature, I found it demoralizing to plod through the grim novels presented here but felt an urgency to finish this project despite its dispiriting effects, since it captures a mood that has settled on much of France. For those of us who do not share the political views of the characters so ubiquitous in degenerative realist fictions, it would be simpler to ignore them. This, however, would be an act of willful blindness and would leave us with an incomplete picture of the current age. Anyone who looks back on the French novel of this period will surely be struck by the insistence of this dark vision. My preference is to study what makes me uncomfortable, to face it with composure and confidence, rather than pretend it doesn't exist or cower in its shadow.

## CHAPTER SUMMARIES

In chapter 1, "Demography and Survival in Twenty-First-Century France," I show the ways in which the social sciences—demography in particular—have returned in the twenty-first century to provide a structural and thematic frame for some contemporary French novels, borrowing from those nineteenth-century counterparts that had relied so heavily on sociology, economics, and population science to build their worlds. Civilizational decline and demographic eschatology are at the heart of the contemporary narratives of interest in this chapter. Whereas nineteenth-century novelists such as Zola or Hugo saw redemptive potential in their tales of human suffering and injustice, the authors featured in this chapter—including Michel Houellebecq, Frédéric Beigbeder, Yann Moix, and Charles Robinson—depict Western civilization as unsalvageable. The apocalyptic vision presented by these authors is a secular one in that God plays no role in the West's death. The dead-end sex in these novels—which is recreational and not reproductive—constitutes a citational recycling of past depictions of the bacchanalia and decadent excesses concomitant with societies in decline. I begin with a brief history of "demografiction" and the relation between the science of demography, which relies on projection models and imaginary cohorts, and the modes of fiction and hypothesis. Next, I show how the aforementioned novelists rely on demography to frame their characters both as members of specific consumer markets and as species in competition for resources. These framings rely on the theories of a variety of figures—such as Arthur de Gobineau, Bénédict Augustin Morel, Max Nordau, and Cesare Lombroso—who had explored demographic questions through the fields of (racist) ethnography, criminology, and even aesthetics. I draw parallels between Max Nordau's notion of *Entartung* or degeneration and the forms of decadence our authors depict[96] and show how more contemporary demographic anxieties—the so-called war of the wombs, national suicide, social Darwinism, and Renaud Camus's theories on the *Grand Remplacement*—are at the crux of these narratives. In a section titled "Stalemate Sex and 9/11 as Castration," I show how the novelists' express anxieties about sex through a critique of radical Islam, the virile immigrant, and the overfeminized Western man who has forfeited his masculinity. Tying together sex, capitalism, religion, and global politics in unexpected ways, novelists like Robinson, Houellebecq, Beigbeder, and Moix depict an *occident émasculé*, a neutered West powerless against its more brawny, more devout adversaries. Finally, in the section "The Future Is Female," I show that the apprehension created by women's increasing social and political status has become a core theme of this strand of contemporary French novel, with its imaginary worlds conjured by distinctly masculine subjectivities. We might describe these narratives as examples of *écriture masculine* in that they rehearse the sufferings of male embodiment in a world in which masculinity has become a liability, at least in their depictions.

In chapter 2, "Endarkenment from the Minitel to the Internet," I show how the arrival of the Minitel—a protointernet developed and funded by the French state—and the internet have led to a confusion between fact and fiction, a theme exploited again and again by our authors. These networks brought with them the possibility of the high-velocity spread of conspiracy theories, false information, and doctored images provided by avatars or anonymous sources, a recipe for the proliferation of destabilizing fictions and even new forms of mysticism. I begin with a brief history of the Minitel and internet and show how these technologies have changed our relationship with truth. It might surprise readers to learn that one of the first Minitel experiments involved the purposeful dissemination of false information. Since then, the way we receive and assess information has changed radically, and our authors have taken great interest in this turn of Copernican proportions and its effects on our ability to distinguish between what is real and what is not. Silicon Valley, the mecca of information science, plays a conspicuous role in many of these narratives as the capital of the twenty-first century, the era in which the lines between real and virtual and between true and false became more blurry. I begin with a close reading of Aurélien Bellanger's novel *La Théorie de l'information* (2012), which offers a history of the Minitel, the internet, and what he calls Web 2.0, a biodigital network that allows humans to exist beyond the death of their bodies. The prodigious novel thematizes France's decline, the virtualization of sex, human mortality, information theory and its posthuman applications, and the virtual aspects of literature. Pairing this novel with Jean-François Lyotard's writings on the possibility of thought continuing without a body, I show how Bellanger marshals the virtual and the fictional in order to preserve a species in decline. I continue with a short segment on Philippe Vasset's *La Conjuration* (2013) on the connection between conspiracy theory and mysticism in the internet age, a glimpse of several of Houellebecq's novels in which digital networks play a conspicuous role, moving at the end of the chapter to Antoine Bello's novel trilogy *Les Falsificateurs* (2007), *Les Éclaireurs* (2009), and *Les Producteurs* (2015), which centers on an organization called the CFR (Consortium de falsification du réel), whose mission is to create and spread apocryphal information, aided in large part by the internet. The degeneration of France happens in synchronicity with the degeneration of the real.

In chapter 3, "Real-Time Realism, Part 1: Journalistic Immediacy," I begin by acknowledging the ever-evolving shape and content of journalistic media brought about by digital technology and the hyperconnectivity of the globalized world, suggesting that these disturbances have necessarily affected the work of realist novelists who seek to catch the contemporary world in their nets. By borrowing from journalism's toolbox, our authors achieve a real-time realism that feeds itself on *actualité* and produces an uncanny effect of immediacy, so close to the present that the future seems to be touched. Practitioners of degenerative realism imitate the techniques of journalistic writing, but they also include journalists and media outlets within the frames of their novels almost compulsively. They do so, I argue, because journalists and media providers are the primary co-constructors of our realities beyond what we can perceive empirically with our own senses. The controversial novel *The Camp of the Saints* (1973), by Jean Raspail, provides a benchmark by which I measure contemporary degenerative realist fictions because of its unrelenting emphasis on the role of the media in crafting reality. Many of the anxieties manifest in contemporary French fiction were already taken up by Raspail in that book, but, as I show in this and the next chapter, its ideological conviction is missing in the more recent novels on demographic angst. In the next section, I show the extent to which contemporary French novelists have adopted—consciously or unconsciously—many of the principles of New Journalism promoted in the late 1960s and early 1970s by writers like Tom Wolfe, Norman Mailer, Joan Didion, and Gay Talese; of the nonfiction novel, as theorized by Truman Capote; and of the new social novel, lauded by Wolfe in his famed 1989 manifesto. Touching on genres such as the *romanquête, autofiction*, and *docufiction*, where fact and fiction share a bed, I show the indebtedness of practitioners of degenerative realism to the journalist's trade. After a survey of a few pertinent works by Alexis Jenni, Yannick Haenel, Michel Houellebecq, Frédéric Beigbeder, Philippe Vasset, and others, I write at length about Jean Rolin's novel *Les Événements* (2015) in order to highlight the shift of focus in degenerative realism away from the smallness of the *fait divers* to the kinds of large-scale global events—usually catastrophic ones—that make the front page. In these fictions, the apocalyptic event is often the trigger for a reflection on the slow

and incremental decay that led to it. I close with a reflection on the implications of the post-truth / fake news / alternative facts era for the novel,
which has always tried to provide a certain kind of truth and which now
finds itself in competition with the fictions that dot the journalistic
mediascape.

In chapter 4, "Real-Time Realism, Part 2: *Le roman post-pamphlétaire*,"
I offer a brief overview of two ideological genres, the *pamphlet* and the
*roman pamphlétaire*, also known as the *roman à thèse*, which thrived
throughout the nineteenth century and into the twentieth, particularly in
moments of social and political upheaval. These combative genres are
unambiguous in their formulation of a consistent and forcefully presented
thesis, meant to convince the reader to "convert" to the author's position.
Using Susan Suleiman's influential book *Authoritarian Fictions: The Ideological Novel as a Literary Genre* (1983), I compare the *romans à thèse* she
describes with contemporary degenerative realist texts, which borrow
many of the formal features of this kind of ideological literature but contain no clear thesis or consistently undermine any doctrinal agenda one
might perceive in their pages. Degenerative realism is post-*pamphlétaire*
in the sense that it readily includes ideological speech in the words and
thoughts of its characters, but its novels are not actually ideological. They
offer no salutary doctrines to aid Western civilization in its convalescence.
No dogma can reverse the decay. Using Michel Houellebecq's *Submission*
(2015) as a case study representing a much broader tendency, I show how
ideological speech features prominently throughout the degenerative
realist novel not in order to convert the reader to adopt the ideologues'
positions but because such speech is omnipresent in contemporary public
discourses. An honest and full literary depiction of the current fraught
sociopolitical landscape is likely to represent these ideological pronouncements, whether or not the author personally agrees with them. *Submission*'s ideological ambivalence is representative of all degenerative realist
novels, which are attuned to the loss of authoritative voices in an era of
irreversible *déchéance*.

*Chapter One*

# DEMOGRAPHY AND SURVIVAL IN TWENTY-FIRST-CENTURY FRANCE

French society is a bit like a beached Beluga whale. It isn't dead yet, but there's an urgency to get it back in the water before the scavengers descend upon the carcass.

—CHARLES ROBINSON, *GÉNIE DU PROXÉNÉTISME*

Gaul is subdued.

—JULIUS CAESAR

In his autobiographical novel *L'Amour dure trois ans* (1997), Frédéric Beigbeder gives romantics a reality check: Love lasts three years. Demography proves it. One cannot argue with this fact. His narrator asserts: "Leo Ferré's song says it all: *'Avec le temps, on n'aime plus.'* [With time, one no longer loves.] How can you possibly argue with glands and neurotransmitters that will let you down as soon as the time comes? I suppose you could try lyric poetry, but faced with the twin forces of science and statistics [*les sciences naturelles et la démographie*], poetry is doomed from the start."[1] In this passage and in many novels analyzed in this chapter, the lyrical voice is muffled by the voice of science, which considers humans as just one species among all others. A treatment of the individual in merely statistical terms, subject to strict demographic and biological laws, is favored. A new realism with a distinctly nineteenth-century flair has emerged, dissolving the last sentimental delusions left from earlier novelistic writing. It recalls Hippolyte Taine's praise of Stendhal, who "treated the sentiments as they should be treated,—in the manner of the naturalist, namely, and of the natural philosopher, who constructs classifications and weighs forces";[2] or the zoological vision of the human as presented by Balzac in his famous introduction to the Comédie humaine; or Zola's experimental novel, which sought to deal with humans following Claude Bernard's methods in experimental medicine; or even to the Goncourt brothers' "clinical picture of Love"[3] they present in the preface to *Germinie Lacerteux*. While in contemporary Anglophone literature critics have noted the rise of what has come to be called the neuronovel,[4] which relies on neuroscience to open new possibilities for the novel, I want to argue that one prevalent tendency in France at the moment is the reliance on demography as the structuring element of plots in many contemporary novels.

The central thesis of this chapter is that demography allows the novelists of concern here to imagine and corroborate the possibility of a secular apocalypse,[5] the endpoint of a process of degeneration heavily feared already in the nineteenth century, made all the more imminent through the certainty and predictive force of statistical proof. This postreligious apocalypse involves only Western civilization, not the world.[6] The force that terminates the West is not God but biological destiny, propelled by *les barbares*, whose population continues to swell. The story woven in this chapter relies on a specific set of concepts—national suicide, social Darwinism, *le Grand Remplacement*, recreational versus reproductive sex, "fictitious cohorts," *l'homme moyen*, countercolonization, the Dusk of Nations, biological determinism, the war of the wombs—and a constellation of names including Thomas Malthus, Charles Darwin, le comte de Gobineau, Jacques Bertillon, Adolphe Quetelet, Cesare Lombroso, Max Nordau, Émile Zola, and the Marquis de Sade. The degenerative realist novel, which has announced its presence in France at the beginning of this new millennium, relies heavily on the science of demography for much of its atmospheric tension and its theses. Demography, a "science of processes,"[7] does not force the scientist to choose between a biological and a sociological conception of the human. Instead, these and other categories, such as the economic, the political, and the psychosexual, are marshaled through demography to make predictions about the future composition of the human race, its future geography, distribution of resources, and ascendant ideologies. The fictional French civilization and its discontents depicted in the realist novels to be discussed in this chapter reside in the same realm as the "fictitious cohorts," also known as "hypothetical" or "synthetic cohorts," used in some demographic methodologies to anticipate the future trajectory of this or that population. The degenerative fiction of today thinks in terms of present or soon-to-arrive reconfigurations of France and Frenchness, making demographic projections about a nearly unrecognizable population that will encroach upon the old one, bound for extinction.[8]

In this chapter, I show how, using a nineteenth-century logic of biological determinism, the new degenerative realism of some contemporary French novels responds to recent population shifts as quantified by present-day demographers. As defined in this book's introduction, degenerative realism is a form of literary mimesis that requires a contemporary setting (contemporaneous with the moment in which the book was written) and that elaborates on existing theories of civilizational decline. A fatalistic belief in statistical projections relieves the novels' protagonists, bound for extinction, of some of their worries because they are part of a system that makes sense, even if they are the losers in this system. If what they imagine as their own civilization is in decline, this is only because it deserves to be, according to the logic of fitness. Instead of stewing endlessly in the indeterminacies that constituted the postmodern era, these authors have drawn their conclusions unilaterally, replacing ambivalence with the certainty of civilizational death. Action cannot stave off this inevitability, and for this reason, the novelists have no salvational dogmas or guiding principles to offer their readers. Their books are devoid of pedagogical intent. There is no need to convince anyone of anything.

The treatment of sex in the novels discussed in this chapter is particularly interesting, especially in its recreational iterations. The maximalism and overstatedness of many of our authors—with their tendency toward textual *surproduction* and their endless staging of page after page of orgiastic sex alternating with lamentations on the slow death of France, of Europe, of the West—seem to function at times as a surrogate of sexual reproduction, as though their gushing ink could stand in for the missing sperm necessary for the survival of their "species": given their "pursuit of vitality at all costs," they might fall under the rubric of what the critic James Wood has called "hysterical realism," which is "characterized by a fear of silence."[9] The connection between textual and sexual production could already be seen in the nineteenth century in such massive novels as Émile Zola's *Fécondité* (1899), whose thesis was prefigured in an article titled "Dépopulation" (1896)[10] and which Rachilde described as "colossal" and "as cumbersome and respectable as the womb of a woman in her ninth month."[11] This sort of metaphorical dissemination allows the author simultaneously to spill out anxieties about the extinction of what he perceives as his own societal line (the narratives are almost invariably written by men) and to leave *something of himself* behind as a kind of mournful *patrimoine*, a residual genetic smudge pressed between the pages of his novel.

The survivalist logic found in these books strays from biological Darwinism in that the impending extinction does not happen on the level of the species but rather on the level of race or other complex identitarian categories that mix religion, social class, and other designations. This is obviously what distinguishes Darwinism from social Darwinism: the substitution of "species" with some other, more specific category in the competitive model. Regarding Jonathan Littell's novel *Les Bienveillantes* (2006), Michael Mack has argued that "Littell's novel confronts us with the stark reality of what happens when real human beings are reduced to non-human categories and rubrics."[12] It is fair to say that all of the novels in this chapter conceive of the human through such rubrics. As the demographer Hervé Le Bras has argued, "Except for the world population—which is that of a biological species—all other populations are cultural constructs. Horde, tribe, people, nation—none has any natural foundation."[13] The West, Europe, France, white males, or Catholics, among other classifications, are imagined in the novels I'll analyze as a species whose unfitness will lead to its demise. In comparing the demography of human populations to that of animals, Le Bras points out that "the elegant models of predation, competition, and spatial dispersal" found in biomathematical models of animal demography "have no equivalent in human societies except at the level of metaphor" (5). But it is precisely this literalization of metaphor that accounts for the social Darwinist projections on which the narratives of these paranoid fictions rely. What does the death of France, of Europe, or of the West actually mean? Is it essentially the death of an idea, not a species? Are culture and ideas subject to the laws of the survival, as certain body-forms are? Can culturally constructed phenomena like the novel or the nation go extinct, or are they capable of developing new traits that guarantee their longevity, at least provisionally?

Several characteristics mark the particular strand of contemporary French fiction of focus in this chapter: the statistical treatment of humans through discourses of demography and marketing; an obsession with national suicide or euthanasia; the expression of a social Darwinist vision of global competition in all its forms; an emphasis on nonreproductive sex; an understanding of 9/11 as the gash that made visible the latent internal contradictions of Western civilization, particularly when juxtaposed with Islam; a preoccupation with paternal and masculine impotence, incompetence, and irrelevance and the suggestion that the future will be female; and a tacit acknowledgment of the existence of an *écriture masculine* whose depicted reality differs from that of *écriture féminine* or other ungendered or differently gendered kinds of writing. These features are characteristic of contemporary French degenerative realism, which we can understand as the attempt to narrate the decay of Western civilization as it happens, often with an implied surrender to this process on the part of the characters. The ailing nation puts itself out of its own misery.

## THE WORRISOME CENSUS: DEMOGRAPHY AND DREAD

If you control the children, you control the future.

—MICHEL HOUELLEBECQ, *SUBMISSION*

While many have noted the conspicuous absence of statistical data regarding the demographic composition of the French population, owing in part to the universalist principle that all French citizens are identical under the law and thus the collection of demographic data is a violation of that principle, there is still a lurking demographic anxiety in France, which is probably not soothed by the absence of concrete figures.[14] With or without accurate data, the world viewed from a demographic perspective has elicited anxieties in Europe, particularly since the late nineteenth century, when this form of statistical analysis gained independence as a discrete field. The original home of demography, a term coined in French by a Belgian statistician named Achille Guillard,[15] was in the field of economics, but gradually it achieved autonomy as a freestanding science and later began to incorporate sociological and anthropological methods and questions into its own.[16] A basic textbook definition announces one of the key problems to be addressed in this chapter: "Demography, the science of population, is a field of study that lies at the intersection of the social and the biological sciences."[17] The novels described in the following sections toggle between a sociological and a biological notion of the human, who is always subject to overlapping—but often conflicting—communal and organic laws. Certain narrative techniques in these novels, such as first-person narration or the third-person-omniscient point of view, offer a glimpse of the psychological interiority of the specimen whose story unfolds in the novel. The strange combination of clinical distancing and subjective interiority characterizes the corpus of novels presented here.

When making forecasts about future population configurations, demography contains a heavily fictional element.[18] In his book *The Nature of Demography*, Hervé Le Bras begins with what he calls *Homo demographicus*, a personification of "a simple and general model of behavior."[19] He explains that *Homo demographicus* "is a gambler who must contend with various risks—those of dying, having a child, migrating, getting married. He and the lifeline linking the events he has experienced are the necessary starting point for demographic analysis" (3). But there is a problem with this imaginary person: "*Homo demographicus* is a Robinson Crusoe–like figure, cut off from his fellow men. When we wish to take account of ties of family or locality, demographic theory quickly loses its effectiveness" (4). Le Bras's use of Defoe's canonical literary figure to describe the imaginary personage required by some demographic models hints at the presence of a fictional element in the science. He continues, evoking the problems of the "fictitious cohort," "microsimulations," and what he calls the "demographic 'novel'" (346), suggesting that "the fiction of the isolated subject becomes untenable when working on marriage or migration" (347). Like Zola's experimental novel, a laboratory in which experiments may be performed on characters, Le Bras's description of demography highlights the problems of fusing science and literature. In their description of how to calculate life expectancy, Lundquist, Anderton, and Yaukey call it a "hypothetical figure," a "mental game" in which the demographer must "conjure up an imaginary set of people and put them through a lifetime of mortality risks," constructing a "hypothetical or synthetic cohort."[20] This conjectural imperative brings demography close to the realm of literature, which crafts characters who don't exist but who perhaps could.

Scholars have taken recent interest in the literary treatment of the statistically rendered human, and with good reason.[21] Perhaps now more than ever, with the global awareness of population growth and the tendency to think of humans in terms of marketing demographics, poll numbers, and economic brackets, any novel that treats problems of family, sociopolitical change, or the role of financial markets in everyday life lends itself to a reading through a statistical framework. Already in 1835, the Belgian statistician and sociologist Adolphe Quetelet, famed for his theory of the *homme moyen*, or average man, dedicated part of a chapter of his well-known book *A Treatise on Man and the Development of His Faculties* (*Sur l'homme et le développement de ses facultés, ou essai de physique sociale*) to the relationship between demography and cultural production such as literature and visual art. For him, the "average man . . . is in a nation what the centre of gravity is in a body; it is by having that central point in view that we arrive at the apprehension of all the phenomena of equilibrium and motion."[22] Only through an understanding of this *homme moyen*—the *femme moyenne* is left aside—can the real truth of a nation be ascertained. In a section titled "Of the Average Man Considered with Reference to Literature and the Fine Arts," Quetelet argues that "the necessity of veracity in faithfully representing the physiognomy, the habits, and the manners of people at different epochs, has at all times led artists and literary men to seize, among the individuals whom they observed, the characteristic traits of the period in which they lived; or, in other words, to come as near the average as possible" (96).

Several issues are at stake here. First, there is the notion that the veracity of a particular literary or visual representation is bound to its degree of focus on what is average for the age. In order to create art and literature that is the *"expression of society"* (97), each writer or painter, in addition to observing his or her own milieu with full attention, would be wise to rely on the statistician's numerically precise rendering of the social realities of a given community. The exceptional person has no representation in Quetelet's model except as one figure among many who tug the average slightly this way or that. The demographer's precision combats the "vague" and "indistinct ideas" (96–97), "erroneous opinions" (96), and "relations determined at a glance" (97) of those who create art without reliance on statistically verifiable patterns. In Quetelet's view, the "predominating elements in any people or any age" (96) constitute the reality of that people or age. Translating ethnographic principles into fiction, Marc Augé implements an idea similar to Quetelet's in his 2011 ethnofiction *Journal d'un SDF*. There, he invents a fictional individual who represents "a social totality of which [the readers] can themselves, over time, form a more or less precise idea from the Press, the news and from conversations they might have with different people."[23] Put in slightly different terms, the imagined "(stereo)types" people create in their minds based on lived and read experiences are constituted by the average of these experiences. Quetelet believed that art and literature are only "capable of moving and agitating the passions"[24] when they are precise and statistically informed. To free themselves from the bonds of the ancients, the contemporary artist and writer must constantly update their portrayals of humanity according to current statistical models, a technique reminiscent of Hippolyte Taine's recipe of *race-milieu-moment*. By recognizing that "the type has changed" (97) and that modern man no longer resembles the one found in classical art and literature, the artist and writer can create a reality customized to the age. An understanding of the average man "would inform [artists and men of literature] more precisely of things which they now know only but vaguely" (97) and would also reveal truths they could never begin to suspect existed. In short, "the truth must always lie between the extremes" (98), and the statistical average reveals this truth. Clearly, the novelists of focus in my study have heeded Quetelet's advice.

These authors share something else with Quetelet, namely, his anxiety toward the demographic shifts to which he is so attentive in his recommendations, asking, "Who . . . can assure himself that the type of the Grecian figure shall not be lost, either in the flight of time, or in some great catastrophe involving the destruction of the Caucasian race? Such overthrows are in the nature of possible things" (97). These fears find new frames with each generation, from the demographer Jacques Bertillon's founding of the Alliance nationale pour l'accroissement de la population française, which sought to reverse France's population plunge at the end of the nineteenth century; to the social Darwinist anxieties in certain *romans à thèse* of the late nineteenth and early twentieth centuries, with protagonists whom Louise Lyle has called *struggleforlifeurs*;[25] to Jean Raspail's novel of demographic dystopia *The Camp of the Saints* (1973) and the contemporary conspiracy theory of the *Grand Remplacement* put forth by the writer Renaud Camus, which both claim that a campaign to purge whiteness from France is well underway. Quetelet's unique pairing of a politics of representational veracity with the hypothetical imaginary provides a clear model for many realist novelists in contemporary France.

Not only does demography include a fictional element in its own methods, but fiction writers seem tempted by the literary promise of demography to shape their novels and short stories. When inserted into fiction, the simple "act of counting" people, whose textual form Elaine Scarry calls the "population tract" or "population treatise,"[26] provides an automatic narrative framework into which a protagonist and characters may be situated. In Anton Kuijsten's analysis, what distinguishes the "demographical novel" or "demografiction" from other types of novels or fictions is that "they do not focus on individual-level vital events as such." In them, "Population dynamics either is their central theme, or is the dominating context in which the theme develops."[27] Borrowing C. Wright Mills's "conceptual distinction between 'personal troubles' and 'public issues,'" Kuijsten argues that the demographic novel blurs these categories. He continues, "What are aspects of individual-level sex, death, and passion in all other novels, are raised to the level of common fate and destiny in the demographic novel: mass-level explosion, extinction, and expulsion" (86). As Lionel Shriver has asserted regarding demographic science, "Because beneath the field's dry statistical surface, there teems an irresistible Pandora's box of paranoia, nationalism, rivalrous ambition, misanthropy, and apocalyptic dread, demography is sure to tempt fiction-writing dabblers to prize open the lid."[28] Shriver's description accurately characterizes the most prominent examples of contemporary French degenerative realism, which use population as a diagnostic tool for the health or infirmity of the civilization they depict.

Already in Zola's naturalist maximalism, a preoccupation with the human conceived in terms of race, population, and the bodily transmission of certain features from one generation to the next was visible:

Physiologically the Rougon-Macquarts illustrate the gradual sequence of nervous and sanguine accidents that befall a race after a first organic lesion and, according to environment, determine in each individual member of the race those feelings, desires, and passions—in sum, all the natural and instinctive manifestations of humanity—whose outcomes are conventionally described in terms of "virtue" or "vice."[29]

The nature of that "organic lesion" of which Zola wrote so ominously transforms in the twentieth century. During the interwar period, there is a split: if Roger Martin du Gard still finds it possible to write a genetico-genealogical family saga in the form of his *roman fleuve* titled *Les Thibault*, published between 1922 and 1940, Jules Romains fails to see the viability of such a project given that family, as a once-meaningful unit to modern man, has dissolved. In the strange, defensive preface to his massive twenty-seven-novel cycle *Men of Good Will* (*Les Hommes de bonne volonté*, 1932–1946), Romains laments the decay of the Western family and the literary impact of this dissolution. As holds true for many realist writers, his objective was to find a "means of expressing collective life,"[30] but in contrast to the novelistic worlds of Zola, Proust, or Martin du Gard, which revolved around the fate of individuals within the web of family, in Romains's twentieth-century world, "families are not of very much importance" (ix). This unhappy familial fragmentation has seeped into the realist novel's form, dissolving its architecture. The twentieth century required a change of perspective to manage what he calls "social multiplicity" (x), which has exploded and diversified even further in our time.

In the nineteenth century, a protodemographic treatment of the human was already visible, for example in Balzac's famed typologies or in Zola's tragic genealogies, but what the twenty-first-century novels bring to the table is a heavy emphasis on the role of demographic *markets*. A pattern is consistent in the novels of interest in this chapter: in them, the human, as consumer and consumed, is a mere statistical unit in a decadent capitalist system, and his or her actions are predetermined by the market to which he or she belongs. This market determinism, combined with an overt biological determinism, virtually negates the free will of the individual. As Frédéric Beigbeder writes in *99 Francs* (2000), his novel about the advertising industry: "You are the products of an age. No, why the age? You are products, full stop. Because globalization is no longer interested in people, you had to become products before society would take any interest in you. Capitalism transforms people into perishable yoghurts, addicted to shows."[31]

A similar vision is apparent in all of Houellebecq's novels, particularly those that celebrate the so-called skin trade. In *Submission* (2015), the protagonist François resists being put into a market demographic, noticing the tendency of women's magazines to think in these terms. In them, "everyone's reduced to some kind of consumer demographic: the eco-responsible urban professional, the brand-conscious bourgeoise, the LGBT-friendly club girl, the satanic geek, the techno-Buddhist. They invent a new one every week." He goes on to argue, "I don't match up with some preconceived consumer profile."[32] The same market-demographic thinking can likewise be found in Charles Robinson's *Génie du proxéné-tisme, ou beautés de la religion péripatéticienne* (2008), which proposes prostitution as the solution to a flagging economy, and Aurélien Bellanger's *La Théorie de l'information* (2012), which illustrates how the digital matrix has allowed for new ways to commodify the body and enrich the already wealthy to a scandalous degree. These and other contemporary novels turn toward print advertisements, travel brochures, television commercials, pop-up ads, social media marketing, and web banner advertising—in short, any media that relies on a "market demographic" notion of the human—to represent the noise of the now. The typical person cannot escape these daily reminders that they are lodged in a market-segmentation system, which places them in the 18-to-34 bracket or the $50,000 to $75,000 income bracket or the divorcée bracket. This very specific form of demographic thinking brings the science of demography full circle, since it was originally developed to better understand purely economic problems. The novels of interest in this study tend to think of the human demographically, both in marketing and economic terms and in terms of general population distribution in a given geography.

Demography can be a fear-inducing science. It elicits anxieties about what the future holds, about the necessity of biopolitical intervention on the part of the state or church to maintain a healthy population equilibrium, and about the questionable independence of individual will in the face of indisputable statistical truths. In the next section, the fear of degeneration through demographic flux will be brought to light.

## DEGENERATION: THE NEW OLD ANGUISH

Tout est foutu.

—DRIEU LA ROCHELLE, "LE CAPITALISME, LE COMMUNISME ET L'ESPRIT"

If journalists, intellectuals, and politicians are to be trusted, France is in a state of irreversible decay. Consider the following declarations:

- "I estimate that France's death is only a matter of years away."
- "The foreigner has taken such a large role in the management of our internal and external affairs that if we want to understand our situation and our politics, we must look abroad to study them."

- "It seems to me that French decadence is distinct from other historical decadences in that France is perfectly self-aware. . . . Never was a woeful population more conscious of its own sufferings."

- "France will collapse under the repeated blows of foreign invasion. . . . France is nothing but a cadaver [whose] decomposition makes terrifying progress each day. [One could] mathematically calculate the day when there won't be a single Frenchman left in France."

- "We are *the most* poorly governed country; or, should I say, so as not to hurt anyone's feelings, we are *one of the most* poorly governed countries to be found in the world."

- "[France,] this glorious and privileged nation, has completely neglected its duty of self-preservation, and the appalling catastrophes that were the cost of this presumptuousness are all too clear."

These quotes express several different kinds of fear, the most prominent of which is angst about the barbarians at the door, or, rather, the barbarians who have filled the foyer. France will lose its national identity to them, watching this loss attentively without taking steps to forestall it. The population has become sensitive, easily offended, incapable of decisive action, reliant on its past glory. The nation faces certain degeneration.

While such declarations are commonplace among contemporary French intellectuals, politicians, and other public figures alarmed by a perceived degradation of the nation, the loss of French identity, the increasing calls for political correctness, and the easy capitulation to a flawed multicultural agenda, the pronouncements just quoted were actually all made in the late nineteenth and early twentieth centuries. These statements—from Joséphin Péladin (1891), Émile Flourens (1906), Jules Lemâitre (1901), Jean du Valdor (1893), Jules Roche (1897), and Léon Bloy (1891), respectively—are illustrative of the French national doom and gloom that characterized the last turn of the century.[33] As Andrew J. Counter has noted, "As anyone familiar with the period knows, identifying, bemoaning, and just occasionally exaggerating the symptoms of national decline was a beloved pastime of the denizens of *fin-de-siècle* France."[34] From its first coalescence as a sovereign body to its revolutionary convulsions, through the horrors of two world wars and the collapse of its colonial aspirations, a fear of nation-death has always found voice in France. Here are a few equivalent voices from twenty-first-century French public figures:

- "The French no longer recognize France. Liberty has become anomie [alien-ation caused by lack of purpose and ideals]; Equality has become affirmative action; Fraternity has become the war against everyone" (Éric Zemmour).[35]
- "Why did I speak of the *suicide of a nation*? Because the French march submis-sively toward the disappearance of their culture and identity, and the nation rushes toward the successive erasure of all that comprised it, without the pos-sibility of a serious movement of refusal of this foreseeable death—with the partial exception of the Front national" (Renaud Camus).[36]
- "Why do I find the French stupid, vulgar, spineless, dull, and offensive? Not only because they renounced their religion but because each day, they trample on their language with the cheerfulness of people who enjoy being loboto-mized" (Richard Millet).[37]
- "France is sinking into the darkness of Europe, and with it the French people, all the people of Europe. France is facing dark times . . . and nothing seems solid underfoot. France is caught in a thick fog of despair of a disenchanted country" (Marine Le Pen).[38]
- "There is a nation that embodies the illnesses of Europe to excess and adds other, more specific ones: France. These days, it is not easy to be French, that is, heirs to a glorious past whose ups and downs bring out our pettiness in con-trast" (Pascal Bruckner).[39]
- "More and more French people, including the elites, are alienated from their own language, literature, history, and landscapes. It is because French civili-zation may be in the process of dying out that this national identity issue concerns so many people even though no one is fooled by the electoral ruse" (Alain Finkielkraut).[40]

If France really is dying, it is taking its sweet damn time doing so. Like Cyrano de Bergerac's protracted death at the end of Edmond Rostand's famous play or the slow death of Ionesco's king in *Le Roi se meurt*, France has filled the moments/years/decades/centuries before its demise with a self-reflective monologue. An always-on-the-horizon but eternally deferred death is perfect literary and journalistic fodder. It would be impossible to calculate how many publishing houses and newspapers have profited from this imminent but ever-tarrying civilization death. The new anxieties about cultural degeneration sound very similar to the fin-de-siècle anxieties, but there was never really a pause between these two moments. My point here is that fretting over degeneration seems to be a favored pastime in modern Europe and the West,[41] with the French being particularly skilled at dwelling on the demise of their own culture. The nation (or postnation, in the case of the European Union) is imagined as an ailing body whose death is imminent. In his book *The Short History of Decay* (1949), published shortly after the end of World War II, E. M. Cioran described a couple of specifically European concepts related to this *déché-ance*: "There is *Weltschmerz*, a *mal du siècle*, which is merely the illness of a generation; there is another which follows upon all historical experience and which becomes the unavoidable conclusion for the time to come. This is what the French call *vague à l'âme*, a melancholy yearning for the end of the world."[42] These concepts are more readily associated with romanticism than with realism, but as I will show, these sweeping generational intuitions are key to the degenerative realist spirit.

In 1957—the year in which Roland Barthes published his famous decryption of bourgeois taste titled *Mythologies*, as anxieties about nuclear proliferation haunted the world and *L'Express* revealed that the French army had been torturing prisoners in its war with Algeria—the journalist and essayist Emmanuel Berl published *La France irréelle*, which begins with this sobering passage: "La politique française me semble évoluer moins comme une histoire que comme une névrose. Son trait dominant, à mon estime, c'est l'affaiblissement progressif du sens du réel qu'elle manifeste, depuis quinze ans."[43] Berl was no stranger to *déclinologie*; he'd collaborated with Drieu la Rochelle on a foreboding periodical titled *Les Derniers Jours* in the 1920s, whose contributors imagined "le Déclin de l'Occident et l'Apocalypse du Progrès."[44] Berl attributes this crumbling sense of the real to a host of factors: the circulation of a political vocabulary bereft of meaning, duplicitous leaders, the progressive entry of France into a global economy, confused alliances, an excessive nationalism and heightened partisanship, and various socially detrimental problems such as alcoholism and the public's inability to adapt to the frenetic pace of technological change. For Berl, a loss of the real meant a loss of crucial orientation points for a population made timorous by war and social upheaval. *La France irréelle* was a bewildered nation vulnerable to both internal and external threats. The contemporary authors of focus in my study manifest many of the same apprehensions regarding the dissolution of the real.

Like their fathers and their fathers' fathers, these authors have assigned to their characters a clear set of anxieties regarding certain degenerative forces that persist in decaying the nation, eating it like a cancer or encrusting it with rot.[45] What will the coroner declare as France's ultimate cause of death? Passive absorption into Europe, capitalist infiltration by America, violent liquidation by radical Islam, feminization, or the genetic dissipation of France into a nation of immigrants are possible culprits to be listed on the death certificate. In his provocative essays and *pamphlets*, Richard Millet catalogues other anxieties in addition to these: linguistic degradation, the abysmal decline of French literature, the loss of taste and historical memory, the oppressive rise of antiracism, the feminization of literary study and of society in general, and the depletion of a Christian identity in France. These troubled expressions of cultural degeneration imply that the nation was once healthy but has contracted a terminal illness. Take Michel Houellebecq's *Submission* as an example. Douglas Morrey writes of it: "The novel's persistent lexical field of fatigue and inertia creates the sense of a nation ground down by an exhausting social system, as well as a soul-destroying bureaucracy."[46] Carole Sweeney calls his novels *The Elementary Particles* and *The Possibility of an Island* "eschatological meditations on modernity in perceived terminal cultural and social decline."[47] As we'll see, Houellebecq is by no means the only miserabilist among contemporary novelists.

The most pressing concern seems to be the nation's changing demographic makeup. Philippe Galanopoulos has noted the role of science in the nineteenth-century vilification of foreigners, which took shape as racist biological theories and treatises on anthropology, epidemiology, and geography.[48] When William Oualid asked in 1927, "Will France become a country of national minorities?"[49] he anticipated the primary European question of the new millennium. Oualid answered his own question with "no," a diagnosis that would have relieved his French compatriots. While it is probably too early to declare *Finis Galliae!*, the demographic shifts invite contemporary citizens to revisit Ernest Renan's famous lecture "What Is a Nation?" (1882), in which he proposes the notion of subjective nationality and calmly declares that "nations are not eternal. They were begun, they will end. A European confederation will probably replace them."[50] For France to continue to survive, it will almost certainly need to redefine "nation" and "nationality" and come to terms with the arrival of a new citizenry that does not resemble the idealized one of the past.

The notion of cultural degeneration, along with decline and decadence, is a very nineteenth-century European idea. In his excellent study *Décadence fin de siècle*, Michel Winock nuances the terms "decline" and "decadence," explaining:

Decline is always a decline of something, of production, fertility rate, or a religious practice. Decadence, which, moreover, can incorporate signs of decline, is above all a vague idea, a pessimistic representation of the world, a nostalgia for what is no more, a creation of the sullen, alarmist, or hopeless imaginary.[51]

Embedded in both terms is a downward gravitational pull, the vector of destiny for all dying things. Degeneration also pulls living things *vers le bas*, but with the added connotation of organic decay. While the fall of empires and civilizational decline are much older preoccupations, the application of biological processes to cultural production originated with scientists and thinkers like Arthur de Gobineau (*Essai sur l'inégalité des races humaines*, 1855),[52] Bénédict Augustin Morel (*Traité des dégénérescences physiques, intellectuelles et morales de l'espèce humaine et des causes qui produisent ces variétés maladives*, 1857), Max Nordau (*Entartung*, 1892), Cesare Lombroso (*Genio e degenerazione*, 1897), and others.[53] While degeneration and decadence are readily associated with nineteenth-century Europe, the concepts have enjoyed a curious revival in contemporary literature, at the turn of this new millennium.[54]

The most famous book to address the collective, cultural fin-de-siècle unraveling as it happened was Max Nordau's influential *Degeneration* (1892). There is a deep irony in the fact that the term "degeneration" (*Entartung* in German)—made so famous by Nordau, who was Jewish and worked alongside Theodor Herzl for the formation of a Zionist state— would be appropriated by the National Socialists in their attempt to pathologize the cultural production of those they saw as their genetic inferiors. The most well-known example of this pathologization was the famous 1937 art exhibit in Munich "Entartete Kunst" (Degenerate Art), which displayed modernist works as examples of cultural degeneration. Using Nordau's own logic, one could say that his notion of degeneration degenerated into a Nazi concept. Leaning heavily on the research of his mentor Cesare Lombroso, the famed Italian criminologist and theorist of criminal atavism, and on the findings of Bénédict Morel presented in his famous treatise *Traité des dégénérescences* (1857), Nordau attributes most of these new symptoms to poisoning (in the form of narcotics, stimulants, tainted food, and environmental pollution), nervousness and fatigue produced by the accelerated pace of life brought about by new communication and transportation technologies, and the social strain produced in urban settings. The nervous system and brain suffer from "organic expenditure,"[55] and this "excessive organic wear and tear" (43) that plagues the individual can also afflict the nation. This suffering seeps from the individual to the collective and begins to manifest itself in what he sees as the degeneracy of realism, naturalism, decadentism, neomysticism, socialism, and Darwinism.

In the book's opening pages, Nordau argues that the concept of fin-de-siècle—an adjective used to describe the "prevalent feeling" of "imminent perdition and extinction" (2) that seemed to dominate the European spirit at the end of the nineteenth century—represents a ridiculous projection of a biological ontology onto an historical era. A belief in fin-de-siècle decline suggests that civilizational time is capable of passing through the various stages of life (birth, childhood, youth, maturity, senility, and death) just as humans and animals do. Since the term "fin-de-siècle" originated in French and has been preserved in this language even when exported to other nations, Nordau argues that it is in France, "the land of its birth that it appears in its most genuine form, and Paris is the right place in which to observe its manifold expressions" (1). He prefers to use the expression *fin-de-race*, the end of the race, careful to note that degeneration manifests itself most prominently in the highest classes and in the cultural production of that slice of the population that might now be called the 1 percent.[56] However, because the tastes of this elite class trickle down to the lower classes, "it appears as if the whole of civilized humanity were converted to the aesthetics of the Dusk of the Nations" (7).

Given Nordau's fixation with the Dusk of Nations, one wonders if he would have viewed the European Union as one form of dusk, given that it articulates a new kind of postnational sovereignty. Or is the Dusk of Nations synonymous with the Dusk of Humanity? The Dusk of the Ruling Class? Or the Dusk of what Paul Bourget called "le mélancolique Occident"?[57] This is not completely clear. The concepts of France, Europe, and the West are often used interchangeably in the narratives at stake in this chapter, which already represents a kind of semantic death of the nation, since it can easily be replaced by some other conceptual unit. If the three ideas slip so easily into one another, their ontological solidity has already begun to dissolve. Some authors focus on the Frenchness of the impending societal death; others, on its Europeanness (or even Western European-ness); still others on its Northern Hemisphereness; and finally others on its general Westernness. These easy slippages allow one alternately to inflate the proportions of the problem or to point to its specificity in a particular place.

For Nordau, nowhere was this decadence more discernible than in lit-erature, music, philosophy, and art. He draws up a long hit list of offenders from his age: the Pre-Raphaelites, Symbolism, Tolstoy, Wagner, the Parnas-sians, the Decadents, Ibsen, Nietzsche, and the new German realists. We find Baudelaire alongside Barrès, Hugo alongside Huysmans, all targets of Nordau's critiques. He reserves a good share of vitriol for Zola and the naturalist school, what he calls a form of "literary canal-dredging [*schrift-stellerischen Kanalräumer-Berufe*]" (13). After dismissing terms like natu-ralism, realism, impressionism, and idealism as meaningless (475), he focuses his critiques on Zola, whose "coprolalia (mucktalk)," "predilection for coarseness" (499), and bluntly sexual themes produce a pornographic realism that is, in Nordau's view, hardly real at all. What would he make of the current millennialism and blasphemous filth of the contemporary novels I will analyze here? Similar to the cultural artifacts he critiqued at the end of the nineteenth century, these new novels show "a contempt for traditional views of custom and morality," "unbridled lewdness," and the "unchaining of the beast in man" (5). The new cultural degenerates are inherently pessimistic, egotistical, perverted, self-loathing, and despon-dent, with virtually no life force visible in their literary production.

The anxieties about the extinction of the French "race" often concur with anxieties about the extinction of the novel.[58] In fact, as I will show, these anxieties have become virtually inseparable. In the notice to the readers of Anatole Baju's first issue of *Le Décadent*, the editors wrote, "It is above all in language that the symptoms [of societal decadence] manifest themselves," and pledged to involve themselves strictly in the literary rather than political aspects of a new Decadent movement.[59] If the novel is seen by many as the literary correlative of democracy[60] or of the nation[61] and the best form in which to represent the life arc of the postrevolution-ary individual, then when the nation suffers, the novel necessarily suffers, too. The terms of interest in this chapter—the Greek *demos* (people) of "demography" and "democracy," the Latin *genus* (birth, descent) of "degeneration," and the Latin *natio* (birth, race, species, or stock of people) of "nation"—are all bound etymologically to biological existence.

The realist novel is particularly susceptible to the vulnerabilities of the body because it is so dependent on *life* for its own form. Realism in its various guises has always been motivated by life and its reproduction, displaying an impulse to make art resemble life or to bring an image or text alive through a set of mimetic techniques. The realist impulse is necessarily vitalist, not in the philosophical sense of the doctrine that life comes about through some force other than physical or chemical ones but, rather, in the survivalist sense of living at all costs. In the broadest terms, I will label as vitalist any effort to make something live or keep living.

The novel—a supremely national literature—has often been imagined as a living, although usually moribund, entity. The novel is always in the middle of dying, it seems, and the language of pathology and biology are constantly summoned to add metaphorical flair to these alarmist diagnoses. Take, for example, the following assertion by Luigi Capuana, one of the fathers of Italian *verismo*, alongside Giovanni Verga. In his 1898 book *The Contemporary -Isms (Gli 'ismi' contemporanei)*, in a chapter called "The Crisis of the Novel," Capuana wrote that "the modern novel is sick," "an infirm creature," and "one of those organisms that falls easily ill."[62] The controversial writer Richard Millet has produced book after book—including *The Disenchantment of Literature* (2007), *The Hell of the Novel: Reflections on Postliterature* (2010), and *Antiracism as Literary Terror* (2012)—mourning the death of the novel and of Western literature and culture, using a similar language of infirmity and putrefaction.[63] In the century that separates Capuana and Millet, one finds countless examples of this language of novelistic degeneration. Yet the novel still thrives in terms of sales figures. Thus it isn't the death of the novel as such that elicits fear but a more specific kind or quality of novel that is at risk.

We are witness to the revival of a certain strain of nineteenth-century vitalism, discernible, for example, in what Andrew Counter calls Zola's "reproductive politics"[64] and, more generally, in what Rita Schober has called the "genetico-genealogical family saga,"[65] novels and novel cycles that rely on the making and transmission of life for their own vital sustainment. However, because the family unit has dissolved, the new survivalist fictions are preoccupied not with familial survival but with the endurance of the race. "The race" is understood alternately as the white race, the French, the Europeans, or Westerners. These books are nonetheless maximalist in both form and content, even without a family tree to provide a sturdy architecture.[66]

In contemporary realism, demography seems to be one of the most prominently represented social sciences. It is clear that a key anxiety in France in the current era is cultural and racial extinction, a fear bolstered by demographic evidence and less-than-scientific declarations made in contemporary *pamphlets* published regularly in France. One wonders whether the sole purpose of France's natalist policies is to birth enough new taxpayers to cover retiree pensions and other forms of *protection sociale* or whether these policies are motivated in part by a latent fear of cultural and racial absorption into the growing pool of immigrants. Contemporary realist fictions have seized upon these demographic anxieties and placed them at the center of their narratives. For example, in Jean-Christophe Rufin's 2007 novel *Le Parfum d'Adam*, ecoterrorists propose a solution to overpopulation, which they attribute to the hyper-reproductivity of the so-called Third World: a toxic substance will kill off the human excess that is causing much of the world's environmental woes. Notwithstanding the clear survivalist thrust in such a book, one recognizes what could be called a poetics of preemptive defeat. Even the most radical, unethical form of population control cannot reroute the course of the future.

In 1999, Henk De Gans argued:

There are two ancient nineteenth-century fears regarding the present demographic situation in different parts of the world which are still at work: the fear of overpopulation (present and future overpopulation in the countries of the Third World; ecological overpopulation in the countries of the Western industrialised world), and that of imminent race suicide in Western societies.[67]

Suicide is central in the French cultural imagination—from the lasting influence of Émile Durkheim's *Suicide* (1897) to the famous suicides that punctuate the French literary corpus, including that of Emma Bovary, the multiple suicides that characterize Houellebecq's corpus, and the writer Edouard Levé's novel *Suicide* (2008), which he handed over to his editor and then killed himself ten days later. Nor should one forget Pierre Chaunu and Georges Suffert's controversial study *La Peste blanche: Comment éviter le suicide de l'Occident* (1976), which enumerated many of the same fears around which practitioners of degenerative realism construct their narratives. Rather than describing France's death as a murder at the hands of immigrants or American capitalism or any number of other treacherous forces, there is a tendency to assign blame to the nation for its own death, labeling it a form of suicide or even euthanasia, as France might need assistance in precipitating its own demise. In a recent feature piece in the *New Yorker* titled "The French Obsession with National Suicide,"[68] Alexander Stille gives countless examples of this tendency, from Éric Zemmour's *Le Suicide français* (2014)—whose first line reads "France is the sick man of Europe"[69]—to declarations over the centuries lamenting the suicidal tendency of French culture by writers like Max Nordau, Édouard Drumont, Raymond Aron, and Marc Bloch. Renaud Camus's *France: Suicide d'une nation* (2014) should be added to this list as well. Compared to the symbolic fullness of Islamist suicide, French cultural suicide seems relatively empty, a pointless self-murder with no higher teleology.[70]

## SOCIAL DARWINISM AND *LE GRAND REMPLACEMENT*

We need only glance at the awesome population figures predicted for the year 2000, i.e., twenty-eight years from now: seven billion people, only nine hundred million of whom will be white.

—JEAN RASPAIL, THE CAMP OF THE SAINTS

In his book *Désenchantement de la littérature* (2007), Richard Millet asks, "Faut-il rappeler que la France est non pas un pays métis ni une société multiculturelle, comme voudraient le faire croire diverses incantations, mais une société de race blanche, de culture chrétienne, avec quelques minorités extraeuropéennes?"[71] This wishful thinking, which manifests strong nostalgia for a lost uniformity of French culture, is characteristic of a mindset that has gained traction in France in recent years. Renaud Camus, the prolific right-wing writer and founder of the In-Nocence Party,[72] has crafted a conspiracy theory that a *Grand Remplacement*, or Great Replacement, is underway, meaning that the white population of *Français de souche*, or native French, is being purposefully replaced by a browner, non-Western population, particularly from the Maghreb and sub-Saharan Africa.[73] He calls this phenomenon a form of countercolonization. In a 2011 interview with *Le Nouvel Observateur*, he explained, "The Great Replacement, the change of a people, made possible by the Great Deculturation, is the most consequential phenomenon in France in centuries and probably ever."[74] He and his followers are opposed to what he calls the *banlocalisation* or *devenir-banlieue* of France, that is, the transformation of the nation into one big, impoverished, immigrant-filled ghetto. Who or what is responsible for the population swap? His answer: The "permanent influx of new arrivals, immigrants, noncitizens, and their massive presence" (18–19) in French territory, the "dogmatic-antiracist" powers (69), the "media-political, multiculturalist, pro-diversity complex" (113), and the active war of the wombs initiated by the Algerians and other Arab and Muslim populations.[75] Camus is nostalgic for a time when his identity as a Frenchman went uncontested, when it was impossible for a "veiled woman who speaks our language poorly, who knows nothing of our culture, and, worst of all, brims with condemnation and animosity, if not hate," to claim, "I am as French as you are" (20). In his view, French identity has been reduced to the status of an "auberge espagnole masochiste" (34). The Third Reich, he claims, ruined perfectly good words like *race*, *patrie*, *patrimoine*, *traditions*, *ancêtres*, *racines*, *héritage*, *nous*, and *notre* (63–64), which, since the Holocaust, have been condemned as Nazi concepts, rendering them unusable. Echoing many of the anxieties found in Jean Raspail's novel *The Camp of the Saints* (1973), which details the conquest of the West by non-Western peoples and which has had a lasting cult following among right-wing and extreme-right-wing readers, Camus's diagnoses ask the "indigenous" French to brace for the worst.[76]

But perhaps the simple accumulation of "non-French" bodies on French soil is not what alarms him the most. Maybe he is more frightened by the potential dissipation of a French "consciousness" into a new collective, multicultural consciousness. Regarding Thomas Malthus's famous alarmist population assessment *On the Principle of Population* (1798), which argued that population increase would eventually outstrip the food supply, Frances Ferguson claims that this "perspective appeared compelling . . . not because there were in 1798 too many people in the world. . . . Rather, . . . Malthus's *Essay*, instead of being a response to the pressure of too many bodies, registers the felt pressure of too many consciousnesses, and his specter of overpopulation represents what might be called a Romantic political economy" similar to the "psychic crowding" put forth in William Wordsworth's descriptions of London.[77] This fascinating argument, when customized and applied to contemporary France and the *Grand Remplacement* narrative, reveals that these new anxieties may have little to do with quantity and everything to do with quality, with the particular features of the perceived alien consciousnesses. If the *Français de souche* as imagined by Camus and others were reproducing at extraordinary rates, such an explosion in numbers would not likely elicit the same anxiety found in the *pamphlets* published in quick succession in France. But a "psychic crowding" by these non-native consciousnesses saps what Maurice Barrès in the late nineteenth century called "l'énergie nationale."[78] The fracturing of a homogeneous consciousness into divergent, quickly multiplying microconsciousnesses could only lead to the death of the nation. In a nation in which universalism is the reigning ideal, the breakdown of the population into competing identity particulates is cause for trepidation. The demographic shifts alarm Camus, but he is equally concerned with erosion of French language, literature, and culture in general and with the shrinkage of historical memory. The genetic overhaul is only the tip of the iceberg.

Camus's theories clearly take inspiration from a social Darwinist model, which has, over the centuries, proved particularly appealing to realist and naturalist writers. As Sébastian Roldan and many others have noted, "Darwinism and naturalist literature seem to go together."[79] The historical overlap of these two phenomena accounts in part for this compatibility, but they also share similar conceptions of the human as a figure of struggle in a hostile world. Life is the temporary hyphen that separates an individual from death, and plenty of predators and competitors would be more than happy to truncate that hyphen. New French fiction relies heavily on the language and logic of Darwinism as well. François-Xavier Ajavon, Delphine Grass, Stephanie Posthumus, and others have shown the extent to which Michel Houellebecq mobilizes a survivalist rhetoric in his novels,[80] and throughout the twentieth century and into the twenty-first, other writers, such as Maurice G. Dantec, Pierre Boulle, and Vercors, have placed evolutionary themes at the center of their fictions.[81] These novels belong in many respects to the category of "biological poetics" as articulated by William Greenslade.[82] In Bruno Viard's view, Houellebecq's oeuvre shows "la compétition vue du côté des perdants."[83] It is not the winners whose stories get told through degenerative realism; it is the losers.

Houellebecq's novel *Submission* (2015) pursues the theme of the *Grand Remplacement* by portraying France in the year 2022, with an ascendant political party called the Muslim Brotherhood at the helm. The country's non-Muslims yield to this peaceful insurrection with little resistance, understanding quickly that the new party's radical propositions are the only path to strong families, a thriving economy, and an invigorated cultural sphere. It is pure reason that leads the citizens of France toward their new Islamized future. Claude Pérez argues that in Houellebecq's novel, "The causes of Islamization are purely endogenous (it's French suicide)."[84] In other contemporary fictions, such enmities explode in physical combat. In Jean Rolin's *Les Événements* (2015), for example, war breaks out in France between a tangle of political forces, including the jihadists, the French army, a UN force, extreme-right-wing militias, a coalition of extreme-left sympathizers, and other smaller factions. In whatever iteration—slow demographic change or violent upheaval—the France of tomorrow will barely resemble the one of today. The survival-of-the-fittest mentality and a certain Lovecraftian racism appear elsewhere in Houellebecq's corpus, for example in *Whatever* (1994)[85] and *Platform* (2001).[86] Robert, a character in the latter, improvises a theory of benevolent racism, with clear Brucknerian overtones that echo *Le Sanglot de l'homme blanc* (1983):[87]

At the time when the white man thought himself superior, racism wasn't dangerous. . . . This benevolent, almost humanist racism has completely vanished. The moment when the white man began to consider blacks as *equals*, it was obvious that sooner or later they would come to consider them to be *superior*. . . . Once white men believed themselves inferior . . . the stage was set for a different type of racism, based on masochism: historically, it is in circumstances like these that violence, inter-racial wars and massacres break out.

(113)

Robert's theory of a waning "humanist racism" reduces the world to a black/white dichotomy, excluding other races from the paradigm and avoiding the question of religion, but radical Islam creeps into the narrative, which culminates in an Islamist terror attack on a sex resort, resulting in the death of the protagonist's lover. He describes the hatred he feels for Muslims after her murder, gaining satisfaction from Muslim deaths seen on TV, as he performs a kind of vengeful math in his mind: "Every time I heard that a Palestinian terrorist, or a Palestinian child or a pregnant Palestinian woman had been gunned down in the Gaza Strip, I felt a quiver of enthusiasm at the thought that it meant one less Muslim" (349). The simple eye-for-an-eye mathematics of the Hammurabi code is replaced here with limitless eyes being taken for one eye. The slow depopulation of Muslims takes shape as one murder at a time in this narrative. As Claude Pérez has argued, "Houellebecq's characters reside entirely in statistics" and acquire the bulk of their information "from sociologists, psychologists, or the summaries of their work found in newspapers."[88] Pierre Jourde has called Houellebecq "une espèce de Droopy du pamphlet sociologique."[89] I believe that Houellebecq's *sociologisme* (116), "lyrical sociology,"[90] or "sociologie-fiction"[91] allows him to add a patina of scientific legitimacy to his arguments, selecting only those sociological theories that support the bleak vision of the world he wants to craft.[92]

What is fascinating about the contemporary novels described in the next section is that they reject the nationalist agendas of those late-nineteenth-century novels that mourned the degeneration of France and instead tacitly admit that France and the West are not the fittest and that if they die it is part of the natural order of things. Such defeatism stands in stark opposition to earlier French examples of *chauvinisme*, which asserted the primacy of this nation over others.[93] Instead of struggling to survive, the protagonists give themselves over to debauchery, masturbation, and fruitless sex, with little life force left to mourn the neutered nation.

## STALEMATE SEX AND 9/11 AS CASTRATION

I'm bored with writing dead-end novels. Bored with sterile post-existentialist meanderings.

—FRÉDÉRIC BEIGBEDER, *WINDOWS ON THE WORLD*

In the narratives I will evaluate next, sex plays a curious role in France's dubious future. On the one hand, in terms of reproductive sex, the nation is demographically doomed. There is nothing to forestall the replacement of the *Français de souche* by the more fertile new arrivals. On the other hand, sex can at least provide a provisional *economic* solution to the nation's financial stagnation. France is the new Third World and will use its bodies the way developing nations sometimes do: as capital.

While sex figures prominently in these contemporary narratives, it is dead-end intercourse. It is interesting to recall that the original title Zola had in mind for his novel *Fécondité* was *Le Déchet*, which means waste or rubbish, referring to nature's useless squandering of its own seed and life force.[94] Nature wastes most of its *semence* through its incorrigible experimentation, its scattering of grain to the wind.[95] A suicidal nation sees no need in proliferating itself; all of its *semence* becomes mere *déchet*. As Gerald Hoffleit has noted, "Orgies and sensual excesses of any kind are privileged elements of literary descriptions of decadent societies, such as Ovid's *Ars Amatoria*, Petronius's *Satyricon*, Gustave Flaubert's *Salammbô*, and Joris-Karl Huysmans's *À rebours*, and there might be no better measurement of the decadence of a society than the latter's relation to the subject of sexuality."[96]

Sade, France's patriarch of perversion, provides the most famous case of literary sex severed from reproduction, and his influence can be found in contemporary narratives of combinatoric sexual frenzy, reminiscent of his *120 Days of Sodom*.[97] In the countless orgiastic, Sade-inspired books published in France since 2000, including Catherine Millet's autobiographical *La Vie sexuelle de Catherine M.* (2001), Michel Houellebecq's *Platform* (2001), Yann Moix's *Partouz* (2004), Charles Robinson's *Génie du proxénétisme, ou beauté de la religion péripatéticienne* (2008), and Jean-Noël Orengo's *La Fleur du capital* (2015), sex has virtually nothing to do with reproduction. In many contemporary realist fictions, this stalemate sexuality is put in contrast with the purposeful and invasive fertility of France's immigrants, who are crafting a demographically new Europe one coupling at a time. Reproduction is viewed as a weapon. If the gropings and sexual assaults in Cologne on New Year's 2015 were just as alarming to the public as other, bloodier forms of terror, this is because they are imagined as a literalization of the rape of Europe in their mediatic representation.

Charles Robinson's polyvocal novel *Génie du proxénétisme, ou beautés de la religion péripatéticienne* (2008), voiced largely in the first-person plural, recounts the construction of a prostitutional empire from the ground up, one that helps save France from itself. The name of this empire is *La Cité*, a word charged with social significance as the dwelling place of the *racaille* (hood thugs) and the epicenter of France's coming, unmanageable future.[98] The managers of this sexual enterprise offer their business as a profitable solution to a floundering region in France afflicted by total pauperization. The narrators point toward the devolution of French society in general, arguing that "in response to globalization, we had found a way to develop the Third World at home."[99] This new institutionalization and commercialization of prostitution addresses many contemporary woes: loneliness, inequality between the sexes, violence in the *banlieue*, economic strife, multicultural self-segregation, and an absence of respect for oneself and others. Bodies become capital, a "patrimoine biologique" (57) that each prostitute uses to gain a new self-respect. The managers of this sexual enterprise are attentive to the demographic profiles of their employees and their clientele, lamenting, for example, that veiled Muslim women only apply for cleaning jobs and not as sex workers. With a larger pool of Muslim prostitutes, they would be able to satisfy the demands of their North African clients and revive the "great culture of prostitution in the Arab-Muslim world" (42) that characterized earlier centuries. Supply and demand do not align perfectly in this new sexual economy, but the optimistic tone of the narrating managers suggests that an equilibrium will be reached in due time. They see the selling of sex as the next cultural revolution and hope the developing nations will be on board: "The poor countries missed the heavy industrialization of the nineteenth century, the technological investment of the twentieth, and it would be a shame if they missed the revolution in the domain of personal services" (43). In their system, everyone wins.

The novel is stamped page after page with a free-market seal of approval, with declarations like "The fundamental difference between capitalism and socialism is that the first one works" (34). The narrator suggests that "Capitalism is a sexual adventure" (32) and that, in contrast to socialism, which requires that an existing cake be divided up among everyone until each piece is microscopic, capitalism involves inventing the "industrial bakery" (16) capable of producing enough cake for everyone. These hyperbolic claims and some of the more ridiculous sexual passages—for example the excerpt in which the narrator enumerates a list of undefined sex acts with ludicrous names like "le 14-Juillet," "le bitch volley," "le moulin anal," and "les orgues de Staline" (147)—serve as clues that we have entered the realm of satire. The reader learns in the book's final pages that the mysterious long passages in italics found throughout the novel are direct citations from François-René de Chateaubriand's *Génie du christianisme* (1802). By replacing the Catholic faith with prostitution, a commercially viable substitute for religion that offers aesthetic, bodily, and even spiritual satisfaction, a new post-Christian utopia is established, renewing France's existential confidence.

Robinson's solutions closely resemble those of Michel Houellebecq, whose advocacy for global sexual tourism and prostitution is well documented. The Aïchas of the world—a characteristically Arab female name given by both Robinson and Houellebecq to some of their sex objects—are invited to colonize the desire of their clients and lovers, symbolically recuperating some of the cultural *patrimoine* stolen from their people. In *The Map and the Territory* (2010), Houellebecq depicts the economically exhausted French countryside, which foreign and local prostitutes and wealthy tourists manage to revitalize. The narrator describes the phenomenon: "Prostitution had even enjoyed, on the economic level, a genuine upturn, due to the persistence, in particular in South America and Russia, of a fantasy image of the *Parisienne*, as well as the tireless efforts of immigrant women from West Africa. For the first time since the 1900s or 1910s, France had once again become a favorite destination for *sex tourism*."[100] In addition to this windfall, waves of wealthy Chinese and Russian immigrants with a high degree of culture and "excessive respect, almost a veneration, for *local customs*" (262) begin to flood into France. The demographic landscape changes in other ways as well: "The birth rate had by this time actually risen in France, even without taking into account immigration, which, anyway, had fallen to almost zero since the disappearance of the last industrial jobs and the drastic reduction of social security coverage imposed at the beginning of the 2020s" (263).

Houellebecq often treats sex as a potential solution for many societal woes, for example in the sex cult in *The Possibility of an Island* (2005) and *Lanzarote* (2003), which compensates for Western spiritual vacuity, or the sex-tourism industry in *Platform* (2001), which provides both economic growth and sexual relief to an otherwise financially strained, undersexed population. Prostitution, however, does not address the demographic problem. As a typically infertile intercourse, this particular kind of sex aims not to increase the population but to quell the sexual restlessness of clients and offer financial security to prostitutes. Michel, the narrator of *Platform*, argues that in the past, when sex was linked to reproduction, the main criteria for sexual selection were youth and physical beauty, but now the removal of a reproductive imperative allows money to skew desire in a different way. The wealthy may purchase sex, but they cannot compete in the reproductive arena with less economically fortunate males. This stalemate sex is the ideal figure for the contemporary West: money is useful in acquiring certain fleeting pleasures but cannot guarantee proliferation of the "race." The sex depicted in these novels is thus purely egotistical, with no higher teleological ambitions for the species. As Patrik Ourednik writes in his novel *La Fin du monde n'aurait pas eu lieu* (2017), the natural order has been disrupted in the West: "La famille occidentale avait perdu sa superbe. . . . Le sperme des hommes finissait plus souvent dans la bouche des femmes que dans leur vagin."[101]

This radical difference between the wealthy, egotistical West and the poor, communal East is dramatized through one event in particular: 9/11, what Susan Sontag called "last Tuesday's monstrous dose of reality."[102] If the birth certificate of the twentieth century was dated 1914, the beginning of the Great War, then for the twenty-first century, it is dated September 11, 2001.[103] By now, it has become a common trope that 9/11 was a kind of castration of the United States—or of the West, with the United States being the jutting phallus. In Hélène Cixous's essay on the Twin Towers, her swirl of psychosexual imagery encapsulates many of the various readings of the event offered by novelists, cultural critics, and philosophers since its occurrence:

In French we have always spoken of twins in the feminine, *jumelles*, the Twin Towers, T.T. being two sisters. So beautiful. Like two indestructible Babels.

And yet what caused the seduction of the T.T., the fascination they exerted in the entire world? Sexual ambiguity. The representation at once obvious and hidden of the mystery of the *Phallus*. The towers *embodied* phallic power in all its ever disquieting complexity: there is nothing as fragile as the erection, properly or *figuratively*. . . .

The terrorists loved [the towers], but *inversely*, with hate: they were not mistaken in their choice of object. To satisfy their castrating rage, the Islamists and their totalitarian-macho ideology, their theophallocratic one-upmanship, could only choose this ambiguous phallus at once *domus aurea*, house of gold, temple of riches, and ivory tower of feminine grace.[104]

Many writers have picked up this imagery in their novelizations of the attacks: the phallic properties of the towers; their twinness; their status as the ultimate symbol of American financial and political power; their resemblance to the Tower of Babel, with its ability to provoke divine anger; and the tangled sentiments of love, hate, erotic attraction, and jealousy that had attached themselves to these architectural structures.

Frédéric Beigbeder's *Windows on the World*, perhaps France's most famous 9/11 novel,[105] is marked not only by the fears of lost Westerners under assault by radical Islam but by paternal anxiety and dismay at the dissolution of a once-useful *patriarcat*. The book offers a twin narrative to match the twinness of the towers that fell on September 11. Two narrators speak in alternating chapters, Beigbeder, narrating from the Tour Montparnasse after the attack on America, and Carthew Yorston, a Texan who, stuck in the restaurant atop the North Tower with his two boys on that September morning, provides a minute-by-minute account of the horror. As one narrator tells us, "It's like being in an apocalyptic J. G. Ballard novel, except this is reality."[106]

This "hyperrealist novel," as Beigbeder calls it, is only half fictional, and the themes of reality and unreality are at the core of the narrative. In an author's note in the English edition, Beigbeder makes the following statement:

A novel is a fiction; what is contained within its pages is not truth. The only way to know what took place on the 107th floor of the North Tower of the World Trade Center on September 11, 2001, is to invent it. Novels, I believe, are a means of understanding history; they can be windows on our world.[107] But merging fiction with truth—and with tragedy—risks hurting those who have already suffered, something of which I was intensely aware when rereading the novel in English— the language in which the tragedy *happened*. There were, I felt, moments when it was starker and perhaps more likely to wound than I intended. Consequently some scenes have been revised for this edition.

(307)

The all-too-real realness of his hyperrealist novel[108] could traumatize those whose family members or friends were victims of the attacks. This particular event poses unique problems for a novelist who abides by the rules of mimetic realism because the attack itself pushed the boundaries of what constitutes the real. His novelized self states: "Writing this hyperrealist novel is made more difficult by reality itself. Since September 11, 2001, reality has not only outstripped fiction, it's destroying it. It's impossible to write about anything else. Nothing else touches us."[109] 9/11 transformed an implausible fiction into a concrete event. Through its self-reflexivity, the novel tries to apologize for its own insufficiencies when juxtaposed with the events that inspired it. Beigbeder confesses that by using 9/11 as the theme for his novel, this tragedy and its ghastly details function as a "a literary crutch" (295), the content being so compelling that the novel will catch the reader's imagination regardless of the quality of the writing. He complicates discourses of reality and fiction further by describing 9/11 as a cinematic event, prophesied by American action movies, which gave the planners of the attacks a blueprint for their offensive. The loop of fictionalization and realization—cycling through cinema, literature, and the actual world—cannot stop; reality is forever tainted by fiction and vice versa.[110] Furthermore, in his reading of the novel, Lawrence Schehr has argued that "Beigbeder's approach to inscribing the events at hand . . . is an attempt, be it successful or not, to displace the ineffability of the Lacanian Real by introducing language where language could not or would not previously go."[111] The events of 9/11 bolstered Jean Baudrillard's prescient theories on the hyperreal, and he had much to say about this even as the dust was settling, arguing that "the events in New York can also be said to have radicalized the relation of the image to reality. Whereas we were dealing before with an uninterrupted profusion of banal images and a seamless flow of sham events, the terrorist act in New York has resuscitated both images and events."[112] He pointed out that "it is the tactic of the terrorist model to bring about an excess of reality, and have the system collapse beneath that excess of reality" (18), and they do so by means of the screen. For anyone who did not witness the events firsthand, access to them was only possible in a mediated form, amplified and looped like a recurrent nightmare. Baudrillard claimed, "The terrorists have exploited the 'real time' of images, their instantaneous worldwide transmission" (27). Drawing a connection similar to Beigbeder's between the confusion of cinema and reality in this event, Baudrillard wrote that "in this singular event, in this Manhattan disaster movie, the twentieth century's two elements of mass fascination are combined: the white magic of the cinema and the black magic of terrorism; the white light of the image and the black light of terrorism" (29–30). The spectacle of terror was destined to be a sellout show.

Beigbeder's probing of the problems of reality and simulation takes other memorable forms as well, notably in his attempts as a Frenchman to make sense of the American *société du spectacle*. For example, from a detached, anthropological perspective, Beigbeder performs a close reading of the American lap dance, a sexless simulation of desire that privileges spectacle over consummation. The recipient of the lap dance is more enticed by a sexually charged image than by actual sex. He describes an event he witnessed in New York, a kind of erotic soirée called SWINGING LITE, which allows couples to flirt with those outside their twosome and engage in "lots of caressing, kissing, fondling, but no penetration" (183). In other words, this distinctly American practice tries to toy with the membrane between real and not real, to allow the body to linger at the threshold of fantasy without crossing it. He evokes the virtual world as well, when, just minutes before the collapse of the North Tower where he and his sons asphyxiate slowly, the character Yorston randomly recalls his attempt at internet dating. He thinks to himself, "I wanted to live in a virtual world; I'm dying in a real one" (248); this said, of course, within the framework of a fiction. The persistent subtext in *Windows on the World* regarding what is real, fictional, simulated, and virtual attests to Beigbeder's self-awareness as a novelist, but unlike those postmodern experimenters who tested the limits of writerly self-inclusion, he seems to want to put himself in psychical proximity with the event itself, imagining what it must have been like to be a father in his thirties, on the verge of dying with his sons at his side.

Fatherhood is problematic in the narrative. The narrators Yorston and Beigbeder see themselves as viruses in the program of filiation. May '68 failed their generation by producing a cohort of deadbeat dads too addicted to freedom to commit to anyone other than themselves. Yorston explains, "Pater familias is a full-time job; the problem is, I know fewer and fewer men who are prepared to take it on. We've been shown too many images of men who are free, poetic, and attractive, exhausted with pleasure; rock'n'roll types running from their responsibilities" (102). Beigbeder proceeds to draws a psychogram of men of his generation, all of them "emotionally crippled thirtysomethings" who want to be like their fathers, and at the same time they're determined not to end up like their fathers, no matter what. Their father abandoned them and they never found him. It's not a criticism: I blame society. The sons of 1968 are men with no role models. Men with no instruction manual. Men with no solidity. Defective men. When they're in a relationship, they're smothered; when they're single, they're miserable.

(175–76)

Yorston reinforces this view: "If society offers you the choice of listening to a baby screaming or going to a party without your wife, it's hardly surprising that there are more and more single mothers in the West" (139–40). Beigbeder, too, mourns this change and its impact on his own life, writing, "Barely forty years ago, we decided to do away with the father, and we want things to carry on as before? I'm the product of that disappearing father. I am collateral damage" (176). Before Yorston realizes that the restaurant where he is sitting will be the place where he dies, he thinks distractedly to himself that he should have a vasectomy (39), that the fact that he's been more or less absent from the lives of his two boys is mildly shameful but not tragic. After the plane strikes the building and the imminence of their death becomes apparent, he feels one last *élan vital* throb through him, a fierce and pathetic love for his progeny, an anger that world affairs about which he knows nothing could truncate his life and his bloodline. In many respects, this is not a novel about an encounter between radical Islam and the West; it is a novel about the West's encounter with itself. The missing Western father figure was a victim of a patricide. Peter Brooks has argued that "paternity is a dominant issue within the great tradition of the nineteenth-century novel (extending well into the twentieth century), a principal embodiment of its concern with authority, legitimacy, the conflict of generations, and the transmission of wisdom."[113] Using *Illusions perdues* as an example, he claims, "The novel presents a France that is in Balzac's view 'malade de son père,' in the sense that it has never recovered from its killing of the father-monarch during the Revolution, the regicide of 1793. France in the nineteenth century lacks a father, lacks any true principle of authority, any authorized system of signs and representations."[114] This pattern repeats itself again and again in twenty-first-century degenerative realist fiction. Douglas Morrey has noted, for example, that "fathers in Houellebecq's universe have always been weak or absent, fundamentally uninterested in their children."[115] According to Bruno Viard, Houellebecq's obsessions are "les générations, la question de la filiation,"[116] with an emphasis on paternal transmission from father to son.[117] Beigbeder's novel, too, shows the continuation of this patricidal trauma into the new millennium.

*Windows on the World* abounds with rough social theories about the degeneration of Western DNA. Children are the new parents in this self-infantilizing society.[118] The traditional family has collapsed: "Freedom had killed off marriage and the family, couples and children. Faithfulness had become a concept that was reactionary, impossible, inhuman. In this new world, love was a three-year thing, max" (137). If Hugh Hefner was the new role model for men in the 1960s, the myth of the international playboy has decayed today as much as the nonagenarian's own body. His template for how to live yielded a self-indulgent, self-destructive batch of men:

The INTERNATIONAL PLAYBOY poses serious questions: what use is love in a civilization based on desire? Why burden yourself with a family if freedom is the ultimate principle? What is the purpose of morality in a hedonistic society? If God is dead, then the whole world is a brothel, and the only thing to do is make the most of it until you buy the farm. If the individual is king, then only selfishness makes sense. And if the father is no longer the sole figure of authority, then the only thing that limits violence in a materialistic democracy is the police. (138)

Was the international playboy a symptom or a cause of Beigbeder's generation's degeneration? This is left unclear. What is certain is that 9/11 was the necessary event that provoked the West to take a hard look at itself. In Beigbeder's pages, the question of Islamist extremism is barely addressed. Instead, he fills his chapters with reflections on the failures of Western society and on the social, political, and cultural circumstances that destroyed the family structure and replaced it with hedonistic self-love.

Echoing some of Beigbeder's critiques, Philippe Muray's controversial book *Chers djihadistes* (2002), a response to 9/11 addressed directly to radical Islamists, argues that while their attack was jolting, the West is reaching the end of a process of self-dismantling, which essentially nullifies the terrorists' efforts. Muray feels as threatened by the "new matriarchal order"[119] as the jihadists must feel. He ridicules recent feminist, multiculturalist, and "homophilic" developments in contemporary French society and politics, which share the common objective of "going ever forward" (32). These include *homoparentalité*, the replacement of patronymic naming by matronymic naming, the rise of political correctness and self-censorship, parity and other attempts to reverse the "natural order," the approval and transmission of new lifestyles via media, the suppression of libido, and the rise of the "adulescent" or self-infantilizing adult.[120] For him, the West has become a fairy-tale world no longer constrained by "the principle of reality" (37). Therefore, for radical Islamists to attack the West is to attack a world that is no longer real, a mere image.

Another French 9/11 novel, far removed from Beigbeder's "hyperrealism" but sharing many of its observations and theories, is Yann Moix's *Partouz* (2004), which wavers between full-blown surrealism—with one character speaking in the afterlife with dead figures like André Breton, James Joyce, and Charles Péguy—long-winded, colorful descriptions of orgies, and a heavy dose of sham psychoanalysis. Moix's response to the explosive dose of reality brought by 9/11 is to improvise, to fill the novel beyond full capacity with histrionic chaos, suggesting that the sobriety of the realist novel cannot possibly contain such an explosive event within its pages. 9/11 destroyed reality and, along with it, the representational mode most intimately bound to the real. *Partouz* recounts the story of a man who sees Mohammed Atta, the primary architect of the 9/11 terror attacks, as a kind of brother in sexual and sentimental suffering, both of them the victims of female rejection. The multilayered narrative—shifting between scenes in a swingers' club and the strikingly similar biographies of these two men, whose romanticism had turned to scorn after a long string of refusals from women—unfurls theory after theory about Islam and sexual frustration; about the similarities and divergences between swingers and jihadists; and about the competitive aspects, in both biological and economic terms, that constitute courtship, mating, and survival. The narrator and Mohammed Atta are doubles, both swingers, the former on earth and the second in the afterlife, with his seventy-two virgins. The narrator takes note of this symmetry, asserting, "The orgy was doubly doubled: terrestrial and celestial, Western and Eastern, Christian and Muslim, ephemeral and eternal" (134). Moix draws other parallels, for example, the relationship between capitalist hyperbole and the hyperbole of the new extremists, tracing the transformation of the *marché* into the *supermarché* and then into the *hypermarché* as comparable to the transformation of terrorism (small-scale kidnappings and murders) into superterrorism (plane hijacking) and, finally, hyperterrorism (using airplanes to take down symbolic architectural structures crowded with people) (67). The scale of the world's tragedies will only grow with the increasing capitalist overreach. And similar to Beigbeder's argument that the grandiosity of American action cinema has found its correlative in the new hyperterrorism, Yann Moix gives the last word of the novel to James Joyce, who says to Mohammed Atta in the afterlife: "I hijacked the classical novel of the nineteenth-century to invent the twentieth century, and you, you've hijacked twentieth-century American cinema to invent the twenty-first century" (404). 9/11 was a cinematic event in which "the political state was confused with the biological state" (49) on a scale so large, it belonged to the realm of *unreality*. Mohammed Atta was a surrealist in that he successfully executed an act of such implausibility, of such *unreality*, that he was able to surpass reality (81).

In 2017, Moix published *Terreur*, which in some respects can be seen as a companion text to *Partouz* because it reformulates many of the novel's theories, this time as a series of meditations on Islamist terror and its targeting of France.[121] These disjointed reflections, separated from one another by blank lines, have an aphoristic quality and were motivated by Moix's personal anguish at living in a country in which the threat of death by terror has begun to hover over daily life. The strands of his thought that focus on the relationship between terrorism and reality are most relevant to the problems addressed here in this book. According to Moix, each attack constitutes a hyperreality—a term that recurs in contemporary discourses involving the event-centered nature of terrorism—and has the unique ability to "déréalise[r] le réel."[122] Just as Beigbeder notes the link between the cinematic imaginary and 9/11, Moix argues that the tendency of terror attacks to push reality beyond its own borders switches on the imagination's science-fiction mode.[123] The terrorist "contaminates reality" (22) phenomenologically by changing our perception of all that surrounds us: nature, the objects and places we know, our own sexuality. He also claims that as the real Isis (Daesh) shrinks in numbers and loses territory, it grows proportionally larger in the imagination and makes *virtual* gains. On the internet, terrorist groups cast shadows larger than themselves. "Today, reality is no longer confined to the real; the virtual is one of its modalities" (13), Moix writes. Arguing that reality can only reach us now through fiction, he suggests that we compare today's evening news reports, which borrow tropes from cowboy westerns—good guys versus bad guys, civilized men versus savages—in order to represent terrorism, with the equivalent news reports from the 1970s, which had not yet begun to use such dramatization.[124] This kind of staging, he suggests, "injects more real into the real" (95). News channels fashion themselves after American TV series, and in turn Isis (Daesh) tries to stage events as spectacular as the ones found in movies.[125] "In the twenty-first century, we flee reality like the plague" (92), he argues. The spectacularization of the real allows us to soften it somehow, even if its effects on the body and the psyche are still as life-threatening.

Moix's originality in *Partouz* comes through in his linguistic play, but his tendency toward maximalism is congruent with the other writers evoked in this chapter. He is a frenetic neologizer with a proliferative style, testing out, in the manner that nature develops new species, every possible modification of a word—*léchage, léchure, léchation, léchance, léchéité* (105) or *ces petits bonhommes érectés, érectisés, érectionnés, érectiles, érectifs* (61). Some of the idiosyncrasies of the text include endless proliferation of acronyms: *les QB et les QBP, les qui-bandaient* and *les qui-bandaient-pas*, those with hard-ons, those without; *les CP (chattes pénétrées)*, penetrated pussies; *le GMS (le grand mystère du sexe)*, the great mystery of sex; *le JNEA (joli nez extrêment arabe)*, the pretty, extremely Arab nose; *la FSG (fille sublime générique)*, generic sublime girl. 9/11 becomes "September 11™," a successful trademark. The birth and death dates of each character are presented consistently, tombstones for the dead and the undead alike. The playful linguistic fecundity and general expansiveness of this novel offset the infertility of the orgy scenes, the sexual failures of both protagonists, and the eternal repetition of female rejection of men since the beginning of time.

This playfulness is counterbalanced by constant theoretical gestures. The main thesis of the book is summed up in this passage, which appears toward its beginning:

The true combat of al-Qaeda is not so much religious as sexual. The Islam of fundamentalists was meant to bring a definitive solution to our Western problems of sentimental suffering, of romanticism, of love stories, of love songs: simply put, its purpose was, through a special reading of the Koran, to restore order to the sexual disorder that threatened to overtake the planet. In short, Bin Laden's Islam offered men the possibility of no longer suffering because of their women. . . . This entailed the mastery of sentimental sorrow by devising a system of enslavement for women, by launching . . . the deranged, bloody, and apocalyptic enterprise of absolute control of the female orgasm.[126]

This declaration that the jealousy of the jihadists was first and foremost sexual rather than economic or cultural aligns with the aforementioned claims of Philippe Muray.[127] Certain ideas in Moix's novel, such as the stupidity of Islam and the sexual frustration that marks the men of this faith, seem lifted straight from Houellebecq's pages. He could be considered one of Houellebecq's many clones, as Frey and Noys have called them,[128] a fact Moix recognizes and perhaps repudiates, given that he gave the title "Michel Houellebecq Is a Dickhead" to one of his subchapters. He develops at length a theory of sexual rejection, suggesting that the source of every true work of beauty or destruction by man was the refusal of his amorous advances by women, who function something like antimuses. The narrator declares, "There is nothing as important in the life of a man as the women who didn't want him" (30). He cites from love letters of some of the most famous men in the history of Western civilization, who received only silence or derision from the beloved women to whom the letters were addressed. Among these romantic, rejected men we find Kafka, Flaubert, Napoleon, Diderot, Musset, Mitterrand, Joyce, Proust, and others. The narrator declares bluntly of these love letters and other sentimental writings addressed to women: "The more you wrote, the more you could be sure of not fucking" (36). He also presents a supplemental theory of the *mec*, the brainless, banal guy whose existence is purely biological, purely sexual, and whom the woman of your dreams will inevitably choose over you: This guy "sticks his dick in the pussy of the love of your life, not you, not you, not you" (52). The war for access to that warm spot is eternally lost by the sentimentalists. If, in the genealogy of literature, realism is imagined to have neatly followed romanticism, the narrator confirms an analogous progression in his theory of the callous smothering of masculine sentimentality through feminine rejection. Even if a man starts out as an idealist, as a romantic, at some point he will wake up to the *real*, to the stark, biological reality of economic and sexual rivalry. The new generation of men in this millennium have shed the old cumbersome emotions and gladly accepted their ruthless, animal nature without reservation. The decadent and sick "romantisme noir" (66) of generations past finally tips over into a cold realism.

Moix's vision of the human is heavily informed by Darwinist theory and biological determinism. His narrator describes in detail the erotic pursuits of the Rabbit (*Le Lapin*), a regular at the swingers' club whose sexual prowess resembles that of nature's creatures, who know what to do automatically, without the human burden of self-doubt or courtship, with its opaque, highly codified rituals. The Rabbit summons his "prey" with a "natural severity" (161), having removed from the sex act "all of its aesthetic, cultural, refined complications, its civilized sophistication," as if "Nature herself were fucking on his behalf." The fascinated narrator watches the spectacle of the Rabbit in action—with women of all shapes, races, and classes lining up to be his next partner—and concludes: "His purified, naïve bestiality was not only more alive; it was life itself" (163). The Rabbit aside, the swingers' club is, in general, a theater where the "secular conditions of human biology" (59) are on display. The narrator describes the aggressive pursuits of competing men who try to couple with the woman you've brought to the party: "Like pigeons scrambling toward a miserable piece of bread, the ballsy men [*types à couilles*] from the whole world rush toward your beauty at full speed if you leave her alone for three seconds" (53). The place swarms with dicks (60). As the narrator contemplates the throbbing landscape of bodies-in-orgy, he notes that in it, "there were vague hints of the end of the world, medleys of death and obscenities. The survival of the race asserted itself in the unreasonable" (59), with the orgy's participants making absurd and violent sexual requests of one another. The narrator, who has little success approaching women in this bacchanal's tangle of bodies, begins to reflect on his own biological degeneration: "I wasn't progressing in my life, I wasn't evolving: only my biology was progressing. Only my biology, my physiology, evolved, and my old age along with them, and all my mortal, fatal, dying [*mortelles, mortifères, mourantes*] cells. But my psychology remained intact. It was stagnating. It was seventeen years old for life" (67). The narrator describes his own biological stagnation or degeneration, but the reader quickly understands that he is a figure for the nation. Again and again throughout the novel's pages, he takes on an almost allegorical significance as the archetypal Frenchman who is too reflective, ill-confident, and self-obsessed to participate in the corporeal market economy of which he is part. He is aware of his own irrelevance in the new global ecosystem. His type will eventually go extinct.

The woman blamed for 9/11 is Pamela Wiltshire, who had rejected the amorous advances of Mohammed Atta, the ringleader of the attacks. The narrator asserts: "September 11ᵀᴹ was a sexual event. The biggest sexual event of all time. Pam emasculated Mohammed. But she emasculated New York as well. She guillotined three cocks: the Twin Towers and Momo's dick" (32). He continues, "September 11ᵀᴹ had been a warning to all the women of the world who had received from all of us romantics love letters to which they hadn't responded" (35). The book ends with what seems like retributive sex, with the narrator anally fisting Pamela in a swingers' club in revenge of Atta. Kamel Daoud, most famous for his recrafting of Camus's *L'Étranger* into the widely praised book *Meursault, contre-enquête* (2013), published an opinion piece in February 2016 titled "Sexual Misery of the Arab World," which offers a theoretical framework for thinking about Moix's brutal story. In it, he argues that throughout the Arab world, "Women are seen as a source of destabilization—short skirts trigger earthquakes, some say" and that the pent-up desire that results from uncompromising religious fundamentalism has led to what he calls "a kind of porno-Islamism," with religious authorities taking to the internet and television to attempt to regulate every possible sexual thought or action. He closes his critique with an emphasis on the disquieting encounter between West and East: "People in the West are discovering, with anxiety and fear, that sex in the Muslim world is sick, and that the disease is spreading to their own lands."[129] For Moix, sexual repression or rejection are not purely Muslim or Arab problems, as men of the West—and, ostensibly, of the entire world—have always suffered physically and psychologically from their unsatisfied desires. In a strange way, the novel implies a kind of future kinship between men of all backgrounds, who might recognize the marks of this suffering in one another. The heavily satirical elements of the novel and its riotous excesses don't allow the reader to take Moix at his word, yet one senses that he is gesturing toward an unspeakable truth, namely, that male embodiment is a liability. Yes, men have ruled the world since the beginning of civilization, but their hearts and testicles are always clutched by the cruel hand of the female. How would the world change if the order of things were reversed?

If the external enemy of Western civilization is Islam, there is also an insidious internal enemy. Western women in the aforementioned narratives are responsible for the sexual misery of Western men. The novels imply this: if Western women would yield their bodies more freely, as women of the East do—as prostitutes, to ease men's pent-up sexual drive, or as mothers, to proliferate the race—perhaps the West, through its imitation of the Eastern model, would be in a better position to survive. Otherwise, women's eagerness to eschew their sexual and reproductive duties and enter into competition with men will lead to certain civilizational death. Or will it? In what follows, an alternative narrative is presented, one that illustrates a future in which only *half* of the West—the male half—will die. The feminization of the West is well under way and takes various forms, all of them inimical to masculinity.

## THE FUTURE IS FEMALE

Today's INTERNATIONAL PLAYBOY is a woman.

—FRÉDÉRIC BEIGBEDER, *WINDOWS ON THE WORLD*

The Young-Girl does not mind miming submission here and there: *because she knows that she dominates.*

—TIQQUN, *PRELIMINARY MATERIALS FOR A THEORY OF THE YOUNG-GIRL*

Je crois que *l'avenir est aux filles,* en art comme en tout . . .

—JOSÉPHIN PÉLADAN

A human form is given to the coming dark days, when the white, Western, straight *homme moyen* theorized by Quetelet will slide into obsolescence. While the past was male, the future is female. Many of the narrators and protagonists in our corpus draw this conclusion, with ambivalent feelings about the femaleness of the future. The reversal is traced back to May '68, the moment when the meek inherited the earth. Sexual liberation provided for women a glimpse of a future beyond their doglike companionship,[130] beyond a submissive and obedient fealty to the men who share their beds. With a few subtle alterations, the theory of benevolent racism put forth in Houellebecq's *Platform* could be modified to describe a benevolent sexism that has recently drifted toward a more cruel and vengeful iteration. Richard Millet draws an equivalence between democratization and feminization, suggesting that the egalitarian spirit embodied by the female will be the downfall of Western civilization because it requires a horizontalization of naturally vertical power structures. The West's increasing tendency to demand inclusiveness, kindness, care, negotiation, and softness will lead to its demise because those outside the West will preserve the older dominant, masculine model and will easily vanquish this new *occident féminisé*. The weakness of the female sex enfeebles all that it touches.[131]

Depictions of this female future take many forms, but the most prominent is to describe it as the obvious endpoint of capitalism, a metonymy for the United States. As Bruno Perreau has shown convincingly in his book *Queer Theory: The French Response* (2016), the French have been historically skeptical of theories of gender and queerness because they are imagined as an intentional American infiltration of French family values and national sovereignty.[132] It is no surprise, then, that a "Future Is Female" movement would be eyed with suspicion, since for many, such a campaign could only represent the inexorable encroachment in France of American political correctness, retributive social justice, and undermining of "natural" gender roles. A full theorization of this American empty, female future—a future of spectacle, of youth, of capitalism, of soul-death—can be found in Tiqqun's *Preliminary Materials for a Theory of the Young-Girl* (1999), which, through heavily Debordian tropes, crafts the young woman as an allegorical figure, a kind of Grim Reaper of male agency.[133] This *fille castratrice* uses her cold scythe to neuter civilization, lopping off the masculine element, perhaps replacing it with a dildo, an industrially manufactured object that cannot protest one's use of it. Her ascent announces the end of men, replaced by technical surrogates. The anonymous authors write, "When the Spectacle proclaims that woman is the future of man, it is naturally speaking of the Young-Girl, and the future it predicts recalls only the worst cybernetic slavery" (25). They are careful to insist on the allegorical nature of their Young-Girl, clarifying that she can just as easily be male as female in her physical embodiment. They describe the evolution of the "traditional woman, assigned to the home with the duty of ensuring survival," who, in the new age, has now transformed into the Young-Girl, whose "disabused stubbornness" is "emancipated from the domestic sphere, and from all sexual monopoly." This cynical obstinacy manifests itself in all of her activities: "in her irreproachable affective impermeability at work, in the extreme rationalization she imposes on her 'emotional life,' in her every step, so spontaneously military, in the way she fucks, car-ries herself, or taps away on her computer" (30–31). Certain passages of this book—those that borrow the language of magazines intended for teenage girls or emphasize the Young-Girl's detachment and professional-ism in the new sexual economy—sound as though they've been penned by Houellebecq. The *minettes* and *beurettes*—always in the diminutive—who populate his novels can be recognized in the Tiqqun portrait. The Young-Girl, who is and has always been what Paul Preciado has called "ejacula-tory capital,"[134] has now professionalized, not necessarily in the prostitu-tional sense but in the sense that her own life is something to be managed. The increasingly managerial nature of Western society, a necessary infra-structural change brought about by the demands of neoliberalism, invites huge brigades of young, neatly groomed, college-educated women to take over the affairs of the planet. She is a supervisor of her own sentimental life and exercises full control over her personnel, the men who seek to pen-etrate her professionalism.

A character in Houellebecq's *The Elementary Particles* (1998) discovers an omen of Europe's future in the pages of a French mail-order catalogue:

The 3 Suisses catalogue . . . offered a more thoughtful, historically informed insight into Europe's current malaise. The impression of a coming mutation in society in its opening pages is finally given precise formulation on page 17. Michel considered for hours the lines that summed up the theme of the collection: "Opti-mism, generosity, complicity, and harmony make the world go round. THE FUTURE IS FEMALE."[135]

These stereotypical values that characterize the female are idealized and celebrated in advertising, the public face of capitalism, because they effectively mask the competitive brutality that is the true essence of the system. Capital-ism is in the process of rebranding, visible in the emphasis in contempo-rary marketing on social and ecological responsibility, fairness, "paying it forward," healthy living, etc., what Ross Douthat has called "woke capital-ism."[136] Its ugliness must be made less disagreeable through a cosmetic or transvestite process, in other words, through the inclusion of a female ele-ment into its appearance. Politics, too, requires a makeover and finds in · the female a perfect, idealized front for a civilization that would rather not talk about war, corruption, exploitation, and inequality. The feminization of the future foretold by the mail-order catalogue is irreversible unless the capitalist system implodes. In his novel *Submission*, this is exactly what happens, as the West and all it has come to stand for—unbridled capitalism, individualism, social democracy, economic liberalism—are reversed by the Islamization of France, which restores "natural" hierarchies that put woman at the foot of man and man at the foot of God. When the protagonist's lover Myriam asks him if he's in favor of a return to the patriarchy, he replies: "You know I'm not *for* anything, but at least patriarchy existed. I mean, as a social system it was able to perpetuate itself. There were families with children, and most of them had children. In other words, it worked, whereas now there aren't enough children, so we're finished."[137] This emphasis on the patriarchy's role in maintaining high birth rates returns again and again throughout the novel. The underlying thesis seems to be that the only society capable of flourishing is one in which men control the bodies of women. A female future is destined to die. Provocatively he says to his lover, "I've never really been convinced that it was a good idea for women to get the vote, study the same things as men, go into the same professions, et cetera. I mean, we're used to it now, but was it really a good idea?" (28). As Douglas Morrey has argued, in Houellebecq's books, "women have essentially no inner life but exist as sexual cyphers, either to titillate or to prove a point."[138] He speaks on their behalf and can only imagine a female future as empty advertising copy meant to conceal the civilizational rot.

In his recent book *Sexagon: Muslims, France, and the Sexualization of National Culture* (2017), Mehammed Amadeus Mack argues that in the popular French imagination, the Arab and other Others of France have been virilized through their mediatization, leading to a concomitant feminization of French culture:

In the eyes of many French observers and commentators, virilism not only animates the "difficult" Arab, black, and Muslim boys featured in sensationalized newscasts, it also defines their neighborhoods in the suburbs or *banlieues*, their religion of Islam, and the notion of immigration itself. This virilization of the Arab *other* naturally requires a feminization, and in some cases androgenization, of the host country: France, which has been called the hexagon (because it has six distinct sides), increasingly has come to resemble what I term a *sexagon*, because of the way its borders increasingly have come to be defined through values such as gay-friendliness, secular feminism, and metrosexuality, on the one hand, and the condemnation of immigrant and working-class machismo on the other.[139]

Mack's argument shares features with the primary claim in Houellebecq's *Submission* but depicts the virilization of the Arab and the feminization of the Frenchman as a process set off in part by the mediatic practices of the West. For Houellebecq, on the other hand, the problem is not produced by mediation but is the inevitable late phase in a "natural" process of existential depletion. By disproportionately fostering the feminine element, once-virile France will ultimately become docile to the still-virile remainder of the world.

In other depictions of the future (and present) female, she has absorbed features of the male into her own ontology. In Moix's *Partouz*, women are the "sex freaks of modern times" (34), and in Houellebecq's *Platform*, the narrator Michel makes the following prediction about women of the future: "Women will probably become much more like men. . . . As women attach more importance to their professional lives and personal projects, they'll find it easier to pay for sex too; and they'll turn to sex tourism. It's possible for women to adapt to male values."[140] In these portrayals, women are not different in essence from men. Having power makes anyone a male, while the lack of power makes anyone a female. In his novel *Windows on the World*, Beigbeder mourns the fact that men like his idol Hugh Hefner have been reconfigured in the new era, this time as women. A realization jolts him:

Today's INTERNATIONAL PLAYBOY is a woman. It's Bridget Jones or Carrie Bradshaw (the heroine of *Sex and the City*). These are the people the fanatical Muslims are scared of, and I can understand why. They scare me shitless too, with their heavy artillery: mascara, lip gloss, oriental perfumes, silk lingerie. They've declared war on me. They terrify me because something tells me that I'll never be able to seduce them all. There's always another one on the horizon, heels higher than the last. It's an impossible task. If they crashed a charter plane onto the city every day, they still wouldn't succeed in eradicating the bevy of dangerous beauties; the sexual imperialism of these sumptuous sluts in their I ESCAPED THE BETTY FORD CLINIC T-shirts; the supremacy of their devastating necklines and their eyelashes, which flutter as they contemptuously write you off: "You're

not on my to-do list. Stop hitting on me, man. I do the hunting tonight. Scram!
Beat it!"

(183–84)

In this brief excerpt, Beigbeder sums up the anxieties of the typical Western male as portrayed in the degenerative realist novel: He fears the "heavy
artillery" of the jihadists and of battalions of impenetrable females. Their
"sexual imperialism" is as big a threat as the "countercolonization" described
by Renaud Camus. Within the narrative, Beigbeder's response to these
women is one of predictable violence; he thinks to himself that all they do
is get his cock hard but they don't throw him head over heels in love, and
thus they do not actuaIly hold any power over him. Male insecurity, which
always existed but which was in the past sublimated in various ways, froths
to the surface in all of these narratives as the authors try to reckon with
the female dominance that has crept up unexpectedly. The Young-Girls,
whose bodies they'd always used as masturbatory fodder, are the new
CEOs, presidents, and managers. Is sexual rejection at the core of this vitriol? Do the realities of these misogynists have anything to do with *real*
reality?

In his *Partouz*, Yann Moix uses an expression that could be applied to
most of the narratives described in this book; their reality is a *réalité de
couilles*,[141] a reality of balls, a testicular reality. They see the world through
sperm-covered glasses. Sex is superimposed on the most banal of life's
events and on the most spectacular ones. The reading public is generally
familiar with Houellebecq's tendency to make these projections, sex being
the primary motivation in his books for nearly all human actions, but
many of his contemporaries seem to share this vision. Even as the room—
the restaurant at the top of the North Tower of the World Trade Center—
fills with smoke after the first plane has cut through the building several
floors below, the trapped protagonist of Beigbeder's *Windows on the World*
can't help but think about sex, as though the threat of death necessarily
triggers the urge to copulate, to leave a splash of semen, a splash of life, in
one's stead. "When I stop thinking about sex, I will cease to be,"[142] the narrator concludes.

From a phenomenological perspective, the consistency and uniformity
of this *réalité de couilles* in contemporary narratives poses certain problems

for our understanding of realism, of subjectivity, and of the discourses of honesty and sincerity that have been bound to realism from its inception. In Paul Preciado's pharmacological autobiography *Testo Junkie* (2008), Beatriz—at the time, she self-identified as female but has since changed her name to Paul, the biblical name of metamorphosis, and began to self-identify as male—recounts her physical and psychological transformation after beginning testosterone injections. Her perceptions of the world changed subtly during this biopolitical experiment. Throughout her account, she insists in Butlerian fashion that "testosterone isn't masculinity," that maleness is rather an assemblage of socially, politically, and aesthetically influenced elements. However, she describes her experience this way: "The microdoses of testosterone . . . produce subtle but decisive changes in my affect, in my inner perception, in my sexual excitation, in the odor of my body, and in resistance to fatigue."[143] While Preciado is unable to fully embody male subjectivity through these injections, her testimony suggests that a *réalité de testostérone* is distinct from a *réalité d'estrogène*.

When Hélène Cixous published her essay "The Laugh of the Medusa" (1975) on *écriture féminine*, her interest was women's writing in general, not realism specifically. But realism holds a special place in literature because in many respects it tries to erase its own status as representation, passing itself off as reality rather than as a depiction of reality. Realist texts constitute their own kind of reality; they attempt not only to describe life but to influence our response to actual life. In the early twentieth century, experiments in subjective realism and the rise of phenomenology showed the ways in which reality is largely filtered through a perceiving apparatus, which ostensibly takes into account the effects of hormones on perceptions of the world among the other possible "filters"—like age, race, disability—imposed by embodiedness. The realities depicted in the novels described in this chapter are not universal, and their novelists tacitly admit as much in their surrender to an *écriture masculine*. While earlier forms of realism did not acknowledge the maleness of their authors' perceptions, there is a new tendency among many of the most widely read contemporary novelists at least to hint at this subjective limitation. The misogyny and objectification of women that characterize these narratives are offset by their cryptoconfessional tone, which tacitly admits the inconveniences and sorrows of male embodiment. These narratives imagine ways to project the male self beyond the crippling *réalité de couilles*, to imagine a future that is female or neuter, digital or posthuman.[144]

The anxiety caused by demographic shifts—from the rising status of women to the influx of immigrants—manifests itself in complicated ways in these novels. In a passage from Houellebecq's *The Elementary Particles*, in which a character declares, "I spent the weekend writing a racist pamphlet—I had a hard-on all the time I was writing it,"[145] the reader recognizes in compressed form all of the patterns I've outlined in this chapter. Here, writing functions as a surrogate for failed reproduction; the writer cannot compete sexually with those he denigrates in his pamphlet, but he imagines his ink as a path forward for his legacy. If his genetic material cannot be transmitted to the future in the form of progeny, at least his words will last beyond him. Racial hatred here prompts an erection, which shows the extent to which a social Darwinist vision of the world is embedded in the narrative. Competition for the womb, a highly politicized space, is responsible in part for this racist vitriol, as members of other races are cast as relentless competitors that vie for the female. In the examples presented in this chapter, the apocalypse has been secularized and communicated in the language of biological survival and demographic inevitability. The statistical certainty of the coming doomsday is met by the authors with a bionihilism that evinces a certain *Tædium Vitæ*, a disgust of life. The novels' protagonists will keep on trying to survive only because they are programmed to, not because they feel a particular zeal for life. As I've shown, the nervous, nationalist response to the degeneration of Western civilization in the late nineteenth century has been replaced in the twenty-first by a tacit surrender to biological fatalism and an abandonment of national pride. Male embodiment is the primary source of the anxieties described here. It is no accident that all of the narratives here were written by men. The particular configuration of fears described in them is a product of the *réalité de couilles* described here. It is nearly impossible to imagine an *écriture féminine* that would depict contemporary France in these terms. This degenerative realism draws a dire, precise portrait of the contemporary world, authenticated by statistical proof, which allows no room for doubt. As Alain Duhamel put it, "La France est fatiguée."[146]

In the next chapter, I describe how the arrival in France of the Minitel—a kind of protointernet—and the transition to the World Wide Web allowed for the accelerated dissemination of the demographic anxieties analyzed here. Through these new networks, reality became pliable, and, to borrow an expression from John D'Agata and Jim Fingal,[147] the lifespan of facts was shortened. Furthermore, apprehensions about life's consequential subjects—death, sex, God—were magnified there. The question posed in the next chapter is: What do such networks do to the novel?

## Chapter Two

# ENDARKENMENT FROM THE MINITEL
# TO THE INTERNET

The train wound its way through Nice's northern suburbs of housing projects full of Arabs, billboards for Minitel sex sites and a sixty percent National Front majority.

—MICHEL HOUELLEBECQ, *THE ELEMENTARY PARTICLES*

The vast digital network that is the internet has permanently transfigured literature. Already in these early years of the twenty-first century, novelists conduct their research differently, readers read differently, and attention to books is marshaled through new forms of digital media. Naturally, digital networks and the new technologies associated with them also drive the plots and characters of many contemporary novels. Furthermore, we see a coalescing body of what could be called Wikipedian literature, which relies on this digital, collectively written encyclopedia for its form and content. The internet has even reshaped the nature of truth in the so-called real world. For example, the *fachosphère*, that part of the Web where far-right fascists craft their narratives of doom, relies on people's weakness for frightening stories and continues to compile its apocalyptic lending library.[1] Well-known right-wing figures like Renaud Camus, Florian Philippot, and Marion Maréchal-Le Pen have been extremely active on Twitter, and the Front national was the first national party to have a website. Literature, too, in the form of storytelling and self-fashioning with a heavy fictional element, has made its mark on the internet. Brands want to tell their stories. People craft themselves as interesting characters through social media. Literary fiction and the internet were made for each other. But when combined, truth begins to degenerate, and the novel is inevitably affected by this degeneration. Enlightenment becomes endarkenment. As

Salman Rushdie put it regarding the spread of fake news on the internet, "You've got so much fiction, so much fantasy, so much distortion and untruth being propagated every day that I think . . . it becomes paradoxically the fiction writer's job to try and reestablish a sense of the truth."[2]

While the concerns of many of the novels mentioned thus far in this study are applicable to the West in general, there is one specifically French matter that haunts degenerative realist fiction in France today: the missed opportunity that was the Minitel. Unveiled in the late 1970s, the Minitel (whose name is a mashup of Médium interactif par numérisation d'information téléphonique) was a kind of protointernet, and it continued to operate until June 2012, when it was laid to rest. What recurs in the narratives I analyze in this chapter is a certain nostalgia for the early erotic innocence of the Minitel, its opening up of new ways for people to find invisible communities, and the underground prominence of all things arcane afforded by this new network. The Minitel was a point of French technocratic pride, pointing the way toward the future but ultimately losing out to the American internet. This missed opportunity, which could have made France the capital of the twenty-first century, gets rehearsed over and over in degenerative realist fictions and cast in a doubly negative light: Not only did France fail to take the necessary measures to ensure the success of its invention; it also suffers from the alienating, deadening effects of the new wired world managed by a different nation. At least if the Minitel had been adopted globally, the French could have claimed an imperial victory even while suffering from the network's detrimental effects on the human spirit.

This chapter will focus primarily on Aurélien Bellanger's *La Théorie de l'information* (2012), a prodigious novel published the same year as the death of the Minitel, which follows various stages of technological and theoretical development, from steampunk to cyberpunk to biopunk, and maps the rise and fall of the Minitel. The novel ends in what seems to be the realm of science fiction—with information (siphoned from social media) representing the quasi-totality of humanity being inserted into the DNA of bees—until one recalls that similar experiments that yoke together biology and digital technology are already under way and that the future will certainly entail the combination of digital network technology and biological engineering.[3] Sci-fi becomes prophecy when its vision is substantiated. In some respects, Bellanger's protagonist, Pascal Ertanger, resembles those of his model, Michel Houellebecq[4]—white, male, empty—but the protagonist seems at times superfluous in the narrative; he is a mere vehicle for the biography of the Minitel.[5] What Bellanger offers, I argue, is a theory of literature based on information science and cognitive science, which puts him in the positivist genealogy of his nineteenth-century forebears like Balzac, Flaubert, and Zola. My larger claim is that with the arrival of each new science or technology, we can expect to find a realist (or, at least, a novelist) who will apply the theories of this new science to the novel or who seeks fresh narratological possibilities provided by the new devices. For this reason, a novel like Houellebecq's *The Possibility of an Island* (2005), about cloning, or Jean-Noël Orengo's novel *L'Opium du ciel* (2017), whose narrator is a drone, were to be expected. The novel becomes a space in which theories are tested and new technologies are put in the service of narrative.

I will also turn briefly to Philippe Vasset's *La Conjuration* (2013) to bring attention to the *existential* problems of our age and their relation to the digital as portrayed in contemporary French fiction. Vasset's text, which depicts a dark reenchantment of the world enabled in part by the internet, explores the potential of religion to revive itself in a wired universe. At its core, the book is about hidden networks and their theological possibilities. In Vasset's depiction, the city of Paris becomes the dark web. The novel's ghostliness is announced in the title, a word that in French can mean either a conspiracy or a spell or incantation. Through this conjugation of the conspiratorial and the mystical, Houellebecq, Bellanger, Orengo, and others share this fascination with the loss of God in a secular society and the possibilities that technologies like the internet afford in offering humans the chance at immortality or at least reenchantment. Vasset invites his readers to notice the extent to which rumor mills and new-age sects use the same unofficial channels.

Finally, I end with a mention of Antoine Bello's trilogy *Les Falsificateurs* (2007), *Les Éclaireurs* (2009), and *Les Producteurs* (2015), which centers on an organization called the CFR (Consortium de falsification du réel), whose mission is the creation and dissemination of apocryphal information, facilitated by the arrival of digital networks and capable of convincing virtually anyone of its authenticity. Presciently, this trilogy, which borrows from genres like the thriller, spy fiction, or mystery-detective novels like *The Da Vinci Code* or esoterism-themed novels like *Foucault's Pendulum*, anticipates many of the themes that arose during the 2016 American presidential election and continued during various European elections of the 2016–2017 season: the spread of fake news, the use of bots and other automated programs to sway public opinion, the attempt to undermine institutions that had seemed stable in the analog world, and the covert operations of international political cabals seeking to usurp control from the current, less murky bearers of power. Bello uses fiction to comment on the potential loss of a healthy membrane between real and invented worlds given the internet's proneness to fabrication and quick dissemination of urban myths and malicious fictions.[6]

## FROM MINITEL TO INTERNET

The Minitel, perhaps the most ambitious French investment in *télématique*, was launched for public use in the early 1980s and was conceived in order to address two problems: the decaying telephone infrastructure and increasing competition from American computer corporations like IBM. As Andrew Feenberg puts it, the French state introduced this new technology "as a means of accelerating the postindustrialization of French society."[7] Completely overhauling the telephone infrastructure, the French government built a high-speed data network that would serve as both a phone network and a telematic network, that is, a network that could transmit computerized information over long distances. The Minitel's terminals were distributed for free to users, and its billing model was extremely simple, two factors that account for the platform's initial success. Its first use for the public was as an electronic phone book, but later, a wide variety of services were added, including weather forecasts, ticket booking, advertising, banking services, university enrollment, chatrooms, horoscopes, and mail ordering. The sex chatrooms of the so-called *Minitel rose* proved particularly popular. With its wide variety of uses and its accessibility to the public, this new space for public interaction had the effect of "indirectly enhancing democratic agency in general" (9). It is worth signaling again here the overlap of discourses of realism and discourses of democracy that have been presented thus far in this book.

It is essential to underscore the importance of the Minitel as a *national* project. Hubert Curien, who held several important governmental roles in the 1980s, such as minister of research and technology and president of the

Conseil scientifique de La Défense, described the Minitel's triumph in this way:

The ever-increasing demand for speed, interactivity, and conviviality, the surge of the audiovisual, and the explosion of information science have overwhelmingly triggered the emergence of new services; the Minitel is one of the most spectacular examples. *We can revel in this authentic French success. Of course, we'd be even more delighted if other nations envied us enough to become our clients.* This will be the next episode in the adventure of the Minitel.[8]

The lines I've italicized show the extent to which the Minitel was conceived as France's chance to reestablish itself as a capital of innovation, thwarting competition from other nations, particularly the United States. Narratives of the Minitel's history published during its formative years belabor this point. The book *Minitel* (1987), written by Marie Marchand, who can rightly be called a "Minitel publicist,"[9] possesses a certain propagandistic quality in its promotion of the platform's successes and its repeated evocations of American jealousy toward it.[10] In this and other pro-Minitel narratives, even when it became clear that the system was not exportable, it maintained its status as a fetish object, even abroad. Marchand writes, "The Minitel remained *franco-français*; it didn't manage to acquire international legitimacy. However, it still fascinates. All it takes is seeing an American or a Japanese consulting the Minitel to understand its ingenuity" (181). The symbolic, nationalistic meanings of the launch of the new system are not lost on Marchand, who describes the moment in 1983 when the Minitel electronic phonebook was inaugurated in Rennes: "Once again, France committed its favorite sin: Showing the entire world that it is the best. That against all obstacles, it knows how to choose the most audacious technical strategies. That it can accomplish this all alone, in the international desert. That its engineers are the strongest" (75). Obviously, the *exception française* applies to tech developments as well. In a comparative study, Lyombe Eko juxtaposes the notions of the "French exception" and "American exceptionalism" as they relate specifically to digital media. He argues that "American exceptionalism is messianic and isolationist, while the French exception is mostly culturalist, identitarian, and protectionist."[11] He shows how these differences have heavily marked the development of legal frameworks related to new digital media, intellectual property in cyberspace, and online privacy. Another argument made by its proponents was that the Minitel and the field of French telematics proved their fitness, to use a Darwinistic term, by surviving the passage in 1981 from a center-right government (under Valéry Giscard d'Estaing) to a socialist government (under François Mitterrand). Marchand argues that the survival of French *télématique* serves as a fine example of "republican continuity," given that it withstood the transfer from an "inventive, dynamic, but a tad authoritarian right-wing government" (69) to a left-wing one.

The report written by Simon Nora and Alain Minc, both inspectors of finance, that led in part to the creation of the Minitel has become, as Aurélien Bellanger puts it, "one of the masterpieces of technocratic literature."[12] Indeed, *L'Informatisation de la société* (1977), written at the behest of then president Giscard d'Estaing to help him craft the best technocratic response to an ailing economy, has markedly literary qualities for a governmental report. In it, we find epigraphs from Montaigne, Woody Allen, Ionesco, and Lewis Mumford. There are also rhetorical flights of fancy, like this one:

As the Sumerians were writing the first hieroglyphs on wax tablets, they were living, probably without realizing it, through a decisive change for mankind: the appearance of writing. And yet it was going to change the world. At the present time, data processing is perhaps introducing a comparable phenomenon. The analogies are striking: extension of memory; proliferation and change in information systems; possibly a change in the models of authority. The astonishing similarities may be far-fetched. The importance of this transformation, however, remains incomprehensible to those who live through it, unless it is considered from the viewpoint of Fabrice at Waterloo.
(129)

This reference to Stendhal's character Fabrice del Dongo from the novel *La Chartreuse de Parme* seems rather out of place in a survey of new computer technologies conducted by two *inspecteurs des finances*. Metaphors abound throughout the report, and the narrative structure might be described as a history of the present, which yields eventually to a history of the future. In the introduction to the English translation of the text, the sociologist Daniel Bell explains why the Nora-Minc report elicited such a lively debate in France when it was made available to the public: "One [reason] was the intrinsic fascination of the subject matter—and its larger rhetorical scope, almost an eschatological fantasy—which had not been covered before by the French press. Thus, it has the impact of a modern Jules Verne story."[13] The looming villain in the text is the United States, of which IBM is the metonym, and the authors note fearfully that French independence on a computerized, internationalized network would be "as easy to outflank as a useless Maginot Line."[14] The report is permeated with fear about France's place in the new interconnected world, but it is equally possibilitarian in its aspirations and shows that France could be a technocratic contender in the centuries to come if it were to make the proper investments in its telecom infrastructure. In a critical review of the Nora-Minc report, Ithiel de Sola Pool writes, "Diffused computing is the *machina* out of which the *deus* in the guise of the French state will descend to produce this significant and much-needed social change."[15] The connection between God and computing becomes all too clear once the internet arrives, as I will show in the next section.

The Nora-Minc report thus paved the way for the choice to embrace the Minitel as a signature project of the French state. Like the arrival of most new media, the Minitel's emergence was accompanied by several foundational myths whose fictional elements are rather striking. For example, the full story—probably apocryphal, at least in part—about the origins of real-time chat through the GRETEL project in Strasbourg remains unconfirmed. One of the system's developers, Michel Landaret, acknowledged that "the first chat system was a user's hack,"[16] but he couldn't confirm the identity of this hacker. Rumor has it that the culprit was a boy—a ten- or eleven-year-old or a teenager, depending on whom you ask—who went by the username Big Panther. Landaret explained:

We were running an experiment with a very small number of users, to determine whether professional associations and institutions would use data banks. . . . We could see how people new to the system could get confused and enter a series of ineffective commands. So we designed a system to communicate with those users by sending a message directly to their screen, and receive messages back from them, to help them learn how to use the system. One of our users just cracked that part of the system and used it to talk with friends. As soon as we found out what was happening, we made improvements on the service and made it a legitimate part of the system.[17]

The story circulated and changed over the years but has remained a fundamental part of the Minitel's self-mythologization. As we will see, this kind of story making and conspiracy craft carries over to the internet and ushers us toward our contemporary fake news moment.

It is also important to note that the rise of information technology has brought with it a whole host of new metaphors, which seem consistently necessary in conveying the mechanisms of any new technology to a non-expert public. The more complex a technology is, the more it lends itself to metaphorization . . . and mystification. Even if its intention is to make complex systems comprehensible, this kind of metaphorization can easily steer us astray, leading to the pursuit of a metaphor beyond its analogical utility and toward a complete misunderstanding of the technology at hand. For example, in his book *A Prehistory of the Cloud*, Tung-Hui Hu attempts to bridge "the gap between the real and the virtual"[18] when it comes to the cloud, "today's dominant metaphor for digital space" (147). Many metaphors for describing the internet have been tried out, such as a series of tubes, an information superhighway, an ecosystem, a commons, a rhizome, and a simulacrum (xxiv), but the cloud is the preferred one at the moment.[19] As for the Minitel, some scholars have described it as a "walled garden" or a "gated community,"[20] as a "labyrinth,"[21] and as a "kiosk,"[22] and Max Read's recent list of ways in which Facebook has been metaphorized continues to expand.[23] For Hu, "the cloud is the premier example of what computer scientists term virtualization—a technique for turning real things into logical objects, whether a physical network turned into a cloud-shaped icon, or a warehouse full of data storage servers turned into a 'cloud drive' " (x). What has gotten lost over time is the metaphoricity of the metaphor; people tend to forget that a cloud has a very concrete correlative: the server cluster. In his conclusion, Hu claims that "the cloud is a neoliberal fantasy about user participation that is so widespread and so ambient as to be universal, but that project is always founded on a volatile layer of insecurity" (145). The cloudiness of the cloud compels the public to forget the infrastructures necessary for the concept to exist. Does the average person really understand how the internet works? No. And in the gap between the technocratic intricacies of the system and the typical person's comprehension of this system, there is a breach that invites magical thinking.[24] Using Aurélien Bellanger's novel *La Théorie de l'information*, I will show this process at work.

Despite the swelling interest in new media and its cultural repercussions, there remain relatively few studies that analyze the Minitel from this angle, with a few notable exceptions. Current studies of the Minitel tend to approach it from an information technology history angle[25] or a sociological angle.[26] Other studies approach the problem from the angles of free speech, digital media law, and public access to information.[27] Andrew Feenberg argues that the introduction of the device into the bourgeois interior allowed for a special kind of infiltration of the home. He writes, "Disguised as a 'cute' telephonic device, the Minitel is a kind of Trojan horse for rationalistic technical codes."[28] The "ultimate deterritorialization" ushered in by the Minitel was only possible because the designers of the system realized that they could not simply put an "incongruous"-looking "large piece of electronic equipment on the bedroom dresser or the dining room table" (162). They opted rather for a subtler design that would allow for the covert introduction of a technocratic, state-run network into the homes of ordinary people. In their book *Minitel: Welcome to the Internet* (2017), Julien Mailland and Kevin Driscoll emphasize the successes of the platform and push back against the commonplace that the internet's victory over the Minitel represents a victory for American neoliberalism over heavy French state control. Alternatively, they claim the Minitel achieved a "balance of public and private interests" (15) and argue that it was not simply a hypercentralized technocratic arm of the bureaucratic state, instead showing how the Minitel provoked a creative surge among developers and entrepreneurs. The ultimate reason for the platform's failure, they argue, was not overbearing state intervention but the impossibility of recuperating the capital needed to replace the aging hardware infrastructure. Still, despite these compelling arguments and the optimistic view presented by the authors, the persistent reputation of the Minitel is still one of French failure.[29] I would argue that the authors I study in this chapter share the more pessimistic attitude about the failure of the Minitel and what can be extrapolated from this failure.

Politics aside, the Minitel certainly left its mark on French culture, more specifically on its art, critical theory, and literature. Annick Bureaud argues that "from the very beginning, the Minitel was the territory of art projects and art experiments,"[30] given that its user interface, connectivity, and pixelated aesthetic allowed for new forms of experimentation. Perhaps the most famous was Jean-François Lyotard's project *Les Immatériaux,* installed at the Centre Pompidou in 1985, which used Minitel terminals to "[facilitate] the questioning of the stability or materiality of cultural forms and automatically [include] the audience in the work of art."[31] As Mark Poster describes, the installation had a particular effect on the public: "Already the position of the audience had changed from the disinterested contemplation of the traditional gallery of paintings to the distracted participation of computerized art" (124–25). Fred Forest's 1983 project *L'Espace communicant* at the Electra show at the Musée d'art moderne de la ville de Paris used Minitels, phone lines, and answering machines, and the artist Eduardo Kac composed his first poems on the Minitel and created a series of Minitel-based art works. Other artists experimented with the new medium's specificities, like its graphic interface, pixelation, connective features, nonlinear navigation, hypertext links, and combination of text and image. The Minitel, with its unique possibilities and constraints, offered fodder to artists, writers, and critical theory alike.

In his book *The Mode of Information: Poststructuralism and Social Context*, Mark Poster draws connections between poststructuralist theorists and the new technologies that arose in the last quarter of the twentieth century. Certain of his pairings include Foucault and databases, Derrida and electronic writing, and Lyotard and computer science. François Cusset, too, has noted the connections between the rise of the Minitel and internet and their developers' reliance on so-called French theory for their vocabulary and conceptual improvisation. He highlights the fact that the "recurring comparison between the Internet and theory, a medium of technical dissemination and a corpus of philosophical texts, can be found across a wide range of Web sites on French theory."[32] French authors such as Deleuze, Guattari, Derrida, Baudrillard, and others were "presented ... as prophets of the Internet" (251–52). He continues: "Certain discussion forums suggested a rereading of every French text as a *network of concepts* and, conversely, that the Net itself be regarded as a successfully implemented program of French theory" (252). This "convergence of technical skill and theoretical backing" (252) is at the thematic heart of Bellanger's novel *La Théorie de l'information*. I will argue that Lyotard's vision is the most compatible with Bellanger's project.[33]

Literature in France has also fallen under the spell of the Minitel, the internet, and other communication networks. These networks play notable roles, for example, in the novels of Guillaume Dustan (*Dans ma chambre,*

1996; *Plus fort que moi*, 1998), Christine Angot (*Les Autres*, 1997), Michka Assayas (*Exhibition*, 2002), and nearly all of Houellebecq's novels. Recall that Houellebecq was at one time a computer administrator. Computing gives an architecture to the plot of his *Whatever* (1994), a kind of postmodern parody of the buddy movie. The narrator is sent on a road trip with an unbearable colleague so that they can train civil servants in a provincial town to use their company's new computer system. At one point, the narrator explains, "In the afternoon I make an appointment with a psychiatrist. There's a system of urgent psychiatric appointments by Minitel; you tap in your schedule, they supply you with the practitioner. All very practical."[34] Maurice G. Dantec's sci-fi novels, such as *Babylon Babies* (1999) and his other cyberpunk narratives, rely on digital networks, and these play a central role in Virginie Despentes's *Vernon Subutex* trilogy as well, with the public using them for everything from medical self-diagnosis to the tracing of lost friends to the obsessive seeking out of images of terror attacks like the one on November 13, 2015, at the Bataclan. The list of wired novels continues, with too many to name here, but the one that stands out among them is Bellanger's *La Théorie de l'information* for its expansive posthuman take on the relation between humans and the digital networks they've created.

## BELLANGER'S INFORMATION SCIENCE REALISM

The fullest literary account of the rise and fall of the Minitel is found in Aurélien Bellanger's maximalist novel *La Théorie de l'information* (2012), ostensibly about the arc leading from the development of the Minitel, then the internet, and finally to what he calls Web 2.0, a network that extends beyond the digital into the realm of the social and then the biological. Dominique Raymond calls the book a "novelesque encyclopedia" and argues that it is the first novel of the "Wikipedia era written in Wikipedian."[35] Nicolas Auray argues that the novel falls somewhere between sociology and fiction and recounts "the emergence of cognitive capitalism,"[36] in which "the definition of reality becomes monopolized by experts, set in their expertise through the support of those in charge who thus lock the chain of authority."[37] In Elisabeth Philippe's words, Bellanger seeks to be "the archaeologist of our modernity, the aloof chronicler of contemporary France."[38] *La Théorie de l'information* dispatches several interconnected "lines of flight," as Deleuze and Guattari might call them, including France's degeneration, information theory and its posthuman applications, the problem of human mortality, and literature as a virtual space. One of the book's central themes, only slightly veiled, is the civilizational degeneration of France. As Vincent Glad notes, "*La Théorie de l'information* is above all the novel of a middle power [*puissance moyenne*] in decline."[39] In August 2017, Bellanger began to try his hand at a different medium—the podcast—launching "La Conclusion" on France Culture. Covering themes such as Wikipedia, the logistics of civilization, the internet, information science, illegal downloading, and "pastoral capitalism," among other topics, Bellanger is clearly a chronicler of the contemporary, often in its degenerating form.

Regarding style, however, Bellanger's work hearkens back to that of his nineteenth-century realist predecessors, for whom simplicity and straightforwardness were essential, at least as articulated in their theories. In an interview with *Les Inrockuptibles*, he explains that he finds the contemporary French novel typically to be "overwritten" (*surécrit*), more poetic than prosaic, and hoped to avoid this pitfall by writing like an artisan rather than like an aesthete. Upon the recommendation of a friend, Bellanger decided to write a Balzacian novel after reading the entire Comédie humaine and falling under its spell.[40] When scrolling down through the online bibliography of novels included in Balzac's monstrous project, one's finger gets fatigued, and the immensity of his "history of manners" is so astounding that it is difficult to imagine a contemporary writer with this kind of stamina. Bellanger's *maximalisme balzacien* comes through in a scaled-down version and was not necessarily celebrated by the critics, many of whom found the novel incredibly boring in its meticulous technical recounting of the history of the Minitel and internet.[41] Defending himself, Bellanger argues that he adopted a style that would allow him to address specific problems in the clearest terms possible: "How to transmit information? How to make it comprehensible?"[42] Information transmission, as we will see, is the crux of the book.

The novel follows the protagonist Pascal Ertanger—at times completely effaced by the nonhuman protagonists, the aforementioned networks[43]—on his life journey as the "child prodigy of the information revolution."[44] Throughout his successful career, he embodies many personas: "the youngest pornographer in France, the youngest millionaire of the Minitel, future tycoon of telematic networks" (136). In short, he is the embodiment of "the French Silicon Valley" (414).[45] Modeled after the real-life French entrepreneur Xavier Niel, Ertanger shows an early talent for programming and channels these skills toward developing explicit chatrooms on the *Minitel rose*, which helps him accumulate a large fortune. Numbered, interspersed micronarratives—written in italics and titled "La théorie de l'information" in the categories of steampunk, cyberpunk, and biopunk—separate the various episodes of Ertanger's *parcours professionnel* and tell of a particular discovery or advancement in science, each turning out to have relevance for the destiny of the protagonist and the human race. Ertanger expands his business and grows his investments until his obsession with the virtual intensifies to such an extent that he eventually surrenders his life to it. Having recognized Facebook as "a biopolitical project" (461) and "a fishnet capable of capturing life" (459), he tries to transform this repository of humanity into a guarantor of immortality. It is worth noting that the ephemerality of the Minitel's content is in large part what left the public so mournful about its end. That the French government and its technocrats did not preserve the Minitel's archive of exchanges is a source of great melancholy for the system's original users. Those exchanges on the *messagerie* were not saved, and thus this missing archive could never be used in the way Bellanger imagines the archival potential of Facebook, another case of failure on the part of the French and success on the part of the Americans. Bellanger's narrator explains: "The billions of Facebook pages offered a complete summary of humanity and, in the case of its sudden extinction, guaranteed its complete restoration" (459). Facebook is a kind of backup drive for our whole species. Toward the end of the novel, Ertanger takes up the challenge put forth by Mark Zuckerberg to continue Facebook's "post-human experiments" (462) and launches Opération Canopée, first creating a mirror version of Facebook and then "implanting the human data . . . into the carapaces [of insects]," repurposing them into "little flying, self-replicating, autonomous data centers" (472). Ertanger eventually selects bees as the ideal bearers of the human information (in the form of DNA-encoded stories), hoping to open up the "closed language" of the apian species by "[contaminating] it with metaphysical human elements" (476). An old IBM factory is transformed into the megahive. Ertanger isolates himself along with the hive, never again sees the light of day, and nourishes himself on honey alone. He is diagnosed with a fatal brain disorder, and parallel with his degeneration, the megahive becomes autonomous, and the human DNA-injected bees "colonize the world" (486). It is discovered that his disease was caused by tampering with the bees' own DNA, and this plague is then spread across the globe by the bees of Opération Canopée, wiping out the human race. However, humanity survives in the "winged combinations of its last messages and could be reborn at any moment. The theory of information would be a time machine" (487). With this sentence, the novel ends.

This finish hearkens back to Lyotard's question, "Can Thought Go on Without a Body?"[46] and to his postmodern fable, in which the human race seeks some way to preserve itself before the inexorable self-extinguishment of Earth's star, the sun. This extinguishment is an obsession of Bellanger's as well,[47] as are the themes of entropy and narrative-as-embalming so central to Lyotard's tale. He writes, "The narrative of the end of the Earth is not in itself fictional, it's really rather realistic. What the final words of this story cause us to ponder is not that the Earth will disappear with the Sun, but that something ought to escape the conflagration of the system and its ashes."[48] He goes on to tell the cosmic tale of the improbable creation of the human race, "the first event whose enigmatic occurrence would condition the rest of the story, and even the possibility of its being recounted" (86). *Homo narrans,* as Kurt Ranke and others have named our species,[49] has attempted to inscribe its history into the world and to forestall its death by crafting a narrative that withstands bodily finitude. In Lyotard's telling, "Mr. Darwin" tells the next part of the story (87), offering a trans-species *Bildungsroman* that tells our own origins back to us. Eventually, Lyotard argues, all progress-oriented research, in fields such as "logic, econometrics and monetary theory, information theory, the physics of conductors, astrophysics and astronautics, genetic and dietetic biology and medicine, catastrophe theory, chaos theory, military strategy and ballistics, sports technology, systems theory, linguistics and potential literature" (91), was marshaled for one purpose: "testing and remodeling the so-called human body, or . . . replacing it, in such a way that the brain remains able to function with the aid only of the energy resources available in the cosmos" (91). Recognizing its impending doom if its energies are not harnessed to prevent it, our species must find a way to transmit itself, in the form of information-energy, to a safer place. After spinning out this cosmic fable, Lyotard switches gears and drives us toward a theme central to my study:

Realism is the art of making reality, of knowing reality and knowing how to make reality. The story we just heard says that this art will still develop a lot in the future. Reality will be changed; making, knowing, and know-how will be changed. Between what we are and what the hero of the final exodus shall be, reality and the art of reality will have been at least as metamorphosed as they have been from the amoebas to us. The fable is real because it recounts the story that makes, unmakes, and remakes reality.

(91)

He pushes further, explaining:

Realism accepts and even requires the presence of the imaginary within it, and that the latter, far from being something foreign to reality, is one of its states, the nascent state. *Science and technology themselves fable no less, and are no less poetic than painting, literature, or film.* The only difference between them lies in the verification/falsification constraint of the hypothesis. The fable is a hypothesis that exempts itself from this constraint.

(95)

I've used italics to highlight Lyotard's use of the word "fable" as a verb to describe one of the operations of science and technology. This verbalization is particularly helpful in reading Bellanger's novel, which pulls out various theories of information and offers them as discrete narratives of progress, often ending in what could be described as a kind of moral. For example, one excursus on the kinetic theory of gases ends with: "Disorder always follows order. It is impossible to turn back time."[50] Another on Claude Shannon's information theory ends with: "The world's indifference is our only apprenticeship. It moves and we move; we are synchronized [*coordonnés*]: The Universe precedes us, makes us live, and erases us. We are completely ignorant of its exact movements. But with information theory, we have a new instrument of control at our disposal" (288). In cybernetic fashion, each new story of scientific discovery causes humanity as a whole to adjust its behaviors and the structure of the larger story of how the world works. Scientific principles, like morals, function as guiding principles.

Both change with time, and both are framed as stories. In my view, the striking compatibility between Bellanger's and Lyotard's understanding of the relationship between narrative and life works as a tool in helping us decipher Bellanger's larger project.

Late in Bellanger's novel, when the human information culled from Facebook turns out to be too cumbersome and messy to transfer to the DNA of bees, Ertanger's programmer friend Xavier Mycenne creates a program that can "transform the chaotic, stuttering narratives into readable biographies that were especially easy to compress," thus converting them "into compact epics" (473). These, coincidentally, contain exactly 140 characters. Here we reach one of the book's metatextual theses, namely, that "literature is in reality nothing more than the applied theory of information" (474). Mycenne argues that novels and poetry are simply "stubborn attempts to encode the maximum information in the minimum number of words" (474). Like Houellebecq's *The Map and the Territory* (2010), this novel is about representation, here, more specifically, literary representation and the possibility of capturing the world in some medium other than itself. *La Théorie de l'information* is also a theory of the novel, à la Lukács, Watt, Mazzoni, and whoever else has ventured book-length hypotheses on the nature of the genre. Bellanger's hypotheses are more covert, hidden in the code, so to speak.

Throughout his novel, Bellanger writes obliquely about the powers of fiction and literary narrative. His protagonist is the archetypal computer wunderkind, and his personal trajectory follows the same epic-like narrative arc of the lives of famous Silicon Valley developers. Ertanger acknowledges this epic quality when he names his company Ithaca, casting himself as Ulysses. (Xavier Niel, the real-life model for the Ertanger character, named his company Iliad.) Ertanger becomes the story of himself; after his death, only those tales about him remain. We are nothing but these stories. At death's door, Ertanger dictates a text to his friend Mycenne, "what he called his memorial and what could have been a science fiction novella (if there had been characters in it) or a scientific article (if it hadn't had strange, mystical digressions). He'd titled it *La Théorie de l'information*" (481). Is this the book we've been reading the entire time? His friend Mycenne—who'd written a dissertation that applied Alan Turing's theories to Stendhal's *Le Rouge et le noir* and William Gibson's *Neuromancer* (414)—had already taken a literary interest in Ertanger's life story and "had been planning for a long time to write a sci-fi narrative inspired by the life of his childhood friend, the details of which—unknown to the public—he knew well" (415). Mycenne's combined interest in philosophy and literature leads him to develop a theory about the two disciplines: "In France, the great comic novel, tragic theater, and the epic poem had taken refuge in philosophy" (415). The triangulation between literature, philosophy (read: French theory), and information theory is not unexpected within the framework of this book. The novel and its imaginative worlds and alternative realities, the headspace of the philosopher full of speculations and theories, and the immaterial realm of information theory are all virtual spaces that allow the human to unshoulder the burden of embodiedness. Bellanger makes this connection explicit when his protagonist Ertanger falls into a "mystical crisis" provoked by reading Baudrillard's book *The Gulf War Did Not Take Place*, an application of the sociologist's simulacra theories. Ertanger writes poems about this period in his life and his reactions to the "de-realization of the reign of images," forgetting himself entirely "in the informational flux" (186). Yet again, we see philosophy, literature, and information theory yoked together, with an added mystical element, which I will examine momentarily.

Literature is one way to re-present or re-produce life, but there are certainly others. Take photography, for example. The relationship between the rise of realist literature and the arrival of the daguerreotype and other photographic processes in the nineteenth century has been studied extensively and could prove helpful in understanding Bellanger's text, since photography and other technologies of the reproduction of life play such a pivotal role in it. Bernard Weinberg sums up the nineteenth-century French debates on realism and photography this way:

What difference is there between a writer who copies nature exactly as it is, without interpretation, and a sensitized plaque exposed momentarily to the light? Many critics saw none whatsoever. Hence article after article equates realism with photography, with a purely mechanical rendition of the object imitated, with the consequent absence of anything recognizable as "art."[51]

When Comte Louis Clément de Ris sarcastically urged writers to "make your brain a daguerreotype lens and everything will be fine,"[52] he mocked would-be realists for their lack of originality and their surrender to the impulse to copy nature rather than make something new. Realism, as a kind of "daguerreotype reproduction proof of daily life,"[53] turned the artist into a machine with a strange penchant for reproducing the ugly, banal elements of existence. Obviously, the realists pushed back against these critiques. Guy de Maupassant argued famously that "the realist, if he is an artist, will not try to show us a banal photograph of life, but to provide us with a vision that is at once more complete, more startling, and more convincing than reality itself."[54] The representational impulse to go beyond simple mimesis is an age-old problem, beautifully illustrated by James Agee in an extraordinary passage from *Let Us Now Praise Famous Men*, his journalistic, photo-essayistic collaboration with Walker Evans: "If I could do it, I'd do no writing at all here. It would be photographs; the rest would be fragments of cloth, bits of cotton, lumps of earth, records of speech, pieces of wood and iron, phials of odors, plates of food and of excrement. . . . A piece of the body torn out by the roots might be more to the point."[55]

While Agee's solution for the transmission of the real relies on a return to the thing represented, Bellanger's vision requires humanity to become pure, bodiless information. His protagonist Ertanger's experiments as a young boy with photography lead him to "master the analogical techniques of the reproduction of the world."[56] When he copies the electronic phone book from the Minitel, he makes a realization: "In contrast to the physical world, in the world of information, the copy could be worth much more than the original" (178). These two moments hint at the final ambitious copy job Ertanger undertakes to rescue humanity from its certain demise. The next step in this process is to launch a new internet access provider called Demon, which allows "the real world and cyberspace to communicate." In the development of this new entity, he refuses to choose between "the real Earth and its technical reproduction" (333). Then, trusting the "most radical theorists of the evolutionist jump," who see on the horizon the *Homo numericus*, the "successful symbiosis of the biological and the electronic" (364), he explores the possibilities offered by Web 2.0. Explaining his final project to an audience that includes Google's founder Sergey Brin, Ertanger compares his rescuing of humanity to analog photography, which involved the passing of "elementary particles" (a very Houellebecquian phrase indeed) through "a dark room to modify the electronic structure of some silver salts" (431). He continues: "I used the Earth and its inhabitants as lenses and the graph of the Internet as a diaphragm. . . . Whereas Google took an objective photograph of the world, with its satellites and Google Cars, I made its subjective portrait: I knew in real time the behavior of my subscribers. I had access to their extra-cranial synapses, to their most unmentionable desires. . . . This time, the photographic plate is immaterial" (431). What was the original source of inspiration for such a project? A poem written by his friend Mycenne about human conservation through information storage.[57] The idea for informational metempsychosis was thus drawn from literature.

Regarding the reproduction of life and the insertion of documentary bits of life into fiction to make it lifelike, it is important to note the role of Wikipedia in *La Théorie de l'information*. Bellanger's book lifts passages directly from Wikipedia,[58] which raises the question whether we might read the book as a kind of documentary fiction that uses bits of realia to strengthen its representational persuasion. This is a generous interpretation and does not address the lack of citation we find in Bellanger and Houellebecq. Wikipedia has brought with it a whole slew of ethical questions.[59] Furthermore, the text offers a kind of dictionary of information technology embedded in the novel, written in italics and signaled as potentially clickable in the same way that the blueness of special words on Wikipedia pages signals to us that these terms are linked to their own pages. For example, the following words are italicized on one page of Bellanger's novel: *start-up, sites personnels, Web native, pure player, on line, dotcom, business model* (253). Many of the words are borrowed from English, which could account for their italicization, but others, like *"sites personnels"* are French terms and thus indicate that something other than Englishness binds the words together. Taken in bulk, they form a kind of lexicon. Bellanger italicizes the kinds of IT or corporate words we would expect to be hyperlinked in a Wikipedia article: *data center, business angels, stockoptions, netéconomie, pépinière d'entreprises, internautes, netentrepreneurs, geek, dégroupage partiel, moteur de recherche, portail,* etc.[60] Bellanger uses this technique throughout the book, every once in a while italicizing nontechnical, nonbusiness terms—such as *crise mystique* (186)—presumably for emphasis. This mixture of technical terms and the language of mysticism and esoterism produces a distinctly uncanny effect.

Wikipedia is also mentioned in the narrative. Its founder, Jimmy Wales, makes an appearance, and at one point Ertanger begins to read Wikipedia at random, using the "random article" feature until he comes across his own page, with the tags: "[this article concerns a contemporary event] [the neutrality of this article is disputed (see discussion)]." He notes that "the discussion thread was endless" (368), implying that the debates on details of Ertanger's life represented negotiations of the truth. The facts regarding the history of French Silicon Valley are as contestable as those of its American counterpart. Wikipedia is one important battlefield for the negotiation of facts in the twenty-first-century truth wars.

Silicon Valley is an imperial force, disregarding national sovereignties and colonizing every aspect of life. Noting its invasiveness, Guillaume Bachelay writes, "With technologies conceived in Silicon Valley, movements are geolocalized, behaviors decrypted, and feelings turned to algorithms."[61] Silicon Valley—embodied by Facebook, Google, Wikipedia, and other California tech companies—has a conspicuous place in Bellanger's narrative, and it is important to recall that this mythologized place also makes a notable appearance in Houellebecq's *The Map and the Territory* published two years earlier. In that novel, one of the most successful paintings of the protagonist-artist Jed Martin is titled "*Bill Gates and Steve Jobs Discussing the Future of Information Technology: The Conversation at Palo Alto.*" In this image, the narrator describes Steve Jobs's portrait as "an embodiment of austerity, of the *Sorge* traditionally associated with Protestant capitalism."[62] Jed Martin depicts Gates as "a creature of faith" possessing the "candor of the sincere capitalist," while Jobs, "made thin by illness, his face care-worn and dotted with stubble, sorrowfully leaning on his right hand, is reminiscent of one of those traveling evangelists who, on finding himself preaching for perhaps the tenth time to a small and indifferent audience, is suddenly filled with doubt. . . . In his eyes still burned that flame common not only to preachers and prophets but also to the inventors so often described by Jules Verne" (118). The language of evangelism here is another feature shared with Bellanger in his depiction of Silicon Valley gurus. In Houellebecq's narrative, the two technocratic leaders face off in a chess match as the California sun sets in the background, "the evening falling on the most advanced part of the world" (119). Having inserted himself in the novel, the fictional Houellebecq's reading of the painting ends this way:

Two convinced supporters of the market economy; two resolute supporters also of the Democratic Party, and yet two opposing facets of capitalism, as different as a banker in Balzac could be from Verne's engineer. *The Conversation at Palo Alto*, Houellebecq stressed in his conclusion, was far too modest a subtitle; instead, Jed Martin could have entitled his painting *A Brief History of Capitalism*, for that, indeed, was what it was.

(119)

The painting raises the encounter between Gates and Jobs to the allegorical level and is consistent with Bellanger's construction of the Ertanger character, whose life means more than the sum of the events that shaped it. As pioneers of posthumanity, these figures have set the world on a perhaps irreversible course toward dis-embodiedness.

## SEX AND *LE MINITEL ROSE*

It is ironic, then, that both the Minitel and the internet have placed such a premium on one of the most ostensibly embodied experiences of all: sex. Through virtualization, however, sex potentially loses its reproductive function and moves further away from an encounter between two bodies and toward an encounter with one's own body, fomented by images and unrealizable fantasies. The virtualization of sex relies on the repository of images and desires stored in the brain's hard drive.

Upon its arrival, the Minitel, a "thicket of sexual encounter,"[63] inaugurated a set of updated social practices related to sex. Shocked by the risqué content available on this new platform, Jean Autin, the former head of TéléDiffusion de France, argued, "You will transform France into one giant porno theater!"[64] Moral anxiety and outrage greeted this new technology, even in a nation imagined as perhaps the most libertine on earth. While the slow-loading, blocky images of naked flesh certainly titillated many, the *messagerie*, which allowed people to chat in real time with complete strangers, offered a new interactive element to fantasy. Julien Mailland and Kevin Driscoll note with some wistfulness the ephemeral nature of the Minitel's content, of which there is virtually no record left: "There is no way to emulate or simulate the experience of hanging out at home alone, dialing 3615, and flirting with strangers all night on a messagerie as we might have done back in 1987."[65] It was a moment of liberalization and a chance for the oldest profession in the world to modernize as well. In her book *King Kong Théorie*, Virginie Despentes describes how she became a prostitute using the network:

The idea of prostitution first came to me in 1991, because of minitel. All modern communication methods are first and foremost used for selling sex. Minitel, a French precursor of the internet, allowed a whole generation of girls to become occasional prostitutes in near-perfect conditions of anonymity, client choice, price negotiation, independence. . . . My first minitel job, in 1989, was in fact to monitor one of the servers. I was paid to disconnect any user employing racist or anti-semitic language, but also paedophiles and, finally, prostitutes.[66]

She explained the process further, saying, "Every time I needed cash I would log on to minitel, on the local-based server of my city, Lyon. It would take me about ten minutes to collect several phone numbers from men looking to score that same day" (57). She was paid handsomely and had the safety and flexibility she needed to live well. When she tried to continue the same work in Paris, dangerous clients and more competition from other prostitutes made things difficult, and "the minitel servers were more heavily policed, and it was hard to be as selective as before" (62). The *Minitel rose* also became a new site of gay sexual sociability. Lawrence Schehr notes the centrality of the Minitel and internet for the characters in the gay fiction novels he analyzes in his book *French Post-Modern Masculinities*: "One could not imagine these characters being themselves without cybercafés, the Internet, easy access to porn, and so forth. The interpellated position of the subject is always *branché*, in both senses of the word: both plugged in and 'in the know.'"[67] With the arrival of the Minitel, the underground suddenly had a whole new network of interconnected tunnels.

While Despentes's experience and the hookups described in gay fiction and personal memoirs involved eventual real-life encounters, most of the exchanges on the *Minitel rose* did not lead to consummation. They remained in the realm of the virtual and allowed for a clinical distancing of desiring subjects. One could remain anonymous and bodiless on the Minitel. As Susan Sontag writes, "Machines supply new, popular ways of inspiring desire and keeping it safe, *as mental as possible*: the commercially organized lechery by telephone (and in France by 'Minitel') that offers a version of anonymous promiscuous sex without the exchange of fluids."[68] I've italicized Sontag's point about how keeping desire strictly mental allows one to skirt the messiness and contaminative disadvantage of the body. Paul Virilio calls this phenomenon "sensory privatization," in other words, "the pleasure of rendez-vous at a distance, of a get-together without getting together, pleasure without risk of contamination offered by the anonymous telecommunications of the erotic Minitel or the Walkman."[69] In a striking comparison, Jean Baudrillard draws an analogy between the Gulf War and the *Minitel rose*: "This war is an asexual surgical war, a matter of war processing in which the enemy only appears as a computerized target, just as sexual partners only appear as code-names on the screen of Minitel Rose."[70] Elsewhere, Baudrillard writes, "The celibacy of the machine entails the celibacy of the Telecomputer Man"[71] and argues that the Minitel lets this man "offer himself the spectacle of his own phantasies, of a strictly virtual pleasure" (54). The screen becomes mirror (54), and thus the Telecomputer Man morphs into the Network Narcissus, patron saint of the contemporary West. Recall that many of Houellebecq's characters seek sex or masturbatory fodder on the *Minitel rose* or the internet, often as a last resort after their real-life conquests fail. Using a specific example, Sandrine Rabosseau writes, "Sexual determinism stems from economic determinism. Without money, no sex for the Western man. As [Houellebecq's] *The Possibility of an Island* shows, he's left only with masturbation or virtual sex via the *minitel rose* or the Internet."[72] Masturbation becomes a kind of societal pressure-release valve.[73]

Bellanger's chronicle of the *Minitel rose* emphasizes its early innocence and subtle eroticism, which eventually yielded to the most illicit kinds of sex. One could argue compellingly that in its early years the *Minitel rose* borrowed from the aesthetic of romanticism but in the late 1980s it yielded to a blunt realism. In its first days, the "cult of the periphrase" (63) dominated the *Minitel rose*. Recall that the early theorists of realism in the nineteenth century railed against the periphrase with particular vitriol.[74] The narrator in Bellanger's novel describes the "spontaneous lyrical callings" (61) that circulated throughout the night but dissipated with the first morning light. Botanical metaphors were used to describe sexual acts (63). As midnight approached, the messages became "mysterious and intimate" (62) and achieved "moments of authentic poetry" (62). The description continues: "People exposed themselves fully, they shared their dreams, and they eventually reached dangerous zones" (62). The protagonist Ertanger cannot give himself over to these romantic embellishments of the early Minitel: "Pascal very quickly preferred the explicit and real language of programming to the poetic ambiguities of the Minitel" (67).

When Minitel users would set up "rendez-vous in real life" (90), there was often a marked discrepancy between the online personas and the actual people who'd created them. Ertanger himself manages twenty pseudonyms at a time: "He loved big dicks and more modestly proportioned ones, he liked doggie style and sodomy. . . . He liked threesomes and double penetrations. Pascal stuck his fingers everywhere, he was wet, biting, or coming" (135). In other words, he was simultaneously male and female, gay, straight, and bi, each of his personas with its own unique tastes. This was a luxury afforded by the anonymity of the Minitel.[75] Over the years, the *Minitel rose* became less a tool for hitting on people—"un instrument de drague"—and more a masturbatory tool, a "technique de jouissance" (90). By the late 1980s, "the era of innocent seduction was over" (89). Women were scared away by the predatory perverts who were no longer willing to accept periphrasis, metaphor, innuendo, and romance. The Minitel flashed its dark underbelly, with all sex gravitating toward the hardcore and the sadomasochistic. It is fair to say that the sex that circulated on the Minitel and continues to circulate on the internet has virtually nothing to do with reproduction. In chapter 1, I illustrated the ways in which the fear of population decline in the West is the precipitant of many of the eschatological narratives we find in contemporary French fiction. The virtualization of sex and its concomitant evasion of the reproductive elements of copulation do not help matters. If a nation of *séducteurs* and *séductrices* becomes a nation of *masturbateurs* and *masturbatrices*, how can the government's natalist policies achieve results?

## FROM MYSTICISM TO CONSPIRACY THEORY

The statement by Ertanger's love interest Émilie that they were "programmed to love" (158) offers a vision of informational determinism and summons up a pervasive theme in the narrative: the idea of God as programmer and the world as a program. Bellanger explains, "My character [Pascal Ertanger] represented a kind of crashtest of this religious system," meaning the new digital networks in which Google is comparable to "an omniscient God."[76] Ertanger "believed in information theory as he would a religious theory."[77] In the section on religion in his book *Houellebecq, écrivain romantique*, which appeared two years before *La Théorie de l'information*, Bellanger writes in a footnote, "An informational history of theology remains to be written, a history of theology as a particular branch of information science."[78] The links between this imagined project and his novel are all too clear. Summing up one of Houellebecq's visions regarding contemporary Western society, Bellanger writes, "Having arrived at the most extreme point of liberalism, men are rediscovering the anthropological necessity of religion" (201). One can also see how Bellanger adapts Houellebecq's thesis to his own project.

The epigraph for one chapter, a quote from a philology professor named Jacques Perret, reminds us of the occluded etymological connection between God and the computer. The French word for computer—*ordinateur*—is also "an adjective that refers to God who puts order into the world" (67). Nora and Minc anticipated critiques against telematics and showed how IT pessimists of the time had a particular vision of the computer: "The machine would no longer be a computer (*ordinateur*), a tool for calculating, remembering, and communicating, but a mysterious and anonymous order-giver (*ordonnateur*)."[79] In Bellanger's novel, the narrator calls Steve Jobs "the founder of a new religion" (14) and describes one of its rituals in this way: "The public presentation of Apple products resembled pagan worship ceremonies, during which Jobs, always dressed in black, exhibited ivory and ebony talismans at the frontier between science and magic" (13). Throughout *La Théorie de l'information*, Silicon Valley becomes "the object of a veritable cult" (94) with its own legends and pilgrimage sites, like the Hewlett-Packard garage in Palo Alto or the childhood home of Steve Jobs in Mountain View. Bellanger reminds us that once Bill Gates became a multibillionaire, he acquired a Gutenberg Bible (201). Following what has come to be called the prosperity doctrine, the billionaires who constructed the technocratic West see their wealth as a *signe d'élection* (11).

In Bellanger's depiction, one of the early uses of the Minitel was to seek answers about God. For example, the diocese of Versailles launches a "telematic survey" on God and discovers that "many people asked themselves questions about the meaning of life and the existence of evil" (55). The act of going on the Minitel is also described as collective psychoanalysis in which France, "Europe's last great literary people," unleashed the poetry from its subconscious, transforming it into the place where people "debated life after death and spiritualist experiences" (63). The Minitel generation "had learned the power of the Word [*la puissance du Verbe*]" (219). In 1997, Marc Augé noted the "compatibility between the Internet and religion," offering examples of how major religions like Christianity, Islam, and Judaism already had begun to take advantage of the reach afforded by the network. However, he predicted a situation in which believers might be tempted to customize their religious experience to their tastes, given the preference-oriented nature of Web navigation and use. He writes:

One can also imagine that, faced with these countless opportunities for "à la carte" religion [on the internet], some would be tempted to practice their own brand of continuous mystical DIY, re-creating for their exclusive use spaces for some mythic place-between analogous to those we think we have pin-pointed in situations of a colonial type. To each, for a while, his own cosmology.[80]

Bellanger—and Philippe Vasset, as I'll show later—creates a fiction in which this customized cosmology plays out in the virtual space of the novel. More importantly, the worship of information itself finds a temple and its own congregation.

Religion, of course, has its architecture, and Bellanger transforms unexpected places into houses of informational worship. At one point in the novel, an abandoned synagogue—left empty after the anti-Semitic attack on the rue Copernic in 1980—is transformed into a sex temple called Sexy Vegas, which Ertanger uses as an investment to support his activities on the *Minitel rose*. He has a mural painted depicting him and his romantic partner Émilie, "the only humans of this landscape of Eden and the Apocalypse" (159), holding hands before a *Blade Runner*–inspired backdrop. The narrator reminds us that France's first flirtations with virtual reality involved its reconstruction of Cluny's Cistercian abbey, known as Project Gunzo (201). The digital archives of the Grand Louvre and the new Bibilothèque nationale become "almost sacred places" where "the civilization of paper and that of immaterial information" were united and meant to survive "long after the end of the world" (200). The internet itself "was conceived in order to resist a nuclear apocalypse" (214). If we had trusted the alarmist and apocalyptic fear campaign at the time, Y2K could have been the end of the world, and this eschatological connection is not lost on Bellanger. Aided by his exorbitant wealth and his increasingly urgent vision of transferring humans' humanity out of their bodies, Ertanger decides to transform the Bourse—also known as the Palais Brongniart and completed in 1826—into a computer science museum that would also "discretely serve as a lab and, even more secretly, would serve as temple devoted to information" (420). A connection might be made between the cloud that holds all of our data and the place where God is often imagined to reside.

In addition to its architecture, religion needs its prophets and demiurges. Along with the Silicon Valley oracle-gods mentioned above, Bellanger includes real-life figures like Thierry Ehrmann—the artist, freemason, and businessman—who makes an appearance in the novel and argues that "Western societies" were "destroyed" and that the only haven from total world *décadence* or decline was "the protected world of information science" (222). Teilhard de Chardin, the French soothsayer prophet-philosopher and Jesuit priest who coined the word "noosphere," makes an appearance in Bellanger's book, just as he does in Houellebecq's *The Possibility of an Island*. He tries to reread the Gospel through the lens of science (219–20). The narrator declares that "new media were the noosphere, the ultimate environment for the men of the future" (219) and that "the Internet was messianic" (221). Of prophets and science, Zola reminds us in *Le Roman expérimental*: "In our scientific age it is a very delicate thing to be a prophet, as we no longer believe in the truths of revelation, and in order to be able to foresee the unknown we must begin by studying the unknown."[81] But Bellanger allows for the reinvigoration of the prophet figure, who takes a new form in the twenty-first century, that of the messianic computer guru.

Because *La Théorie de l'information* delves so deeply into the theological and because Bellanger relied so heavily on the Comédie humaine as a catalyst for the writing of this novel, it might be helpful to recall the question raised by Balzac in the preface of his massive project. He asks, "In what way do the phenomena of brain and nerves, which prove the existence of an undiscovered world of psychology, modify the necessary and undoubted relations of the worlds to God? In what way can they shake the Catholic dogma?"[82] For Bellanger, the brain and nerves form a system whose function will eventually be consigned to a different kind of system—a postcorporeal, purely informational one—precisely at a moment when God has ceased to exist. I see a strange chiasmus here, in which for Balzac the new discoveries about the brain could potentially shake the certainties of the faithful while for Bellanger the transfer of consciousness outside the body manages to reenchant the world and make God a possibility once again.

In a fascinating comparative article on Houellebecq's *The Possibility of an Island* and Bellanger's *La Théorie de l'information*, Emmanuel Buzay argues that both authors use computational writing—that is, the writing of code—as a means for reflecting on the limits of humanity, which holds a "teleological conception of writing and its mythologies."[83] He shows the lineage that leads from Houellebecq to Bellanger, noting the transmission of specific features: sci-fi elements, a cyberpunk aesthetic, Comtean positivism, and the "metaphysical dread" of the philosopher-mathematician Blaise Pascal "on the subject of the infinite through a reflection on computer coding, the sciences, and poetic language" (93). It is no coincidence that the protagonist of Bellanger's novel shares the name Pascal with Blaise Pascal, the mathematician, philosopher, and creator of calculation machines that could be considered the forerunners of modern computers. The famed Jansenist is omnipresent in *La Théorie de l'information*, an obvious inheritance from Michel Houellebecq.[84] Pascal Ertanger makes the following claim toward the end of the novel: "Every calculator since Blaise Pascal's has been an attempt to enumerate the infinite name of God, his mathematical name."[85]

At the heart of his argument, Emmanuel Buzay suggests that the protagonists of the aforementioned novels function as programs (in the information science sense of the word) "in order to show the way in which posthumanist ideology would lead to a reification of the world in a near future" (94). Both books pose the question: Is digital mortality possible? We perceive in the act of writing a will to create, to code the human out of its dilemmas imposed by bodily finitude. It goes without saying that the novelists also actively resist time through their writing, creating the possibility of extending their singular selves beyond death. The novel is a container of humanity, a time capsule, and a mechanism for the transmission of information about one generation and its singular moment to the next generation. The transmission of life stories from one generation to the next in all their fullness means in these novels the transmission of *actual* life.

These reflections on God, immortality, and digital life are paramount themes in Houellebecq's and Bellanger's novels, but there is another crucial element, which appears in other contemporary French novels as well. In this final section, I would like to show a set of shared mechanisms between the process of (re)mystification brought about by networks like the Minitel and the internet and the dissemination of conspiracy theories and fake news via these same networks. What is so different, after all, between the attempt to unveil the hidden metaphysical forces that shepherd our universe and the attempt to unmask the arcane political forces that govern us?[86] While the term "fake news" has only recently entered popular parlance, its utility was already being tested in the early days of the Minitel. Michel Landaret, one of the platform's developers, describes an early social experiment he conducted with his team: "We found that we could feed a small piece of deliberately false information to one of these people, and it spread throughout all different groups, to as many as four thousand people within two days."[87] Yes, you've read correctly. Long before the Russian disinformation campaign that impacted the 2016 American presidential elections and before the internet, with its superabundance of untruths, the French were already toying with the propagation of falsehoods through a digital network. Using Bellanger's *La Théorie de l'information* alongside novels by two other writers—Philippe Vasset and Antoine Bello—I will show the proximity of these processes (the development and spread of arcane knowledge and of false information and conspiracy theories) and how they relate to the contemporary realism I describe throughout this book.

In his book *Antinomies of Realism*, Fredric Jameson argues, "Realism as a form (or mode) is historically associated, particularly if you position the *Quijote* as the first (modern, or realist) novel, with the function of demystification."[88] Elsewhere, he describes realism's task as "a demystification of some preceding ideal or illusion"[89] and argues that the object of realism is "that desacralized, postmagical, common-sense, everyday, secular reality" (122). What is strange in the novels I've been describing is their entertainment of a process of remystification, spurred in part by the Minitel and the internet, networks that allow for and indeed encourage a reenchantment of the world. One could even say that in these novels, the real in realism no longer holds up, leading the novels to tip in their last pages into science fiction or other modes of otherworldliness. Who could forget, for example, the end of Houellebecq's *The Elementary Particles*, which spins out from a depressing narrative about a pair of dull-lifed men to a distant future in which clones have eliminated the need for sex? In his reading of several cyberpunk and sci-fi novels, Andrew Feenberg relies on Stanislaw Lem's notion of "actualysis," or "the breaking down, the eroding of reality."[90] The novels in the corpus Feenberg chooses "are all based on a sense of the fragility of the real" and "exhibit a disturbing undercurrent of worry about the unity and reality of the subject caught in a hyperbolic doubt that now embraces the *cogito* itself. Total technical mediation has destabilized both personal identities and objective reality."[91] I want to suggest that as the perforated membrane between reality and fiction splits open, we can expect more and more novels that begin in the realist mode to "degenerate" into sci-fi or some other nonrealist mode as they move toward their conclusions.

First, the Minitel apparatus itself brought about new configurations of immediacy and remoteness, of visibility and invisibility, a tension that naturally invited a mystical experience of the machine. Andrew Feenberg writes, "Like the telephone, the Minitel too acquired new and unexpected connotations as it became a privileged instrument of personal encounter. In both cases, the magic play of presence and absence, of disembodied voice or text, generates unexpected social possibilities inherent in the very nature of mediated communication" (165). The spectral absence of one's interlocutors and of the consultable databases made the machine a kind of oracle and the user, a querent who would pose it questions and wait for responses. Bellanger says as much: "The Minitel was oracular" (63). He also notes that Steve Jobs and the protagonist Ertanger "were treated as paradigmatic geniuses gifted with oracular faculties" (308). Furthermore, because the cables were underground, their formation of a subterranean network made it simple to associate them with other forms of mystical clandestinity. As Nicolas Auray puts it, "An unprecedented link was formed there between the network and the secret."[92] It doesn't take much imagination to see the connection between the cryptic and encryption and to note the proliferation of mystical terms in IT (cargo cult programming, magic strings, oracle machines, etc.). Because their mechanisms are so difficult for the average person to understand, the intricacies of complex technologies seem to the average person as unknowable as whether God, ghosts, or aliens exist. They are destined to be approximated with the enigmatic. The ethernet suggests the presence of an æther on earth. The plasma screen becomes ectoplasmic. The modem's staticky screams resemble the shrieks of otherworldly banshees.

The early pioneers of the Minitel and internet were young men, awkward and isolated, living in fantasy worlds of their own creation. Bellanger highlights the connection between future programmers and the arcane world of Dungeons & Dragons, role-playing games, and other "obscure ceremonial games in secret" (72). "They were the first shamans of prehistoric ages, driven out of the tribe but endowed with unknown powers, the first Christians who took refuge in the catacombs but ready to conquer the Empire, the last monk scribes, besieged by wars and epidemics but saving the forgotten masterpieces of ancient philosophy" (72). Excluded from the social world, they "dreamt of revenge" (72). The protagonist Ertanger lives by one of the tenets of Arthur C. Clarke, namely, that "every sufficiently advanced technology is indiscernible from magic" (74). Among these alienated men, Ertanger's childhood friend Xavier Mycenne launches a project combining the work of H. P. Lovecraft, an author dear to Houellebecq,[93] and the mathematical constant π and shows that "behind ordinary mathematics, there existed an esoteric science of the number" (50). Hacker ethics and aesthetics freely circulate the notion of the hacker as a savior, a member of the Illuminati, a necromancer, a cosmic trickster, and a possessor of arcane skills meant only for the initiated. Like the magician of the Tarot deck, the first trump in the Major Arcana, the hacker avails himself of all the tools he's learned to use in order to mediate between the cloud or æther and the immanent world of the typical mortal user. As the narrator of Bellanger's novel puts it, "The Minitel could reenchant the social world" (63).

The Minitel, a nonplace where the coexistence of real and fantasy was encouraged, was a perfect site for the flourishing of esoterism. Tarot, ufology, horoscopes, numerology, clairvoyance, and divination thrived there, as did the tools of such trades, like ionizing lamps, incense, manuals, tarot cards, pendulums, runes, and medallions (153). There, one could find debates about "paranormal phenomena" (154), "healing by the laying on of hands, telepathy, telekinesis, magnetism, . . . reincarnations" (155). In Maurice G. Dantec's *Babylon Babies*, similar esoteric materials circulate on the web.[94] The hyper-rationality of information science had in some ways provoked this backlash. As the narrator puts it, "The medium of engineers brought along with it the emergence of an entire anti-Cartesian industry" (153). Sociologists of the time called this industry a "quest for meaning" and argued that the rise of astrology "gave evidence of the successful de-Christianization of French society" (153). Another cause of this rise in esoterism was the relativization of the sciences; the narrator mentions in passing "the relative character of scientific truths and . . . the history of science as a *metanarrative* and a great postmodern myth stripped of founding principles" (155). At the moment of the Minitel's arrival, a slice of the population has a respect for the hard truths of science while still entertaining an interest in the inexplicable. Ertanger believed that the strict rejection of all unexplained phenomena is not a scientific attitude but rather a religious one (160–61). He preferred to keep a more open mind.

This "revenge of vernacular knowledge over official knowledge" (59) on the early Minitel leads easily to a general distrust of sanctioned stories—that is, information provided by journalistic outlets and by the state—and a freedom to create alternative facts. In Philippe Vasset's strange novel *La Conjuration* (2013), the Fantômas-like protagonist haunts the peripheral and forgotten zones of Paris and eventually forms a religion around fiction-made-to-resemble-fact, borrowing some of the methods used by purveyors of urban legends, conspiracy theories, and junk science on the Minitel and internet. Vasset, who is both a novelist and a journalist, has displayed his fascination with computers and the digital realm in a variety of formats. His novel *Exemplaire de démonstration* (2003), translated into English as *ScriptGenerator*, tells of the obsolescence of the human in creating literature. Computers have replaced people in the writing of books, an idea proposed already by Italo Calvino, for example in his lecture "Cybernetics and Ghosts" (1967) and in his novel *If on a Winter's Night a Traveler* (1979). Vasset's novel *Carte muette* (2004), which combines his fascination with maps and with the web, tells the tale of the attempt to create the first complete map of the internet. His most recent book, *Armes de déstabilisation massive: Enquête sur le business des fuites de données* (2017), a nonfiction study coauthored with Pierre Gastineau, was written in the wake of the 2016 American elections and explores large-scale data breaches and the weaponization of information. Regarding Vasset's novel *La Conjuration*, it is significant that in French the word *conjuration* means both "conspiracy" or "plot" and an "incantation," "spell," or "conjuration," the double meaning toward which the book's themes and plot insistently gravitate. Roaming the *zones blanches* of the city, "the zones left blank on the map of the Île-de-France"[95]—a theme explored already in nonfiction form in his book *Un*

*Livre blanc* (2007), analyzed in the next chapter—the protagonist laments the encroachment of shopping malls and housing developments into these lost, magical crevices, the useless and vacant spaces where he wanders day and night. However, he has no interest in founding an "autonomous zone" (10), a term borrowed from Hakim Bey.[96] Instead, he sees them as the last bastions of mysticism, sacred sites where one might learn the art of total self-effacement. He seeks others who are also drawn to the enigmatic margins of Paris and describes his first attempt to ally himself with such a collective, "a group of strange characters dressed in cloaks and mismatched hats, their faces covered with veils of gauze" (26). For them, the white or blank zones meant "areas not covered by mobile telephone networks" (27), and after spending more time with them, he starts to understand the nature of their hauntings, describing them as contemporary, isolated souls reminiscent of Defoe's Robinson Crusoe: "My Robinsons in training were in reality schizophrenics who imagined they suffered from an intolerance of electromagnetic fields and who sought in the wastelands hypothetical protection from the radiation of relay masts" (27). Unfortunately, they discover that the entire Île-de-France can be reached by the networks: "everything was covered 100%, no one was sheltered from a call" (27). The protagonist makes an important observation about who counts as a legitimate source of information: "You couldn't trust schizophrenics, which was really too bad because they had excellent ideas" (27).

In his explorations of the city, the protagonist turns to an important resource, a website offered by France's Institut national de l'information géographique et forestière (IGN): "On the virtual globe of the Institute (www.geoportail.gouv.fr), the satellite images of the most sensitive sites had been discreetly blurred (indeed, in certain cases, completely obscured), which prevented you from seeing them but nonetheless allowed you to locate them" (28–29). I visited the URL provided by Vasset to see if it was functional, and indeed, it leads to the Géoportail, which gives visitors access to satellite images of the world, cadastral parcels (a map showing property lines), road maps, and other visual representations of our globe.[97] Vasset's use of the Géoportail in his narrative is reminiscent of Bellanger's highlighting of the relationship between satellite imagery and worldmaking in *Théorie*. In an extraordinary passage of Vasset's book, the protagonist comes across "mysterious warehouses" belonging to "computerized data storage companies" or "data centers" (39), which he infiltrates without revealing how. Inside, a thought troubles him. What is the connection between "this machinery and its action on the city" (40)? What exactly was the purpose of the strange pods? "Sending messages? Stock market transactions? Keyword searches? Ordering of files?" (40). The sheer epistemological impenetrability of these boxes makes them mysterious, closed chests. (Recall that the etymological root of the word "arcane" is chest, *arca* in Latin.) The thought crosses his mind to tamper with the system and shut it down, and he wonders what the result might be. They are protected from the outside, he notes, but what would happen if an internal threat presented itself? A rat, for example. He states, "I liked the thought that a rodent could reduce a city to nothingness by nibbling on its digital reserves" (41). He hesitates to act on his impulse to crash the system, noting that in this "time of anti-terrorist hysteria" (41), such an infraction would pose too much of a personal risk of possible arrest and prosecution. Next to these data centers, he finds evangelical churches, a theme that acquires greater and greater significance as the narrative unfolds.

By chance he meets in the street an old acquaintance named André, who reveals a new business scheme: to found a religion. Citing George Orwell from 1938, André explains that "creating your own religion must be a very profitable business" (49) and describes the details of his new endeavor. "My idea, it's a sort of cult, but adapted to the needs of today: no totalizing theory or brainwashing, but secrets, rituals, and spectacular ceremonies" (50). The protagonist recognizes compatibilities between André's vision and his mystical exploration of the hidden folds of Paris. They team up. They begin to search for possible benefactors, explicitly suggesting Thierry Ehrmann and Pierre Bellanger, real-life entrepreneurs who both play mentionable roles in Aurélien Bellanger's *La Théorie de l'information*. During an interview with Miviludes (Mission interministérielle de vigilance et de lutte contre les dérives sectaires), an actual state-sponsored organization that tries to prevent cults in France,[98] the protagonist and his partner pose an important question to the representatives: "Why forbid Raël from doing what Bill Gates did?" (134). Raël is, of course, the founder of the French UFO cult known as the religion of Raëlisme, which played a central role in Houellebecq's novel *The Possibility of an Island*.[99] As we saw in Bellanger's text, Bill Gates, Steve Jobs, and other Silicon Valley entrepreneurs constitute a kind of cult leadership, capable of mesmerizing masses of people to do their bidding and live by their doctrines.

In a taxonomy of the four types of "ecstatic group experiences" (78) articulated by Vasset's protagonist, he includes: Evangelical churches, which preach the "success theology," also known as the prosperity doctrine; cults like Scientology, the Raëlist movement, or transcendental meditation; schools of thought that call themselves "cultural movements" or philosophies, thus avoiding the religious label, and that recruit from "the highest socioprofessional levels" (79); and new self-help, therapy, and life-coach movements that combine psychology, sociology, and asceticism. I want to mention here in passing that the reason I believe such emphasis is placed on cults, or what we might call "alternative belief systems," in contemporary French fiction—in Houellebecq, Bellanger, and Vasset, for example—is because this theme allows us to entertain the possibility that rationality can never really defeat mystical thinking, even in an age of reason. Cults are miniature, cybernetic religions that adjust to the epistemological necessities of the age. I also believe such novels are talking obliquely about Islam, a religion imagined by those unfamiliar with it as being if not from another dimension then at least from a dark age long ago, out of joint with the so-called enlightened, modern West.

Through the protagonist's study of these various forms of religion and esoterism, he and his partner begin to formulate a kind of recipe for getting people to believe, even in an age of reason. The recipe is simple: "You begin with a simple, irrefutable scientific fact. . . . Then, you embroider" (108). To embroider here means to add exaggerated or fictitious details. Every story must have "the greatest appearance of scientificity" (109). In an age of reason, a scientific veneer works as a Trojan horse with mystical thinking hidden inside it. Toward the end of the novel, after the protagonist has parted ways with his co-conspirator, the narrative transforms into a kind of how-to manual for the followers of a process the narrator calls *conjuration*, a word whose double meaning I've already highlighted. The conspiracy or incantation that is the ultimate objective of the practitioners of this singular mysticism involves total self-erasure, invisibility, and a dissipation of the self into a bodiless nothing. As the manual states, "Humanity only accesses the sublime by disappearing" (161). The group, which "progresses from building to building like a computer virus" (191), begins to lose its bodily form and become omnipresent, capable of watching and hearing everything while being watched and heard by everything at the same time: "Our surveillance is total, our listening perpetual, and our impotence absolute. Each piece of information, barely perceived, is immediately forgotten: We prefer the blissful spasm of the rumor to knowledge" (192). Vasset's description—of a powerless population under complete surveillance while voyeuristically surveilling others, preferring rumors and the shiver they deliver to more substantial knowledge, without the capacity to remember anymore in this deluge of information—sounds eerily like a community to which most of us belong, that of the vast pool of internet users. Only hinting at this connection throughout the book, Vasset is, I believe, gesturing toward the wired masses, whose bodies lose consistency through the internet and who can pass through walls, into the homes of strangers, without being detected. The spectrality I mentioned earlier in relation to various networks (the phone, Minitel, and internet) arrives in full force at the end of the book, when the members of the cult of *conjuration* fuse together and disappear.

*Conjuration* is the ideal word to describe the dual problem I am raising in this chapter, namely, the relationship between mysticism and conspiracy theory that we find with the arrival of Minitel and internet culture and in contemporary narratives about this moment. A final example I'll mention, Antoine Bello's trilogy of global intrigue and fake news (*Les Falsificateurs*, *Les Éclaireurs*, *Les Producteurs*), revolves around a problem: how to convince the public to believe what is not true. As we saw in Vasset's novel, the solution was to begin with scientifically verifiable facts and then to embellish them, potentially transforming them into a metaphysical system with the potential to attract a body of believers. Scientificity was the key. In Bello's trilogy, however, the trick is exhaustiveness and multiplicity. The three novels recount the rise of the CFR (Consortium de falsification du réel), which spreads apocryphal stories but without a clear ultimate objective for doing so. Their method is to craft a superabundance of evidence of different kinds and of varying levels of legitimacy, which all work in unison to deceive. The artisans of this false information are divided into two groups: the *scénaristes*, responsible for crafting an overarching story that makes the pieces fit together, and the *falsificateurs*, whose primary responsibility is to generate fake documents. Their methods of distraction and of dissemination and credibilization of falsehoods include altering translations without touching the original; manipulating the press into spreading their falsehoods; disseminating rumors; stocking archives with fake documents, such as doctoral theses, obituaries, and reports written by experts; and spreading multiple stories that resemble one another but that are not identical. If the stories align too neatly, they begin to seem false. As the narrator explains, "When several versions of the same story are circulating, the observers struggle so much to sort out the circumstances of the event that they forget to ask themselves if this event actually took place."[100] The best dossiers are those that gain a life of their own and that *s'auto-entretiennent*,[101] or maintain themselves. A special genre of CFR dossiers is the saga, an epic lie whose originator may revisit and embellish from time to time. Sometimes the work of the CFR agents takes on a predictive function; they intend simply to "anticipate [*dévancer*] reality" (40). During rigorous training sessions, the agents study the art of deception and of the manipulation "of the collective unconscious" (296–97). Believable stories, they discover, rely on the authority of the person telling the story and whether it confirms what one already believes (164). The group's scale is global and their epistemological operations—messing with people's heads—involve every possible kind of information one can know, from scientific facts to court testimonies, historical chronicles, and newspaper articles. In short, they tamper with truth.

As I've shown, the act of storytelling as a process of reality construction is central to the novels of interest in this chapter, and Bello's trilogy is no exception. Again, a theory of literature is embedded in these novels about the artisans of fake news, a theory whose force involves what we might call laminations of reality and fiction, the layered and alternating superposition of these epistemological categories. We discover in the final section of the last novel that the entire trilogy was a fiction written by one of the characters—an old trick—who'd "used her novelistic work to test *in vitro* her ideas"[102] on the world of NGOs and nonprofits for which she works, but she eventually loses the need for the "crutch of fiction" (571). The trilogy ends with the sentence: "Nothing resists literature" (572). In the acknowledgments at the end of *Les Éclaireurs* (2009), Bello writes, "A big thanks to the thousands of anonymous contributors of Wikipedia, these triumphant conspirators of the human spirit."[103] Wikipedia is a valuable resource for any contemporary writer, but Bello's whole trilogy goes further than simply using the service to conduct research; the entire underground operation he describes is a network uncannily similar to Wikipedia in spirit and function. The CFR involves the collaborative drafting of dossiers—comparable to a Wikipedia article on a given event, such as Columbus's discovery of America or the Baader-Meinhof affair in Germany in the late 1970s—which are subsequently cited as truth by those who refer to these dossiers. The disputed nature of so many Wikipedia entries and the status of the site as a place where partisan interests clash through litigations of what is and isn't true make it the ideal arena for a cage match between reality and fiction.

The trilogy's first novel, *Les Falsificateurs* (2007), offers reflections on virality, even before the internet, as well as on the formation of *théories du complot*, or conspiracy theories. The protagonist/narrator Sliv Dartunghuver gets credit from the consortium of which he is a top agent for his suggestion that the organization should abandon physical falsification, that is, the falsification of paper documents or other tangible materials. With new technologies like DNA analysis and powerful microscopes and other precise instruments of artifice detection, the CFR was running greater and greater risks of being caught in its trickery. Instead, Sliv suggests the group should perfect the art of digital falsification, thus anticipating the era of internet-disseminated conspiracies and fake news. The three novels trace this arc as the CFR moves from specializing in the analog to the digital. The arrival of the internet offers new possibilities to the agents: "The falsifiers had perhaps even more to gain: the starting of rumors, the creation of reference sources, the corruption of data bases was becoming child's play for whoever mastered the mysteries of the networks [*les arcanes des réseaux*] and knew how to cover his tracks."[104] The novels offer example after example in which the bait is taken and the public absorbs the CFR's fake news and apocryphal stories and willingly disseminates them as truth.

In the final novel of the trilogy, *Les Producteurs* (2015), the protagonist notes the benefits and the drawbacks of their enterprise, now reoriented mostly toward digital falsification. With hackers lurking everywhere, they spend more and more of their financial capital on security. In contrast to rumors spread by word of mouth, rumors circulate on the internet at an uncontrollably fast pace. After giving a few examples of the kinds of conspiracy theories circulating online—like the idea that the FBI carried out 9/11 or that the American government helped spread the AIDS virus in black communities—the protagonist-narrator Sliv expresses his reservations about the internet as it relates to his agency, the CFR:

This twaddle was nothing new but the Internet had both accelerated its propagation and supported its legitimacy. The concept of truth had never seemed so relative. The Web provided arguments to the champions of every cause. . . . Everything was true and thus nothing was true; everything was false and thus nothing was false. For the CFR, whose stock in trade relied on this fundamental distinction, the rise of the Internet represented a catastrophe.[105]

What had seemed a godsend for the group becomes instead a devilsend, for them and for everyone else. The novelists I've discussed in this chapter channel a deep anxiety about this relatively new technology, whose manageability has already proven onerous. What is to be done when it is no longer a question whether this or that story can be verified but whether the difference between reality and fiction has any meaning whatsoever?

In his essay "Beyond the Cave: Demystifying the Ideology of Modernism," Fredric Jameson wrote, "Objective reality—or the various possible objective realities—are . . . the function of genuine group existence or collective vitality; and when the dominant group disintegrates, so also does the certainty of some common truth or being." It is clear that the twentieth century represented a slow disintegration of collective vitality and, along with it, common truth. But when he published that essay in 1975, the internet and the Minitel did not yet exist. The following declaration from Jameson's piece made sense before the arrival of these two networks, but their arrival has somewhat reversed his claim: "Capitalism destroys genuine human relationships, but also for the first time liberates humankind from village idiocy and the tyranny and intolerance of tribal life."[106] As we have confirmed—terrifyingly—in recent years, an occupying army of village idiots—of the most tyrannical, intolerant, and tribal sort—has invaded the internet with a vengeance. In this chapter, I've tried to illustrate the relationship between reality's degeneration and the rise of new forms of mystification made possible by networks like the Minitel and the internet. Our authors in this chapter are conscious of their role as fiction makers who tell us stories about other fiction makers who've fueled conspiracy theories, cults, fake news, and new forms of mystical engagement. If the best novelists are experts at building believable worlds, their task is not so dissimilar from that of the cult leader, the guru-like tech executive, the head ogre at the troll farm, or the conspiracy theorist. Our authors seek to remind us of these kinships.

The mutual permeability of fact and fiction, one of the internet's key features, seems to be facilitated in part by the public's demand for factual information packaged in forms developed by fiction writers from the epic to the nineteenth-century realist novel. In the next chapter, I turn toward American New Journalism and the New Social Novel, whose techniques have been borrowed by contemporary French realist novelists, to show some of the mechanisms at work in the mutual penetration of the novel and journalistic writing. In the final chapter, I will show how the polemical *pamphlet* has enjoyed a renaissance in France—at least on a formal level—and how, through its embeddedness in contemporary novels, its controversial claims are softened and its author relieved of much responsibility . . . since it is, after all, just fiction.

---

## Chapter Three

# REAL-TIME REALISM, PART 1

## Journalistic Immediacy

In journalism whatever is probable is true.

—HONORÉ DE BALZAC, *LOST ILLUSIONS*

The internet has blurred or erased the generic markers that once separated various forms of information and has recanalized the existing channels through which such information was historically legitimized and circulated. Nowhere is this upheaval more evident than in the categories of news and opinion, which now often flow freely between one another. It is increasingly difficult to tell where one ends and the other begins, to determine whether the bearer of this information has any authority on the matter at hand. In his book *Premediation: Affect and Mediality After 9/11*, Richard Grusin writes, "The real is no longer that which is free from mediation, but that which is thoroughly enmeshed with networks of social, technical, aesthetic, political, cultural, and economic mediation. The real is defined not in terms of representational accuracy, but in terms of liquidity and mobility."[1] The speed and dynamism of these flows have increased, carving out new information ducts capable of reaching publics that were inaccessible before. The internet has proven to be a democratizing force in the circulation of news, opinion, and other information formats, but the drawbacks are all too evident. In the previous chapter, the Minitel and the internet were presented as hyperconduits of (mis- and dis-)information. These networks are sites where multiple, contradictory accounts of what happened flourish and where opinions—anonymized and amplified—compete for validation. This chapter and the next focus on two genres that have been reinvigorated and complicated by the internet's arrival: journalistic writing and the *pamphlet*. Indeed, it is difficult to move from a chapter on the Minitel and internet to distinct chapters on journalism and the *pamphlet*, as though these phenomena have not become mutually imbricated. However, I want to argue that whether the journalist's or *pamphleteer's* spirit takes shape as a newspaper article or political tract, a blog or online op-ed, or as a journalistic or *pamphlet*-like excursus within a novel, social urgency and a desire to register the contemporary are still its core features. I claim that the temporal urgency of both journalistic writing and the *pamphlet* is subsumed into the degenerative realist novel, which tries to cope as quickly as possible with what its author depicts as impending doom. The breakdown of the real is tracked in real time in its pages as well. For this reason, these two chapters will highlight the relationship between time and the degenerative realist novel.

So far, I have shown the various resources used by the degenerative realist novel—such as the social sciences, particularly demography, or Wikipedia, for example—to do its work. In this chapter and the next, I will add two more, namely, journalistic writing and the polemical *pamphlet*. It is not coincidence that Frédéric Beigbeder opens his novel *Windows on the World* with an epigraph from Tom Wolfe, the most forceful advocate for New Journalism and the New Social Novel: "A novelist who does not write realistic novels understands nothing of the world in which we live."[2] Journalism and the *pamphlet* have a twin interest in the contemporary, in registering and even bending its arc. But, as the lines between fact, fiction, and opinion have become increasingly indistinct, a generic uncertainty has touched these various forms.[3] If the novel, journalistic writing, and the *pamphlet* seem to borrow from one another more and more readily, one wonders if this muddied transdisciplinarity will result in a kind of uniformization, with all fields abandoning their specificity and becoming mashups indistinguishable from one another.

I begin with a case study: Jean Raspail's *The Camp of the Saints* (1973), a precursor to the other novels of focus in this chapter. Journalistic media and the *pamphlet* are essential components of this demographic dystopia, whose central claims revolve, consciously or not, around the problem of the representation of what is real. Raspail uses journalism in several ways. First, he uses real-life headlines—on refugees, immigration, demographic change, and the projects of charitable organizations—as fodder for his novel's thesis: that Western civilization will collapse under the weight of throngs of refugees who abuse Europe's hospitality. Second, to produce a sense of urgency, Raspail stages various scenes in which mediatic velocity—specifically the rush to publicly advocate compassion toward waves of arriving refugees and to condemn all dissenters as racists—is paradoxically responsible for the slowing down of *action* on the part of the government and the people to obviate the impending demographic apocalypse. In Raspail's depiction, the media is the key accelerator and facilitator of Europe's death drive, and it uses its various modes of communication to accelerate the end of Western civilization. To assure that this message is not lost in the book's endless proliferation of grotesque carnage, Raspail inserts miniature *pamphlets* into the mouths of his characters throughout the narrative. *The Camp of the Saints* is a *roman à thèse* whose message is abundantly clear. Like the other authors I discuss here, Raspail uses the immediacy afforded by journalism and pamphleteering to lend urgency to his thesis. The novel, like others analyzed in this chapter, creates what I'll call an immediacy effect (*effet d'immédiat*), modifying Roland Barthes's famed *effet de réel*, through several writerly techniques.

The next section of this chapter will highlight the journalistic elements of some contemporary French degenerative realist novels, which, I argue, emphasize the decisive role of journalistic media in determining what the public considers to be real. Responding to new mediatic velocities, one of the most significant conceptual problems in French literary realism since the 2000s has been the creation of the immediacy effect. This effect is achieved through what we might name "real-time realism," which has devised its own temporality to match the new pace of fast journalism, social media, and rapid-fire opinion-giving in the form of comments and tweets. It seems that novels and television have been tempted to live on Twitter time and embed themselves in daily civilian life as deeply as the journalists who report from the world's hubs of conflict. The authors analyzed in this chapter remind us implicitly of the sometimes forgotten connection between the words "novel," "*nouveau*," and "news," what is new or just breaking. For the practitioner of degenerative realism, current events have currency. A pattern emerges in the documentation of the present: Our authors move away from the smallness and localness of the *fait divers* that inspired many nineteenth and twentieth-century novelists and toward the grand and global events that promise to change the face of France forever. Using the work of several contemporary French novelists, I will show how they accelerate time to such a degree that real-life events that hadn't happened yet when the book was written seem to have been anticipated by the text, creating an effect of prophecy. I will then analyze the relationship between *reportage* and the novel and will show how the event has become a primary conceptual tool for the writers in our corpus, using the works of journalist-novelists like Jean Rolin (*Les Événements*, 2015) and Philippe Vasset (*Un Livre blanc*, 2007; *La Conjuration*, 2013) as examples. I will show how the novels not only borrow various stylistic techniques from journalism but also thematize media and mediatization, focusing less on the events and more on how the media documents and fashions them. In this chapter, I will show which techniques the journalist-novelists of real-time realism have borrowed from their counterparts from earlier centuries—for example, Zola, Jules Vallès, Barbey d'Aurevilly, Léon Bloy, Octave Mirabeau, Gustave Geffroy, or François Mauriac—and how they have adapted them to the new mediatic conditions of the age.

## JEAN RASPAIL'S *THE CAMP OF THE SAINTS* (1973): A PRECURSOR

Thanks to the freedom of the press, you can print any trash you want, and poison the heads of a million damn fools.

—JEAN RASPAIL, *THE CAMP OF THE SAINTS*

Already mentioned as a predecessor of contemporary demographic dystopian fictions, Jean Raspail's *The Camp of the Saints* (1973) is also a forerunner of the degenerative realist novels I discuss in this book in both its treatment of the media and its insertion of miniature *pamphlets* in the speech and thoughts of character after character. Incidentally, it was published the same year as Konrad Lorenz's famed *Civilized Man's Eight Deadly Sins* (*Die acht Todsünden der zivilisierten Menschheit*), which argues that civilization will crumble in part from overpopulation and what he calls "genetic decay" (*Genetischer Verfall*). Given its fevered racism and sexism, its brutality toward the French Left, its sustained critique of the media, and its general gruesomeness, Raspail's novel provoked a scandal shortly after its publication on both sides of the Atlantic and gained new relevance during the 2015 refugee crisis in Europe when far-right groups held the novel up as prophecy.[4] In that year, a post about *The Camp of the Saints* appeared on the blog *Radix*, run by the white nationalists Richard Spencer and Andrew Joyce, arguing that Raspail's "narrative, howsoever exaggerated for effect, was a distillation and condensation of observable reality."[5] The book's childish caricatures—including May '68 hippies, "Latin Quarter kids,"[6] race traitors and race baiters, victimized *Français de souche*, women as mere sexual vessels, conspiring intellectuals and media kingpins, and diseased, orgy-prone, writhing masses on the invading "fleet from the Ganges" (96)—would be laughable were they not shared by a vast number of paranoid individuals bearing an inordinate amount of political power in our own time. As Andreu Domingo has argued, Raspail's novel "is a compendium of modern racism, its insurrectional thesis absorbed by neo-Nazi movements in Europe and the United States."[7] Like Houellebecq's *Submission* (2015), *The Camp of the Saints* suggests that the timorous West is to blame for its own demise, that the loss of tradition, religion, and old familial and social structures has produced a demographic crisis as well as an existential one. The language of decadence and decay abound in the novel. The Enlightenment led us here, Raspail argues. As he sees it, the genealogy that connects the *Lumières*, the rabble-rousers of the Revolution, the custodians of liberalism, the instigators and beneficiaries of May '68, and the global capitalists constitutes a decaying family tree. With its string of Christological associations running through the novel[8] along with references to the invasion as "the Crusades in reverse" (27), the Apocalypse is the obvious structural model of Raspail's narrative. Indeed, the title *The Camp of the Saints* comes from the Book of Revelation in the New Testament.[9] Raspail has refracted demographic change through a biblical prism.

The plot of the novel goes like this: At some unspecified date, probably in the late twentieth century, the narrator tells of the events leading to the fall of the West. He spins his dark tale from the temporary safety of Switzerland, which had, up to the point of the telling of the story, survived the onslaught of foreigners. This demise takes shape as an invasion by hordes of people from India—whom he depicts as shit-eating humanoids[10]—who spontaneously board ships to invade Europe, with other "Third World" nations quickly following suit and inundating wealthier nations across the globe. The narrator describes his tale as an "anti-epic" and an "epic in reverse, or upside down, or loser-take-all" (203). With his constant refrain of "That could be one explanation," the narrator tries to account for why and how the West's charity—in its Christian iteration or its hippie globalist variant—and its loss of traditional values created the conditions of its own annihilation. Scapegoat after scapegoat is paraded before the reader in livestock-show fashion in between grisly scenes of rape, murder, suicide, and graphic descriptions of rotting corpses, gang bangs, the deformed bodies of Indian children, and white men being butchered, turned into "pâté," and canned by African workers in a French pork-packing plant. The novel seems to be a manifestation of the author's own psychosexual complexes—particularly regarding homosexuality and the "stealing" of white women by black and brown men—and the description of the "Third World" intruders as various animals, insects, diseases, bacteria, and invasive growths[11] borrows from the tired playbook of National Socialism. Centering on the complicity of the press in promoting the Left's antiracist agenda, nearly every chapter of *The Camp of the Saints* alludes to the media and its supposed calculated construction of an illusory "reality." While critiques of the novel have focused primarily on its racist and misogynistic elements, I would like to draw attention to the novel's sustained diatribe against the media and its implications for subsequent degenerative realist fictions. Much of Raspail's energies are invested in vilifying what the narrator names "that whore called Mass Media" (59). As I will show, contemporary degenerative realist fictions tend to focus not only on the cataclysmic events that will end France but how they are represented through—and sometimes caused by—the media. The problem of journalistic representation is a central preoccupation of these novels. I will analyze this strange *mise-en-abîme* of journalistic representations within the "realist" representation—the novel— that presents itself as prophetic truth.

*The Camp of the Saints* attacks the media on a number of fronts. (It is a bit ironic, then, that the English edition contains page after page of praise from various media outlets that reviewed Raspail's book, suggesting the media has value on the condition that it endorse his dark vision.) First and foremost, the media is responsible for pulling the heartstrings of the public and depicting the approaching fleet as primarily a humanitarian crisis solvable through kindness, empathy, and charity.[12] Magazines and newspapers avoid publishing images that might horrify the public and instead opt to disseminate humanizing photographs of women, children, and the elderly suffering. This asymmetrical representational economy, in which the facts of the situation do not match their depictions, means that consumers of media have lost touch with reality and will receive a rude awakening when the ships reach Europe's shores. These representations have become cinematic, a form of entertainment that allows for passive absorption into the phantasmagoria with no call to action. Who creates this phantasmagoria? Of course he names the bleeding-heart liberals who run media organizations—and who profit from the spectacles they peddle—but Raspail also calls out a more specific group. Leaning on an anti-Semitic trope, the narrator describes Israelis as "entertainers of the Western World" (60), distracting and deceiving the unwitting Gentiles. The leftists and the Jews will bring about the downfall of Europe, in his portrayal. In a particularly colorful scene, the narrator describes what will happen on the day the fleet arrives, when the televised illusion will be destroyed and the French public will be under assault by what they thought were just actors in a troubling but distant human drama:

But now let's imagine a rude awakening, a plunge into reality, with everyone caught in the soup, like nothing since World War II. The serial suddenly breaks through the screen, smashing it to pieces into the steak and fries. And all at once the hordes of characters stream into the living room, looking the way they did in the fishbowl, doing their tricks a few moments before, only now they're not acting, and the glass wall is shattered, and they're armed with their woes, their wounds, their groans, their grievance, their hate. Their machine guns too. Now they rip through the apartment, jar it out of its orderly calm, stun the families caught short in mid-digestion, spread through the town, the country, the world, pictures come to life, living, breathing problems on the march, newsfilm actors turning on their director in unbridled frenzy, and suddenly telling him "shit!" to his face. (60)

The dull-brained French, dining slack-jawed on *steak frites* in front of the TV, have become hypnotized by the manipulative spectacles broadcast before them. The passage suggests that the remoteness of the tragedy is an elaborate illusion created and sustained by the media, which benefits from the public's passive consumption of the spectacle. Epistemologically, Raspail's novel structures itself as a wake-up call or reality check, whose features include the revelation of an unknown, hidden reality, instructions for awaking from one's blindness to it, and an enumeration of the consequences should the reader remain asleep, with sleep standing in as a figure for ignorance and inaction.

Raspail's novel can be seen as a kind of "J'accuse!" targeting all of the mediatic co-creators of the misrepresentation of the real and mobilizing all of the same discourses of reality, truth, fiction, verisimilitude, deception, and lie we've seen again and again throughout this study.[13] The narrator and various characters in the book critique the overrepresentation of leftist thought on television, radio, and in print media, claiming that right-wing media has become all but nonexistent. The few dissenting voices that express centrist or conservative perspectives are censored or shamed into silence. To strengthen his case, Raspail attacks the media genre by genre: from radio with its "free, objective thinkers" (80) and all-doubting skeptics as hosts to colluding advertisers and editorialists, from "glossy, full-color spreads" (80) in leftist weeklies to satirical newspapers, from televised news to low-print-run independent newspapers. The journalist who receives the most brutal—and racist[14]—treatment in the narrative is "Ben Suad, alias Clément Dio" (68), a leftist reformer and public figure. He is depicted as a sower of discord and an antiracist instigator whose mediatic interventions never fail to move popular opinion. Calling him an "anti-Joan of Arc" (69), the narrator writes of Dio, "The journalist's pen gave him many a size and shape, but one thing never changed: his contempt for tradition, his scorn for Western man per se, and above all the patriotic Frenchman" (69). True to Raspail's maximalist style and his tendency toward enumeration, he proceeds to spin out a whole list—too long and disgusting to repeat here—of the various aggrieved victims Dio embodies in his journalistic writings, such as "an Arab workman, snubbed and insulted," "a student terrorist," "a schoolgirl on the pill," "a protester crapping on the Unknown Soldier," "a Vietnam deserter," "a faggot with a medical excuse," and "an Indian dying from a tourist's measles" (69). The narrative ultimately punishes Dio for his transgressions, first by having his wife raped and murdered by a gang composed of those he'd defended in his writings and then by having him strangled and trampled by the Indian mob that has just come ashore. The novel sets up its straw man and summarily burns him.

In contrast, another journalist, the tell-it-like-it-is Machefer, is celebrated for his independence of spirit and his willingness to go against the grain by telling the blunt truth to the public. As is customary in right-wing narratives of victimization and grievance, Machefer is depicted as a courageous but scorned individual martyred for defending his minority ideals. His small-scale paper *La Pensée Nationale* struggles to compete with more mainstream papers: "A poor, eight-page daily, with no pictures, practically no ads, badly printed, and more badly sold, it owed its survival to the combined efforts of a few anonymous benefactors" (74). The novel constantly references an underground community of like-minded patriots, shamed into hiding but finding ways to subvert the dominant leftist ideology secretly. The narrator goes on to explain, "Machefer's paper was neither right nor left, nor even lukewarm middle of the road. It would lash out, often where least expected, tilting at the windmills of hackneyed opinion, rather dogmatically sometimes, to be sure, though Machefer's followers always felt that he hit the mark" (75). Given Machefer's blunt truth-telling crusade and his distaste for otherness, I cannot help but see a parallel between this character and the French politician Pierre Poujade, who founded a short-lived anti-intellectual, antitax, pro–small business movement in the 1950s and helped launch the political career of Jean-Marie Le Pen.[15] Machefer's anti-ideological disposition is celebrated throughout the narrative. In an argument with an editor of *La Grenouille*, "a satirical weekly of the altruistic Left" (90), perhaps a softer version of *Charlie Hebdo* or *Le Canard Enchaîné*, Machefer accuses him of "sapping the strength of the nation, quietly tearing it down brick by brick, behind [his] convenient satirical mask" (91). He claims that any supposed public confrontation of ideas is a sham: "To get [the people] to swallow what you feed them, you need something vaguely resembling an opposition" (91). He recognizes himself in this role. This is why he is allowed to enter Left-dominated debates: to create the illusion of authentic intellectual exchange. Throughout the narrative, various scandalous incidents occur, which the media refuses to report accurately.[16] One in particular stirs Machefer to report the testimony of an eyewitness that directly contradicts reporting from all other news outlets. The backlash is swift, with accusations of racism and white supremacy being hurled back in the direction of Machefer and the witness. He ultimately dies in a bomb attack alongside the other heroic *résistants* who did their best to fight the Indian hordes, the antiracist social justice warriors, the "Third World" workers in France, and the spineless church, media, and government.

One of the morals of the story is provided by a character named Perret, the undersecretary of state, who is also killed in the attack: "Let's just talk about the media, so called, and the shameless way certain people, under the guise of freedom, took a tool meant for mass communication, twisted and warped it, and used it to bully the minds of the public. The few clear thinkers left tried to warn us. But we wouldn't listen" (190). Raspail, of course, classifies himself as one such "clear thinker." He is trying to warn his readers with this dystopian fiction that the media is engaged in a permanent gaslighting campaign against the public, but no one will listen, he claims. His account is so focused on the journalistic media because it is one of the primary mechanisms through which reality is constructed. Our world picture is largely formed not from things we have experienced ourselves but from images and texts generated by journalists who try to offer an all-encompassing picture of the state of current global affairs. The only way we can access these places and events is through their mediation. Raspail tries to counter what he sees as mediatic misrepresentations and replace them with "reality," told paradoxically through fiction. This is always the work of the dystopian novel: it is both prophecy and reality check, a call to action and a corrective to indifference or to more optimistic assessments of the world's future trajectory.

In addition to the media focus of *The Camp of the Saints*, the novel can also be described as a *roman pamphlétaire*, in that it includes within it miniature *pamphlets* on various topics, from immigration policy to gender, from race relations to the reprehensibility of the Left. Most often, these opinions are expressed through direct dialogue between characters or in the narrator's direct disclosures to the reader. *The Camp of the Saints* is a *roman à thèse*, much in the same vein as books like Maurice Barrès's *Les Déracinés* (1897). In the next chapter, I will explore the *pamphlet* and its novelized versions in detail and show the extent to which the degenerative realist novel has turned again and again to specific formal strategies of the *roman à thèse*, but here I'd like to give some concrete examples in order to highlight Raspail's unremitting insistence on his novel's thesis. One could not imagine a more closed-ended book. He constructs the narrative in such a way that the reader has zero interpretive freedom.

In a short note before the opening of the book, Raspail writes: "I should at least point out, though, that many of the texts I have put into my characters' mouths or pens—editorials, speeches, pastoral letters, laws, news stories, statements of every description—are, in fact, authentic. Perhaps the reader will spot them as they go by. In terms of the fictional situation I have presented, they become all the more revealing" (xviii). This maneuver allows Raspail to frame his novel as a container of truth. By strategically borrowing from public debates of the time, he is able selectively to feature the grounded, common-sense "truth" of one side and simultaneously to lampoon and misrepresent the other. This introduction suggests the novel possesses a certain documentary value, that it is a small-scale archive of the sociopolitical commentary of the period. The book can only shock its audience if it maintains a consistent level of "truthiness," and this is one strategy to achieve this.

Pascal Bruckner's *Sanglot de l'homme blanc: Tiers-Monde, culpabilité, haine de soi* (1983) is more or less the *pamphlet* version of Jean Raspail's *The Camp of the Saints* published ten years earlier. William R. Beer's description of Bruckner's book could be applied word for word to Raspail's as well:[17]

*The Tears of the White Man* [*Le Sanglot de l'homme blanc*] is a critique of "Third-Worldism," a set of attitudes toward underdeveloped countries and the West that has flourished, mainly among left-wing intellectuals and journalists, over the last twenty years. It is based on a conviction that the countries of the Third World . . . have long been victims of the West. They have had their resources stolen by imperialist colonialists or multinational corporations, their cultures destroyed by commercialism and exploitation, their pastoral sensitivity toward nature corrupted by industry and pollution. But Bruckner's thesis is that it is the passionate Third-Worldist who is most often exploiting the poor nations. Starving people are carefully chosen or ignored, depending on whether they can be portrayed to suit specific political programs.[17]

Several of Raspail's characters voice opinions identical to those Bruckner presents in his controversial book. For example, the consul at the Belgian consulate in Calcutta shouts at the bleeding-heart liberals who stand before him: "Your damned, obnoxious, detestable pity! Call it what you please: world brotherhood, charity, conscience . . . I take one look at you, each and every one of you, and all I see is contempt for yourselves and all you stand for."[18] In a ministerial meeting, the French undersecretary says of the refugees:

The richer we are, the more jealous they'll be, and the more we'll be billed. But so what? We're used to all that. Don't we do the same thing now when the Third World kicks up and we want to make peace? We pay. We bitch a little, but we pay. And we get our peace for a couple of food packages from UN Relief and some aspirin from World Health. Cheap enough, don't you think?

(63)

The narrator makes clear from the beginning that he sides with these cynical opinions. The asymmetry and acedia into which the West has fallen have led to an uncomfortable equilibrium: The West must purchase its peace from a parasitic "Third World" whose self-renewing tribulations will never be resolved. Instead of systemic change, the West is happy to make this costly investment to maintain its status as world power. The undersecretary continues, lamenting the flipping of values that he has witnessed in his lifetime:

Day by day, month by month, doubt by doubt, law and order became fascism; education, constraint; work, alienation; revolution, mere sport; leisure, a privilege of class; marijuana, a harmless weed; family, a stifling hothouse; affluence, oppression; success, a social disease; sex, an innocent pastime; youth, a permanent tribunal; maturity, the new senility; discipline, an attack on personality; Christianity . . . and the West . . . and white skin.

(92–93)

Implicitly, this excerpt is about a loss of touch with reality as institutions and beliefs that had held solidly for centuries if not millennia have suddenly come undone. The conservative message of the excerpt is all too obvious, with its preference for tradition and the stewardship of family, the police and military, religion, and other hierarchical institutions. The passage is a direct repudiation of May '68 values. All of the older guiding principles have become damaged goods in the new progressive era. It is under these conditions of cultural confusion that the wretched of the earth are able to plan their invasion. Another character says that the influx of unarmed refugees constitutes a new form of warfare: "This might well be some new, sophisticated form of warfare: a pathetic enemy, who attacks without firing a shot, and who counts on our pity to protect him" (157). The president of the republic, reticent to voice his true views on the crisis, eventually makes a demographically inflected argument:

Five hours from now, a million refugees will peacefully begin to set foot on our soil. Refugees whose race, religion, language, and culture are different from our own. For the most part they will be women and children, jobless and needy peasants, all fleeing from famine, and misery, and despair. Dramatic examples of that ever-growing store of surplus humanity, victims of the soaring birthrate that has long been the curse of our century's waning years. (210)

On the other side, Raspail presents the opinions of the Left as hyperbolically and reductively as possible. An atheist philosopher named Ballan shouts, "Passports, countries, religions, ideals, races, borders, oceans . . . What bloody rubbish!" (28). As France's government leaders debate what to do about the incoming flood of refugees, the left-wing minister Jean Orelle argues that "France owes it to herself to respond in a clear, compassionate voice, and to plan a heartfelt welcome, here and now, in keeping with both our material wealth and our moral resources" (65), and other leftists argue that the fleet's mission is "to cleanse and redeem the capitalist West" (83). These opinions are, in the mind of the narrator and other right-wing characters, caused by Enlightenment and "the noxious gases of modern thought" (216).

If there were any doubts that Raspail's novel is a *roman à thèse*, these are dispelled by the book's paratextual elements, such as the brief introductory note that appears in the original, the added introduction to the 1985 French edition, the afterword added ten years after the original publication, and the June 2004 essay "Fatherland Betrayed by the Republic" ("La Patrie trahie par la République") written by Jean Raspail for *Le Figaro* and included in the 2018 Social Contract Press edition of the book. These present Raspail's thesis in no uncertain terms. This prefatory statement appears in the novel's first edition:

I had wanted to write a lengthy preface to explain my position and show that this is no wild-eyed dream; that even if the specific action, symbolic as it is, may seem farfetched, the fact remains that we are inevitably heading for something of the sort. We need only glance at the awesome population figures predicted for the year 2000, i.e., twenty-eight years from now: seven billion people, only nine hundred million of whom will be white. (XVIII)

In his preface to the 1985 edition, he enumerates the central themes of *The Camp of the Saints* ("boat people, the radicalization of the North African community and of other foreign groups in France, the strong psychological impact of human rights organizations, the inflamed evangelism of the religious leadership, a hypocritical purity of consciences, refusal to look truth in the face, etc." [xiv]) and describes his novel as a "parable" (xv) whose purpose is to wake up lethargic France from its naïveté. His conviction that "the fate of France is sealed" (315) is widely shared today and informs the shifts of discourse regarding what is real and how mediatic representation fails to portray accurately the degenerating state of things. Using a compensatory logic, Raspail sees his book as the counterbalance to the misrepresentations he detects in journalistic reporting and commentary from public intellectuals, suggesting that his narrative must be so bluntly and brutally real, exceeding the category of the believable, that it forces the reader to acknowledge the dire reality of the circumstances. In its customary sense, the label "realist novel" would never be applied to a book like Raspail's; it is too over the top, too reliant on caricature and hyperbole, too stylistically ridiculous. But it is realist in the sense that it attempts to jolt the reader into a forced recognition of what the author sees as all-too-evident reality, veiled by mediatic lies. Paradoxically, often the most outlandish novels are the most insistent in their calls for awareness of a sobering reality. Yes, the novel could simply be called a demographic dystopia, verging on sci-fi in its fantastical vision, but Raspail's emphasis throughout the book on the politics of representation and the real positions the book as a precursor to the more contemporary novels of focus in this study. Whereas the project of nineteenth-century French realists and naturalists sought, in part, to represent the heretofore gritty unrepresented, they did not call into question reality itself. The real was taken as a given, as an inflexible backdrop before which a wide variety of plotlines could unfold; it was simply a question of expanding what the novel as a representational tool could depict among existing realities. These novelists' social and aesthetic aims had little to do with questioning what is real. Raspail does not use his novel to garner sympathy for the refugees through a depiction of their painful reality; instead, he uses his pages to suggest that the reality sold to the French public by the media and other purveyors of misrepresentation is a corrupted one. The ability to distinguish between reality and fiction has been destroyed, and Western civilization will be the main casualty of this reality rot.

I strategically chose this epigraph for the section on *The Camp of the Saints*: "Thanks to the freedom of the press, you can print any trash you want, and poison the heads of a million damn fools" (91). The irony is that while it endlessly critiques the media's abuse of press freedom, Raspail's trash-novel—itself a product of freedom of expression—is racist propaganda meant to "poison the heads of a million damn fools," which it has done quite effectively. Raspail frames his novel as a container of the truths that the media is unwilling to reveal, making its case through miniature *pamphlets* couched in worst-case-scenario fiction. Despite its crude hyperbole and frequent departures from anything we might recognize in the actual world, *The Camp of the Saints* markets itself as a reality check. Like most dystopian fiction, it aims to stir the reader from his or her apathy or ignorance and to prompt, in the best case, some kind of action to stave off looming ruin. The novels I will explore in the next sections share some of these features, at least on a formal level. However, their authors seem to have given up hope that preventive measures can change anything. While the media plays a conspicuous role in their plots and is critiqued implicitly and explicitly throughout the narrative, the will to resolve the problem is lacking, as though the novelists are merely recording the death of their civilization with full attention rather than engaging in fruitless efforts to impede this death. The redemptive potential of these fictions is lost.

## JOURNALISM AND THE NEW SOCIAL NOVEL

Nous avons tout parfaitement fact-checké.

—FRÉDÉRIC LORDON, "POLITIQUE POST-VÉRITÉ OU JOURNALISME
POST-POLITIQUE?"

In *Imagined Communities* (1983), Benedict Anderson argued that the novel and the newspaper "provided the technical means for 're-presenting' the *kind* of imagined community that is the nation."[19] Typically, they accomplish this "re-presenting" of the nation at different paces. While the newspaper delivers detailed accounts of specific, actual events unfolding on the local, national, and international levels as they happen, the realist novel averages these events and composts them slowly into an imaginary world. Throughout most of its history, the novel has moved in a slower, literary time that has little to do with the high velocity of print periodicals and much less with the acceleration brought about by online journalism, social media, or blogging. Even in the nineteenth century, when print journalism quickened the pace and immediacy of the novel's events, decreasing the temporal interval between real-world events and their novelistic representation, that acceleration is no match for contemporary journalism's speed. Televised series, too, had until recently lagged slightly in their response to current events, but a new responsiveness to the demands of an update-hungry body of culture consumers is the signature of television and literature of this last decade. For contemporary engineers of realism, the central challenge is to create immediacy, which combines both time and directness of experience, conveying the nearness of the most pressing issues of global consequence. The power of this kind of fiction resides in its manipulative appropriation of *actualité*, or current events, made possible only through the development of social media and the new exigencies of online journalism. These developments have permanently altered our understanding of the relationship between time and representation, and this change is reflected in the tendency of literature, television, and other forms of art and media toward real-time realism.

Until the internet's arrival, the *jour*, or day, was the primary unit of time by which *jour*nalism functioned. The minute, or better, the second, is the new unit of preference, inviting us to identify and analyze the features of this new minutalism or secondalism. In its online iteration, journalism has become increasingly cybernetic in that it constantly receives and adjusts itself according to feedback, with a single article being edited throughout the day and moved perpetually around the website based on the number of views it has received, how many times it has been forwarded, and how many comments it has elicited. I have argued elsewhere that an uptick in speculative journalism, which involves "reporters and editors making guesses at what might happen rather than reporting what did happen,"[20] is a signature of American journalism in this millennium so far, although this tendency is by no means limited to journalism in the

United States. Some French real-time realists—and I am thinking here specifically of Beigbeder, Moix, Vasset, Rolin, and Houellebecq—have imported some of this spirit into literature, writing novels that are so contemporary, they feel nearly like *romans d'anticipation*—not following the usual definition of the term, which refers to anticipatory sci-fi, but being contemporary to the point of successfully simulating a correct prediction of major world events. Peter Brooks has noted that "Balzac could be said to create the novel of modern society by decreasing the gap between the moment of writing (and reading) and the moment represented, making the historical gap a matter of a decade rather than some centuries,"[21] and the time between the event and the reading of its representation has continued to shorten. Tom Wolfe praised himself for having produced "prophetic fictions" merely by paying close attention to the world around him and writing in advance about the historical vector that was obvious to him from these civilizational studies. Among contemporary French examples, Yannick Haenel's *Les Renards pâles* (2013), about an uprising among refugees and *sans-papiers* in France, was prescient in its anticipation of the 2015 refugee crisis in Europe. In the case of Houellebecq, whom Adam Gopnik has called "a wannabe Nostradamus,"[22] what gives his fictions a prophetic character is the timing of their publication. *Platform*, in which the protagonist's lover is murdered by Islamist extremists, was published a few weeks before 9/11; *Submission*, which tells of the Islamization of the French state, came out the very day of the Charlie Hebdo attacks in Paris; and *Serotonin*, which describes France's pauperization, appeared just as the yellow-vest protests were exploding. Are these fictions prophetic or merely attentive to inevitabilities?[23] Of these predictions, Houellebecq stated, "Je ne suis pas un prophète, je ne l'ai jamais été, mais j'ai gardé de ma longue fréquentation de la science-fiction le goût de lancer des hypothèses."[24] In the case of Houellebecq's *Submission*, Claude Pérez has argued that the "future of *Submission* is entirely *nominal*. The temporal site of the story is not tomorrow; it is now. It's 2015 renamed 2022; a today upon which a sign with *tomorrow* written on it hangs. . . . *Submission* is not a predictive novel; it's a novel on current events. The year 2022 is a way of talking about 2017, as the upcoming election rumors begin to swell."[25] This technique—of putting the label "tomorrow" on the events of today—produces an immediacy effect, making the future feel hauntingly familiar only because it is the now in disguise. Adam Gopnik frames Houellebecq's enlistment of the future in slightly different terms: "[Houellebecq] likes to take what's happening now and imagine what would happen if it kept on happening. That's what satirists do."[26] This is true, but more is at stake in the narratives I'll present in this chapter, in which time is manipulated in order to produce anxieties about the various degenerative forces putting the nation's health at risk, in the view of some.

The ability to create an illusion of hypercontemporaneity is what aligns these texts with both New Journalism and the New Social Novel, called for in the famous manifesto published by Wolfe in 1989. Lamenting the state of the novel in late-1980s America, Wolfe issued a challenge to writers of his generation: "At this weak, pale, tabescent moment in the history of American literature, we need a battalion, a brigade, of Zolas to head out into this wild, bizarre, unpredictable, Hog-stomping Baroque country of ours and reclaim it as literary property."[27] In his call for the New Social Novel, he argued, "The imagination of the novelist is powerless before what he knows he's going to read in tomorrow morning's newspaper" (55), and it is clear that the French real-time realists have heeded his call. Notice Wolfe's emphasis on what is to come, not on what is. The novelist does not compete with today's news but with tomorrow's. For a novelist to write journalistically, he or she must write about the now as it happens or even in anticipation of what is to come, highlighting the names and events characteristic of the moment. This journalistic consciousness manifests itself not only in the pace of narration and the global consciousness of the events—they think globally even when speaking locally—but in the seemingly unavoidable inclusion of journalistic media in the narratives themselves. Without fail, these books include media representation within their own representation, a mimetic *mise-en-abîme*.

Among the most famous American practitioners of New Journalism, which thrived in the 1960s and 1970s, were Truman Capote, Norman Mailer, Joan Didion, and a host of others. Crediting one of them, the Pulitzer-winning American journalist Jimmy Breslin, with the importation of novelistic techniques into long-form journalism, Wolfe described his approach: "Breslin made it a practice to arrive on the scene long before the main event in order to gather the off-camera material, the by-play in the make-up room, that would enable him to create character. It was part of his *modus operandi* to gather 'novelistic' details, the rings, the perspiration, the jabs on the shoulder, and he did it more skillfully than most novelists."[28]

This, Wolfe argues, helped American journalists who'd just discovered "the joys of detailed realism and its strange powers" (28) to realize that "it was possible to write accurate non-fiction with techniques usually associated with novels and short stories" (15). Claude Grimal has described New Journalism as a hybrid genre, "un mélange difficilement définissable d'éthnographie, de sociologie ou de reportage d'investigation et de fiction."[29] Wolfe writes that what attracted these New Journalists to literary realism was its "'immediacy,' its 'concrete reality,' its 'emotional involvement,' its 'gripping' or 'absorbing' quality."[30] He describes four specific devices the New Journalists borrowed from realist novelists: "scene-by-scene construction"; the recording of "dialogue in full" (31); "third-person point of view" (32); and finally: "the recording of everyday gestures, habits, manners, customs, styles of furniture, clothing, decoration, styles of traveling, eating, keeping house, modes of behaving toward children, servants, superiors, inferiors, peers, plus the various looks, glances, poses, styles of walking and other symbolic details that might exist within a scene. Symbolic of what? Symbolic, generally, of people's *status life*" (32).

For its detractors, New Journalism was a bastard genre, dismissed as "parajournalism" (24) whose ornamentation was not to be taken seriously. This kind of "novelization" of real life has brought with it certain slippages and projections, blurring the boundaries between fact and fiction. As Dwight Macdonald argued in his review of Wolfe's book *The Kandy-Kolored Tangerine-Flake Streamline Baby* (1965): "Parajournalism seems to be journalism—'the collection and dissemination of current news'—but the appearance is deceptive. It is a bastard form, having it both ways, exploiting the factual authority of journalism and the atmospheric license of fiction. Entertainment rather than information is the aim of its producers, and the hope of its consumers."[31] The two-way borrowing—the novel borrowing from journalism and journalism borrowing from the novel—was destined to produce new epistemological confusions about what constitutes truth. Wolfe made a fascinating prediction about how the novel, too, would be infiltrated by journalism:

I think there is a tremendous future for a sort of novel that will be called the journalistic novel or perhaps documentary novel, novels of intense social realism based upon the same painstaking reporting that goes into the New Journalism. . . . There are certain areas of life that journalism still cannot move into easily, particularly for reasons of privacy, and it is in this margin that the novel will be able to grow in the future.[32]

In the United States, there is some dispute about whether Wolfe's prophecy has borne out,[33] but in France, many contemporary novelists have helped fulfill it. I do not claim that there is a direct genealogy between these novelists and Wolfe or other American New Social Novelists or that they were even aware of this innovation in American literature and journalism, even if, as Isabelle Meuret has argued, many contemporary French novelists "share the same preoccupations as their American colleagues, these famed new New Journalists."[34] As Wolfe said regarding these sudden developments in the United States, it was as though a strange collective intuition had set in, leading writers all to the same conclusion: that journalism and the novel should couple. Perhaps the same could be said of the French novelists, who responded to something in the air, calling to them all at once. In his *Windows on the World* (2003), which belongs to the coalescing genre of the 9/11 novel,[35] Frédéric Beigbeder does, however, explicitly announce his predilection for the techniques of New Journalism and the New Social Novel, quoting Wolfe: "A novelist who does not write realistic novels understands nothing of the world in which we live."[36] One could say that Beigbeder's novel, which unfolds minute by minute on the morning of 9/11, borrows in literary form the effects of what Guido Isekenmeier has called in his essay "Visual Event Realism" a "realism of commotion," characterized by a "handycam aesthetic of blurred and grainy pictures."[37] In alternating chapters, the book fills with smoke, noise, and chaos as the collapse approaches. The real-time realists need not embed themselves like reporters in some far-off warscape. The remote world comes to them through screens. Even better, since war has come to the West, the journalist-novelist need only sit at his desk and type as the room vibrates from a nearby explosion, the walls pockmarked with shrapnel.

If the real-time realists have heeded Wolfe's call for the New Social Novel, they've also been attentive to his appeal for a New Journalism.[38] Philippe Vilain has noted the tendency in twenty-first-century postrealist French fiction toward "le journalisme littéraire qui, par le docufiction, réactualise les formes de la littérature populaire, comme le roman-feuilleton, le roman du faits divers, le roman-reportage, la *nonfiction* version Tom Wolfe et le gonzon-journalisme [*sic*]."[39] In 2003, Bernard-Henri Lévy gave

the label *romanquête*, a portmanteau combining novel (*roman*) and investigation (*enquête*), to his *Who Killed Daniel Pearl?* [40] A more recent example is *Journal intime d'un marchand de canons* (2009), written by the journalist and novelist Philippe Vasset and described this way on its back cover:
"A cannon dealer, he is the fictional hero of real adventures. The transactions
described, the weapons sold, the names of the manufacturers and buyers,
the details of the contracts: Everything is true. With his journalistic expertise, Philippe Vasset reveals a hidden side of the globalized economy." [41]

Other examples include Frédéric Beigbeder's autofiction *Un roman
français* (2009), described in the book's third chapter as "un reportage sur
la banalité française," [42] and his *Une vie sans fin* (2018), which is identified
as a novel on its cover page but which the author describes in the preface as
an "enquête sur l'immortalité de l'homme" and "un ouvrage de 'science
non-fiction.'" [43] Beigbeder's book begins with a quote and a question: "'La
différence entre la fiction et la réalité, c'est que la fiction doit être crédible,'
dit Mark Twain. Mais que faire quand la réalité ne l'est plus?" (11). The label
*romanquête* hints at a parentage between it and the nonfiction-novel genre
that Truman Capote claims to have invented, a close cousin to Wolfe's
New Journalism, but in book form. Capote was certainly not the first to
theorize the nonfiction novel; Stendhal begged clemency for his famed
novelist-as-bearer-of-mirror from his 1830 *Le Rouge et le noir*, who merely
depicts society's vices as they are; [44] already in the 1832 preface to *Indiana*,
Georges Sand names the novel "a very simple story in which the writer has
invented almost nothing"; [45] and in their 1864 preface to *Germinie Lacerteux*, the Goncourt brothers wrote that the typical reader "likes false novels;
this novel is a true one." [46] Capote believed that journalism and *reportage*
"could be forced to yield a serious new art form" that "employed all the techniques of fictional art" but would be "nevertheless immaculately factual." [47]
He sought to undo the belief that "journalism is only literary photography,
and unbecoming to the serious writer's artistic dignity" (48). But skeptics
have challenged such blending of fiction and fact. For example, critics of
Lévy's *romanquête* argued that it was simply lazy journalism hiding
behind the novel to avoid being held accountable for its investigative defi-
ciencies and contradiction of the facts. [48] Such murk is to be expected when
fact and fiction fraternize.

These more recent negotiations between journalism and realist fiction
are not the first instance in French literary circles of a deliberate blurring

of the line separating fact and fiction. Ever since Serge Doubrovsky coined the term "autofiction" in 1977, which he defined as "fiction d'événements et de faits strictement réels" and likened to a kind of literary masturbation,[49] writers and scholars have not ceased disputing the meaning of the term, whether it constitutes its own genre, and what the ethical and epistemological implications of true fiction might be.[50] In describing the features of one of his novels, the writer and journalist Jean Rolin explains: "Dans le cas du *Ravissement de Britney Spears*, ce qui me permet de dire que c'est un roman, c'est le caractère fictif du narrateur. En revanche, à peu près tout ce que je décris dans ce livre s'est réellement produit."[51] The narratorial framing allows Rolin to call the book a novel, despite its heavy reliance on *reportage*. In a review, Isabelle Rüf writes that in Rolin's novel, "la fiction et le reportage s'y mêlent" and argues that "Ce roman est aussi un superbe reportage sur un Los Angeles inconnu, ses parkings, ses jardins secrets, ses lignes de bus."[52] One puts down this fiction having acquired the same sort of knowledge one could obtain from a purely journalistic account of the concrete realities of contemporary Los Angeles. This coupling of journalism and the novel has bidirectional benefits, as articulated by Claude Grimal:

He allows journalism to abandon stereotypical writing habits and, by encouraging it to use novelistic techniques, to reach a fictional dimension; he brings back the novel, lost in vain formalisms and idle subjects, toward methods and preoccupations he'd forgotten, namely realism and current events.[53]

Among current trends in the contemporary French novel, Antoine Jurga has noted an upsurge in "romans vrais," or true novels, observing a "tendance récente d'invention de romans qui refusent en partie les artifices du récit classique pour se tourner vers la narration gagée sur des faits ou événements liés à l'expérience personnelle ou collective. Romans qui, avant tout, visent le vrai et l'authenticité."[54] As I've noted, the novels of focus here rely not only on the real—*les choses vues et vécues*—but on a more specific sub-branch of the real: the *actuel*. This fixation on *actualité*—a word that implies not just the sum total of contemporary events that will eventually become History with the passage of time but that suggests a certain political urgency and mediatic relevance—is perhaps the most essential component necessary in creating an immediacy effect. To render something immediate is to remove any separating interval of time or space, to depose what might insinuate itself between us and event.

It is perhaps for this reason that journalists, those perennial purveyors of *actualité*, make such conspicuous appearances in degenerative realist fiction.[55] News and novel—etymologically bound by novelty—share an encounter not just in the plethora of "romans de reporter" identified by Myriam Boucharenc, in which reporters feature as protagonists or narrators,[56] but in a general emphasis on the omnipresence of journalistic media in the everyday lives of characters, shaping their sense of reality. The protagonist Charles Avril of Alexis Jenni's *Nuit de Walenhammes* (2015) is a freelance journalist whose search for a story takes him to a dying industrial city in the country's north, a site emblematic of France's decline. Grégoire Leménager has described the novel as "un étrange polar philosophique sur les ravages du libéralisme,"[57] and Nicolas Léger classifies it as a "novel of inequality," describing it thus:

An account of the dereliction and cynicism that ravage deindustrialized zones, the novel plunges a precariously employed journalist, a fragile observer, into a fictional town in northern France. Discoveries, encounters, the intertwining of political rhetoric, slogans, the words of residents, globalization's losers or winners—all these are attempts to hold within the dense structure of the novel a phenomenon that forever spills out of its grasp. Burning swimming pools and murders add a cruel, carnivalesque dimension to the chaos and despair assured to those whose dignity is stripped away by economic globalization.[58]

Yannick Haenel's *Les Renards pâles* (2013) makes similar critiques of an economic system that generates more than profit for the already wealthy; it generates "les sans-abri, les sans-emploi, les sans-papiers."[59] The homeless, jobless narrator Jean Deichel, who features in several of Haenel's novels, lives in his car and gets France's bad news through the radio. "J'ai entendu à la radio qu'en France, le taux de suicide ne cesse de progresser" (33), he hears. Not realizing it was the day of the presidential election, he unexpectedly hears the winner give his acceptance speech through the same radio. Having not voted, Deichel explains his political indifference: "Bien sûr, je n'étais pas allé voter—mais ce n'était pas un oubli: j'avais choisi de *ne pas voter*. Cette décision, elle remontait à plusieurs années déjà, à une époque où ce qu'on nomme la 'politique' en France avait commencé à se décomposer" (19). As he listens to the newly elected president spew the same platitudes over the radio, Deichel imagines a breakdown of the system that has pushed him to its margins: "Et si chacun parvenait à en finir avec sa propre docilité—à briser dans sa vie la sale habitude d'obéir? Une grève générale éclaterait enfin, qui plongerait le pays dans le tumulte. Avec un plaisir ambigu, j'imaginais la France étouffée dans son chaos" (21). An uncanny mysticism creeps into the novel, leading the narrator on a strange path: chance puts Marx's *La Guerre civile en France* in his hands, leads him to reflections on France's revolutionary past, and folds him into a group of *sans-papiers* who revolt against their irregular status by urging people to wear masks and abandon their identities, what journalists begin to call "l'insurrection des masques" (170). A commentary on police brutality, discrimination, surveillance, unbridled capitalism, and media deceit is embedded in Haenel's novel:

And it is indeed about war: a civil war that divides France, like all countries that suspend certain individuals' rights by criminalizing their mere existence. It sets in opposition the "undesirable" foreigners . . . and the police. Most often, civil war is concealed for political reasons; thus it remains partly secret. But it does happen that for the same reasons, we show it: it degenerates into spectacle, and the media, by presenting the undocumented as delinquents who break the law, paints this war as a fight for security.[60]

(146)

The media aids and abets the political and economic oppressors, facilitating their exploitative practices. Michel Houellebecq's oeuvre, fixated as well on the deleterious effects of globalization, is consistent in its emphasis on the mediatization of decline. As Claude Pérez has argued compellingly, Houellebecq's *Submission* is a "mediatic novel" in which the act of turning on the television or other media devices amounts to a voluntary surrender to an alternate reality.[61] Pérez goes on to argue that the novel speaks the language of media so fluently because it *is* the eight o'clock news, only reformatted as a novel.[62] He writes, "What *Submission* borrows from the media is not just its subject matter but its language. The novel's language is prescribed by the newspapers."[63] Thematically, the media plays a prominent role in Houellebecq's *Submission*, as key shifts in the narrative involve mediatic representation, and famous French journalists make cameo appearances or are mentioned throughout the novel, including David Pujadas, Michèle Cotta, Jean-Pierre Elkabbach, Christophe Barbier, Renaud Dély, Yves Thréard, and Alain Duhamel. The derisiveness with which he treats the media, particularly the left-leaning media, is not far removed from that of Raspail. The narrator displays particular ire against "the *soixante-huitards*, those progressive mummified corpses—extinct in the wider world—who managed to hang on in the citadels of the media."[64] Echoing the Machefer character in Raspail's *Camp of the Saints*, Houellebecq's protagonist argues that "the existence of political debate, however factitious, is necessary to the smooth functioning of the media—and, perhaps also, to keep people feeling that they live, at least technically, in a democracy" (164). His characters and narrator allude to various print, digital, and radio outlets, including *Figaro*, *Le Monde*, *Libération*, CNN, YouTube, RuTube, *Observateur*, iTélé, BFM, LCI, France Info, Europe 1, Radio Monte-Carlo, and RTL, and the news reaches them through a variety of channels: car radio, transistor radio, tablets, smartphones, TV news, newspapers. One cannot really flee the mediatic universe. Politics is pure spectacle in the world Houellebecq creates. His narrator declares:

I've always loved election night. I'd go so far as to say it's my favorite TV show, after the World Cup finals. Obviously there was less suspense in elections, since, according to their peculiar narrative structure, you knew from the first minutes how they would end, but the wide range of actors (the political scientists, the pundits, the crowds of supporters cheering or in tears at the party headquarters . . . and the politicians, in the heat of the moment, with their thoughtful or passionate declarations) and the general excitement of the participants really gave you the feeling, so rare, so precious, so telegenic, that history was coming to you live. (58)

It is worth noting the circularity of Houellebecq's own relation to the media, in that he is a constant maker of news—his various controversies earning incalculable revenue for media outlets in France and across the globe—and all the while relying on the media as "content creators" for his own novels. In many of the novels already analyzed throughout this book, the media returns again and again as a degenerative force, manipulating reality for profit. In some cases, specific outlets are named—CNN is a favorite, the sine qua non of global news providers within the framework of contemporary French fiction[65]—and in others, vague mediatic forces misrepresent the world and take advantage of the public's willingness to accept what they say as truth. I contend that so much energy in these novels is invested in depicting journalistic media's transgressions because these media outlets provide the only access possible to *actualité* beyond our own lived experience. If we are to gain an understanding of the realities of the world beyond our own turf, journalists are among the few who can provide it. When what they offer is tainted, then our reality is also tainted.

Let us return to Tom Wolfe's prediction in 1973 that "the future of the fictional novel would be in a highly detailed realism based on reporting, a realism more thorough than any currently being attempted, a realism that would portray the individual in intimate and inextricable relation to the society around him."[66] A strong example can be found in the work of Philippe Vasset, a journalist and novelist who has used several projects to test the boundaries between the two genres in which he writes most freely. I mentioned his novel *Journal intime d'un marchand de canons*, in which "everything is real."[67] Another example, *Un Livre blanc* (2007), originates in Vasset's personal fascination with the blank spaces on maps of Paris. He gave himself a challenge: For one year, he would explore those empty spaces, visiting a new one each week. The excursions were recorded in *Un Livre blanc*, which can be described as a *reportage*—although Vasset resists this label—and a research document whose material later would be given a fictional frame in his novel *La Conjuration* (2013), described in chapter 2. Jean-François Duclos notes that the book was "conçu puis réalisé à la manière d'une enquête,"[68] though the genre of *Un Livre blanc* is difficult to name. The book's subtitle calls it a *récit avec cartes*, and the book does indeed include map details every few pages that show areas Vasset explored during his expeditions to the ostensibly empty spaces of Paris. Regarding the *récit* element of the book, Vasset details his methods and preparations for his ambiguous project, whose aims are never clearly defined. He proceeds in tentacular fashion, assaying various approaches to the problem of what to do with the observations and experiences he's collected in the unrepresented spaces in Paris. What thesis could he argue through his findings? Should he make a guide book? Should he lead group expeditions to these places? Should he incorporate the material into a novel? Into an art project? In the end, *Un Livre blanc* turns out to be a book about representation and unrepresentability, about margins and the marginalized, and about what constitutes reality. Even while protesting the label of *reportage*, this *récit* is more or less a narration of just that: the methods and experiences of a reporter looking for a story. The second half of the project involves transferring the content of this *récit* into the aforementioned novel *La Conjuration*.

Similar to Zola's project and that of the social and socialist realists, Vasset attempts to democratize representation. Those who haunt the blank spaces on Parisian maps—immigrants, prostitutes, drug addicts, Roma and other migrants and transients, the homeless, graffiti artists, members of alternative religions, the poor—deserve representation, he argues. As Églantine Colon has argued, Vasset's narrative deploys a "poetics of precarity,"[69] highlighting the most vulnerable individuals in French society, those who live on the margins of it. As his project neared completion, Vasset experienced a strange sensation while watching a CNN report on the *banlieue*: "It seemed that the film of my twelve months of expeditions was passing before me in accelerated fashion."[70] He notes the way the CNN presenters talk about the *banlieues* as a uniform phenomenon, not drawing distinctions between various suburbs at the edge of Paris. This glossing over of difference is for Vasset a key feature of marginalization in all its forms. What exists in the *banlieue* is bad, uniformly bad, and uniformly unworthy of representation. Visiting Washington, DC, he noticed a peculiar absence on maps of the city: "The black and poor zones were simply not represented" (130). He argues that the terra incognitæ of the world are no longer the jungles, deserts, and mountains in faraway places but rather the cities' in-between places that have remained unmapped for questionable reasons. In his recuperative project, which he calls a form of *documentaire engagé* (27), Vasset seeks to represent the heretofore unrepresented. Once he realized that the unrepresented spaces contained within them the "shameful, the unacceptable, the barely believable," he decided to write "a kind of documentary, a text that would say: 'Look, here's how people live in your city, and you, you see nothing; even worse, you structure it to hide them'" (23).[71] He describes his project as one focused on observation, one that seeks "not to do reportage" (104) but to imitate the skateboarder who, in his wild jumps down stairs, on ramps, and across low walls, struggles all the while to keep his balance. Vasset clearly recognizes that the average reader will take his text for pure *reportage*, but he doesn't want it to be *just* that. Fiction tempts him at several moments, particularly when he looks at the blank spots on Google Earth and the satellite maps on the website of the Institut géographique national and is enticed to fictionalize their content. He explains: "The temptation to invent what I didn't manage to identify was considerable, but yielding to that temptation would have led me to write a novel and I wanted something else: a brittle reality riddled with holes and infinitely more mysterious than any made-up story" (102). Of course, Vasset eventually did write a novel using the same material, but he circumscribed a discrete space for it, separated by several years from the original project. After finishing *Un Livre blanc*, Vasset also launched an experimental working group whose objective was, in part, to see whether the world as represented through technologies like Google Earth corresponds to the actual world. He and his team tried to compare reality to the blocky satellite images, what he describes as "irréelles démarcations géométriques," visiting their real-life locations "pour voir si elles correspondaient à des véritables frontières et pouvaient révéler une réalité invisible à l'œil nu."[72] The tension between the real and the represented is clearly a central preoccupation of Vasset's in his various endeavors.

Vasset borrowed several *reportage* methods in compiling the materials for *Un Livre blanc*. He studied a wide variety of maps in print and digital form from different eras and produced by different institutions. Trespassing on private property in order to discover what was hidden there, he took countless photographs and made audio recordings of the sounds of the netherplaces he was exploring. He conducted interviews with people he happened to meet there. He filled notebooks with extremely detailed observations jotted down on site and, after the fact, analyses and thoughts about what he'd seen. In the notebooks, he also sketched what he saw before him. He reached out to professional and amateur geographers, including those who manage the Atelier de géographie parallèle and its website unsiteblanc.com. He read theories of space and place (Marc Augé, Gilles Deleuze, Félix Guattari, Mike Davis [*City of Quartz: Excavating the Future of Los Angeles*, 1990], Alain Corbin, Pierre Sansot) and novels that focus on these questions. He brought along a GPS tracker to help him locate his destinations more efficiently. He consulted reports written by specialists. He avoided studying the history of these sites, to keep himself from reducing the places to mere dates and anecdotes. In the fashion of the nineteenth-century French realists and the New Journalism feature writers, he accumulated objects and piled them up in his text: porno magazines, bullet casings, old refrigerators, burnt-out cars, skittish animals, hovels, graffitied walls, piles of garbage, scrap metal, broken bottles, light bulbs, empty packages, wires, stained carpets, and rusty pipes. We have moved outside of the bourgeois interior into the street, the home of the homeless. This "excès de réel" (50) began to produce what he calls the *fantastique urbain* in a city periphery overcome with incongruous objects and people. If the descriptive *élan* we find in Balzac, Zola, or Flaubert is impoverished in Vasset's text, which tends toward the blunt and the concrete (in all of its meanings) and away from the superfluities and baubles that adjectives sometimes bring, it is because what he describes is not ornament but detritus.[73] There is far more junk in the text than there are people. How would historical detractors of realism's scandalous ugliness have responded to this new representational low?

Degenerative realism possesses the journalist's acuity in its registering of the contemporary world, particularly its most troubling and intractable aspects. The techniques of the New Social Novelists and New Journalists have proven useful to practitioners of degenerative realism, who track social decay in real time by amassing the minutiae of everyday life that convey this rot. The result is an atmospherics of dread and a helpless urgency to attend to unsolvable problems, to study them intently yet listlessly. Far more interested in the losers of French society than in its winners, the social consciousness of degenerative realism is not redemptive, making no attempts to save these losers, only to chronicle their plight. These journalist-novelists are bearers of bad news.

## THE GLOBAL EVENT: BEYOND THE *FAIT DIVERS*

With its long-winded stamina and descriptive fervor, the kind of *reportage* favored by the New Journalists and New Social Novelists is excellent at producing atmosphere and fleshing out "characters," but how do journalists deal with singular events, and what can novelists learn from them? The place where the event receives its most pithy treatment—often with powerful effect—is that journalistic microgenre known as the *fait divers*. Dominique Kalifa describes *faits divers* as "a multitude of lifeless occurrences: brawls or altercations, pickpocketing or fraud, minuscule and often ordinary conflicts" and "assaults, burglaries, and family dramas."[74]

Their power, he argues, resides in part in their accumulation and repetition (1348), which reveals essential behavioral patterns of the human. Most operate in the factual register, although some occupy a space "between fiction and information" (1349). Typically, these local stories do not reach far beyond their site of occurrence. They have no global impact and involve mainly the individual perpetrators and victims, who function as characters in these narratives. Jean Touzot created a laundry list of the various *faits divers* out of which François Mauriac constructed his novels, the tragedies somehow made small in the pages of the daily paper: "Many cases of suicide by hanging, drowning, jumping out of windows, using barbiturates or, more often, by gunshot; we occasionally encounter murderous villains, a sexual crime perpetrated against a teenager, road accidents, in short everything that belongs, by metonymy of the species for the genre, to the rubric of crushed dogs [a French term for small town news]."[75]

Kalifa has further noted that in late-nineteenth-century France, the *faits divers* and the *roman criminel*[76] "signaled the country's progressive entry into the mediatic regime."[77] In other words, journalistic media and the novel began to recognize the permeability of the membrane between life and literature and to readily exploit it. In these two forms, fictionality and facticity were easily and often blended together. What complicated the *faits divers* further was the demand on the part of the publishers to have their writers not only entertain readers by injecting "literarity" into the descriptions of the events but *anticipate* the events to come, in order to outflank the competition.[78] The master of *faits divers* in France was Félix Fénéon (1861–1944), who elevated this small journalistic form to the status of literature. The collection of his writings called *Nouvelles en trois lignes*, rendered in English by Luc Sante as *Novels in Three Lines*, illustrates the compressed beauty of the human drama in all its police blotter perfection. Here is an example of his talent: "Pauline Rivera, 20, repeatedly stabbed, with a hatpin, the face of the inconstant Luthier, a dishwasher of Chatou, who had underestimated her."[79] And another: "Atop the station in Enghien a painter was electrocuted. His jaws could be heard clacking, then he fell on the glass roof" (56). While we've seen examples in which the material of the *fait divers* can be useful for practitioners of degenerative realism,[80] the proportions of the *fait divers* are far too small to accommodate the expansive, global-scale worlds they create. Because their shared theme is civilizational decline, a single case of domestic abuse, theft, or murder is too small to drive these narratives, even if such cases do tend to accumulate within them. We might think, for example, of the proliferation of suicides in Houellebecq's oeuvre, recognizing that not one of them is enough to sustain the novel in its entirety.

The *fait divers* attends to little events; the front page, to big ones. Degenerative realism is all about the front page, *la une*, as it is known in French. In degenerative realism, civilizational decline occurs as both slow-moving incremental change and as sudden convulsion, encapsulated in *the big event*. That event might be a terror attack, an election, a *manifestation agricole* gone awry, or, in the case of Jean Rolin's *Les Événements* (2015), published the year of the refugee crisis in Europe, an undisclosed set of events that triggers a civil war in France and something resembling World War III for the rest of the globe. Whereas in Annie Ernaux's *L'Événement* (2000) the reader can easily recognize that the event in question is the protagonist's (and author's) illegal abortion, in Rolin's novel, the events that plunged France into a global war are never disclosed. The book withholds the typical details that news reports offer us—the who, what, when, where, how, and why. All is lost in the fog of war. That France has transformed into a warscape is signaled from the first sentence of the novel, with the narrator stating that one of the small pleasures of wartime is to speed the wrong way down the boulevard de Sébastopol in Paris at full velocity. Much like Houellebecq's *Submission*, this cryptic book tries to describe France in the second decade of the twenty-first century, when the fallout from today's political choices has settled.

As the narrator crosses the French countryside, he encounters French refugees, militias of the Far Right and Far Left, a Christian militia of the Lebanese Forces, jihadists, locals—he mentions, for example, the "population clermontoise"[81]—journalists, humanitarian groups, regular armies, and all manner of dissidents and deserters. The cast of characters is remarkably international, with factions issuing from Ghana, Finland, Chechnya, the Netherlands, Venezuela, Chile, and a host of other nations roaming across the war-torn French countryside. Various organizations, each with its own agenda, clash with one another, including the FINUF (la Force d'interposition des Nations unies en France), the AQBRI (Al Qaïda dans les Bouches-du-Rhône islamiques), or the UNHCR (Haut Commissariat des Nations unies pour les réfugiés). As in other novels I've described here, journalists traverse the landscape—CNN, BBC, and the *New York*

*Times* are mentioned explicitly—trying to understand what is happening as it happens in circumstances marked by rumor, confusion, dissimulation, false flags, war-crime secrecy, propaganda, and unreliable witnesses. As an intervening narrator explains early in the novel:

In times of war, and even in the context of a full curfew—but who really knows how much it's obeyed and whether it applies everywhere—most of the information collected remotely on the particular situation of a given route or a certain spot ends up being inaccurate, either because it was communicated to you casually, or in bad faith, or because the situation has changed in one way or the other between the moment these pieces of information were collected and the moment they reach you.[82]

(28)

This kind of blur characterizes the entire narrative. We know very little about the protagonist, and even as we track his movements, it is clear that the barely sketched plotline attached to him is not the central focus of the story. It is a mere vehicle for the thought experiment that asks us to imagine a new civil war in France, one whose features resemble those of other intranational conflicts like the Reformation (wars instigated by religious difference) or the French Revolution (a class-based struggle) and more recent European hostilities like the Yugoslav wars. The story includes a mention in passing of a failed attempt by an Algerian Islamist militant to attack the Eiffel Tower, a gesture toward the Franco-Algerian War, whose scars are still unhealed, and scenes of battle and torture linger throughout the narrative. The various ways in which humans divide themselves into quarreling groups—political affiliation, ethnicity, religion, social class—are combined to create a superwar in Rolin's dark universe. One can't help but interpret his inclusion of specifically *French* refugees in his story as an attempt to humanize the influx of refugees to Europe in 2015 from places like Syria, Afghanistan, Iraq, Eritrea, Nigeria, Somalia, and a host of other embattled nations for a French reading public. Unlike Charles Robinson's novel *Fabrication de la guerre civile* (2016), which asks the reader to imagine a French civil war between the gentrifiers and the gentrified of the *banlieue parisienne*, Rolin moves beyond class warfare to describe a total war tearing France asunder from inside and out.

The narration alternates between chapters in which the protagonist tells his own story and chapters in which an unnamed narrator intervenes. This second narrator, a *voix-off* from nowhere who addresses readers directly, draws our attention to the scaffolding of the story and outs the protagonist—whom the second narrator names "the narrator"—as what he is: a character in a book. Here is just one example of this strange narratorial diplomacy: "As for the reason the narrator ends up on Highway 721 when we left him on the edge of Highway 20, it turns out that he exited at the moment when it reaches the Étampes crossing, trusting unreliable information that indicated a resumption of fighting in the capital of Essonne, where the Chalouette and Juine rivers merge" (27–28).[83] We know even less about the second narrator than the first, and Rolin's narratorial ambiguity adds one more level of abstruseness to an already perplexing story. Why this "apparemment" in the second narrator's clarification? What does he know and why? These details are never divulged.

While the story is set in the future—the 2020s to be precise—history plays a fascinating role in Rolin's narrative, with past conflicts haunting almost every page. The novel displays what Sophie Ménard has called a "frénésie patrimoniale et monumentale": as the protagonist moves across the country, he encounters various *lieux de mémoire*, to use Pierre Nora's term, that dot the landscape, most often war memorials dedicated to the dead of countless wars. He finds a monument commemorating the execution of Jean Cordin, a monument dedicated to the communist Ambroise Croizat, a pine tree supposedly planted by Yuri Gagarin, and countless plaques, statues, and other commemorative sites. An implicit commentary in Rolin's novel is that all of this memorialization—the call to remember history in order to keep from repeating it—has not prevented another bloody war from breaking out over and over again. As Ménard writes, "Histoire d'un patrimoine régional: s'il y a du réalisme à l'œuvre chez Rolin, il se terre dans ces zones culturelles et topographiques, qui n'ont rien de terminal," and argues that an "ethnological realism" is what drives the narrative.[84] This realism is produced in part by the endless toponymic references—indeed, the entire novel could be mapped out place by place—and by mentions of more consumerist reference points recognizable to today's readers, like restaurant chains (Buffalo Grill, Léon de Bruxelles, and McDonald's, for example). There is surely a critique of collective memory loss in the face of neoliberal distractions embedded in Rolin's novel, which juxtaposes national monuments to the dead (a metonymy for *la patrie*) with fast-food chains (a metonymy for capitalism).

In a 2012 interview, Rolin described a novel he was trying to write but couldn't:

I wanted to write a novel of a slight anticipatory nature. By this I mean a book whose action and plot would have taken place in France, but in an indeterminate near future. But how can one describe the places exactly the way they will be in a few years? And if I describe the place the way it is now, it is not because the plot is set in an indeterminate future. I was paralyzed by what seemed to be a small obstacle, a sort of molehill, which made me stumble because the exactitude, the rendering of things seen in their exactitude, in their precision, was lacking.[85]

I believe that Rolin finally overcame these obstacles and managed to write this book. *Les Événements* is precisely a "roman de légère anticipation" whose events take place in France, and description of "les lieux"[86] is the novel's nearly obsessive focus. Rolin apparently succeeded in his struggle to create a convincing realism of tomorrow based on observations of today. His novel performs a fascinating maneuver: by taking the France familiar to us now and superimposing atop it the news events from elsewhere— various *coups d'état*, guerilla conflicts, rebel insurgencies, and civil wars that dominate our screens—Rolin has made a composite picture of the contemporary world. He brings the horror home. He has described his process of collecting materials for a novel as dragging a rake across the world,[87] seeking out things from real life that already look and feel like literature and film.[88] This could explain why Rolin's bleak tale feels so familiar. It has assimilated every conflict from the twentieth and twenty-first centuries— gleaned from news reports, documentaries, and fictionalizations of real events into TV dramas or feature-length films—and integrated them into one composite picture. This, perhaps, is what the title *Les Événements* refers to, not just the specific, unknown fictional events that produced the novel's warscape but the earlier real-life geopolitical conflicts that have led to France's current precarity and to a general sense of disquiet in the world. Older conflicts never really ended; they simply spawned new events that still contain within them kernels of the old ones. Ruth Cruickshank has noted that tropes of crisis dominate French fiction at the turn of the

millennium, and this has largely to do with a media landscape that benefits from a constant threat of civilizational annihilation. She writes: "Such
media crises [like May '68] are . . . not 'real' events but discourses structured as 'reality.' As the news media structure reality as crisis, so com-
modified apocalypse becomes part of daily life."[89] Rolin's novel embodies
this spirit and asks his readers to be haunted by it.

As we have seen, the novels discussed in this chapter treat the media
with a general suspicion, mainly because the news shapes the world into a
spectacularized reality often disconnected from the actual world. In short,
it is representation that tries to erase its status as such. The current conditions
under which news is produced and distributed have allowed disingenuous
actors to daze and deceive the public. As Jean Baudrillard wrote regarding
the media's response to 9/11 and other acts of terror, "There is no 'good' use
of the media; the media are part of the event, they are part of the terror,
and they work in both directions."[90] He continues with an example: "Internet terrorism, biological terrorism, the terrorism of anthrax and rumour—
all are ascribed to Bin Laden. . . . It is like an 'automatic writing' of terrorism, constantly refuelled by the involuntary terrorism of news and
information" (33). The "involuntary terrorism of news and information" is
the perfect phrase for describing the current media dynamic in which the
nerves of the public are constantly subject to the irritants of world distress,
often delivered in spectacular format. In his treatise *Les Peurs françaises*
(1993), Alain Duhamel depicted the French people as particularly susceptible to disinformation and mediatic manipulation even before the arrival
of the internet. He wrote:

The fear of information may seem more anecdotal: it is not the case. In the midst
of the depressive period, the temptation of irrationality, subjectivity, approximation or sensationalism wreaks havoc. Television increasingly weighs on the morale
of the French. It has an amplifying effect. The cult of instantaneity, the risk of
superficiality, contribute to shaping an image of society that is literally illegible
and indecipherable.[91]

The increasingly duplicitous mediatic landscape only exacerbates a
problem that was already there, namely, the epistemological stubbornness
of a population that believes what it wants to believe rather than what is
true.[92] There is also the problem of journalistic laziness in the digital age,

which Michel Onfray summed up this way: "En France, les journalistes parlent souvent d'un livre qu'ils n'ont pas lu en glosant sur les textes de confrères qui ont d'abord consulté le Net qui ne vit que de rumeurs."[93] The superabundance of information at our fingertips has decreased the capacity or willingness of some journalists—if this label can still be applied to the type Onfray describes—to read and research carefully and deeply. A chapter on journalism in the degenerative realist age would be incomplete without a short detour into the world of post-truth and alternative facts. Shortly after the election of Donald Trump, Frédéric Lordon—the French economist and *maître à penser* of Nuit debout[94]—wrote an opinion piece titled "Politique post-vérité ou journalisme post-politique?," in which he argues that the sudden appearance of a post-truth vocabulary was only the symptom of a decay that had been underway for a long time. He writes, "Ça fait très longtemps que la décomposition est en marche, mais c'est que nous avons affaire à un genre particulier de système qui ignore ses propres messages d'erreur-système."[95] He then embarks on an extended critique of the French media, which responded to shock moments like Brexit, the American election, and various electoral successes of the Far Right throughout Europe with the creation of fact-checking outlets (he names *Le Monde*'s Décodeurs and *Libération*'s Désintox as examples) and the deployment of fevered "return to reality" discourses. Lordon argues:

The frenzy of fact-checking is itself the late but most representative derivative product of post-political journalism, which has in fact existed for a very long time, and in which there is *nothing* more to discuss, except the factual truths. The spontaneous philosophy of fact-checking is that the world is only a collection of facts and that, not only, like the earth, the facts do not lie, but they exhaust all that there is to say of the world. The problem is that this post-political truth, opposed to post-truth politics, is entirely false. Properly established facts will never be the terminus of politics but barely its beginning, because facts *never said anything of themselves*, nothing! Facts are only established through the work of mediations not proper to them.[96]

Contextless facts do not speak for themselves, and they can be massaged to fit agendas or selectively ordered to create biased stories. In journalistic contexts, facts are always mediated, Lordon stresses. Facts, too, have a curious way of curtailing debate, given that they bring a certain finality and fatality with them: *This is how things are*, facts imply, *untransformable by whatever imaginary*. France's lawmakers have begun efforts to pass laws banning fake news and the spread of false information, particularly during election cycles,[97] but no law can remedy the injuries to the public's permanently damaged sense of reality. Degenerative realism uses fiction to work through the epistemological and ethical dilemmas that arise in a post-truth mediascape.

As I've shown in this chapter, practitioners of degenerative realism turn again and again to the field of journalism, borrowing its techniques and concerns in order to sketch a convincing picture of contemporary life in France. The media make conspicuous appearances in degenerative realist novels, which highlight the representational aspect of mediatic production and suggest a shared vocation between the novel and the news. The news creates meaning and orders the world, tracing constellations from disparate events and extrapolating significance out of these configurations, while the novel assembles material from the actual world to build its representational double within the frame of the book. In recent years, as the credibility of the traditional news media has been called into question and as dubious new outlets have emerged, it is not surprising that certain contemporary novelists have deployed journalistic dilemmas in their own work in order to advance their interrogations on the nature of reality. They wonder: Who has license to tell us what is real? How can media outlets, which belong to corporations with an agenda and profit-driven ambitions, pretend to present a neutral picture of the contemporary world? Are the worlds that novelists build inferior to those of journalists? Or do they deliver more fundamental truths? The double maneuver of taking up institutionalized forms—journalism in this case—only to show their insufficiencies and failures is a primary characteristic of degenerative realism. As I will show in the next chapter, the formal features of the *pamphlet*—the polemical genre par excellence—have been subsumed by the degenerative realist novel, even as the conviction and bravado of the form have been diluted by the uncertainties of the age.

## Chapter Four

# REAL-TIME REALISM, PART 2

## *Le roman post-pamphlétaire*

I spent the weekend writing a racist pamphlet—I had a hard-on all the time I was
writing it.

—MICHEL HOUELLEBECQ, *THE ELEMENTARY PARTICLES*

The *pamphlet* and the *roman pamphlétaire*—sometimes known as the
*roman à thèse* or the *roman idéologique*—share many features, including
their readiness to respond with vehemence to political *actualité*, to take an
unambiguous and polemical position on a chosen topic of contemporary
relevance, and to convince the reader to side with the author using various
rhetorical and stylistic strategies. As Frédéric Saenen wrote of the *pamphlet*, "Son auteur hume l'air du temps, s'enflamme pour une actualité
forcément brûlante."[1] In her influential study *Authoritarian Fictions: The
Ideological Novel as a Literary Genre* (1983), Susan Rubin Suleiman offered
a list of historical conditions under which the *roman à thèse* thrives particularly well. Noting the rise of this subgenre of the realist novel during
and shortly after the Dreyfus affair in France, she explains, "It should not
surprise us if this ideologically polarized period constitutes one of the
'strong' moments of the *roman à thèse* in France. The *roman à thèse* is a
genre that thrives on ideological polarization, which becomes both a fundamental theme and an organizing principle."[2] Michel Hastings, Cédric
Passard, and Juliette Rennes have made a similar claim regarding the
*pamphlet*, arguing that spikes in the publication of *pamphlets* correlate
with "periods of conflict or agitation,"[3] while such writings are less common in relatively calm political circumstances. These declarations prepare
us to *expect* to find *romans à thèse* and *pamphlets* galore in contemporary

France, a period and place marked by the social and political strife out-lined in chapter 1, what Suleiman would certainly identify as a "climate of crisis" (16). Many of the clashes that marked the Dreyfus affair era remain unresolved, and a host of new sites of conflict have joined those of the late nineteenth century. Such ground seems fertile for what we might call an *urgence pamphlétaire* and for a healthy crop of ideological fictions.

The *pamphlet* and the *roman à thèse* are certainly thriving today in France.[4] But what is the relation between these forms and degenerative realism? Given the fixation of all three on what is wrong with contempo-rary society, one might anticipate a confluence, with degenerative realism borrowing from these genres to express its discontent with the current state of things. In reality, what we find is that degenerative realism samples the forceful language and rhetorical strategies of the *pamphlet* and the *roman à thèse* but cannot manage to muster the conviction inherent in these forms. Taking Houellebecq's *Platform* (2001) as an example, some critics have not yet decided whether it should be read as a *roman à thèse* or as a "satirical pastiche of a *roman à thèse*."[5] Agathe Novak-Lechevalier has called *Platform* and the rest of Houellebecq's novels "étranges romans à thèse sans thèse."[6] This undecidability leads us to conclude that these books *cannot* be *romans à thèse*, which, according to Susan Rubin Suleiman's defi-nition, must "formulate, in an insistent, consistent, and unambiguous manner, the thesis (or theses)" that they seek to illustrate.[7] *Platform*'s ambiguous messaging does not allow readers to walk away from it with a clear assessment of its argument, despite the presence in the narrative of several mutually reinforcing theses delivered by various characters.[8] Sev-eral critics have noted Houellebecq's general tendency toward didactic, thesis-centered narratives, but these do not work in the same way as the theses in earlier *romans à thèse* such as Paul Bourget's *L'Étape* or Paul Nizan's *Le Cheval de Troie*. While some characters in Houellebecq's books make clear-eyed pronouncements about why the West is crumbling, these novels lack the certitude of the *roman à thèse* and leave vast space for highly varied readings. These and other degenerative realist fictions are happy to include staunch voices—often reactionary ones—within their narratives, if for no other reason than to show the omnipresence of ideo-logues in the current mediascape. Any honest depiction of the real must feature such obdurate doomsayers, highlighting their role in the creation of an atmospherics of angst. I will argue that degenerative realist novels may be classified as *romans post-pamphlétaires* in that they borrow from and radically subvert the *pamphlet* and its literary relatives like the *roman à thèse*. They have moved past ideology into acedia.

This final chapter will highlight the instances in which the contemporary French novel borrows *formal* conventions from the *roman pamphlétaire*. Although embedded polemical assertions offer the primary architecture of these books, they can no longer be interpreted without ambiguity in the way that, say, Raspail's *The Camp of the Saints* could. Using Susan Suleiman's term, what seem at first to be the new "authoritarian fictions"—I am thinking, for example, of Houellebecq's *Platform* and *Submission*, which contain countless *pamphlet*-like claims and thesis-filled excurses, what Dominique Rabaté has identified as "des sortes de traités pleins d'affirmations et de sentences"[9]—seem to have lost their conviction. Unlike the writers of *romans à thèse* Suleiman studied—including Zola, Nizan, and Sartre on the left side of the political spectrum and Barrès, Bourget, and Drieu La Rochelle on the right—Houellebecq has been read as a satirist, which implies a doubleness of meaning in his work, and the ambiguity inherent in his writing and that of some of his contemporaries does not allow for a closed-ended reading. While it is true that Houellebecq's politics have been labeled as reactionary based on the content of his novels and his controversial statements in interviews, it is actually quite difficult to interpret him with such certainty. Writing of the "persistent political ambivalence of Houellebecq," Gavin Bowd has described the author as one who "observes and comments, rarely without humour, on his own situation: the ungraspable 'totality' of an atomised and enclaved society, marked by a crisis of political representation and stratification by education and income, all soaked in a climate of fear."[10] In contrast to strong proponents of *littérature engagée* such as Sartre, who thrived in "the heroic period of the universal intellectual" (23), Houellebecq limits his engagement to mere observation and commentary without calls for action or the construction of a cohesive political vision. Adam Gopnik has called Houellebecq a Francophobic satirist,[11] and others, such as Karl Ove Knausgaard, Graham Matthews, Guy Berger, and Alex Preston, have recognized satirical elements in his recent books.[12] "La satire houellebecquienne," writes Bruno Viard, "tire son efficacité de son réalisme autant que de son outrance."[13] While *pamphlétaires* certainly avail themselves of satire in their writings, the possibility of multiple readings in Houellebecq's work suggests uncertainty, something prohibited in *littérature pamphlétaire*.

What manifests itself in the novels of interest in this chapter is a polyphonic competition between various theses, rather than a clear-cut single thesis or the setting up of various weaker voices, usually handily destroyed, to counter the main thesis, thus bolstering the novel's argument. Above all, the *roman à thèse* requires certainty and conviction on the part of its author, something altogether lacking in the works analyzed here. These novels offer a kind of reality check, but a reality that is so convoluted and self-contradictory that the realist novel form, historically so intent on creating wholeness and a meaning, breaks down. This is the realism that returns after postmodernism's self-referential, citational experimentations, a realism that acknowledges its own shortcomings even while emptily repeating older formal conventions, themes, and narrative arcs. I begin with a brief exposé on the *pamphlet* and the *roman à thèse* and then move to a specific case study, Michel Houellebecq's *Submission*, whose ambiguities are representative of the general loss of conviction we find in the degenerative realist novel.

## THE FEATURES OF *LITTÉRATURE PAMPHLÉTAIRE*

The *pamphlet*'s pugilistic spirit is evident in its nickname: "la littérature de combat."[14] Its vituperative energy and linguistic violence can be felt on every page of this kind of prose.[15] Yves Avril defines the *pamphlet* as "un écrit de circonstance, attaquant plus ou moins violemment, unilatéralement, un individu ou un groupe d'individus, une idée ou un système idéologique dont l'écrivain révèle, sous la pression d'une vérité urgente et libératrice, l'imposture."[16] The emphasis on *circonstance* makes clear the importance of context for the *pamphlet*, which comments forcefully on the specific circumstances in which it was produced. In this sense, like the journalistic writing surveyed in the last chapter, it is a parasitic literature that feeds off *actualité*. It is quite difficult, in fact, to imagine a *pamphlet* that is not a direct and urgent invective against something happening in real time. As Cédric Passard puts it, "Le caractère convulsif du pamphlet révèle sa sensibilité à l'événement."[17] The event-centered aspect of pamphlet literature is crucial to understanding both its urgency and its transitory nature. In their article on the contemporary *pamphlet*, Michel Hastings, Cédric Passard, and Juliette Rennes argue that the *pamphlet* is essentially an ephemeral literature, fighting against time, which erases it once the circumstances in which it was written have changed.[18] Journalism, as we have seen, also shares this expirational quality. In his seminal study *La Parole pamphlé-taire* (1982), Marc Angenot identifies two other genres—the *polémique* and the satire—as forms contiguous to the *pamphlet*,[19] although the slippage between these three genres makes it difficult to discern where the boundaries of one end and where those of the next begin. Like most genres, the *pamphlet* is not exempt from borrowing freely from its neighbors.[20] *Pamphlétaires* themselves, "situés au carrefour de la littérature, de la presse et de la politique,"[21] wear many hats simultaneously and help themselves to the various discourses at their disposal. On the spectrum of written and oral discourse, this eristic literature, centered on debate or argumentation, hovers somewhere in the middle, with carefully structured logical associations and verbal bombast coupled in one text. France's list of more famed *pamphlétaires* of the late nineteenth and early twentieth centuries includes Henri Rochefort, Jules Vallès, Édouard Drumont, Léon Bloy, Octave Mirabeau, Émile Zola, Charles Péguy, Robert Brasillach, and Louis-Ferdinand Céline, to name just a few. What these kickers of hornets' nests share is a strong conviction in their political principles, be they of a left- or right-leaning disposition, and the eagerness to make their private discontent a public matter. These and other authors published their *pamphlets* in various formats, from short-form tracts to newspaper or *revue* articles to speeches published subsequently in print form. New forms of distribution have accelerated the spread of the *pamphlétaire*'s opinions. In a book on France's neoconservatives, or "les antimodernes," Pascale Tournier notes the new *possibilités pamphlétaires* afforded by digital media, which permits them to express their displeasure "à coups de tweets ou d'articles-fleuves,"[22] often published online, allowing for quick propagation and a stirring up of public sentiment. The *pamphlet* has maintained—and perhaps increased—its status as real-time literature.

Historically, the *pamphlet* was also readily embedded in the novel, accomplished by using characters or narrators as mouthpieces for the author's eristic discourse. The advantage for an author of couching his claims inside a fictional world is that he is able to shape the narrative outcomes to bolster his own assertions, and, should criticisms arise, he could

dodge responsibility, claiming his writing is "just fiction." In the con-
trolled environment of the novel, what Zola has famously called a laboratory, his experiment always returns the results he wishes. In the last chapter, I showed the many strategies used by Jean Raspail in his *Camp of the
Saints* to prove himself right by staging the worst possible fates for the
characters who disregarded his intra- and extradiegetic warnings, which
bear out in the end. This is what happens to people who do not believe me,
the novel implies. Susan Suleiman has defined this kind of novel, the
*roman pamphlétaire*,[23] or its more common name, the *roman à thèse*, as "a
novel written in the realistic mode (that is, based on an aesthetic of verisimilitude and representation), which signals itself to the reader as primarily
didactic in intent, seeking to demonstrate the validity of a political, philosophical, or religious doctrine."[24] In her terms, such novels "formulate, in
an insistent, consistent, and unambiguous manner, the thesis (or theses)
they seek to illustrate" (10). After the publication of Suleiman's *Authoritarian Fictions* (1983), few if any extensive studies of the *roman à thèse* genre
have followed.[25] The date of the book's publication is important. As Suleiman articulates in the introduction, her project pushes against the tendencies in literary criticism of the period, what she calls the "modern 'textual'
revolt," which represented "an attempt to systematically suppress the ref-
erential element in writing, and corollarily to emphasize its self-referential
element. It has been a revolt against (a single) *meaning*."[26] The Jakobsonian
categories of poetic and communicative function helped lead to a situation
in the 1980s in which criticism became "tremendously wary of any literary
work that 'means to say something' (that has a 'message'), and of any critic
or reader who reads literature as an 'attempt to say something'" (18). This
is where the *roman à thèse* complicates matters. Because this subgenre of
the realist novel does indeed attempt to say something and does so insistently and unambiguously, critics with a distaste for didactic literature
would naturally turn their backs on it. Suleiman writes that "it is precisely
because it is founded on that aesthetic [of verisimilar representation]—as
well as on the equally 'outmoded' notion that literature is an act of communication between writer and reader—that the *roman à thèse* is interesting, and provocative" (18). The *roman à thèse* is absolutely not a plural text.
It is univocal and non-negotiable, so to speak. It "aims for a single meaning and for total closure" (22). Moving into the twenty-first century, while
degenerative realist novels all dwell on the fact of France's decline, they

lack this didactic intent. We learn no lessons from them; we are simply infected by their gloom.

Of the many interesting problems set forth by her book, the most relevant to my project is the relationship between the *roman à thèse* and reality. Suleiman noted the strange paradox that arises with this type of realism: "Because of its desire to 'prove' something, the *roman à thèse* was unfaithful to reality: instead of being based on impartial observation, the *roman à thèse* presented a distorted image of the world, an image constructed with a demonstration in mind" (4). She calls this tendency its "repressive righteousness" (10). This is precisely the quality that led the novelist Laurent Binet to say of the *roman à thèse*, "I dislike authoritarian fictions ('*romans à thèse*') that resort to fiction to prove something: I consider this to be truly manipulative."[27] More specifically, the *roman à thèse* manipulates the reader's emotions. Recall the heavy-handed way in which Raspail's novel triggers the reader's fear response by staging scenes of utter horror, all to corroborate his thesis on foreign encroachment. In Claire Bompaire-Evesque's view, the *roman idéologique* relies on a particular balance between the plot and the "emotion provoked by the play of ideas."[28] Interestingly, she claims that the realist elements—in her analysis this seems to mean heavily descriptive passages—are not well developed in ideological novels.[29] Instead, the emphasis is placed on dialogue, one natural habitat in which a thesis may grow. As we will see, Houellebecq and others rely greatly on dialogue to convey their characters' ideological beliefs. Bompaire-Evesque's study of the oeuvre of Maurice Barrès—who, she notes, used the expressions "roman idéologique," "roman de la métaphysique," and "roman de la vie intérieure" to describe the kinds of texts he hoped to produce—shows an author who tries to speak on behalf of "une génération dégoûtée de beaucoup de choses, de tout peut-être."[30] In short, he believes that his generation already intuits the predicaments of the age but needs someone to voice them and bring them to consciousness. A skeptic would say that Barrès's reality is a constructed one, carefully crafted to herd readers toward only one set of emotions and one conclusion about the world.

The general tendency in contemporary French literature is *away* from this kind of manipulative practice, away from the domineering messaging of the *roman à thèse*. Dominique Viart writes of the shift in contemporary fiction away from the "authoritarian fiction" described by Suleiman: "L'autorité n'y est plus si autoritaire que cela, mais bien plus incertaine; et la fiction se nourrit moins de discours et plus des realia du temps."[31] But can't discourse also be realia? Wouldn't a realistic account of the current age, fraught with political consternation, necessarily include those snippets of univocal speech upon which the *pamphlet* and the *roman à thèse* are built? To show what I mean, I've selected a few examples of what we might call "thesis statements" inserted by contemporary French writers into their fiction. The reader will note that these thesis statements have neither a narrative function (they are not components of the plotline into which the novels' characters are braided) nor a descriptive function (their role in setting the scene is only secondary) but belong rather to the category of eristic discourse:

• In Michel Houellebecq's *Platform* (2001), many theses are asserted, but a couple of examples include: "There seems to be . . . a near-perfect match between the Western men, who are unappreciated and get no respect in their own countries, and Thai women, who would be happy to find someone who simply does his job and hopes to come home to a pleasant family life after work. Most Western women do not want such a boring husband."[32] And "The closer a religion comes to monotheism, . . . the more cruel and inhuman it becomes; and of all religions, Islam imposes the most radical monotheism."[33]

• In Frédéric Beigbeder's 2003 novel *Windows on the World*: "By dint of being so compassionate, Judeo-Christian democracies are easy to crush."[34] The book also argues that women have won and that their reward for having won is to grow old alone.

• In Yann Moix's 2004 novel *Partouz*: "The true combat of al-Qaeda is not so much religious as sexual. The Islam of fundamentalists was meant to bring a definitive solution to our Western problems of sentimental suffering, of romanticism, of love stories, of love songs: simply put, its purpose was, through a special reading of the Koran, to restore order to the sexual disorder that threatened to overtake the planet. In short, Bin Laden's Islam offered men the possibility of no longer suffering because of their women. . . . This entailed the mastery of sentimental sorrow by devising a system of enslavement for women, by launching . . . the deranged, bloody, and apocalyptic enterprise of absolute control of the female orgasm."[35]

• In Michel Houellebecq's *The Possibility of an Island* (2005): "To increase desires to an unbearable level whilst making the fulfilment of them more and more inaccessible: this was the single principle upon which Western society was based."[36]

- In Alexis Jenni's *L'Art français de la guerre* (2011): "It's good that there are yellow, black, and brown Frenchmen. This shows that France is open to all races and that the country has a universal vocation. But only on the condition that they remain a small minority. Otherwise, France would no longer be France. After all, we are a European people of white race, Greek and Latin culture, and Christian religion."[37]
- In Bernard-Henri Lévy's theater piece *Hôtel Europe* (2014): "Europe is succumbing to an overdose of mediocrity, bitterness, cowardice. . . . They exasperate us with all this talk of 'national identity in jeopardy,' when it's Europe, not France, that's collapsing."[38]
- In Michel Houellebecq's *Sérotonine* (2019): "This is how a civilization dies, without bother, without danger, without tragedy, and with very little carnage. A civilization dies just out of weariness, out of disgust for itself."[39]

These statements surely sound familiar. They are facsimiles of the alarmist discourse so omnipresent in the contemporary French mediascape. How would it be possible to create a full picture of the now in France without alluding to such declarations as these? While these kinds of assertions pepper the fictions I've described throughout this book, they do not deliver the ideological sureness we've come to expect from the *roman à thèse*. They are not prescriptions but rather melancholic, descriptive time capsules in which the atmospherics of the moment remain preserved. Degenerative realist novels have moved beyond ideology toward resignation.

## A CASE STUDY: MICHEL HOUELLEBECQ'S *SUBMISSION* (2015)

John Attridge has neatly summed up the general aim of Michel Houellebecq's fictions: "Houellebecq's novels are all devoted to describing one or another aspect of the supposed decadence of contemporary French society,"[40] and he notes the author's "obsession with enumerating the maladies of the French body politic and castigating the pusillanimity of its governing classes" (65). His "depressive realism," as Ben Jeffrey has named it,[41] dwells on the downward pull of the degenerative forces I've described throughout this book. Houellebecq has gained a reputation as "a diagnostician of French national decline,"[42] but the public knows him also as an instigator. The pugnacious character of his oeuvre and his public interventions is evident. He is—or was—spoiling for a fight. His early works *Extension du domaine de la lutte* (1994) and *Le sens du combat* (1996) announce this spirit in their titles, and the fight for survival is one of the main organizing themes of his fictions, essays, and poetry. His published email exchange with Bernard-Henri Lévy titled *Ennemis publics* (2008), marketed in English with the phrase "dueling writers take on each other and the world" and a drawing of the two writers fencing with writing utensils, acknowledged the provocateur status of both men and allowed them to bicker and banter while the public watched. The cover of Jean-François Patricola's book *Michel Houellebecq ou la provocation permanente* (2005) uses an image of boxing gloves to drive home the point. Houellebecq's argumentativeness is surely informed by one of his favorite philosophers, Schopenhauer, who published a book titled *Eristic Dialectic: The Art of Winning an Argument* (*Eristische Dialektik: Die Kunst, Recht zu behalten* [1831]), the advice of which some of Houellebecq's characters seem to have taken to heart. He has done his fair share of name-calling—feminists are "aimables connes,"[43] Islam is the "stupidest religion"[44]—and has instigated countless *affaires.* On the face of it, Houellebecq would seem to be a born *pamphlétaire.*

Yet his oeuvre has been met with critical ambivalence regarding its ideological component. Is he producing *littérature pamphlétaire?* Many critics believe he is not. For example, moving chronologically through Houellebecq's novels, Douglas Morrey claims that "*Extension du domaine de la lutte* may be, in a sense, a *roman à thèse*, at least in so far as it seeks to involve the reader in the demonstration of its thesis; yet the black humour and parodic tone undermine the establishment of a doctrine."[45] Regarding *The Elementary Particles*, Robert Dion and Élisabeth Haghebaert have noted how the genre of *roman à thèse* is subverted in the novel: "Le monologisme du roman à thèse est contrecarré par le dialogisme des diverses formes qui cohabitent dans le livre, par les multiples bifurcations qui menacent sans arrêt de faire dérailler le récit. On obtient ainsi le paradoxe d'un roman à thèse ambigu, protéiforme, hybride."[46] This ambiguity of form led Liesbeth Korthals Altes to call *The Elementary Particles* a "roman à thèse postmoderne." She argues that given the novel's polyvocality, the presence of parody and "double speak,"[47] and other ambiguating elements, the novel does not fit Suleiman's definition of the *roman à thèse*. Benoît Denis described *Platform* as "un roman récent à forte teneur idéologique" that seems at first to present a clear thesis,[48] but he argues that the novel's complicated blend of ideology and irony requires a more discerning and nuanced appraisal. Adam Gopnik wrote, "French reviews and American previews of *Submission* might leave one with the impression of a sardonic, teeth-baring polemic about the evils of Islam, the absurdities of feminism, the terrible demoralization of French life. In truth, the tone of the book is melancholic rather than polemical."[49] David Speiser-Landes has argued that the postmodern qualities of *Submission* foreclose readings of the novel as an Islamophobic *pamphlet*.[50] Regarding the same novel, Douglas Morrey writes, "Houellebecq satirizes a polyphony of second-hand, ill-thought-out views that are the symptom and result of an ingrained consumer culture in which values have become thoroughly detached from any real ethical ground and irrevocably tied to the dictatorship of short-term pleasure and gain."[51] In Agathe Novak-Chevalier's view, this ambivalence applies to all of Houellebecq's novels:

Although Houellebecq's novels often display the formal characteristics of the ideological novel, the thesis itself seems paradoxically to vanish in it: the juxtaposition of inconsistent perspectives and tones, the work of parody, and the constant games of ambivalence undermine all univocity and prevent the various statements of the novel from hardening into an identifiable doctrine.[52]

Labeling Houellebecq's oeuvre as an "écriture de l'ambiguïté,"[53] Bruno Viard wrote an entire book in which he stages fictional conversations between a variety of imaginary readers who debate the meaning of the novelist's work. This undecidability moves us away from the *roman à thèse*, even if some scholars have been quick to label his novels as such.[54]

I will use Houellebecq's most recent novel, *Submission*, which describes France's swift transfiguration into an Islamic state within the next decade, as an example of his subversion of the *roman à thèse*. In his implausible yet nonetheless politically galvanizing story, France has finally found a solution to its enduring failure to synthesize the profamily, patriarchic yearnings of the Far Right and the postnational religious and cultural tolerance of the Left: A new political party called the Muslim Brotherhood manages to wrest the presidency from the hands of the Front national (FN) and the battered post-Hollande Socialist Party with a message of strong families, economic prosperity, and the will to transcend the nation-state.[55] This weird Hegelian synthesis essentially puts an end to the West or at least transforms it so radically that it becomes barely recognizable. Under the

Islamic presidency, the European Union grows southward, absorbing the Maghreb and Egypt, and eastward, inviting Turkey to join and beginning the process of including Lebanon and Syria. With women out of the workforce—as they have returned to their roles as mothers and wives solely— the unemployment rate plunges. The new embrace of distributism, the economic theory by which the ownership of the means of production is spread as widely as possible, replaces Big Corp with small business. Shop owners multiply and thrive. Delinquency in the *banlieues* vanishes virtually overnight. The secular course curriculum in public schools is replaced by Quranic education, and Sharia law is implemented progressively in the courts. Contrary to what readers might anticipate, the book does not depict a violent seizure of power by Salafists or other extremists. Rather, it seems to suggest that Europeans in the near future will recognize that fully embracing a moderate form of Islam is the only way to rescue decadent Europe from itself. Michel Onfray has argued that the main theme of the novel is collaboration, and the guiding question of the narrative is: "Comment devient-on *collabo* d'un régime qui bafoue les libertés?"[56] This is only one of many possible interpretations put forth by critics and journalists in the weeks following the publication of *Submission*.

Predictably, the thematic relevance of the novel and the timing of its release on the day of the Charlie Hebdo attacks resulted in astounding sales figures and countless commentaries by the professional media and across the blogosphere. In a *New Yorker* article from late January 2015, Adam Gopnik calmly describes Houellebecq as simply an innocuous and sincere satirist who is not an Islamophobe but a Francophobe.[57] His take on the novel is at odds with the majority of public opinions, which place much more cultural weight on the dangerous assertions of *Submission*. Journalists and bloggers debated over Houellebecq's clairvoyance, over his long legacy as a *provocateur*, and over whether his alarming tale would strengthen the position of the FN, France's far-right political party, and influence other conservative, nationalist movements, such as the German Pegida (Patriotische Europäer gegen die Islamisierung des Abendlandes, Patriotic Europeans Against the Islamization of the West). One thing is clear: *Submission* fed France its own most acute fears.

The novel's intertextually rich title *Submission* derives from one of the protagonist François's conversations with a proponent of France's Islamization, in which they discuss *The Story of O* (1954), by Dominique

Aury/Pauline Réage (the pseudonym of Anne Desclos, who wrote the book for her lover Jean Paulhan, who had a particular taste for the works of Sade), about a Parisian photographer's unconditional masochistic submission to her lover. The Dutch filmmaker Theo van Gogh used this same title *Submission* for his 2004 film about the abuse of Muslim women, a project that got him murdered. In response to the film and its critique of Islam, a fundamentalist named Mohammed Bouyeri shot and stabbed van Gogh multiple times as he biked to work in November 2004 in Amsterdam and pinned to the body a death threat intended for Ayaan Hirsi Ali, the film's screenplay writer. Perhaps the most obvious meaning of the title and the reason for van Gogh's and Houellebecq's use of it is that the word "submission" is one possible translation of the word "Islam." In their conversation, the protagonist François and his interlocutor Robert Rediger agree that Aury's erotic book has a compelling force, which Rediger attributes to its implicit thesis that "the summit of human happiness lies in the most absolute submission" (212). Indeed, if the novel pretends to have a thesis, it is this. Rediger continues, arguing, "There's a connection between woman's submission to man, as it's described in *Story of O*, and the Islamic idea of man's submission to God" (212). The triangle formed between the feminist film of Theo van Gogh, the sadomasochistic erotica of Aury, and the Quran creates a framework for the rest of Houellebecq's plot, which details the submission of "feminine" Christianity to "masculine" Islam.[58] The problem with civilizational conclusions drawn by the West is that they disregard the "natural" hierarchies that put woman at the foot of man and man at the foot of God, the novel suggests. *Submission* solves the West's plight by putting everyone back in their proper place. The vector of transcendent verticality is thus restored.

A primary technique used by Houellebecq in this and other novels of his is the insertion of theses like this one in the speech and thoughts of his fictional characters, which, like nonfiction polemical essays and *pamphlets*, still have the potential to sway public opinion even though they are couched in fiction. As Agathe Novak-Chevalier has written of Houellebecq's flair as a *pamphlétaire*, "Qu'il soit capable d'avoir une plume incisive, railleuse et parfois redoutablement drôle lorsqu'il s'essaie au genre du pamphlet est une évidence."[59] He has mastered the formal techniques of the *pamphlet*. However, while most *pamphlétaires* use these techniques— the manipulative appropriation of *actualité* or current events, an appeal to historical evidence, and the reliance on certain rhetorical figures and a forcefulness of speech—in order to persuade the reader, Houellebecq's work evinces no will to change the status quo. No redemption is possible for the decaying world he describes, even if some of the characters featured in his books believe it is. As mentioned in the introduction, Houellebecq distances himself from reactionaries, who readily turn to the *pamphlet* as an expressive outlet of choice because they believe it has the power to return the world to a better past:

A reactionary is someone who favors some previously existing social configuration—something it is possible to return to—and someone who militates in favor of such a return. Whereas, if there is an idea, a single idea that runs through all of my novels, which goes so far as to haunt them, it is the *absolute irreversibility of all processes of decay* once they have begun. . . . It is more than organic, it is like a universal law that applies also to inert objects; it is literally entropic.[60]

*Submission* follows the same principle as his other novels, which describe the decay of Western civilization without aspiring to animate the public to make changes to reverse it.[61] You cannot unmold a rotting peach. Believing that Houellebecq expects his novels to produce a civilizational volte-face is, I believe, a projection.

In *Submission*, on the eve of the first round of the French presidential election in the year 2022, polls suggest that the FN has the majority of votes at 34.1 percent, with the PS (Parti socialiste) in second place at 21.8 percent, and the Muslim Brotherhood at 21.7 percent. Sarkozy's former party, the center-right UMP (Union pour un mouvement populaire, or Union for a Popular Movement), and the center-right UDI (Union des démocrates et indépendants, or Union of Democrats and Independents) have become political nonentities with virtually no share of the power. The first-round results shock the nation: The presidency will belong either to the far-right FN or to the Brotherhood. The subsequent scrambling to build coalitions to defeat the nationalists creates strange political bedfellows. In the end, the support of the PS, UMP, and UDI goes to the Brotherhood, and the final election round is won by the Islamic party. It is in this setting that we meet the book's protagonist. François—what more French a name could Houellebecq have chosen for a character who embodies *l'Hexagone*, the French state?—is a professor at the Sorbonne and a specialist on the nineteenth-century writer Joris-Karl Huysmans, most known for his decadent character from *À Rebours* (1884) named Des Esseintes, who leads a life of solitary aesthetic contemplation.[62] François's own life mirrors that of Huysmans (and often that of Des Esseintes, as well), and the novel draws constant parallels between the philosophical preoccupations of both men and their religious conversions. In an interview with Sylvain Bourmeau, Houellebecq reveals that originally the book was meant to show François's conversion to Catholicism, not Islam.[63] Houellebecq uses his hopeless, middle-aged, French, white male protagonist—a signature of his fiction[64]—to suggest obliquely that such a pathetic and empty man, the lovechild of neoliberalism and late Enlightenment, might actually have a partial chance at contentment were he to convert to Islam, keep his professorship, accept the generous salary offered by the Saudi petromonarchy that now funds the Sorbonne, and marry at least two wives, a young one for the bedroom and an old one for the kitchen. Thematically, *Submission* fits snugly in Houellebecq's corpus, with its global scale; its graphic sex scenes and treatment of women as ontologically lesser; its lengthy, thesis-filled orations by authoritative men; its typical Camusian references (François is informed by letter that his mother is dead and that he must handle the logistics of her burial) and existentialist emphasis on the problem of individual choice; and its bleak nihilism regarding Europe, the status of the white male, and the sexual economy between women and men. The theme of Islamist terror is not new to Houellebecq's corpus either; for example, in the culminating scene of his 2001 novel *Platform*, the protagonist's lover Valérie is murdered in Thailand when a group of armed Islamist extremists storms the sex tourism club they've just established there. There are brief flashes of violent terror in *Submission*, but by and large, Houellebecq relies perhaps more on the metaphor of the slow shadow than the bright explosion. The new president Mohammed Ben Abbes has imperial ambitions and does not intend to build his Islamic empire with suicide bombers and small-scale shootouts but through reeducation and the management of family life and reproduction. Explaining the long-term strategy of the Muslim Brotherhood, a secret service agent tells François, "If you control the children, you control the future."[65] This divergence from the characteristic brutalities of ISIS, Boko Haram, Hezbollah, al-Qaeda, and the Taliban—beheadings, kidnappings, suicide bombings, attacks on crowded public spaces—is nonetheless depicted in a language of ominous inevitability. The slow steadiness of the demographic transformation, a fear evoked already by Jean Raspail's *The Camp of the Saints* (1973) and through Renaud Camus's notion of the *Grand Remplacement*, makes it all the more forbidding. Yet the novel never tips over into dystopianism, at least not for men. On the contrary, the narrator declares that the new Muslim president's rule has brought "the most optimistic moment that France had known since the Thirty Glorious Years half a century before" (162). This is what would potentially frighten a certain kind of reader: the thought that an Islamized France would be a better France. French nationalism and Enlightenment values would be demolished with one blow, to everyone's benefit.

From a literary perspective, Houellebecq makes shrewd use of numerous tension-building rhetorical strategies, pacing techniques, and well-timed, cliff-hanging cuts. He uses weather as the objective correlative of the turmoil residing in the collective consciousness. He mobilizes history to show that France's absorption into Islam has always been ineluctable. He populates his book with famous contemporary French politicians and journalists, which buttresses the novel's already persuasive realism, adding many plausible, fictitious characters to their company. This aggregate of techniques produces an *effet d'immédiat*, or immediacy effect, described in the previous chapter. In contrast to the reality effect, achieved through a strategic scrutiny of the material details of a particular scene in order to signal "realness," the immediacy effect adds urgency to the reality effect, emphasizing the close proximity in time and space of the events at hand. Furthermore, the novel's particular blend of fact and fiction and of real and hypothetical events invites the reader to smudge the line between what is happening and what could happen. The interpenetration of the actual and the hypothetical is the most prominent feature of the *pamphlet*-inspired passages of the book.

A strong example of this interpenetration occurs when the first-person narrator François describes France's progression toward a "new kind of society" (165). A young sociologist in the story named Daniel Da Silva publishes a book called *One Day, All This Will Be Yours, My Son* (*Un jour, tout cela sera à toi, mon fils*), which argues for a return to the model of the marriage of convenience, that is, marriages constructed around mutual economic interest rather than love.[66] François declares, "My own family history was a perfect illustration of Da Silva's arguments" (167). This fictional book and sociologist were inspired by a very real book from 2010 titled *Has Marriage for Love Failed?* (*Le mariage d'amour a-t-il échoué?*), by the living French philosopher Pascal Bruckner, whose arguments have repeatedly influenced Houellebecq's own writing and thinking.[67] In many of his novels, he has appropriated the central thesis of Bruckner's 1983 book *Tears of the White Man: Compassion as Contempt* (*Le Sanglot de l'homme blanc: Tiers-monde, culpabilité, haine de soi*).[68] As is clear in the French subtitle, Bruckner rails against the (leftist) white man's guilt and self-hatred provoked in him by his contact with the so-called Third World. A rehashing of the white man's burden, Bruckner proposes a Reagan-era renewal of the attitude toward "your new-caught, sullen peoples, half-devil and half-child," formulated by Kipling in his 1899 poem.[69] Houellebecq has articulated in many contexts his shared disdain for the kind of leftism denounced by Bruckner. For example, in his letter to Bernard-Henri Lévy, dated May 20, 2008, in their published exchange of letters called *Public Enemies*, Houellebecq writes that the "unholy collusion between the far-left and radical Islam" is not a fantasy but a reality. He continues: "I leave the accountability of those who find excuses for Islam because it's the 'religion of the poor,' or who look for points of agreement between Marxist thought and Sharia law, but I will say that every anti-Semitic attack or murder in the French *banlieues* owes something to them."[70]

Houellebecq's use of Bruckner in this latest novel and the transmission of his ideas from the real world to a fictional one, in which the imaginary sociologist Da Silva pays homage to Bruckner in the introduction to his own book, confirm his belief in the formal power of the *pamphlet*. *Submission* alludes to other conspiracy theories that have provided the framework for a number of contemporary *pamphlets*, including those of Bat Ye'or (Gisèle Littman) on *dhimmitude* and the Eurabian conspiracy (127), the British historian Arnold Toynbee's "idea that civilizations die not by murder but by suicide" (208), and the English historian Edward Gibbon's theories presented in his late-eighteenth-century six-volume work *The History of the Decline and Fall of the Roman Empire* (210). Houellebecq's inclusion of a variety of sociological and economic theories in his novels is well documented.[71] But this citational gusto only shows the extent to which the construction of reality is a manufactured process, with individuals from a variety of fields hypothesizing about the nature of the world. As David Nowell Smith has argued, "Houellebecq's great formal innovation lies in his blurring of the distinction between fiction and socio-economic argument, such that each fiction stands as symptom, or exemplum, of the broader historical forces at work."[72] Houellebecq parrots various social science discourses and more incendiary political language, knowing full well that a certain kind of reader might mistake them for doctrine.[73] A more careful reading, however, reveals the mutability of meaning within his novels.

In part, *Submission* consists of a kind of listening tour, with aimless François paying visits to various interlocutors who deliver to him their theories on the world. Among the bearers of such *thèses* are a right-wing intellectual and new university colleague of François's named Godefroy Lempereur; Alain Tanneur, a retiring secret service agent and husband of François's colleague Marie-Françoise Tanneur; and Robert Rediger, the new pro-Muslim president of the Sorbonne. The roles of these men as polemicists are not so different: they diagnose the radical upheavals before their eyes in France. As François watches his own world begin to unravel—with his position at the university under threat and his sentimental and sexual life deteriorating—he seeks someone to construct a reality that will make sense to him and in which he might carve out a space for himself. He offers his own observations about the world, but they are unstable and often self-contradictory. As Claude Pérez has noted, "[Le personnage-narrateur] multiplie les assertions de vérité, les abstractions généralisantes, les *thèses* tantôt triviales et tantôt provocantes, sur un ton d'évidence lassée."[74] François is no ideologue. If anything, he is a container of commonplaces and half-baked conjectures about the world. Only external discourses can help his reality gel. He seeks them out.

Lempereur, a young, wealthy, conservative intellectual who once belonged to a nativist group including Catholics, royalists, nostalgics, and "romantics," invites François to his luxurious home, where he delivers the key thesis of the "indigenous peoples of Europe" regarding the demographic demise of secular societies, including France:

Belief in a transcendent being conveys a genetic advantage: that couples who follow one of the three religions of the Book and maintain patriarchal values have more children than atheists or agnostics. You see less education among women,

less hedonism and individualism. . . . Atheist humanism—the basis of any plural-
ist society—is doomed. Monotheism is on the rise, especially in the Muslim
population—and that's even before you factor in immigration. European nativists
start by admitting that, sooner or later, we'll see a civil war between the Muslims
and everybody else. They conclude that, if they want to have a fighting chance, the
war had better come as soon as possible—certainly before 2050, preferably much
sooner.

(53–54)

Lempereur continues with theories regarding the French military,
Scandinavian-style multiculturalism, and rising extremism. After their
conversation, François admits that he'd spent decades "hearing people
talk about these things" (55) but always pushed the thought away because
he couldn't possibly believe that any consequences of the dynamic
described by Lempereur and others could possibly affect his own life.[75]
"What if the deluge came before I died?" (55), he wonders. "Was [Lempe-
reur] being an alarmist? I didn't think he was, unfortunately. The kid
struck me as a deep thinker" (56). This pattern of reflection during and
after each of François's conversations shows him to be of malleable opinion, with each speaker capable of swaying him. Just after their talk, a
thought occurs to him suddenly: "If there was an ethnic conflict, I'd automatically be lumped together with the whites, and for the first time, as I
went out to buy groceries, I was grateful to the Chinese for having always
kept the neighborhood free of blacks or Arabs—or pretty much anyone
who wasn't Chinese, apart from a few Vietnamese" (56).[76] Lempereur's
arguments have succeeded in altering François's sense of reality. He begins
to feel his whiteness, which he'd never done before.

In a conversation between François and Alain Tanneur, a colleague's
husband, history is summoned up to bolster the thesis. Given his inside
knowledge of the political scene as a secret service agent, Tanneur specu-
lates about what will happen after Ben Abbes becomes president, what his
logic will be as a ruler, and where his allegiances lie. He gives François—
his apathetic, apolitical, and uninformed interlocutor—a history lesson
about France's encounters with Islam, even as early as Charles "The Ham-
mer" Martel's defeat of the Umayyad Caliphate army in the Battle of Tours
in 732. Tanneur begins to speculate about what France's future will be,
making the observation that "for these Muslims, the real enemy—the

thing they fear and hate—isn't Catholicism. It's secularism. It's laicism. It's atheist materialism" (125). Christians will convert to Islam in large numbers, he predicts, and the next step will be to construct a postnational Islamic empire reaching across the Mediterranean and toward the East. He convinces François to make a sort of pilgrimage to the Black Virgin of the Church of Notre Dame de Rocamadour to witness the superiority of the medieval Christian empire over the meek and short-lived French Republic. His implicit argument is that only *religion* can unite large swaths of diverse peoples in a lasting way.[77] Ben Abbes has understood what the secular humanist and godless state makers could not, namely, that only religion, not statehood, can guarantee longevity to a heterogeneous community. All of Tanneur's theses, speculations, and opinions, the rhetorical power of which is strengthened by his confidential knowledge, coax François toward conversion. Tanneur's access to privileged state secrets and his astuteness as a political analyst are the sources of his authority on the subject of Islamization. And in his response to this authority, François's intellectual malleability is confirmed again.

The loudest *voix pamphlétaire* is that of Robert Rediger, a controversial figure known for his pro-Palestinian stance, who becomes president of the Sorbonne after Ben Abbes's electoral victory. He invites François to his home to persuade him that his best options are to keep his post at the university and convert to Islam. Once inside Rediger's home, François accidentally sees one of the man's wives, the fifteen-year-old Aïcha, in a Hello Kitty T-shirt and with her hair uncovered, for which she is reprimanded. He also meets another of Rediger's wives, Malika, a plump woman in her forties who takes care of the cooking. These two women have a nearly archetypal significance for François, who had already contemplated at length the decline of woman in the contemporary West.[78] Aïcha is the "fille"; Malika is the "femme pot-au-feu." The "fille," or young girl figure, takes care of her body and her looks and is there primarily to satisfy her partner in bed. The "femme pot-au-feu" is an older woman responsible for satisfying her husband's *gourmandise*, his taste for delicious meals, and for sustaining his general level of domestic comfort. Rediger explains the benefits of such a household for a man like François. He enumerates the other advantages of converting and gives François a copy of his book *Ten Questions on Islam*, whose main thesis is that "Europe had reached a point of such putrid decomposition that it could no longer save itself" (225) and that Islam is the only solution.

Rediger's argument is ultimately this, summed up by the narrator: "This wave of new immigrants, with their traditional culture—of natural hierarchies, the submission of women, and respect for elders—offered a historic opportunity for the moral and familial rearmament of Europe. These immigrants held out the hope of a new golden age for the old continent" (226). Rediger makes his pronouncements with the calm assurance of someone on the side of destiny. Of course François will see the light. Rediger's role in the narrative is to offer experience-based, autobiographical authority. He is a living example of the success of Islamization. François does recognize the rhetoricity of Rediger's pronouncements. He notes, "What struck me during our meeting—and struck me even more now as I read his book—was that sense of hearing a *well-rehearsed speech*, which inevitably made Rediger sound like a politician" (221). Politicians are, like journalists, mages of reality construction. Nonetheless, Rediger sketches for him an appealing world picture in whose reality he might be willing to invest.

François's listening tour brings him to a fork in the road. He must decide whether to convert to Islam. Houellebecq does not offer his reader the satisfaction of knowing which choice the protagonist makes. The narrative leaves us in suspension at the end, signaled by the sudden use of the conditional tense in the final chapter. The last lines of the novel are: "Rather like my father a few years before, I'd be given another chance; and it would be the chance at a second life, with very little connection to the old one. I would have nothing to mourn" (246). As Agathe Novak-Chevalier has noted of this switch to the conditional:

The narrator does not convert at the end of *Submission*; he considers conversion and its consequences as a (tempting) possibility. Thus from its title to its last pages, the novel will remain unstable and in suspense. No support, no closure will guarantee the reader a meaning beyond the reach of a threat of incessant reversibility. Wherein *Submission* cannot in any way be considered an ideological novel, nor be classified under any heading.[79]

The contingencies that arise through conditional speech foreclose the possibility of a *certitude pamphlétaire*, and this same undecidability characterizes all of Houellebecq's fictions. For each, we can trace the general thematic field on which he comments: in *Whatever*, it is the "disaggregating effects of post-Fordism on the intimate spaces of human affect";[80] in

*Elementary Particles*, the indissociability of sex, science, and economy[81] and the ways in which "liberation, sexual and otherwise, smashed not only authority and a sense of responsibility, but love itself";[82] in *The Possibility of an Island*, the human desire for immortality, achieved through cloning; in *Platform* and *Lanzarote*, "the dream leisure of the Western tourist" and the "de-localization of pleasure";[83] in *The Map and the Territory*, "the total subsumption of the society under capital";[84] in *Submission*, the "religious, and, specifically, Islamic solution to human suffering and civilisational decline";[85] and in *Serotonin*, the connection "between body and state, between the declining health of the protagonist and the health of French society."[86] However, the books are more mournfully descriptive than forcefully prescriptive. We find in them no staunch calls for a renewed nationalism, no full-throated promotion of this or that ideology, no set of demands for specific policy changes. We find only despondency.

It is true that Houellebecq's decaying worlds are full of people who attempt to shape reality, often motivated by self-gain: cult leaders peddling eternal life and sexual ecstasy, capitalists, deceitful politicians and media figures, ideologues and proselytizers, marketing specialists and advertisers, prostitutes who feign desire, psychopharma execs pushing happy pills. In essence, they all offer "the chance at a second life," or, to put it another way, they present an alternative reality where happiness is a possibility. They take aim at the weak-minded, spiritless masses who slouch from cradle to grave with no clear convictions, living pointlessly like the lumps of organic matter they are. In this vein, Louis Betty has argued that Houellebecq's "materialist horror" is fixated on showing "societies and persons in which the terminal social and psychological consequences of materialism are being played out."[87] The alternative realities presented to these decaying individuals only destabilize their sense of the real. Houellebecq describes the pathetic middle-aged women who turn to Tarot cards or cobbled-together mystical practices to soothe their pain without really believing any of it and the consumers who place faith in products or tourist packages to grow their joy, knowing full well that any happiness derived from consumption will be fleeting. The institutions that once provided form and purpose to life—the family, the church, the state—have degenerated, along with the assurances they provided.

It is extraordinary the extent to which Houellebecq's novels dwell on the discrepancy between reality and representation, or between reality as it is constructed and *le réel* external to this construction. The most obvious example is announced in the title of his novel *The Map and the Territory*, a novel about representation and the loss of reality that occurs once global capital has infiltrated every aspect of life. The role of art and literature as representational practices plays a central role there, and again and again, Houellebecq returns in the novel to themes of mimesis, copies versus originals, and the cleft between what is real and what represents the real. In his meditations on clones—in *The Elementary Particles*[88] and *The Possibility of an Island*—Houellebecq invites us to study the fine membrane that separates science fiction from scientific reality and to think about the ways in which new technologies can radically modify our definitions of reality. Addressing new discoveries in neurochemistry, Houellebecq explained in an interview, "Nous n'échapperons pas à une redéfinition des conditions de la connaissance, de la notion même de réalité; il faudrait dès maintenant en prendre conscience sur un plan affectif."[89] His neuronovel *Sérotonine* uses its energies to document the disintegration of reality for a man taking an antidepressant that pushes him toward psychosis and suicide, probing along the way the unbearable realities of *agriculteurs* and other losers in social democracy and economic liberalism. In his world, the realities of various groups—men and women,[90] economic victors and victims—are completely distinct, yet they exist simultaneously, rubbing uncomfortably against one another and making all parties involved question which of these realities is ascendant. The narrator's own reality disintegrates throughout the narrative[91] as he keeps increasing his dosage and isolating himself from the external world. For Houellebecq, the deterioration of the real makes the ideologue's task an impossible one. Who, after all, can claim any certainty in a world whose reality has gone soft?

The features of Houellebecq's *littérature post-pamphlétaire* are consistent with those found in the other novels presented throughout this study. If we try to pin down a thesis in, say, Aurélien Bellanger's *Théorie de l'information* or Frédéric Beigbeder's *Windows on the World* or Philippe Vasset's *La Conjuration*, we will fail. While certain characters in these books may provide forceful pronouncements on the causes and cures of civilizational decay, the novels as a whole lack the *pamphlétaire*'s conviction on these matters. The theses put forth are subverted by polyvocality, with competing discourses canceling one another out, or by a pervasive sense of ineluctable decline that makes any proposed solution seem like make-believe.

Degenerative realist novels evince a general suspicion of all discourses, even if they borrow readily from political tracts, sociological theories, or journalistic writing. Furthermore, they express a disenchantment with contemporary intellectual life, which has been sapped of its authoritative force. An early critique of the decay within the European intellectual class was offered in Julien Benda's *La Trahison des clercs* (1927),[92] but recent titles have also probed the problem in its contemporary, specifically French iteration. The Israeli historian Schlomo Sand's *La Fin de l'intellectuel français? De Zola à Houellebecq* (2016), tracks the slow *déchéance* of the French intellectual from the nineteenth century to today, and in Nicolas Truong's *Le Crépuscule des intellectuels français?* (2016), a wide range of public figures weigh in on the changing role of the intellectual in France as a mediator and interpreter of new sociopolitical realities. The consensus among the contributors seems to be that the fast-paced way that intellectuals are summoned to respond to a particular event requires an empty performativity and a simplification of complicated matters into absurdly reductive sound bites. The question marks in both of these titles suggest that no verdict has been reached on the survival of this once-lustrous archetype, but readers finish each book with the sense that the sun is indeed setting on the French intellectual, who has historically been heavily relied upon to deliver reality-shaping judgments on social and political life. As Jean Bothorel put it, "Cet affaissement—cet enterrement, devrait-on dire—du débat d'idées est des plus singuliers dans un pays comme le nôtre."[93] In short, yet another authoritative source for truth has gone missing.

Throughout this study, I have tracked a number of casualties within the framework of degenerative realism, including the loss or weakening of once-strong discursive authorities and other points of reference necessary for an establishment of a sense of reality. Readers might have disagreed with the arguments presented in certain *pamphlets* or *romans à thèse*, but they may have been stimulated nonetheless by the vibrancy and vitality of a person still imbued with the will to fight. Degenerative realism does not offer this recompense.

# NOVEL AS NATION

## Forms of Parallel Decay

Our sickness is autoimmune, our war is civil.

—MARC AUGÉ, *THE WAR OF DREAMS*

If the nation really is sinking, the novel—the literary genre most bound to nation—is going down with the ship. This is, at least, the assessment of Richard Millet, in whose *pamphlets* all of the fears described throughout this book crystallize. He is just one of France's many reactionary doomsayers, but the concerns he describes map particularly well onto those of degenerative realist fiction. France is changing and, along with it, the nature of reality. Millet laments "une inversion générale des valeurs,"[1] which has resulted in the rise of "le métissage, l'homosexualité, l'antiracisme, le show-business politique, les lobbies minoritaires, les faussaires de tout genre, les travestis de l'information, les transsexuels de la parole publique" (25). To this list of poisons, he adds other signs of national decay: "les progrès de l'ignorance, le naufrage de l'enseignement public, les redéfinitions minoritaires (sexuelles, ethniques, raciales, religieuses, linguistiques, mémorielles) de l'humanité" (33), all of which have corrupted the public's sense of *le réel*. Again and again in his *pamphlets*, Millet decries the death of reality through "la falsification du réel" (29) and argues that no great thinkers or writers are left in France to analyze with honesty the forged reality that has been foisted on everyone through journalistic *mensonge*, internet duplicity, deceptive advertising, and the peddling of falsehoods by public figures in politics and the media. He argues, "le journalisme est, avec la mauvaise conscience et la publicité, le destin mortifère de la littérature" (48–49). Along with the corruption of reality, the French language and literature written in it have been similarly debased. Millet writes, "Le jeu de la langue et du territoire étant une autre définition de la littérature, on peut, de ce point de vue, dire aujourd'hui que la France est morte, vue qu'il n'y a plus nul écrivain pour en déployer le paysage ni en rendre sensible le filigrane historique" (26). France has lost its historical memory, and as the West becomes "mosaïfié par les minorités" (59), its other cultural orientation points will be lost as well. These grim appraisals are, as I've shown throughout this study, pressed between the pages of all degenerative realist fiction, whose characters express similar anxieties. While their authors track the progress of this decay and the angst it produces in their characters, they take no firm ideological position on these matters. They tacitly acknowledge that whatever forces are causing the withering of the nation are also breaking down the novel, the literary genre best equipped to "think" the individual through the lens of nationhood.

There is a unique tendency in France to describe the nation's history as a *roman national*, that is, a cohesive, linear narrative that depicts the nation's past events as a unified story, meant to bring a sense of solidarity and patriotism to French citizens. The *roman national* weaves together well-known events and heroic figures—Vercingétorix and Jeanne d'Arc, for example—in an uninterrupted flow, adding symbolic valence to the whole of it as novelists often do. The historical figures become characters in a story with a teleology. Developed during the Third Republic and transmitted through the educational manuals of Ernest Lavisse, the *récit national* has a specific purpose, according to Sébastien Ledoux, "de nourrir un imaginaire historique devant être partagé par l'ensemble des citoyens pour former ainsi la communauté nationale."[2] One could imagine all of France's children gathered around the restorative fire in the homeland's hearth to hear the story of the nation, a tale meant to build solidarity among citizens. In an article from 2016, Anne-Aël Durand pointed out the prevalence of the term "roman national" or "récit national" in political speeches given by center-right-wing politicians—she specifically names Nicolas Sarkozy and François Fillon—and notes that even the Left had begun to deploy this phrasing on occasion.[3] The people, it seems, are hungry for a good story. The problem with the *roman national* is, like all national histories sanctioned by governments, that its vision of France is idealized, leaving out the dark side of French history. As Ledoux writes, "Une telle production narrative a . . . omis des faits historiques dont l'État français s'est rendu responsable (traite et esclavage, violences coloniales, persécution des juifs par Vichy)."[4] It is also quite limited in its definition of who is allowed to count as a hero of the nation's glorious past. Sarkozy made headlines in 2016 when he suggested that the *tirailleurs sénégalais* should be included among France's esteemed *ancêtres* who drive the plot of the *roman national*. The fictional elements, exaggerations, idealizations, or omissions of the *récit national* have come under increasing scrutiny, and the epistemological implications of this shift are substantial, in my view. If this story had a standardizing function—indoctrinating each citizen with a shared vision of France's past—and allowed national subjects to construct their realities based in part on a common, unshakable knowledge of the historical foundations of the country, then its unraveling necessarily undermines one's ability to determine what is real and what isn't. If the story you've been told since childhood does not hold up under scrutiny, you begin to wonder where to turn for truth.

Regarding France's history, the Far Right has taken a preservationist position. They see the *récit national* as a set of embalmed facts whose transmission from one generation to the next is a civic duty.[5] But even as a rise in nationalist enthusiasm has marked these first years of the twenty-first century, a simultaneous disillusionment with nationalist thinking has appeared as well. In a critique of the nationalists representative of a general deflated spirit regarding French pride, Michel Houellebecq declared, "Developing an overweening national pride is always a sign, to my mind, that you have nothing much else to be proud of."[6] Imagining himself as a postnational citizen, he has claimed, "I have never felt any duty or responsibility toward France and choosing which country I live in has about as much emotional resonance for me as choosing which hotel I stay in" (115). His cynicism regarding national pride has no limits: "All things . . . die, including mental constructs, and as for the French nation, French patriotism, they are already dead" (112).[7] In terms of what France will be like in the future, he declares, "Do I really want to turn France into a dead, mummified country, a sort of *tourist brothel*? . . . Without a second thought, I say YES" (117). As I have shown throughout this study, this sentiment extends beyond France's borders to Europe and to the whole of Western civilization.

The authors I've presented here have lost faith not only in France's *roman national* but also in the *roman occidental*, if there ever was one.

Degenerative realism is a mode through which a perceived national and civilizational decay can be registered and where anxieties about the collapse of reality are given voice. I began by showing how demographic change has destabilized cultural hierarchies that had seemed fixed, setting off a survival-of-the-fittest mentality as the guiding logic of many contemporary novels. Identity-based apprehensions, with a particular focus on race and gender, obsess the characters and narrators, who see themselves as losers in this new globalized, horizontalized configuration. As margin becomes center, new perspectives—and thus new "readings" of reality—multiply, and fewer and fewer assumptions about objective truth seem possible. The social sciences might be helpful in describing and explaining the fluctuations our characters fear, but they cannot reverse them. These changes arrive in a moment of informational upheaval, as I showed in the chapter on the Minitel and the internet, when arcane networks created the conditions for new forms of mystification. From conspiracy theories to marketing manipulations, from avatars and anonymous actors to fringe groups who live in alternate realities, the wall dividing what is real and what seems to be real has only become more permeable in the digital age. Practitioners of degenerative realism are sensitive to this interference and understand its potential within fiction to force us to rethink what we believe we know and how we know it. This is why journalism and other forms of mediatized information feature so heavily in degenerative realist novels. These, after all, are among the key sources of understanding about the world beyond our doorstep. Our authors call attention again and again to the constructed nature of our world picture, underscoring the fact that media outlets are never disinterested parties who strive to provide objective truths. The novels I've analyzed deliver the same *actualité* we find on the front page, borrowing techniques from the New Social Novelists and the New Journalists, but they are suspicious of journalism's ability to offer an account of the world, given its sometimes dubious motivations, its focus on profit margins and clicks, and its need to satisfy entertainment-hungry consumers. The confidence of the *pamphlétaire*, whose unequivocal pronouncements made it seem as though he'd figured it all out, has been sapped from these books. Degenerative realism lacks conviction, able only to record the decay, not to stop it or even to curse it. No ideology is capable of solving the intractable problems of the twenty-first century.

Degenerative realism is part of a larger trend within contemporary French literature, namely, the calling into question of what constitutes the real. In his book *La Littérature sans idéal* (2016), Philippe Vilain argues that the postrealist trend in the contemporary French novel suggests a "mise en doute du réel."[8] The world it sees, marked by "l'inhumanité et la barbarie," is bleak: "Si ce qui caractérise le post-réalisme est bien sa passion du réel, cette passion, négative, incline pour un certain type de réel, un réel apocalyptique, endémique, dont le sensationnel fascine" (53). He argues that what typifies these novels is a "fascination pour l'apocalypse de l'homme, son déclin et ses drames, ses malheurs et ses mauvais penchants, dans laquelle il puise le sensationnel nécessaire à sa fiction" (54). In studying the patterns I've described in this book and reading them alongside the turbulent sociopolitical events that have marked the first decades of the twenty-first century, it seems natural that a degeneration of the nation, of the novel, and of reality would coincide. The realist novel, whose history parallels the coalescence of the nation and modern European democracy, has always had a special relationship to the world it represents. While nineteenth-century realists and naturalists believed in the novel's capacity to influence the social world, this idealism has vanished in degenerative realism. Throughout this study, we have seen example after example of narratives that begin in a realist mode and then depart from it—toward science fiction or horror or complete narrative dissolution—as though this mimetic practice can no longer sustain its energies even for the length of a novel. The real simply does not hold up under the downward pull of degeneration. In the past, realism at times served a socially redemptive purpose, seeking to raise consciousness about veiled injustices and perhaps change them. The realism I describe throughout this book no longer makes such attempts. Regarding this shift, Nicolas Léger has identified a growing tendency in the contemporary French novel, what he calls the "literature of inequality" (*la littérature des inégalités*). He writes:

Although there is a French tradition of social narrative that follows in the footsteps of Émile Zola's naturalism or Victor Hugo's epics, contemporary novels no longer seem to have their sights set on a radiant, just future. Many of them are more disillusioned in tone and tap into a collective sense of the loss of an ideal while attempting to explore the genealogy and effects of that loss.[9]

This loss of idealism is perhaps a result of the heightened sense of crisis that Ruth Cruickshank and others have detected in French turn-of-the-millennium literature. Crisis narratives of this period recount the catastrophes of past and present and anticipate even worse ones to come. Drawing a triangle between this atmosphere of crisis, various calls for realism in politics, and the realist novel's social role, Stéphane Bikialo and Julien Rault argue:

In some contexts, the use of the word *crisis* may serve a more reactionary ideology, linked to decline, to decadence. In the fields of literature and linguistics, for example, the word often appears in instances of regressive speech; (dramatizing) phrases such as "the crisis of the French language" or "the crisis of the novel" usually occur only in the form of purist, reactionary tension, activating the anxiety-inducing idea of degradation, in accordance with a background template: For those who use it, the word *crisis* often signals a regressive ideology, a nostalgic, retrospective gaze, setting up an implicit earlier standard by which disparities and deviations may be better assessed. But obviously this "crisis" is a fundamental and even foundational auxiliary of the realist dictum. Without it, realism loses some of its character of self-evidence.[10]

Crisis and calls for a return to the real go hand in hand. In moments of panic, one naturally seeks orientation points to help thwart what seems like impending doom. The adage that those who do not understand history are doomed to repeat it suggests that studying the past might be the key to surviving into the future. History, for our authors, provides no such edification. Nor does deep analysis of the present. Science, politics, economy, technology, humanities: None can reverse the degenerative forces breaking down the nation, the novel, and the real. Even writing cannot regenerate what has already deteriorated.

In Patrik Ourednik's short novel *La Fin du monde n'aurait pas eu lieu*, the narrator states, "Selon les psychologues, l'idée de la fin du monde permet d'accepter sa propre disparition."[11] One wonders the extent to which the tales of civilizational decline described throughout my study are manifestations of the authors' fears of personal physical decline, a loss of status in the new global order, and of a potential creeping irrelevance of their work and philosophies. The obsessive circling around themes of bodily collapse, the ineptitude and banality of contemporary literary production (literature written by others, of course), and other helpless grievances lead us to the conclusion that practitioners of degenerative realism are using the decline of France, Europe, and Western civilization as a proxy for talking about their own decline as organic beings and as writers past the halfway point in life. To attribute all of the patterns I've described throughout this book to this phenomenon would be reductive, but there is undoubtedly a connection between the authors' own sense of finitude and the various forms of cultural putrefaction that fill their books.

Degenerative realism, like all developments within a given cultural field (in this case, literature), simultaneously adheres to tradition and breaks from it. I've shown what degenerative realism has inherited from its nineteenth-century forebears and what it has sloughed off, but the most interesting and radical innovation it offers is the destabilization of reality. This undermining of the real is by no means a strictly French phenomenon. As geographical borders become more porous, so do ontological categories—the difference between what is real and what isn't—and epistemological categories—the difference between what is true and what isn't. The authors whose work I analyzed throughout this study experience these new forms of porosity as an existential threat, and because the phenomenon of reality loss is global and not national, their fears are shared across the planet by a motley assemblage of discontents with widely varying political beliefs. Among the writers studied here, Michel Houellebecq is by far the most internationally known and translated, and this global success can be attributed in part to his skill at naming and describing a *feeling* that has draped itself over much of the world. Yes, there is something quintessentially French about Houellebecq's brand of culture critique, but there is also a postnational intuition in his pages felt by his most committed readers outside France. Something about his cynicism is beguiling across political lines. A leftist, feminist colleague recently summed up in one sentence what I've heard in longer iterations over the years from many friends and colleagues: "I kind of hate Houellebecq but I can't stop reading him." Why is that? In my view, it is because he gives literary form to the general malaise produced by a world too fast and fluctuating to be understood in real time. The other practitioners of degenerative realism I've presented have a much smaller global reach—most of their works remain untranslated—but they, too, try to capture the dread generated by the acceleration of culture and the concomitant loss of once-shared orientation points. Though I am less familiar with other contemporary Western prose literatures than with the contemporary French novel, it would not surprise me to find writers across borders who use their books to track the same collective loss of bearings pursued by the writers I've presented here. There is great potential, I think, for the category of degenerative realism to be applied across national novelistic traditions, and I hope literary scholars in other subfields will follow the model I've tried to provide here. The real, like the ground, used to be taken for granted as the foundation upon which all culture, politics, and social life could be built. What happens when it decays? Degenerative realism attempts to answer this question through both the content and form of the novel.

# NOTES

## INTRODUCTION: WHAT IS DEGENERATIVE REALISM?

1. A. Peytel, "Le Roman réaliste en Amérique," *Gazette Littéraire* (June 25, 1864): 98.
2. Henry Maudsley, *Body and Will* (New York: Appleton, 1884), 240.
3. Robert Barnhart, ed., *The Barnhart Concise Dictionary of Etymology* (New York: HarperCollins, 1995), 192.
4. See Aristide Leucate, *Dictionnaire du grand épuisement français et européen* (Paris: Dualpha, 2018). Also see Jean-François Mattéi, *Le Regard vide: Essai sur l'épuisement de la culture européenne* (Paris: Flammarion, 2007). An echo of these titles is found in John Barth's famous 1967 essay "The Literature of Exhaustion," one of many postmodern *manifesti*, about the "used-upness" of certain forms of literary representation, including realism. John Barth, *The Friday Book* (Baltimore, MD: Johns Hopkins University Press, 1997), 53.
5. Like many authors in this study, Spengler conceived of culture and history as organic entities, a feature he emphasized throughout both tomes of *Decline*. He wrote, "I see world-history as a picture of endless formations and transformations, of the marvellous waxing and waning of organic forms. The professional historian, on the contrary, sees it as a sort of tapeworm industriously adding on to itself one epoch after another" Oswald Spengler, *The Decline of The West*, 2 vols., trans. Charles Francis Atkinson (New York: Knopf, 1950), 1:21–22. For an assessment of the book's legacy upon the hundredth birthday of the first volume (1918–2018), see Gilbert Merlio, *Le Début de la fin? Penser la décadence avec Oswald Spengler* (Paris: Presses universitaires de France, 2019). The American historian Brooks Adams beat Spengler to the punch by over twenty years with his book *The Law of Civilization and Decay: An Essay on History*, which appeared in 1895 (London: Swan Sonnenschein & Co.). Also see Samuel Huntington, *The Clash of Civilizations and the Remaking of World Order* (New York: Simon and Schuster, 1996).

6. Peter Brooks has underscored this paradox, arguing that realist fictions "have to lie in order to tell the truth: they must foreshorten, summarize, perspectivize, give an illusion of completeness from fragments." Peter Brooks, *Realist Vision* (New Haven, CT: Yale University Press, 2008), 6. Philippe Hamon has also rightly pointed out the conspicuous number of nineteenth-century realist novels that rely on a thematics of falsehood and artificiality, naming *Madame Bovary* and *L'Éducation sentimentale* as examples: "Tout est faux, tout n'est que paraître ou faux semblant, tous les personnages, leurs goûts, leurs rêves, sont sous influence. Ils sont, littéralement, intoxiqués de facticité." Philippe Hamon, *Puisque réalisme il y a* (Geneva: Éditions La Baconnière, 2015), 28. Champfleury argued, "Le romancier ne juge pas, ne condamne pas, n'absout pas. Il expose des faits." Champfleury, "Encore quelques mots à propos de *M. de Boisdhyver*," *Figaro*, August 7, 1856, 4.

7. These include Florence Delay (elected in 2000), Chinese-born François Cheng (2002), Algerian-born Assia Djebar (2005), Simone Veil (2008), Lebanese-born Amin Maalouf (2011), Danièle Sallenave (2011), the Haitian Canadian author Dany Laferrière (2013), and Dominique Bona (2013).

8. A few examples: Prix Goncourt for the novel (Leïla Slimani, 2018; Lydie Salvayre, 2016; Marie Ndiaye, 2012; Atiq Rahimi, 2010); Prix Goncourt for poetry (Vénus Khoury-Ghata, 2011; Abdellatif Laabi, 2009; Andrée Chedid, 2002; Liliane Wouters, 2000); Prix Goncourt for the novella (Marie-Hélène Lafon, 2016; Fouad Laroui, 2013; Brigitte Giraud, 2007; Catherine Paysan, 2000); Prix Renaudot (Yasmina Reza, 2016; Delphine de Vigan, 2015; Scholastique Mukasonga, 2012; Virginie Despentes, 2010; Tierno Monénembo, 2008; Alain Mabanckou, 2006; Nina Bouraoui, 2005; Irène Némirovsky, 2004; Martine Le Coz, 2001; Ahmadou Kourouma, 2000); and Prix de Flore (Nina Yargekov, 2016; Monica Sabolo, 2013; Abdellah Taïa, 2010; Amélie Nothomb, 2007; Christine Angot, 2006; Joy Sorman, 2005).

9. A few impressive recent examples of these categories of study are Annabel L. Kim, *Unbecoming Language: Anti-Identitarian French Feminist Fictions* (Columbus: Ohio State University Press, 2018); Yves Clavaron, *Francophonie, postcolonialisme et mondialisation* (Paris: Classiques Garnier, 2018); Jennifer Yee, *The Colonial Comedy: Imperialism in the French Realist Novel* (Oxford: Oxford University Press, 2016); and Bruno Perreau, *Queer Theory: The French Response* (Stanford, CA: Stanford University Press, 2016).

10. For more on cynicism in French literature, see Pierre Glaudes and Jean-François Louette, eds., *Cynismes littéraires* (Paris: Classiques Garnier, 2018).

11. While women have also produced novels that describe and diagnose France's pathologies—the first that comes to mind is Virginie Despentes's *Vernon Subutex* trilogy—I have yet to find an example in which both the novel's content *and* form are marked by the category of the degenerative. This is not to say that examples drawn from the work of female novelists absolutely don't exist, only that I was able to find a preponderance of examples among male authors.

12. Sabine van Wesemael argues that the books of Michel Houellebecq and other authors whose writing shares features with his (she explicitly names Fabrice Pliskin, Florian Zeller, Yann Moix, Simon Liberati, Eric Reinhardt, Philippe Djian, Frédéric Beigbeder, Vincent Ravalec, Pierre Mérot, and Bret Easton Ellis) are essentially nonredemptive: "Ils ne proposent pas de solutions: à la littérature salvatrice, ils opposent la littérature vaine dans laquelle la névrose, l'hystérie, la

maladie deviennent les sujets essentiels." Sabine van Wesemael, "Michel Houel-lebecq, figure de roman," in *Lectures croisées de l'œuvre de Michel Houellebecq*, ed. Antoine Jurga and Sabine van Wesemael (Paris: Classiques Garnier, 2017), 34.

13. Shortly after Y2K, in a collective mood of augmented fear regarding climate change, nuclear proliferation, instability in the Middle East, global terror, and other seemingly intractable problems, Jean-Pierre Dupuy published his book *Pour un catastrophisme éclairé*, in which he argued that instead of approaching these problems with ignorance and fear, "on peut construire un catastrophisme cohérent et conforme à la raison la plus exigeante." Jean-Pierre Dupuy, *Pour un catastrophisme éclairé: Quand l'impossible est certain* (Paris: Seuil, 2002), 81.

14. Frédéric Beigbeder, *Windows on the World*, trans. Frank Wynne (New York: Hyperion, 2004), 144.

15. Antoine Bello, *Les Éclaireurs* (Paris: Gallimard, 2009), 58.

16. Alexandre Devecchio has drawn a parallel between young jihadists and young *identitaires*: "Ils ont vingt ans. Ils sont islamistes et partent pour le jihad. Ils sont souverainistes ou identitaires et s'enrôlent au Front national. Ils sont conservateurs, catholiques et animent la Manif pour tous. Tout les oppose, mais ils s'opposent tous à la globalisation, au libéralisme, à la fin de l'histoire. Par leurs révoltes et par leurs fractures, ils sont le miroir de la France d'aujourd'hui et de demain." Alexandre Devecchio, *Les Nouveaux enfants du siècle* (Paris: Éditions du Cerf, 2016), n.p.

17. "The perception of a threat to French national identity is articulated in anti-American critiques of the cultural relativism perceived in the discourses of the *politiquement correct* and the *tout culturel*." Ruth Cruickshank, *Fin de Millénaire French Fiction: The Aesthetics of Crisis* (Oxford: Oxford University Press, 2009), 47.

18. A character in Beigbeder's *Windows on the World* states, "In the United States, life is like a movie, since all movies are shot on location. All Americans are actors, and their houses, their cars, and their desires all seem artificial. Truth is reinvented every morning in America. It's a country that has decided to look like something on celluloid" (21).

19. See the excellent book by Philippe Roger, *L'Ennemi américain: Généalogie de l'antiaméricanisme français* (Paris: Seuil, 2002).

20. Haenel was an ideal guest in the trial because his own work and its mixing of truth and fiction had caused a stir a few years earlier. A controversy erupted involving his novel *Jan Karski* (2009), part faithful transcription of the eponymous Polish resistance fighter's testimony and part fictionalization, which prompted Claude Lanzmann to speak out against what he called Haenel's "truquage de l'homme" and his "falsification de l'Histoire." Claude Lanzmann, "*Jan Karski* de Yannick Haenel: Un faux roman," *Les Temps Modernes* 657 (2010): 4.

21. "1) Le brouillage, l'effacement de la frontière entre fait et fiction [conduit] à élider la différence entre la vérité et les faits alternatifs avec de graves conséquences démocratiques; 2) Effacer la frontière entre faits et fiction [conduit] à un confusionnisme historique avec de graves préjudices épistémologiques et éthiques; 3) Faisant le constat d'une judiciarisation croissante de la littérature, la recrudescence de procès d'écrivains soulignait qu'effacer la différence entre faits et fiction pouvait conduire à blesser les personnes qui s'identifiaient comme personnages dans les œuvres de fiction et que la recrudescence de ces procès attestait de la nécessité

du maintien de cette frontière; 4) Souligner que la différence entre faits et fiction est la condition pour admettre une véritable pluralité ontologique, pluralité des registres de réalité, condition non seulement pour s'informer sur le monde tel qu'il est mais pour tirer plaisir des œuvres de fiction en les distinguant, bel et bien de la réalité telle que nos sens, nos informations nous la présentent; 5) Souligner que mélanger, confondre deux régimes cognitifs, l'un orienté vers le réel, l'autre vers la fiction, constituait une erreur à la fois philosophique avec de lourdes conséquences politiques et une erreur scientifique, au regard des avancées des neurosciences." A recording of the entire trial is available at https://www.youtube.com /watch?v=C3HdoiQP-fk.

22. See Robert Dion, *Des fictions sans fiction ou le partage du réel* (Montreal: Presses universitaires de l'Université de Montréal, 2018); Abdelaziz Amraoui and Marie-Rose Abomo-Maurin, eds., *Littérature et réalité: Regards croisés* (Paris: L'Harmattan, 2018); Alison James and Christophe Reig, eds., *Frontières de la nonfiction: Littérature, cinéma, arts* (Rennes: Presses universitaires de Rennes, 2013); and Alexandre Gefen and René Audet, eds., *Frontières de la fiction* (Quebec: Éditions Nota Bene, 2002). For more on a similar tendency in the visual arts, see Paulo Cirio, ed., *Evidentiary Realism: Investigative, Forensic, and Documentary Art* (Berlin: Nome, 2017). An earlier precedent to these books is the essay collection edited by Gérard Genette and Tzvetan Todorov, *Littérature et réalité* (Paris: Seuil, 1982).

23. Françoise Lavocat, *Fait et fiction: Pour une frontière* (Paris: Seuil, 2016), 12.

24. Lionel Ruffel, "Un réalisme contemporain: Les narrations documentaires," *Littératures* 166 (2012): 14.

25. Marie-Jeanne Zenetti argues that a body of factual literature composed of works that "proposent . . . une alternative au récit comme forme dominante de mise en ordre du réel et de l'expérience, appelant d'autres interrogations que celles qui dominent ce domaine d'étude et qui touchent principalement à deux questions: celle des critères éventuels de distinction entre récit fictionnel et récit factuel d'une part, celle de la littérarité des textes factuels d'autre part." Marie-Jeanne Zenetti, *Factographies: L'enregistrement littéraire à l'époque contemporaine* (Paris: Classiques Garnier, 2014), 19.

26. Dominique Viart, *Le Roman français au XXe siècle* (Paris: Armand Colin, 2011), 159.

27. Philippe Forest, *Le Roman, le réel, et autres essais* (Paris: Éditions Cécile Defaut, 2007), 29.

28. In their edited volume on twenty-first-century narrative fiction, Narjoux and Stolz write, "Le recueil se penche donc sur ces questions, avec des études qui s'efforcent de montrer comment de nouvelles définitions de la fiction se cherchent dans une relative dénégation du romanesque au profit d'une fictionalisation du réel et de nouveaux traitements de l'Histoire." Cécile Narjoux and Claire Stolz, eds., *Fictions narratives du XXIe siècle: Approches rhétoriques, stylistiques et sémiotiques* (Rennes: La Licorne, 2014), 9.

29. Using three contemporary French novels as examples—Philippe Vasset's *Un Livre blanc* (Paris: Fayard, 2007), Olivia Rosenthal's *Viande froide* (Paris: Centquatre, 2008), and Thomas Clerc's *Paris, musée du XXIe siècle* (Paris: Gallimard, 2007)—Trudel argues that these narratives "display formal strategies that attempt

to capture something singular, strange or in excess, in short everything that in the 'real' resists or challenges representation." He calls this a "precarious real, (precarious because it is often nearly invisible, inaudible or already fading away)." Éric Trudel, "Passions du réel (sur Philippe Vasset, Olivia Rosenthal et Thomas Clerc)," *Australian Journal of French Studies* 54, no. 2–3 (2017): 113.

30. Joshua Armstrong, "Empiritexts: Mapping Attention and Invention in Post-1980 French Literature," *French Forum* 40, no. 1 (Winter 2015): 96; original text italicized.

31. Jacinto Lageira, *La Déréalisation du monde: Réalité et fiction en conflit* (Nîmes: Éditions Jacqueline Chambon, 2010), 21.

32. Philippe Vilain, *La Littérature sans idéal* (Paris: Grasset, 2016), 43.

33. "[Le post-réalisme] se charge d'explorer une nouvelle dimension du réel, sa troisième, non plus en le figurant à la manière d'un Balzac, ni même en le sublimant à la manière d'un Breton, mais en investissant subjectivement le réel pour le réinventer, en réécrivant sa mythologie personnelle (autofiction), les mythologies collectives (biofiction), en faisant de la littérature le lieu d'un immense reportage de l'actualité, en alimentant une documentation fictive du monde (docufiction)" Vilain, *La Littérature sans idéal*, 45. Translated from French to English by Saadia El Karfi, indicated henceforth as SE.

34. See Johan Faerber, "Contre la Zemmourisation de la critique littéraire," *Diakritik*, October 15, 2018, https://diacritik.com/2018/10/15/contre-la-zemmourisation-de-la -critique-litteraire/. Here is the full call for papers: "À l'heure de la littérature-monde et de sa géographie étendue, le roman de langue française n'a cessé ces dernières décennies de penser l'identité française, que ce soit celle du territoire ou de ses périphéries. Dans les écritures de terrain comme dans les enquêtes mémorielles, dans les récits de filiation comme dans ceux de métissage, le territoire français, l'histoire nationale, les passions françaises, ont fait retour en fiction. En traversant l'histoire du XXe siècle, de la guerre de 14 à la décolonisation, en parcourant la 'France profonde,' en s'installant dans les terrains vagues industriels et dans les banlieues, nombre d'écrivains ont tenté de formuler un nouveau regard sur l'identité française. La fiction littéraire renoue ainsi avec la question politique, entre reconstruction nostalgique, déconstruction critique et utopie. Pierre Bergounioux et Alexis Jenni, Aurélien Bellanger et Pascal Quignard, Anne-Marie Garat et Hédi Kaddour, Renaud Camus et Marie NDiaye, Tierno Monénembo et Léonora Miano, Boualem Sansal et Abdourahman Waberi, sans oublier Richard Millet et Michel Houellebecq, ont éprouvé le besoin, à l'heure où l'Union européenne, le multiculturalisme et les flux migratoires sont au centre du débat, de penser à nouveaux frais une identité traditionnellement conçue comme nationale et les différentes formes d'appartenance à une langue et à un territoire. Cette identité n'est pas saisie seulement depuis le centre 'franco-français'; elle est aussi projetée, parfois imaginée, depuis ses voisinages francophones à l'échelle du monde. Loin de n'être que l'appui d'un grand récit, ou de se complaire à nourrir une culpabilité collective, la fiction est ainsi devenue l'espace même où ces interrogations se formulent, le lieu où s'élabore ou se conteste une conscience commune de la 'francité.' " See http://www.revue-critique-de-fixxion-francaise -contemporaine.org/rcffc/announcement/view/74.

35. See Elisabeth Philippe, "La Critique littéraire est-elle en voie de 'zemmourisa-tion'?," *BibliObs*, October 16, 2018, https://bibliobs.nouvelobs.com/idees/20181015.OBS3953/la-critique-litteraire-est-elle-en-voie-de-zemmourisation.html.

36. See Alexandre Gefen, Oana Panaïté, and Cornelia Ruhe, "Savoir lire: Un droit de réponse," *Diakritik*, October 16, 2018, https://diacritik.com/2018/10/16/savoir-lire-un-droit-de-reponse/.

37. Martin Crowley has written elegantly on the synecdochic relationship between Houellebecq and France: "It is particularly appropriate that Houellebecq's perti-nence should be considered through the figure of the synecdoche (whether posi-tive or negative): for the relation between a given social context and its more or less realist or naturalist representation—such as we find in Houellebecq's novels—is necessarily synecdochic. By definition smaller than its context, a work stakes its claim to realism by purporting to offer a credible sample, a selection of details which may reliably be scaled up to produce an accurate account of the wider world they imply." Martin Crowley, "Houellebecq's France," *Australian Journal of French Studies* 56, no. 1 (2019): 25.

38. "Pendant de trop longues années, le déclinisme et la tentation du repli, la pusil-lanimité et la xénophobie ont dominé le paysage médiatique et culturel français. Comme si le pays de Voltaire et de Montaigne, de Gary et de Hugo, de La Boétie et de Zola s'était résigné à n'être que la maison de Maurras et de Maistre, Barrès et Drieu. Comme si la nation qui proclama un jour que tous les hommes naissaient libres et égaux avait cédé la place à une assemblée de copropriétaires égoïstes et égo-tistes. 'Droit-de-l'hommiste' est devenu une insulte sur les terres du 26 août 1789: voilà jusqu'où nous ont menés nos faiblesses et nos paresses." Raphaël Glucksmann, "Tout reste à écrire," *Le Nouveau Magazine Littéraire*, December 16, 2017, https://www.nouveau-magazine-litteraire.com/manifesto. Already in 2015, Glucksmann had published a book titled *Génération gueule de bois: Manuel de lutte contre les réacs* (Paris: Allary Éditions, 2015), in which he argues, "Face aux tentations islamistes et xénophobes, nous devons transformer nos sentiments vaguement humanistes, notre attachement fainéant à la liberté, nos paresseuses intuitions mondialistes en une vision, un project, une idéologie. Le reveil a sonné. Notre génération endormie par les fables de Wall Street ou Stanford sur la globalisation heureuse est sommée de descendre dans l'arène" (15–16).

39. See Agnès Poirier, "Is There No End to Books on the 'End of France'?," *Spectator*, April 21, 2018, https://www.spectator.co.uk/2018/04/is-there-no-end-to-books-on-the-end-of-france/. Poirier's article responds specifically to the publication of Schlomo Sand's book *The End of the French Intellectual: From Zola to Houellebecq* (London: Verso, 2018), but a few other pertinent titles on French *déclinisme* include Nicolas Bavarez's *La France qui tombe* (Paris: Perrin, 2003); Alain Duhamel's *Le Désarroi français* (Paris: Plon, 2003); Jean-Marie Rouart's *Adieu à la France qui s'en va* (Paris: Grasset, 2003); Marc Bélit's *Le Malaise de la culture: Essai sur la crise du modèle culturel français* (Biarritz: Séguier, 2006); Tony Chafer and Emmanuel Godin's edited volume *The End of the French Exception? Decline and Revival of the "French Model"* (New York: Palgrave Macmillan, 2010); Robert Frank's *La Han-tise du déclin: la France de 1914 à 2014* (Paris: Belin, 2014); and Nicolas Truong's edited volume *Le Crépuscule des intellectuels français?* (La Tour d'Aigues: Éditions

de l'aube, 2016). In chapter 1, I write extensively about the notion of national suicide, a term that has had a strong resonance in the France of the new millennium.

40. See Pablo Servigne and Raphaël Stevens, *Comment tout peut s'effondrer: Petit manuel de collapsologie à l'usage des générations présentes* (Paris: Seuil, 2015).

41. While the book's main focus is the inheritance from nineteenth-century psychiatry, Hochmann argues that a biblical logic also guided applications of many
theories of degeneration: "La théorie de la dégénerescence, fil conducteur de
notre recherche sur la pensée réactionnaire, ne surgit pas de nulle part. Elle
succède à la réactualisation, au lendemain de la Révolution, par des penseurs
catholiques intégristes, ennemis des Lumières, du dogme du péché originel, lui-
même issu, à l'aube du christianisme, de la transformation de la transgression
morale d'un interdit en une souillure héréditaire de la chair." Jacques Hochmann,
*Théories de la dégénerescence: D'un mythe psychiatrique au déclinisme contempo-
rain* (Paris: Odile Jacob, 2018), 17; italics in original.

42. Mark Lilla makes the following distinction between conservatives and reactionaries: "Conservatives have always seen society as a kind of inheritance we receive
and are responsible for; we have obligations toward those who came before and to
those who will come after, and these obligations take priority over our rights. Conservatives have also been inclined to assume … that this inheritance is best
passed on implicitly through slow changes in custom and tradition, not through
explicit political action." In contrast, he describes two types of reactionary, the
"restorative reactionary," who "dreams of a return to some real or imaginary state
of perfection that existed before a revolution," and the "redemptive reactionary,"
who "take[s] for granted that the revolution is a fait accompli and that there is no
going back." This type "believe[s] that the only sane response to an apocalypse is
to provoke another, in hopes of starting over." Mark Lilla, "Republicans for Revolution," *New York Review of Books*, January 12, 2012, https://www.nybooks.com
/articles/2012/01/12/republicans-revolution/.

43. In one bullet point of its 2017 platform, the Front national used the trope of a return
to reality in its appeal for the elimination of affirmative action: "Rétablir l'égalité
réelle et la méritocratie en refusant le principe de 'discrimination positive.'" See
https://www.rassemblementnational.fr/pdf/144-engagements.pdf.

44. Mark Lilla, "Our Reactionary Age," *New York Times*, November 6, 2016, https://
www.nytimes.com/2016/11/07/opinion/our-reactionary-age.html.

45. On the debate between Maurice Barrès and André Gide on cultural rootedness
in a homeland, see the section "Talk of Roots in the Air: *La querelle du peuplier*,"
in Christy Wampole, *Rootedness: The Ramifications of a Metaphor* (Chicago: University of Chicago Press, 2016).

46. For a concise modern history of French conservatism, see Kevin Passmore, *The
Right in France from the Third Republic to Vichy* (Oxford: Oxford University Press,
2013).

47. On their website, the Manif pour tous organizers express their support for a return
to reality regarding sex and sex difference: "La Manif Pour Tous défend le mariage et la filiation en cohérence avec *la réalité sexuée de l'humanité*, dont la con-
séquence est à la fois la différence et la complémentarité des sexes, incontournable
pour concevoir un enfant et assumer la différence père-mère, paternité-maternité."

See https://www.lamanifpourtous.fr/qui-sommes-nous/notre-message/. My emphasis added.

48. See Étienne Achille, "Fiction 'néo-réactionnaire' avec Richard Millet," *Modern and Contemporary France* 26, no. 4 (2018): 370–79.

49. See Nicholas Hewitt, *Literature and the Right in Postwar France* (Oxford: Berg, 1996).

50. Michel Houellebecq and Bernard-Henry Lévy, *Public Enemies*, trans. Miriam Frendo and Frank Wynne (New York: Random House, 2011), 111. For more on Houellebecq and reactionary thought, see Wendy Michallat, "Modern Life Is Still Rubbish: Houellebecq and the Refiguring of 'Reactionary' Retro," *Journal of European Studies* 37, no. 3 (2007): 313–31.

51. To the list of literary reactionaries, the editors of the volume *Le Discours "néo-réactionnaire": Transgressions conservatrices* add Maurice G. Dantec, Marc-Édouard Nabe, Denis Tillinac, Éric Neuhoff, and Patrick Besson. See Pascal Durand and Sarah Sindaco, eds., *Le Discours "néo-réactionnaire": Transgressions conservatrices* (Paris: CNRS Éditions, 2015), 15.

52. Sapiro writes, "La vision apocalyptique de la fin du monde—c'est-à-dire la fin d'un ordre social hiérarchisé, dans lequel leurs capitaux d'hommes blancs cultivés avaient encore une valeur symbolique distinctive, et où ils incarnaient 'l'identité française'—revêt en effet des formes spécifiques à chacun de ces pôles: à la politisation de l'esthétique qui caractérise le discours critique des 'polémistes' répond l'esthétisation du politique au pôle 'esthète.'" Gisèle Sapiro, "Notables, esthètes et polémistes: manières d'être un écrivain 'réactionnaire' des années 30 à nos jours," in *Le Discours "néo-réactionnaire": Transgressions conservatrices*, ed. Pascal Durand and Sarah Sindaco (Paris: CNRS Éditions, 2015), 46.

53. Daniel Lindenberg's controversial book *Le Rappel à l'ordre: Enquête sur les nouveaux réactionnaires* (Paris: Seuil, 2002) attached the label to several public intellectuals who vehemently rejected Lindenberg's characterizations of their thought, such as Pierre-André Taguieff, who wrote a response titled *Les Contre-Réactionnaires: Le progressisme entre illusion et imposture* (Paris: Denoël, 2007), in which he accuses the Left of a "discours vigilantiel" (84), a form of speech policing. Others wear the label of reactionary with pride. See, for example, Denis Tillinac, *Du bonheur d'être réac* (Sainte-Marguerite-sur-Mer: Équateurs, 2014).

54. See Étienne Achille, "En marge du discours 'néo-réactionnaire': Le rap identitaire," *French Cultural Studies* 29, no. 3 (2018): 218–27.

55. Experts on the *fachosphère* argue that a sharp discrepancy exists between "real life" and the coexisting world of far-right online communities, where participants— often young men—who are "honteux ou solitaires dans la 'vraie vie' . . . se découvrent membres d'une grande communauté d'idées." Dominique Albertini and David Doucet, *La Fachosphère: Comment l'extrême droite remporte la bataille du net* (Paris: Flammarion, 2016), 51.

56. Harold Bernat, *Vieux réac! Faut-il s'adapter à tout?* (Paris: Flammarion, 2012), 21.

57. Among the most common are: "critique de Mai 68 et notamment de la libération des mœurs et d'un féminisme institué en dogme; critique de l'égalitarisme démocratique et des phénomènes de nivellement, de massification et de relativisme culturel qu'il induirait; critique du 'droit-de-l'hommisme' et du primat

accordé aux minorités; critique de la société 'métissée' et de l'"antiracisme institu-tionnel,' etc." Durand and Sindaco, *Discours*, 13.

58. Durand and Sindaco, *Discours*, 13.

59. Cruickshank, *Fin de millénaire French Fiction*, 43.

60. Mona Chollet posed the question in 2011: "Twitter est-il un réseau social permet-tant d'échanger avec ses amis, comme Facebook, ou plutôt une agence de presse où chacun a la possibilité d'être à la fois émetteur et récepteur?" Mona Chollet, "Twitter jusqu'au vertige," *Le Monde Diplomatique*, October 2011, https://www .monde-diplomatique.fr/2011/10/CHOLLET/21103.

61. Chollet, "Twitter." "La twittosphère brasse un mélange inédit d'information, de bavardage et de commentaire, activités autrefois bien distinctes, ce qui suscite sou-vent la méfiance et le mépris de ceux qui n'en sont pas familiers. . . . Mystifications et fausses rumeurs sont en effet rapidement identifiées: le tâtonnement et le travail de vérification des données, qu'autrefois seuls les journalistes se coltinaient, reposent désormais sur tous les internautes, et se déroulent au grand jour" (translated by SE).

62. The narrator in Patrik Ourednik's *La Fin du monde n'aurait pas eu lieu* (Paris: Édi-tions Allia, 2017) explains: "Dans le monde devenu global, les blagues impliquant la race, l'ethnie, la nationalité, la condition sociale, l'aspect physique ou l'orientation sexuelle ont été considérées comme désobligeantes et blessantes. Pour promou-voir une société harmonieuse, les interdits se sont multipliés; pour éviter toute stig-matisation, il a fallu ne pas heurter la sensibilité des autres; pour ne pas heurter la sensibilité des autres, on a inventé le *politiquement correct*" (102).

63. "La société française est en proie à un pessimisme, à un malaise, à une juxtaposi-tion impressionnante d'appréhensions si souvent irrationnelles et démesurées qu'elles en présentent les caractéristiques d'une dépression collective." Alain Duhamel, *Les Peurs françaises* (Paris: Flammarion, 1993), 12.

64. A few of these controversies include Houellebecq's statement that Islam is the stu-pidest religion, Yann Moix's declaration that he could never be attracted to a woman his own age, and Richard Millet's praise of Anders Breivik's murder of seventy-seven people in July 2011 as perfect in form.

65. Erich Auerbach, *Mimesis: The Presentation of Reality in Western Literature*, trans. Willard R. Trask (Princeton, NJ: Princeton University Press, 2003), 491.

66. Champfleury, paraphrased in Bernard Weinberg, *French Realism: The Critical Reaction, 1830–1870* (Oxford: Oxford University Press, 1937), 121.

67. Marie Scarpa describes naturalism as "une intensification d'un premier réalisme," in which the artist or writer's intuition is replaced by "les procédures du savant," such as new observational techniques, photography, and experimental methods. Daniel Fabre and Marie Scarpa, *Le Moment réaliste: Un tournant de l'ethnologie* (Nancy: Presses universitaires de Nancy, 2017), 12. Yves Chevrel has noted the ten-dency to consider naturalism as "un point extrême du réalisme, donc comme un hyper-réalisme." Yves Chevrel, *Le Naturalisme* (Paris: Presses universitaires de France, 1982), 13.

68. Guy de Maupassant, *Pierre et Jean*, trans. Julie Mead (Oxford: Oxford University Press, 2001), 14.

69. Honoré de Balzac, *Honoré de Balzac in Twenty-Five Volumes*, 25 vols. (New York: Peter Fenelon Collier, 1900), 1:15.

70. Victor Hugo, *Les Misérables*, trans. William Walton (New York: George H. Richmond & Co., 1893), n.p.

71. Edmond de Goncourt and Jules de Goncourt, *Germinie Lacerteux*, trans. Leonard Tancock (Middlesex: Penguin, 1984), 15.

72. Émile Zola, *The Fortune of the Rougons*, trans. Brian Nelson (Oxford: Oxford University Press, 2012), 3.

73. George J. Becker, *Realism in Modern Literature* (New York: Frederick Ungar, 1980), 16.

74. Henry Thurston Peck, *Studies in Several Literatures* (Freeport, NY: Books for Libraries Press, 1968), 205.

75. Luc Herman, *Concepts of Realism* (Columbia, SC: Camden House, 1996), 14.

76. Matthieu Baumier, "Penser la modernité post-démocratique," *Controverses* 5 (June 2007): 141; italics in the original. Also see Matthieu Baumier, *La Démocratie totalitaire: Penser la modernité post-démocratique* (Paris: Presses de la Renaissance, 2007).

77. Devin Fore, *Realism After Modernism: The Rehumanization of Art and Literature* (Cambridge, MA: MIT Press, 2012), 11.

78. Fredric Jameson, *The Antinomies of Realism* (London: Verso, 2015), 11.

79. Jean-Louis Hippolyte, *Fuzzy Fiction* (Lincoln: University of Nebraska Press, 2006), 7.

80. D. S. Likhachev, *The Poetics of Early Russian Literature*, trans. Christopher M. Arden-Close (Plymouth: Lexington, 2014), 150.

81. ". . . le réel est fragmenté, irrécupérable par les systèmes globaux d'explication (capitalisme, marxisme, etc.—les 'grands récits' de Lyotard), composé à la fois de données observables et mesurables et de courants de sensibilité innombrables et incommensurables; c'est un mixte de faits et de rumeurs, de culture légitime et de sous-cultures, de représentations et d'affects, de savoirs techniques et de croyances, d'information continue et de désinformation galopante, etc." Dion, *Des Fictions sans fiction*, 17; my translation.

82. Hal Foster, *The Return of the Real: The Avant-Garde at the End of the Century* (Cambridge, MA: MIT Press, 1996), 132. Also see Hal Foster, "Real Fictions: Alternatives to Alternative Facts," *Artforum International* 55, no. 8 (April 2017), https://www.artforum.com/print/201704/real-fictions-alternatives-to-alternative-facts-67192.

83. In their edited volume *Le Roman français contemporain face à l'Histoire* (Macerata: Quodlibet, 2016), the editors Gianfranco Rubino and Dominique Viart and contributors highlight the ways in which historical events such as the Terror, the Commune, the Grande Guerre, the Second World War, the Franco-Algerian War, May '68, and other events *do* leave their traumatic residue on contemporary fiction.

84. Marc Augé, *No Fixed Abode: Ethnofiction*, trans. Chris Turner (London: Seagull, 2013), vii. In his 1997 book *The War of Dreams: Exercises in Ethno-Fiction*, trans. Liz Heron (London: Pluto, 1999), he offers a slightly different definition. Ethno-fiction is, "on the one hand, an attempt to analyse the status of fiction or the conditions of its emergence in a society or at a specific historical point; on the other hand, an attempt to analyze the different fictional genres, their connection with the forms of the individual or collective imagination, with representations of death, etc., in different societies and at different conjunctures" (118).

85. Nelly Kprièlan, "*Sérotonine* de Michel Houellebecq, premières impressions avant la suite . . . ," *Les Inrockuptibles*, December 15, 2018, https://www.lesinrocks.com /2018/12/15/livres/serotonine-de-michel-houellebecq-premieres-impressions-avant-la -suite-111152153/.

86. See, for example, Lauren Provost, "Dans *Sérotonine* de Michel Houellebecq, voici ce qu'il y a de 'gilets jaunes,'" *Huffington Post*, January 3, 2019, https://www .huffingtonpost.fr/2019/01/03/dans-serotonine-de-michel-houellebecq-voici-ce -quil-y-a-de-gilets-jaunes_a_23632459/; Alexandre Devecchio, "*Sérotonine* de Houellebecq, un roman qui fait écho à la France des 'gilets jaunes'?," *Le Figaro*, December 27, 2018, http://www.lefigaro.fr/vox/culture/2018/12/27/31006-20181227 ARTFIG00008--serotonine-de-houellebecq-un-roman-qui-fait-echo-a-la-france -des-gilets-jaunes.php; and Geoffrey Lejeune, "Nous avons lu *Sérotonine*, le nou-veau roman de Houellebecq sur la France des gilets jaunes," *Valeurs Actuelles*, December 27, 2018, https://www.valeursactuelles.com/culture/nous-avons-lu -serotonine-le-nouveau-roman-de-houellebecq-sur-la-france-des-gilets-jaunes -102110.

87. The singer Pierre Perret, a supporter of the *gilets jaunes*, argued in a radio inter-view that "les dirigeants du pays sont déconnectés de la réalité." Pierre Perret, "Interview," *Le Progrès*, November 16, 2018, https://www.leprogres.fr/france-monde /2018/11/16/pierre-perret-je-soutiens-les-gilets-jaunes-il-y-a-un-ras-le-bol-general. In response to Macron's speech regarding the *gilets jaunes*, the spokesperson of the Républicains, Laurence Sailliet, argued on Twitter that Macron "a récité un texte sans émotion, sans conviction et si loin de la réalité des Français." Twitter, @ lsailliet, December 31, 2018, https://twitter.com/lsailliet/status/10798241218176 94208.

88. One finds yet another example in the discourses surrounding Islamophobia in con-temporary France. As the cover of Thomas Guénolé's book *Islamopsychose: Pour-quoi la France diabolise les musulmans* (Paris: Fayard, 2017) argues, "Entre haine et paranoïa, la société française se fait de sa minorité musulmane et de l'islam fran-çais une représentation collective délirante, c'est-à-dire *déconnectée de la réalité*" (n.p.; my emphasis).

89. See Gianni Vattimo, *Of Reality: The Purposes of Philosophy* (New York: Columbia University Press, 2016); Alain Badiou, *À la recherche du réel perdu* (Paris: Fayard, 2015); Jean-François Kahn, *Philosophie de la réalité: Critique du réalisme* (Paris: Fayard, 2011).

90. Mark Fisher defines capitalist realism as "the widespread sense that not only is capitalism the only viable political and economic system, but also that it is now impossible even to *imagine* a coherent alternative to it." Mark Fisher, *Capitalist Realism: Is There No Alternative?* (Winchester: Zero, 2010), 2. Also see Alison Shonkwiler and Leigh Claire La Berge, eds., *Reading Capitalist Realism* (Iowa City: University of Iowa Press, 2014); and Alison Shonkwiler, *The Financial Imaginary: Economic Mystification and the Limits of Realist Fiction* (Minneapolis: University of Minnesota Press, 2018). On the financialization of contemporary French litera-ture, see Aurore Labadie, *Le Roman d'entreprise français au tournant du XXIe siè-cle* (Paris: Presses Sorbonne Nouvelle, 2016).

91. See Graham Harman, *Speculative Realism: An Introduction* (Cambridge: Polity, 2018); Peter Gratton, *Speculative Realism: Problems and Prospects* (London:

Bloomsbury, 2014); and Quentin Meillassoux, *Après la finitude: Essai sur la nécessité de la contingence* (Paris: Seuil, 2006).

92. See Colin Marshall, *Compassionate Moral Realism* (Oxford: Oxford University Press, 2018).

93. See Tonio Kröner et al., eds., *Post-Apocalyptic Realism* (Cologne: Walther König, 2018).

94. Stéphane Bikialo and Julien Rault, *Au nom du réalisme: Usage(s) politique(s) d'un mot d'ordre* (Paris: Éditions Utopia, 2018), 11.

95. Jean-François Kahn, "Le réalisme est un pétainisme," *BibliObs*, January 7, 2011, https://bibliobs.nouvelobs.com/essais/20110531.OBS4250/jean-francois-kahn-le -realisme-est-un-petainisme.html.

96. Signaling the renewed relevance of this book, a new German commented edition by Karin Tebben was released in 2013. See Max Nordau, *Entartung* (Berlin: De Gruyter, 2013).

## 1. DEMOGRAPHY AND SURVIVAL IN TWENTY-FIRST-CENTURY FRANCE

1. Frédéric Beigbeder, *Holiday in a Coma* and *Love Lasts Three Years: Two Novels*, trans. Frank Wynne (London: Fourth Estate, 2007), 178.

2. Hippolyte Taine, *History of English Literature*, trans. H. van Laun (New York: Holt & Williams, 1871), 1:19.

3. Edmond de Goncourt and Jules de Goncourt, *Germinie Lacerteux*, trans. Leonard Tancock (Middlesex: Penguin, 1984), 15.

4. In 2009, referring to recent developments in the Anglo-American novel, Marco Roth wrote, "What has been variously referred to as the novel of consciousness or the psychological or confessional novel—the novel, at any rate, about the workings of the mind—has transformed itself into the neurological novel, wherein the mind becomes the brain." Marco Roth, "The Rise of the Neuronovel," *N+1*, Fall 2009, https://nplusonemag.com/issue-8/essays/the-rise-of-the-neuronovel/. Also see Natalie Roxburgh, Anton Kirchhofer, and Anna Auguscik, "Universal Narrativity and the Anxious Scientist of the Contemporary Neuronovel," *Mosaic* 49, no. 4 (December 2016): 71–87; Stephen J. Burn, "Neuroscience and Modern Fiction," *Modern Fiction Studies* 61, no. 2 (Summer 2015): 209–25; Frank Kelleter, "A Tale of Two Natures: Worried Reflections on the Study of Literature and Culture in an Age of Neuroscience and Neo-Darwinism," *Journal of Literary Theory* 1, no. 1 (2007): 153–89. Also see the special issue on neuroscience and fiction in *Substance* 45, no. 2 (2016).

5. In Aurélien Bellanger's novel *La Théorie de l'information*, the narrator claims, "Postmodernism was...a secular millenarianism, coupled with a reactionary progressionism," constituted by "an unbridled desire for historical recapitulation." Aurélien Bellanger, *La Théorie de l'information* (Paris: Gallimard, 2012), 196–97.

6. "Although secularized, the Enlightenment narrative, Romanticist or speculative dialectics, and the Marxist narrative deploy the same historicity as Christianity, because they conserve the eschatological principle." Jean-François Lyotard,

*Postmodern Fables*, trans. Georges Van Den Abbeele (Minneapolis: University of Minnesota Press, 1997), 97.

7. Hervé Le Bras, *The Nature of Demography* (Princeton, NJ: Princeton University Press, 2008), 345.

8. For more on demographic projections in literature, see the chapter "The 'Arithmetic of Futurity': Poetry, Population, and the Structure of the Future" in Maureen N. McLane, *Romanticism and the Human Sciences: Poetry, Population, and the Discourse of the Species* (Cambridge: Cambridge University Press, 2000), 109–58.

9. James Wood, "Tell Me How Does It Feel?," *Guardian*, October 6, 2001, https://www.theguardian.com/books/2001/oct/06/fiction.

10. ". . . la statistique constate que la population en France n'augmente plus que dans des proportions sans cesse déclinantes, qui font prévoir le jour prochain où elle diminuera." Émile Zola, "Dépopulation," *Le Figaro* 144 (May 23, 1896): 1.

11. "*Fécondité*, c'est colossal, scandaleux, pitoyable, bête à pleurer, tout aussi encombrant et tout aussi respectueux que le ventre d'une femme à son neuvième mois." Rachilde, "Les Romans. Émile Zola, *Fécondité*," *Le Mercure de France* 119 (November 1899): 485–86. My translation.

12. Michael Mack, *Philosophy and Literature in Times of Crisis: Challenging Our Infatuation with Numbers* (New York: Bloomsbury, 2014), 206.

13. Le Bras, *The Nature of Demography*, 349.

14. On this question, see Maxime Cervulle, "The Uses of Universalism: 'Diversity Statistics' and the Race Issue in Contemporary France," *European Journal of Cultural Studies* 17, no. 2 (2014): 118–33.

15. In his book *Éléments de statistique humaine, ou démographie comparée* (1855), Guillard defines demography, which he also calls "la statistique humaine," "populationistique," and even "science économique" this way: "C'est, dans son sens plus étendu, l'histoire naturelle et sociale de l'espèce humaine. Dans le sens restreint où nous devons la prendre ici, c'est la connaissance mathématique des populations, de leurs mouvements généraux, de leur état physique, civil, intellectuel et moral." Achille Guillard, *Éléments de statistique humaine, ou démographie comparée* (Paris: Guillaumin, 1855), xxvi. He closes his book, writing, "La Démographie est la connaissance, donnée par l'observation, des lois suivant lesquelles les Populations se forment, s'entretiennent, se renouvellent et se succèdent" (367).

16. In his book *Le Problème de la population en France* (1929), Léon Rabinowicz wrote, "Après avoir pris naissance aux sources de la vie économique des peuples primitifs comme une simple et instinctive politique de la population, transformée ensuite en science véritable, bien qu'annexe de l'économie politique, elle s'est débarrassée ensuite de cette enveloppe économique et est devenue une science autonome, celle de la démographie. Elle doit entrer maintenant dans sa quatrième phase, que nous appellerons celle de la Sociologie de la Population." Léon Rabinowicz, *Le Problème de la population en France* (Paris: Marcel Rivière, 1929), 33. For a compressed history of demography, see Hervé Le Bras, *Naissance de la mortalité: L'origine politique de la statistique et de la démographie* (Paris: Hautes Études, 2000).

17. Jay Weinstein and Vijayan K. Pillai, *Demography: The Science of Population*, 2nd ed. (Lanham, MD: Rowman & Littlefield, 2016), 5.

1. DEMOGRAPHY AND SURVIVAL IN TWENTY-FIRST-CENTURY FRANCE

18. Michel Vilette, who has noted the rhetorical and representational features of the social sciences and makes a connection between the *roman à thèse* and the sociological thesis, poses the question, "What is the status of the *récit* in social science texts?" He pursues the argument this way: "Considérez les descriptions empiriques (qu'elles soient chiffrées ou littéraires) comme des éléments ayant pour fonction la persuasion ou l'illustration pédagogique: la Sociologie devient aussitôt une branche de la rhétorique. L'art du sociologue est de faire advenir et de rendre crédible une représentation de la vie en société." Michel Vilette, "Thèses de sociologie et romans à thèse," *Sociedade e Estado* 17, no. 2 (2002): 542.
19. Le Bras, *The Nature of Demography*, 3.
20. Jennifer Hickes Lundquist, Douglas L. Anderton, and David Yaukey, *Demography: The Study of Human Population*, 4th ed. (Long Grove, IL: Waveland, 2015), 147.
21. See Andrew J. Counter, "Zola's *Fin-de-siècle* Reproductive Politics," *French Studies* 68, no. 2 (April 2014): 193–208; the subchapter "The Place of Statistics in Aesthetics: The Normal Idea," in Rüdiger Campe, *The Game of Probability: Literature and Calculation from Pascal to Kleist*, trans. Ellwood H. Wiggins Jr. (Stanford, CA: Stanford University Press, 2012), 346–51; Paul Fleming, *Exemplarity and Mediocrity: The Art of the Average from Bourgeois Tragedy to Realism* (Stanford, CA: Stanford University Press, 2009); Nancy Armstrong and Leonard Tennenhouse, "The Problem of Population and the Form of the American Novel," *American Literary History* 20, no. 4 (Winter 2008): 667–85; *Birth and Death in Nineteenth-Century French Culture*, ed. Nigel Harkness et al. (Amsterdam: Rodopi, 2007); and Brian P. Cooper, *Family Fictions and Family Facts: Harriet Martineau, Adolphe Quetelet, and the Population Question in England, 1798–1859* (London: Routledge, 2007).
22. Adolphe Quetelet, *A Treatise on Man and the Development of His Faculties*, English trans. (Edinburgh: W. and R. Chambers, 1842), 96.
23. Marc Augé, *No Fixed Abode: Ethnofiction*, trans. Chris Turner (London: Seagull, 2013), viii.
24. Quetelet, *A Treatise on Man and the Development of His Faculties*, 97.
25. "Reactionary authors Maurice Barrès and Paul Bourget sought to capitalize on such anxieties in certain *romans à thèse* featuring rapacious social Darwinist protagonists, or *struggleforlifeurs*." Louise Lyle, "*Le Struggleforlife*: Contesting Balzac Through Darwin in Zola, Bourget, and Barrès," *Nineteenth-Century French Studies* 36, no. 3–4 (Spring/Summer 2008): 306.
26. Elaine Scarry, ed., *Literature and the Body: Essays on Populations and Persons* (Baltimore, MD: Johns Hopkins University Press, 1988), viii.
27. Anton Kuijsten, "Demografiction," in *The Joy of Demography . . . and Other Disciplines*, ed. Anton Kuijsten, Henk De Gans, and Henk de Feijter (Amsterdam: Thela Thesis, 1999), 86. For more on the topic of demodystopias, see Andreu Domingo, "'Demodystopias': Prospects of Demographic Hell," *Population and Development Review* 34, no. 4 (December 2008): 725–45.
28. Lionel Shriver, "Population in Literature," *Population and Development Review* 29, no. 2 (June 2013): 160.
29. Émile Zola, *The Fortune of the Rougons*, trans. Brian Nelson (Oxford: Oxford University Press, 2012), 3.
30. Jules Romains, *Men of Good Will*, trans. Warre B. Wells (New York: Knopf, 1933), x.
31. Frédéric Beigbeder, £9.99, trans. Adriana Hunter (London: Picador, 2002), 220.

32. Michel Houellebecq, *Submission*, trans. Loren Stein (New York: Picador, 2015), 29.
33. The quotes have been modernized and slightly tweaked for maximum effect. Here are the originals, in order of their appearance above. (1) "Je juge que la fin de la France n'est plus qu'une question d'années." Péladan, in Jules Huret, *Enquête sur l'évolution littéraire* (Paris: Charpentier, 1891), 41. (2) "L'étranger a pris une telle part dans la direction de nos affaires intérieures et extérieures, que si nous voulons nous rendre compte de notre situation et comprendre notre politique, c'est à l'étranger qu'il faut l'étudier." Émile Flourens, *La France conquise* (Paris: Garnier Frères, 1906), 1. (3) "Il me semble que la décadence française se distingue des autres décadences historiques en ceci, qu'elle se connaît parfaitement. . . . Jamais peuple malheureux n'a été plus conscient de ses maux." Jules Lemaître, *Opinions à répandre*, 4th ed. (Paris: Société française d'imprimerie et de librairie, 1901), 10–11. (4) "La France s'effondrera sous les coups répétés de l'invasion étrangère. . . . La France n'est plus qu'un cadavre. . . . La décomposition du cadavre fait tous les jours des progrès effrayants. . . . On pourrait . . . calculer mathématiquement le jour où il n'y aura plus un seul Français en France." Jean Du Valdor, *Les Signes de la fin d'un monde*, 2nd ed. (Saint Amand: Société anonyme de l'imprimerie Saint-Joseph, 1893), 277, 299. (5) "Nous n'en sommes pas moins le pays le plus mal gouverné—ou l'un des plus mal gouvernés, pour n'humilier personne—qu'on puisse voir dans le monde." Jules Roche, "La Révision de la constitution," *Figaro* 162 (June 11, 1897): 1. (6) "Cette nation glorieuse et privilégiée a vraiment trop oublié qu'elle avait le devoir de se secourir elle-même et vous savez quelles effroyables catastrophes ont été le salaire de sa présomption." Léon Bloy, *Les Funérailles du naturalisme* (Paris: Les Belles Lettres, 2001), 5.
34. Counter, "Zola's *Fin-de-siècle* Reproductive Politics," 193.
35. Éric Zemmour, *Le Suicide français* (Paris: Albin Michel, 2014), 9. The following quotes are my translations.
36. Renaud Camus, *France: Suicide d'une nation* (Paris: Éditions Mordicus, 2014), 11.
37. Richard Millet, *L'Opprobre* (Paris: Gallimard, 2008), 131.
38. Marine Le Pen, cited in Cécile Alduy and Stéphane Wahnich, *Marine Le Pen prise aux mots: Décryptage du nouveau discours frontiste* (Paris: Seuil, 2015), 69.
39. Pascal Bruckner, *The Tyranny of Guilt: An Essay on Western Masochism*, trans. Steven Rendall (Princeton, NJ: Princeton University Press, 2010), 168.
40. Alain Finkielkraut, in Alain Badiou and Alain Finkielkraut, *Confrontation*, trans. Susan Spitzer (Cambridge: Polity, 2014), 2.
41. In *The Decline of the West*, Oswald Spengler describes the soul of Western culture as Faustian (in contrast to the Apollonian—the cultures of Mediterranean antiquity—and the Magian—Jews, Christians, Muslims, and their Semitic and Persian forebears) and argues that the West has reached its terminal phase: Civilization. "The Civilization is the inevitable *destiny* of the Culture. . . . Civilizations are the most external and artificial states of which a species of developed humanity is capable. They are a conclusion, the thing-become succeeding the thing-becoming, death following life, rigidity following expansion, intellectual age and the stone-built, petrifying world-city following mother-earth and the spiritual childhood of Doric and Gothic. They are an end, irrevocable, yet by inward necessity reached again and again." Oswald Spengler, *The Decline of The West*, 2 vols., trans. Charles Francis Atkinson (New York: Knopf, 1950), 1:31.

42. E. M. Cioran, *A Short History of Decay*, trans. Richard Howard (New York: Arcade, 2012), 116–17.

43. Emmanuel Berl, *La France irréelle* (Paris: Grasset, 1957), 11.

44. Berl, *La France irréelle*, back cover.

45. In his book *Sauve qui peut!*, Éric Brunet employs the usual degenerative or medical metaphors for describing France's decay: "La France s'est encroûtée." Éric Brunet, *Sauve qui peut!* (Paris: Albin Michel, 2013), 10; "C'est une pathologie. Un cancer national qui nous consume lentement mais sûrement" (11); and "La littérature française, longtemps considérée comme la plus riche du monde est atteinte du même syndrome avec le triomphe des romans intimistes et égocentrés . . ." (279).

46. Douglas Morrey, "The Banality of Monstrosity: On Michel Houellebecq's *Soumission*," *Australian Journal of French Studies* 55, no. 2 (2018): 207. Morrey also notes the demographic paranoia omnipresent in the novel: "In Houellebecq's quasi-scientific language, this cultural pessimism is given a demographic framing: once neo-liberalism has undermined the social and moral authority of the family, its days are demographically numbered" (215).

47. Carole Sweeney, *Michel Houellebecq and the Literature of Despair* (London: Bloomsbury, 2013), 164.

48. Galanopoulos argues that science played a central role in "la rationalisation des sentiments de méfiance, de rejet, voire de répulsion, exprimés à l'égard des étrangers." Philippe Galanopoulos, "L'Étranger: Une figure de la décadence? Les discours scientifiques et politiques sur les races, en France, dans la seconde moitié du XIXe siècle," in *La Décadence dans la culture et la pensée politique. Espagne, France et Italie (XVIIIe–XXe siècle)*, ed. Jean-Yves Frétigné and François Jankowiak (Rome: École française de Rome, 2008), 322.

49. See William Oualid, "La France deviendra-t-elle un pays de minorités nationales?," *Le Musée Social* 5–6 (1927): 160–84.

50. Ernest Renan, *What Is a Nation?*, trans. Wanda Romer Taylor (Toronto: Tapir, 1996), 49.

51. Michel Winock, *Décadence fin de siècle* (Paris: Gallimard, 2017), 7. "Le déclin est toujours déclin de quelque chose, d'une production, d'un taux de fécondité, d'une pratique religieuse. La décadence, qui au demeurant peut intégrer des signes de déclin, est avant tout une idée vague, une représentation pessimiste du monde, une nostalgie de ce qui n'est plus, une création de l'imaginaire maussade, alarmiste ou carrément désespéré." Translated by SE.

52. De Gobineau called his research a form of "géologie morale" that sought to excavate the deep history of "des races, des sociétés et des civilisations diverses" instead of that of nation-states. Arthur de Gobineau, *Essai sur l'inégalité des races humaines*, 2nd ed. (Paris: Firmin-Didot, 1884), 1:viii.

53. For comprehensive nineteenth- and twentieth-century histories of the notions of degeneration and decadence, see Vincent Sherry, *Modernism and the Reinvention of Decadence* (Cambridge: Cambridge University Press, 2015); Matthew Potolsky, *The Decadent Republic of Letters: Taste, Politics, and Cosmopolitan Community from Baudelaire to Beardsley* (Philadelphia: University of Pennsylvania Press, 2013); Jean de Palacio, *La Décadence: Le mot et la chose* (Paris: Les Belles lettres, 2011); Charles Bernheimer, *Decadent Subjects* (Baltimore, MD: Johns Hopkins

University Press, 2002); William Greenslade, *Degeneration, Culture, and the Novel 1880–1940* (Cambridge: Cambridge University Press, 1994); Richard D. Walter, "What Became of the Degenerate? A Brief History of a Concept," *Journal of the History of Medicine and Allied Sciences* 11, no. 4 (1956): 422–29; Barbara Spackman, *Decadent Genealogies: The Rhetoric of Sickness from Baudelaire to D'Annunzio* (Ithaca, NY: Cornell University Press, 1989); Julien Freund, *La Décadence: Histoire sociologique et philosophique d'une catégorie de l'expérience humaine* (Paris: Éditions Sirey, 1984).

54. See Regenia Gagnier, "The Decadence of the West in Huysmans and Houellebecq: Decadence in the Longue Durée," *English Literature in Translation, 1880–1920* 60, no. 4 (2017): 419–30.

55. Max Nordau, *Degeneration* (Lincoln: University of Nebraska Press, 1993), 39.

56. In a footnote (2n2), Nordau notes he only intended to mean the "upper ten thousand," arguing, "The peasant population, and a part of the working classes and the *bourgeoisie* are sound. I assert only the decay of the rich inhabitants of great cities and the leading classes. It is they who have discovered *fin-de-siècle*, and it is to them also that *fin-de-race* applies."

57. Paul Bourget, *Essais de psychologie contemporaine* (Paris: Plon, 1901), 1:xvii.

58. See Alexandre Gefen, " 'La Muse est morte, ou la faveur pour elle': Brève histoire des discours sur la mort de la littérature," in *Fins de la littérature: Esthétiques et discours de la fin*, ed. Laurent Demanze and Dominique Viart, 1:37–49 (Paris: Armand Colin, 2011).

59. "C'est dans la langue surtout que s'en manifestent les premiers symptômes. . . . Nous ne nous occuperons de ce mouvement qu'au point de vue de la littérature." Anatole Baju, "Aux lecteurs!," *Le Décadent* 1 (April 10, 1886): 1.

60. "Le roman apparaît à nos yeux comme une véritable analogie de la démocratie, en ce sens qu'il fournit, dans ses fictions, ses modes narratifs et sa langue, un équivalent des expériences fondatrices de celle-ci." Nelly Wolf, *Le Roman de la démocratie* (Saint-Denis: Presses universitaires de Vincennes, 2003), 6.

61. See the special issue of *Canadian Review of Comparative Literature* 42, no. 4 (December 2015) on the topic of "Novel Beyond Nation"; the chapter "When Novels Made Nations," in Nancy Armstrong, *How Novels Think: The Limits of British Individualism from 1719–1900* (New York: Columbia University Press, 2005), 53–78; and Pericles Lewis, *Modernism, Nationalism, and the Novel* (Cambridge: Cambridge University Press, 2000).

62. Luigi Capuana, *Gli 'ismi' contemporanei* (Catania: Giannotta, 1898), 61.

63. For example, Millet writes, "Le roman ne va pas plus mal que la littérature n'est en crise: cette dernière est morte de la prolifération démocratique du premier, comme des métastases d'un cancer à l'estomac." *L'Opprobre*, 40. "Le roman postlittéraire est toujours déjà mort. Nous reniflons son cadavre, manions des membres décomposés, contemplons des fosses communes." Richard Millet, *L'Enfer du roman: Réflexions sur la postlittérature* (Paris: Gallimard, 2010), 187. "Le jeu de la langue et du territoire étant une autre définition de la littérature, on peut, de ce point de vue, dire aujourd'hui que la France est morte, vu qu'il n'y a plus nul écrivain pour en déployer le paysage ni en rendre sensible le filigrane historique." Richard Millet, *Désenchantement de la littérature* (Paris: Gallimard, 2007), 26.

64. See Counter, "Zola's *Fin-de-siècle* Reproductive Politics."

65. Rita Schober, "Vision du monde et théorie du roman, concepts opératoires des romans de Michel Houellebecq," in *Le Roman français au tournant du XXe siècle*, ed. Bruno Blanckeman, Aline Mura-Brunel, and Marc Dambre (Paris: Presses Sorbonne nouvelle, 2004), 511.

66. A few examples of this contemporary maximalism include Orengo's *La Fleur du Capital* (764 pages), Yann Moix's *Partouz* (Paris: Grasset, 2004; 402 pages) and his *Naissance* (1,143 pages), Alexis Jenni's *La Nuit de Walenhammes* (405 pages), and Maurice G. Dantec's *American Black Box* (690 pages). For more on the maximalist novel, see Stefano Ercolino, *The Maximalist Novel: From Thomas Pynchon's Gravity's Rainbow to Roberto Bolaño's 2666*, trans. Albert Sbragia (New York: Bloomsbury, 2014).

67. Henk De Gans, "Vision, Future, Forecaster: On Demons and Soothers in Long-Range Demographic Prediction," in *The Joy of Demography . . . and Other Disciplines*, ed. Anton Kuijsten, Henk De Gans, and Henk De Feijter (Amsterdam: Thela Thesis, 1999), 108.

68. The *New Yorker* has shown a marked interest in the French far right's discourses in decline, with recent articles such as Thomas Chatterton Williams, "The French Origins of 'You Will Not Replace Us,'" *New Yorker*, December 4, 2017, https://www .newyorker.com/magazine/2017/12/04/the-french-origins-of-you-will-not -replace-us; Adam Gopnik, "The Second Coming of the French Far-Right Tradition," *New Yorker*, March 31, 2017, https://www.newyorker.com/news/daily -comment/franco-american; and Elisabeth Zerofsky, "France's Frenzy Over the Discourse of Decline," *New Yorker*, December 17, 2014, https://www.newyorker .com/news/news-desk/frances-frenzy-discourse-decline-zemmour.

69. Zemmour, *Le Suicide français*, 9. Bernard Maris pokes fun at Zemmour's cynicism, writing that as he was reading Zemmour's *Le Suicide français*, Patrick Modiano and Jean Tirole won the Nobel Prize and Artur Avila, a Franco-Brazilian, won the Fields Medal in math after two other Frenchmen had won it. This led Maris to quip: "Pas mal, pour un pays de suicidés." Bernard Maris, *Et si on aimait la France* (Paris: Grasset, 2015), 34–35. The book in which this anecdote appears was left unfinished, as Maris was murdered in the Charlie Hebdo attacks while still writing it.

70. Bérénice Levet called for a reversal of this dynamic in the closing pages of her book *Le Crépuscule des idoles progressistes*: "Aux passions meurtrières de l'islam, opposons les passions fécondes qui ont fait la France et l'Occident." Bérénice Levet, *Le Crépuscule des idoles progressistes* (Paris: Stock, 2017), 262.

71. Millet, *Désenchantement*, 34–35.

72. Camus explains his use of the word "In-Nocence": "*l'in-nocence* n'est pas *l'innocence*, c'est la *non-nocence*, la *non nuisance*. . . . Elle tient dans ce nom et dans cet idéal: *ne pas nuire*—ni à la terre, ni au territoire, ni aux biens, ni aux personnes, aux concitoyens, aux voisins, aux compagnons de planète." Renaud Camus, *Le Grand Remplacement* (Paris: David Reinharc, 2011), 110.

73. For a concise summary of the various responses to Camus's theory, see Frédéric Joignot, "Le fantasme du 'grand remplacement' démographique," *Le Monde*, January 23, 2014, http://www.lemonde.fr/politique/article/2014/01/23/le-grand -boniment_4353499_823448.html. Also see Jean-Claude Chesnais, *Le Crépuscule de l'Occident: Démographie et politique* (Paris: Robert Laffont, 1995).

74. Camus, *Le Grand Remplacement*, 112.
75. Camus cites a declaration delivered by the Algerian president Houari Boumédiène to the United Nations in New York City on April 10, 1974: "Un jour, des millions d'hommes quitteront l'hémisphère sud pour aller dans l'hémisphère nord. Et ils n'iront pas là-bas en tant qu'amis. Parce qu'ils iront là-bas pour le conquérir. Et ils le conquerront en le peuplant avec leurs fils. C'est le ventre de nos femmes qui nous donnera la victoire." *Le Grand Remplacement*, 50.
76. For an analysis of Raspail's alarmism in *The Camp of the Saints*, trans. Norman Shapiro (Petoskey, MI: Social Contract Press, 2018), see Matthew Connelly and Paul Kennedy, "Must It Be the West Against the Rest?," *Atlantic Monthly* 274, no. 6 (December 1994): 61–84. In 2017, Raspail's book gained new attention when it was revealed to be a favorite book of Steve Bannon, Donald Trump's former chief strategist. For more on this controversy, see Paul Blumenthal and J. M. Rieger, "This Stunningly Racist French Novel Is How Steve Bannon Explains the World," *Huffington Post*, March 3, 2017, https://www.huffingtonpost.com/entry/steve-bannon -camp-of-the-saints-immigration_us_58b75206e4b0284854b3dc03; Ben Mathis-Lilley, "Bannon, Adviser Behind Travel Ban, Is Fan of Novel About Feces-Eating, Dark-Skinned Immigrants Destroying White Society," *Slate*, March 6, 2017, http://www.slate.com/blogs/the_slatest/2017/03/06/steve_bannon_and_the _camp_of_the_saints.html; Cécile Alduy, "What a 1973 French Novel Tells Us About Marine Le Pen, Steve Bannon, and the Rise of the Populist Right," *Politico*, April 23, 2017, http://www.politico.com/magazine/story/2017/04/23/what-a-1973 -french-novel-tells-us-about-marine-le-pen-steve-bannon-and-the-rise-of-the -populist-right-215064.
77. Frances Ferguson, "Malthus, Godwin, Wordsworth, and the Spirit of Solitude," in *Literature and the Body: Essays on Populations and Persons*, ed. Elaine Scarry (Baltimore, MD: Johns Hopkins University Press, 1988), 106.
78. Maurice Barrès titled his trilogy of late-nineteenth-century nativist novels *Le Roman de l'énergie nationale*. For more on the literal expenditure of national energy and its relation to new discoveries in thermodynamics, see Mason Tattersall, "Thermal Degeneration: Thermodynamics and the Heat-Death of the Universe in Victorian Science, Philosophy, and Culture," in *Decadence, Degeneration, and the End: Studies in the European* Fin de Siècle, ed. Marja Härmänmaa and Christopher Nissen (New York: Palgrave Macmillan, 2014).
79. Sébastian Roldan, "Victimes d'eux-mêmes ou de l'espèce? Darwin et les suicidés du roman naturaliste," in *Les voies de l'évolution: De la pertinence du darwinisme en littérature*, ed. Jean-François Chassay, Daniel Grenier, and William S. Messier (Montreal: Presses de l'Université de Québec, 2013), 75.
80. See François-Xavier Ajavon, "Michel Houellebecq et la notion de 'sélection sexuelle,'" *Le Philosophoire* 18 (2002–3): 167–73; Delphine Grass, "Domesticating Hierarchies, Eugenic Hygiene, and Exclusion Zones: The Dogs and Clones of Houellebecq's *La Possibilité d'une île*," *L'Esprit Créateur* 52, no. 2 (Summer 2012): 127–40; and Stephanie Posthumus, "Les Enjeux animaux (humains) chez Michel Houellebecq, du darwinisme au post-humanisme," *French Studies* 68, no. 3 (July 2014): 359–76.
81. See Vercors's *Les Animaux dénaturés* (Paris: Albin Michel, 1952); Pierre Boulle's *La Planète des singes* (Paris: Julliard, 1963); Douglas Morrey, "Natural and

Anti-natural Evolution: Genetics and Schizophrenia in Maurice G. Dantec's *Babylon Babies*," *L'Esprit Créateur* 52, no. 2 (Summer 2013): 114–26; and Philippe Clermont, *Darwinisme et littérature de science-fiction* (Paris: L'Harmattan, 2011). For nineteenth-century examples, see Laurence A. Gregorio, *Maupassant's Fiction and the Darwinian View of Life* (New York: Peter Lang, 2005).

82. See the chapter "Biological Poetics," in Greenslade, *Degeneration, Culture, and the Novel*, 32–46.

83. Bruno Viard, *Houellebecq au scanner: La faute à Mai 68* (Nice: Éditions Ovadia, 2008), 46.

84. Claude Pérez, "Houellebecq, le vingt-heures et l'art du roman: À propos de *Soumission*," *Revue Critique de Fixxion Française Contemporaine* 11 (2015): 114.

85. "Economic liberalism is an extension of the domain of the struggle, its extension to all ages and all classes of society. Sexual liberalism is likewise an extension of the domain of the struggle, its extension to all ages and all clases of society." Michel Houellebecq, *Whatever*, trans. Paul Hammond (London: Serpent's Tail, 1998), 99. For more on the treatment of economy in Houellebecq, see Bernard Maris, *Houellebecq économiste* (Paris: Flammarion, 2014).

86. "As a wealthy European, I could obtain food and the services of women more cheaply in other countries; as a decadent European, conscious of my approaching death, I could see no reason to deprive myself of such things. I was aware, however, that such a situation was barely tenable, that people like me were incapable of ensuring the survival of society, perhaps more simply we were unworthy of life." Michel Houellebecq, *Platform*, trans. Frank Wynne (London: Heinemann, 2002), 299.

87. For more on Pascal Bruckner's influence on Houellebecq, see Alain-Philippe Durand, "Pascal Bruckner et Michel Houellebecq: Deux transécrivains au milieu du monde," in *Michel Houellebecq sous la loupe*, ed. Murielle Lucie Clément and Sabine van Wesemael (Amsterdam: Rodopi, 2007), 157–67.

88. Pérez, "Houellebecq," 112.

89. Pierre Jourde, *La Littérature sans estomac* (Paris: L'Esprit des péninsules, 2002), 234.

90. Svend Brinkmann, "Literature as Qualitative Inquiry: The Novelist as Researcher," *Qualitative Inquiry* 15, no. 8 (2009): 1378.

91. To define "sociologie-fiction," Mezioz explains: "Je propose ce néologisme sur le modèle de 'science-fiction': mise en scène de théories sociologiques prospectives (pastichées à divers degrés) pour comprendre un présent ou anticiper un futur." Jérôme Meizoz, "Le roman et l'inacceptable: Sociologie d'une polémique: Autour de *Plateforme* de Michel Houellebecq," in *L'œil sociologue et la littérature* (Geneva: Slatkine Érudition, 2004), 131n15.

92. For an excellent analysis of the relationship between mid-nineteenth-century sociological surveys and realist literature, see Judith Lyon-Caen, "Enquêtes, littérature et savoir sur le monde social en France dans les année 1840," in *Le Moment réaliste: Un tournant de l'ethnologie*, ed. Daniel Fabre and Marie Scarpa (Nancy: Presses universitaires de Nancy, 2017). For more on the connection between sociology and contemporary French novel, see Philippe Baudorre et al., eds., *Littérature et sociologie* (Bordeaux: Presses universitaires de Bordeaux, 2007); the special issue titled "Le roman parle du monde: Lectures sociocritiques et

211

1. DEMOGRAPHY AND SURVIVAL IN TWENTY-FIRST-CENTURY FRANCE

sociologiques du roman contemporain," ed. Émilie Brière and Mélanie Lamarre, *Revue des Sciences Humaines* 299 (October 2010). Robert Sayre has argued that "La France représente sans doute le pays où le discours socio-littéraire a connu le développement le plus marqué, le plus soutenu et le plus diversifié." Robert Sayre, *La Sociologie de la littérature: Histoire, problématique, synthèse critique* (Paris: L'Harmattan, 2011), 18.

93. For more on the nationalist novels of writers like Barrès, Brasillach, Drieu la Rochelle, and Rebatet, see David Carroll, *French Literary Fascism: Nationalism, Anti-Semitism, and the Ideology of Culture* (Princeton, NJ: Princeton University Press, 1995).

94. "Que de forces, que de semences perdues dans la nature! J'avais été frappé de la quantité de pollen que renferme le calice des fleurs pour assurer la perpétuité de l'espèce, du nombre d'œufs que portent les poissons et qui est si disproportionné avec le nombre de ceux qui éclosent. Il y a là un déchet énorme. Dans l'humanité, c'est bien pis." Zola, qtd. in Xavier Mélet, "*Fécondité*," *Le Temps*, October 13, 1899, 2.

95. In his article "Dépopulation," Zola writes of the failed attempts at life, those seeds that never germinate: "Ce sont les frais d'ébauche, d'essayage, les pertes de toute grande besogne, quitte à refondre les miettes tombées, à les reprendre et à en refaire plus tard d'autres œuvres" (1).

96. Gerald Hoffleit, "Progress and Decadence—Poststructuralism as Progressivism," in *Decadence in Literature and Intellectual Debate Since 1945*, ed. Diemo Landgraf (New York: Palgrave Macmillan, 2014), 67.

97. In 2001, the Prix Sade was created in France by Frédéric Beigbeder and Lionel Aracil, described on the official website as a "prix littéraire dédié à la littérature contemporaine dans la juste filiation de l'héritage sadien." See http://prix-sade.over-blog.com.

98. Robinson recognizes the symbolic cultural power of the *cité*, setting two of his other recent massive novels there, his 525-page *Dans les cités* (Paris: Seuil, 2011) and his 636-page *Fabrication de la guerre civile* (Paris: Seuil, 2016).

99. Charles Robinson, *Génie du proxénétisme, ou beautés de la religion péripatéticienne* (Paris: Seuil, 2008), 9. All translations mine.

100. Michel Houellebecq, *The Map and the Territory*, trans. Gavin Bowd (New York: Vintage International, 2011), 261. Houellebecq's narrator also mentions a passage written by the "fascist author Drieu La Rochelle" in which "he laments French decadence and the fall in the birth rate (already in the news in the 1930s)" (188).

101. Patrik Ourednik, *La Fin du monde n'aurait pas eu lieu* (Paris: Éditions Allia, 2017), 77.

102. Susan Sontag, "9.11.01.," in *Susan Sontag: Later Essays*, ed. David Rieff (New York: Library of America, 2017), 709.

103. "C'était tout le 20ᵉ siècle qui avait été résumé en quelques minutes ce mardi-là. Ce serait donc là l'acte de naissance du 21ᵉ siècle comme 1914 l'avait été pour le 20ᵉ." Moix, *Partouz*, 48. For more on 9/11's influence on literature, see Charlie Lee-Potter, *Writing the 9/11 Decade: Reportage and the Evolution of the Novel* (New York: Bloomsbury, 2017); and John C. Duvall and Robert P. Marzec, eds., *Narrating 9/11: Fantasies of State, Security, and Terrorism* (Baltimore, MD: Johns Hopkins University Press, 2015).

104. Hélène Cixous, "The Towers: *Les tours,*" *Signs* 28, no. 1 (Autumn 2002): 431.
105. Others include Luc Lang, *11 septembre mon amour* (Paris: Éditions Stock, 2003); Didier Goupil, *Le Jour de mon retour sur Terre* (Paris: Le Serpent à Plumes, 2003); and Moix, *Partouz*. Regarding the French-language 9/11 novels that proliferated after the event, Tim Gauthier has argued that "if these texts appeal primarily to French readers, it is because they speak of contemporary France itself, of its self-proclaimed role as resister and regulator of the global ambitions of the US, but also of its anxiety concerning its own decline or growing inconsequentiality." Tim Gauthier, "French Fiction, Empathy, and the Utopian Potential of 9/11," *Studies in Twentieth- and Twenty-First-Century Literature* 37, no. 1 (2013): 114.
106. Frédéric Beigbeder, *Windows on the World*, trans. Frank Wynne (New York: Hyperion, 2004), 98.
107. Windows on the World is the name of the restaurant perched in the North Tower of the World Trade Center, but the reference to windows is significant here. Peter Brooks, in *Realist Vision* (New Haven, CT: Yale University Press, 2008), reminds us, "Windows are always important in realist fiction, as in realist painting" (56).
108. For more on the hyperrealist element of Beigbeder's novel, see Jenn Brandt, "9/11, Hyperreality, and the Global Body Politic: Frédéric Beigbeder's *Windows on the World,*" *Studies in Twentieth- and Twenty-First-Century Literature* 39, no. 1 (2015): article 4, https://doi.org/10.4148/2334-4415.1578.
109. Beigbeder, *Windows on the World*, 8. His novel quotes a real witness, Medhi Dadgarian, a survivor who had been on the seventy-second floor: "I couldn't stop thinking: it's not real, it's a film. It can't be real" (271).
110. Also see Jean-Philippe Mathy, "Seeing Is Disbelieving: The Contested Visibility of 9/11 in France," in *9/11 in European Literature*, ed. Svenja Frank (Cham: Palgrave Macmillan, 2017), 105–29.
111. Lawrence Schehr, "Effondrements: Frédéric Beigbeder's *Windows on the World,*" *French Cultural Studies* 21, no. 2 (2010): 136.
112. Jean Baudrillard, "The Spirit of Terrorism," in *The Spirit of Terrorism and Requiem for the Twin Towers*, trans. Chris Turner (London: Verso, 2002), 26–27.
113. Peter Brooks, *Reading for the Plot: Design and Intention in Narratives* (Cambridge, MA: Harvard University Press, 1992), 63.
114. Brooks, *Realist Vision*, 39.
115. Morrey, "The Banality of Monstrosity," 209.
116. Viard, *Houellebecq au scanner*, 45.
117. The narrator of his *Sérotonine* quips: "Des familles recomposées pour ma part je n'en avais jamais vu, des familles décomposées oui." Michel Houellebecq, *Sérotonine* (Paris: Flammarion, 2019), 312.
118. In Olivier Adam's *Les Lisières* (Paris: Flammarion, 2012), the narrator wonders, "Pourquoi ma génération se révélait à ce point incapable de grandir, de se comporter en adulte? . . . Nous avions tous au moins dix ans de retard. Nous ne savions rien faire de nos mains. Ni de nos vies" (346).
119. Philippe Muray, *Chers djihadistes* (Paris: Mille et une nuits, 2002), 17.
120. In his meditations on terrorism, Moix argues that the war against Isis (Daesh) is a war against "adulescents," immature, childish warriors whose logic for attacking the West does not surpass that of a primary school playground dispute. He

calls this war "the first immature war of humanity" and an "infantile war." Yann Moix, *Terreur* (Paris: Grasset, 2017), 16–17.

121. Also see Florian Zeller's novel *La Fascination du pire* (Paris: Flammarion, 2004), which touches in part on the theme of "le conflit à venir entre les civilisations occidentales et musulmanes" (197).

122. Moix, *Terreur*, 27.

123. "L'attentat est si réel, si infiniment réel, qu'il semble ne jamais avoir eu lieu. Il y a, dans l'évidence de certains faits, une manière de science-fiction qui s'installe, dont seule l'imagination peut fidèlement rendre compte." Moix, *Terreur*, 23.

124. "La fiction est devenue le seul canal par lequel la réalité ait encore le moyen de se faufiler pour nous parvenir, nous joindre, nous *concerner*. Pour s'en persuader, il suffit de regarder, en allant sur le merveilleux site de l'INA, n'importe quel journal télévisé de 1975, époque où la réalité apparaissait sous des allures réelles, sans apparat, sans robe de soirée, sans mise en scène, sans suspense, sans compte à rebours—il n'y avait point encore cette westernisation des actes terroristes . . . , il n'y avait point encore de *dramatisation*." Moix, *Terreur*, 98.

125. "*Daech plagie la fiction pour produire la réalité.* La fiction est devenue tellement plus réelle que le réel, qu'il s'agit de s'appliquer à reproduire les imperfections de la fiction à la perfection. De reproduire, le plus fidèlement possible, ses aberrations, ses tics, ses approximations—ses ficelles. Seule la parodie du réel parvient à l'effet de réel recherché." Moix, *Terreur*, 96. He also argues that Isis reinvented the snuff movie (94), a film genre in which real murders occur on screen.

126. Moix, *Partouz*, 24.

127. Muray, *Chers djihadistes*, 24.

128. "In the cultural sphere, it seems easier for editors to promote Houellebecq and his clones than to find new writers or subjects." Hugo Frey and Benjamin Noys, "Introduction: More Reactionary Times: Culture," *Journal of European Studies* 3, no. 4 (2007): 250.

129. Kamel Daoud, "Sexual Misery of the Arab World," *New York Times*, February 12, 2016, https://www.nytimes.com/2016/02/14/opinion/sunday/the-sexual-misery-of -the-arab-world.html.

130. In *The Possibility of an Island*, Houellebecq's narrator from far in the future posits: "The advantage of having a dog for company lies in the fact that it is possible to make him happy; he demands such simple things, his ego is so limited. Possibly, in a previous era, women found themselves in a comparable situation—similar to that of domestic animals." Michel Houellebecq, *The Possibility of an Island*, trans. Gavin Bowd (New York: Vintage, 2005), 5.

131. For more on this concept, see Michael O'Sullivan, *Weakness: A Literary and Philosophical History* (London: Continuum, 2012).

132. "While [the opponents of gender theory] see it as a conspiracy hatched in the United States to undermine the traditional family and national identity, its main backers stress the American origins of queer theory in order to effect a rupture with the prevailing norms in France." Bruno Perreau, *Queer Theory: The French Response* (Stanford, CA: Stanford University Press, 2016), 13.

133. In this section's epigraph, taken from this book, the second half of the original French sentence permits a rich ambiguity: "La Jeune-Fille ne répugne pas, çà et

là, à mimer la soumission: *car elle sait qu'elle domine*." Tiqqun, *Premiers matéri-aux pour une théorie de la Jeune-Fille* (Paris: Éditions Mille et une nuits, 2001), 65. The English translation takes *elle* to mean "submission"—"*because she knows that it* [submission] *dominates.*" Tiqqun, *Preliminary Materials for a Theory of the Young-Girl*, trans. Ariana Reines (Los Angeles: Semiotext(e), 2012), 64, but I take it to mean "she," the Young-Girl. For an excellent critical reading of the Tiqqun text, see Moira Weigel and Mal Ahern, "Further Materials Toward a Theory of the Man-Child," *New Inquiry*, July 9, 2013, https://thenewinquiry.com/further -materials-toward-a-theory-of-the-man-child/.

134. Paul Preciado, *Testo Junkie*, trans. Bruce Benderson (New York: Feminist Press, 2013), 50.

135. Michel Houellebecq, *The Elementary Particles*, trans. Frank Wynne (New York: Vintage, 2000), 102.

136. Ross Douthat, "The Rise of Woke Capitalism," *New York Times*, February 28, 2019, https://www.nytimes.com/2018/02/28/opinion/corporate-america-activism .html.

137. Houellebecq, *Submission*, 28.

138. Morrey, "The Banality of Monstrosity," 205.

139. Mehammed Amadeus Mack, *Sexagon: Muslims, France, and the Sexualization of National Culture* (New York: Fordham University Press, 2017), 1–2.

140. Houellebecq, *Platform*, 146.

141. Moix, *Partouz*, 60.

142. Beigbeder, *Windows on the World*, 180.

143. Preciado, *Testo Junkie*, 141.

144. For an excellent overview of the concept of *masculinisme*, see Francis Dupuis-Déri, "Le 'masculinisme': Une histoire politique du mot (en anglais et en français)," *Recherches Féministes* 22, no. 2 (2009): 97–123.

145. Houellebecq, *Elementary Particles*, 161–62.

146. Alain Duhamel, *Les Peurs françaises* (Paris: Flammarion, 1993), 275.

147. See John d'Agata and Jim Fingal, *The Lifespan of a Fact* (New York: Norton, 2012).

## 2. ENDARKENMENT FROM THE MINITEL TO THE INTERNET

1. For an excellent analysis of the far-right webscape, see Dominique Albertini and David Doucet, *La Fachosphère: Comment l'extrême droite remporte la bataille du net* (Paris: Flammarion, 2016). They argue that the dominant discourse of the *fachosphère* is one of decadence, which allows them to call for a recuperation of the lost golden age to help us out of "our present misery" (15).

2. Salman Rushdie, *Real Time with Bill Maher*, September 15, 2017.

3. For example, see Geoff Manaugh, "Concrete-Printing Bees and Other Living 3D Printers," *Gizmodo*, December 6, 2013, https://gizmodo.com/concrete-printing -bees-and-other-living-3d-printers-1477853742.

4. Aurélien Bellanger's academic interest in Houellebecq impelled him to write *Houellebecq, écrivain romantique* (Paris: Scheer, 2010).

5. René Audet and Nicolas Xanthos argue that Bellanger's "decentering of the figure of the protagonist" conforms to "a tendency in literature that evokes contemporary social changes to the detriment of the main character." René Audet and Nicolas

Xanthos, "Le roman contemporain au détriment du personnage: Introduction," *L'Esprit Créateur* 54, no. 1 (Spring 2013): 6.

6. Yann Moix, *Terreur* (Paris: Grasset, 2017), offers another example of the disappearance of the membrane separating real life and virtual life: "À l'heure où le réel et le virtuel se conjuguent et souvent se confondent, comme en atteste puissamment le Pokémon Go, ce serait un réflexe tout juste digne du précédent siècle que d'affirmer qu'un pays qui n'existe pas dans la réalité n'existe pas tout court" (13).

7. Andrew Feenberg, *Alternative Modernity: The Technical Turn in Philosophy and Social Theory* (Berkeley: University of California Press, 1995), 132.

8. Curien, in Marie Marchand, *Minitel* (Paris: Larousse, 1987), 8. My translation.

9. Richard Kramer, "The Politics of Information: A Study of the French Minitel System," in *Between Communication and Information*, vol. 4: *Information and Behavior*, ed. Jorge R. Schement and Brent D. Ruben (New Brunswick, NJ: Transaction, 1993), 467.

10. For example: "Ce qui fait l'admiration des étrangers, surtout des Américains, qui raffolent des 'success stories', c'est qu'autour du Minitel s'est forgé un secteur économique rentable. *French Videotex Makes Money*, tirait le *Wall Street Journal*, manifestement interloqué, au début de l'été 1986." Marchand, *Minitel*, 12. "Les étrangers, une fois l'annuaire électronique étendu à l'ensemble de la France, ne ménageront pas leurs compliments. La presse américaine se fera largement l'écho de cette *success story* française." Marchand, *Minitel*, 75.

11. Lyombe Eko, *American Exceptionalism, the French Exception, and Digital Media Law* (Plymouth: Lexington, 2013), 5. He furthers the distinction this way: "American exceptionalism is the proclamation that the United States is a singular nation whose superior democratic system is ordained by God, a system whose unparalleled libertarian values set it apart from the rest of the world. For its part, the French exception is a declaration of Gallic linguistic and cultural specificity."

12. Aurélien Bellanger, *La Théorie de l'information* (Paris: Gallimard, 2012), 35.

13. Daniel Bell, in Simon Nora and Alain Minc, *The Computerization of Society: A Report to the President of France* (Cambridge, MA: MIT Press, 1981), xiv.

14. Nora and Minc, *The Computerization of Society*, 73.

15. Ithiel de Sola Pool, "*The Computerization of Society* by Simon Nora and Alain Minc (Review)," *Technology and Culture* 22, no. 2 (April 1981): 353.

16. Howard Rheingold, *The Virtual Community: Homesteading on the Electronic Frontier* (Boston: Addison-Wesley, 1993), 227.

17. Landaret, quoted in Rheingold, *The Virtual Community*, 227–28.

18. Tung-Hui Hu, *A Prehistory of the Cloud* (Cambridge, MA: MIT Press, 2016), x.

19. "No single metaphor completely conveys the nature of cyberspace. Virtual communities are places where people meet, and they also are tools; the place-like aspects and tool-like aspects only partially overlap." Howard Rheingold, "Daily Life in Cyberspace: How the Computerized Counterculture Built a New Kind of Place," in *Social Media Archeology and Poetics*, ed. Judy Malloy (Cambridge, MA: MIT Press, 2016), 77.

20. Julien Mailland and Kevin Driscoll, *Minitel: Welcome to the Internet* (Cambridge, MA: MIT Press, 2017), 73. See also 87–91 on the nuancing of these terms.

21. See André Lemos, "The Labyrinth of the Minitel," in *Cultures of Internet: Virtual Spaces, Real Histories, Living Bodies*, ed. Rob Shields (London: Sage, 1996), 33–48.

22. Julien Mailland, "Minitel," in *Paid: Tales of Dongles, Checks, and Other Money Stuff*, ed. Bill Maurer and Lana Swartz (Cambridge, MA: MIT Press, 2017), 175.

23. "Over the past year I've heard Facebook compared to a dozen entities and felt like I've caught glimpses of it acting like a dozen more. I've heard government metaphors (a state, the E.U., the Catholic Church, *Star Trek*'s United Federation of Planets) and business ones (a railroad company, a mall); physical metaphors (a town square, an interstate highway, an electrical grid) and economic ones (a Special Economic Zone, Gosplan). For every direct comparison, there was an equally elaborate one: a faceless Elder God. A conquering alien fleet." Max Read, "Does Even Mark Zuckerberg Know What Facebook Is?," *New York Magazine*, October 1, 2017, http://nymag.com/selectall/2017/10/does-even-mark-zuckerberg-know-what-facebook-is.html. Read also mentions Facebook imagined as a television broadcaster and an NGO. Mona Chollet notes that Twitter is often thought of as a Swiss army knife—"un couteau suisse"—given "l'extrême diversité de ses utilisateurs et des usages qu'il permet." Mona Chollet, "Twitter jusqu'au vertige," *Le Monde Diplomatique*, October 2011, https://www.monde-diplomatique.fr/2011/10/CHOLLET/21103.

24. A synonym for "technical" in the *Oxford American Writer's Thesaurus* is "esoteric."

25. See Antonio Gonzalez, "Minitel: Histoire du réseau télématique français," *Flux* 47, no. 1 (2002): 84–89.

26. See Tamara Chaplin, "Lesbians Online: Queer Identity and Community Formation on the French Minitel," *Journal of the History of Sexuality* 23, no. 3 (2014): 451–72; Anna Livia, "Public and Clandestine: Gay Men's Pseudonyms on the French Minitel," *Sexualities* 5, no. 2 (2002): 201–17; Denis Périer, *Le Dossier noir du Minitel rose* (Paris: Albin Michel, 1988); and Martine Vantses, *Sexe et mensonge: Enquête sur la sexualité féminine auprès d'utilisatrices du minitel, des petites annonces et agences matrimoniales* (Paris: Éditions Joëlle Losfeld, 1993).

27. Eko, *American Exceptionalism*; Lyombe Eko, "New Technologies, Old Mentalities: The Internet, Minitel, and Exceptionalist Information and Communication Technology Policy," in *New Media, Old Regimes: Case Studies in Comparative Communication Law and Policy* (Plymouth: Lexington, 2012); H. L. Moulaison, "The Minitel and France's Legacy of Democratic Information Access," *Government Information Quarterly* 21 (2004): 99–107; and Gunnar Trumbull, *Silicon and the State: French Innovation Policy in the Internet Age* (Washington, DC: Brookings Institution Press, 2004).

28. Feenberg, *Alternative Modernity*, 162.

29. Vincent Glad begins his review of Bellanger's *La Théorie de l'information* with this: "The Minitel is a shameful page of French industrial history. France, ahead by a generation at the beginning of the 1980s, would be behind in the revolution in the mid-1990s when the information highways opened up." Vincent Glad, "La théorie du déclin français," *Slate*, September 18, 2012, http://www.slate.fr/story/61857/aurelien-bellanger-la-theorie-de-linformation.

30. Annick Bureau, "Art and Minitel in France in the 1980s," in *Social Media Archaeology and Poetics*, ed. Judy Malloy (Cambridge, MA: MIT Press, 2016), 139. For more on such experiments, see Roy Ascott, *Telematic Embrace: Visionary Theories of Art, Technology, and Consciousness* (Berkeley: University of California Press, 2007), 257–75.

31. Mark Poster, *Information Please: Culture and Politics in the Age of Digital Machines* (Durham, NC: Duke University Press, 2006), 124.

32. François Cusset, *French Theory: How Foucault, Derrida, Deleuze, and Co. Transformed the Intellectual Life of the United States*, trans. Jeff Fort (Minneapolis: University of Minnesota Press, 2008), 251. For more on the convergence of the internet and French theory, see the section of the book titled "A Temporary Autonomous Zone" (250–53). Cusset describes the two main benefits of this convergence: "It provided Internet pioneers with language and concepts with which they could consider their practices, and it offered French theorists a much broader and more affordable channel of distribution than the publishing industry, which helped them gain readers outside the academic sphere" (253).

33. For Bellanger's take on the connection between (post)structuralism and the Minitel and Internet—or at least the take of one of his characters on this connection—see the sections "Structuralisme, cybernétique et fin de l'histoire," "La French Theory, le devenir-machine de l'homme et sa libération," and "La singularité comme théorie littéraire" in the character Xavier Mycenne's article "La singularité française." Bellanger, *Théorie*, 403–8.

34. Michel Houellebecq, *Whatever*, trans. Paul Hammond (London: Serpent's Tail, 1998), 131.

35. Dominique Raymond, "Trois instances et un roman: *La Théorie de l'information* d'Aurélien Bellanger," *L'Esprit Créateur* 54, no. 1 (Spring 2014): 115. Sylvain Bourmeau writes that Bellanger sees "Wikipedian" as an entirely new language, like "IT engineers writing in Pascal [a programming language]." Sylvain Bourmeau, "*La Théorie de l'information*, un puissant avatar de l'époque," *Libération*, August 22, 2012, http://next.liberation.fr/livres/2012/08/22/la-theorie-de-l-informa tion-un-puissant-avatar-de-l-epoque_841306.

36. Nicolas Auray, "Les plis du capitalisme cognitif," *Multitudes* 52 (2013): 147.

37. "La *définition* de la réalité devient alors monopolisée par les 'experts', installés et assis dans leur expertise par l'appui de 'responsables' qui verrouillent ainsi la chaîne d'autorité" (149).

38. Elisabeth Philippe, "Aurélien Bellanger remporte le prix de Flore," *Les Inrockuptibles*, November 13, 2014, http://www.lesinrocks.com/2014/11/13/livres/aurelien -bellanger-remporte-prix-flore-11535357/.

39. Glad, "La théorie du déclin français."

40. Elisabeth Philippe, "Aurélien Bellanger, le nouveau Houellebecq?," *Les Inrockuptibles*, August 20, 2012, http://www.lesinrocks.com/2012/08/20/livres/aurelien -bellanger-le-nouveau-houellebecq-11287237/.

41. For example, see Jérôme Dupuis, "Aurélien Bellanger, ennuyeux comme un annuaire électronique," *L'Express*, August 23, 2012, http://www.lexpress.fr/culture /livre/la-theorie-de-l-information_1151599.html.

42. Philippe, "Aurélien Bellanger, le nouveau Houellebecq?"

43. Dominique Raymond argues that the protagonist is pushed to the margins of the *récit* by two other entities: the narrator and "la machine." Raymond, "Trois instances," 116.

44. Bellanger, *Théorie*, 14.

45. In Luc Lang's novel *Au commencement du septième jour* (Paris: Stock, 2016), the protagonist Thomas Texier is a software developer who creates a technology

218

. ENDARKENMENT FROM THE MINITEL TO THE INTERNET

called NUXITEMPO, which allows for the real-time tracking of people's movements. The novel abounds with anxieties about what is untrackable—that is, unknowable—in life. Despite the utopian rhetoric of Silicon Valley, the technologies it offers have distinct limitations and even pose threats to civil liberties and democracy, a fact noted by many French novelists.

46. See "Can Thought Go On Without a Body?" in Jean-François Lyotard, *The Inhuman*, trans. Geoffrey Bennington and Rachel Bowlby (Cambridge: Polity, 1991), 8–23.

47. In *Houellebecq, écrivain romantique*, 11, Bellanger describes the moment when he discovered that "the sun would be extinguished in five billion years," which caused him to cry the entire night. He was consoled by reading Houellebecq's *The Elementary Particles*.

48. Jean-François Lyotard, *Postmodern Fables*, trans. Georges Van Den Abbeele (Minneapolis: University of Minnesota Press, 1997), 84.

49. For more on the genealogy of Ranke's *Homo narrans* concept, see Albrecht Lehmann, "Homo narrans—Individuelle und kollektive Dimensionen des Erzählens," in *Erzählkultur: Beiträge zur kulturwissenschaftlichen Erzählforschung*, ed. Rolf Wilhelm Brednich (Berlin: Walter de Gruyter, 2009), 59–70.

50. Bellanger, *Théorie*, 79.

51. Bernard Weinberg, *French Realism: The Critical Reaction, 1830–1870* (Oxford: Oxford University Press, 1937), 134.

52. Comte Louis Clément de Ris, *Critiques d'art et de littérature* (Paris: Didier, 1862), 307.

53. Elme-Marie Caro, "Études morales sur le XIXe siècle," *Revue contemporaine* 13 (April 1854): 432.

54. Guy de Maupassant, *Pierre et Jean*, trans. Julie Mead (Oxford: Oxford University Press, 2001), 7.

55. James Agee and Walker Evans, *Let Us Now Praise Famous Men* (New York: Houghton Mifflin, 2001), x.

56. Bellanger, *Théorie*, 25.

57. One stanza goes: "Toutes les données du monde sont déjà rassemblées / Dans des hangars dédiés à la métempsychose / Où des bras mécaniques rassemblent par octets / Les voix et les messages, le savoir et les choses" (416).

58. A short description of Stéphane Richard, the CEO of Orange (formerly France Télécom), "was located on his Wikipedia page" (347), from which Bellanger cites directly. This is only one of many instances of direct cut-and-paste from Wikipedia and other sources as well. For a detailed accusation of Wikipedia plagiarism against Bellanger, see Dominique Bry, "La *Théorie de l'information*, c'est wiki qui dit qu'y est," *Mediapart*, August 27, 2012, https://blogs.mediapart.fr/edition/bookclub/article/270812/la-theorie-de-l-information-c-est-wiki-qui-dit-qu-y-est. Houellebecq, too, was caught plagiarizing Wikipedia in *The Map and the Territory*. See Vincent Glad, "Houellebecq, la possibilité d'un plagiat," *Slate*, February 9, 2010, http://www.slate.fr/story/26745/wikipedia-plagiat-michel-houellebecq-carte-territoire. In later editions of the book, he writes in the acknowledgments, "I also thank Wikipedia (http://fr.wikipedia.org) and its contributors, whose entries I have occasionally used as a source of inspiration, notably those concerning the housefly, the town of Beauvais, and Frédéric Nihous." Michel

Houellebecq, *The Map and the Territory*, trans. Gavin Bowd (New York: Vintage International, 2011), 271. Dominique Raymond sees both *La Théorie de l'information* and *The Map and the Territory* as constituting a "'collage' wikipédien." Raymond, "Trois instances," 115.

59. For example, regarding terrorism, Yann Moix writes, "It isn't very acceptable (it's even very obscene) that Salah Abdeslam has a Wikipedia page, as do Albert Camus, Chopin, Ghandhi, and Shakespeare." Moix, *Terreur*, 45. Noting that some terrorists have Wikipedia pages while others don't, he asks, "What are the criteria for being Wikipedified?" (46).

60. In her chapter "La fiction littéraire à l'assaut de la novlangue d'entreprise," Aurore Labadie argues that a key feature of the twenty-first-century French novel, particularly the *roman d'entreprise*, is the omnipresence of the specialized language of business speak. She offers a list of terms for this kind of language: *novlangue néoliberale, langue du capital, discours néolibéral, LQR, langue économique, langue de coton, novlangue française, novlangue d'entreprise, langue du néomanagement*. Aurore Labadie, *Le Roman d'entreprise français au tournant du XXIe siècle* (Paris: Presses Sorbonne nouvelle, 2016), 179.

61. Guillaume Bachelay, *La Politique sauvée par les livres* (Paris: Stock, 2016), 20. My translation.

62. Houellebecq, *The Map and the Territory*, 117.

63. Paul Levinson, *Digital McLuhan: A Guide to the Information Millennium* (London: Routledge, 1999), 58.

64. Autin, in Mailland and Driscoll, *Minitel*, 65n80.

65. Mailland and Driscoll, *Minitel*, 17–18.

66. Virginie Despentes, *King Kong Theory*, trans. Stéphanie Benson (London: Serpent's Tail, 2009), 49–50.

67. Lawrence Schehr, *French Post-Modern Masculinities: From Neuromatrices to Seropositivity* (Liverpool: Liverpool University Press, 2009), 138.

68. Susan Sontag, *Illness as Metaphor and AIDS and Its Metaphors* (New York: Farrar, Straus and Giroux, 1990), 167. Emphasis added.

69. Paul Virilio, *A Landscape of Events*, trans. Julie Rose (Cambridge, MA: MIT Press, 2000), 62.

70. Jean Baudrillard, *The Gulf War Did Not Take Place*, trans. Paul Patton (Bloomington: Indiana University Press, 1995), 62.

71. Jean Baudrillard, *The Transparency of Evil: Essays on Extreme Phenomena*, trans. James Benedict (London: Verso, 2002), 53.

72. Sandrine Rabosseau, "Houellebecq ou le renouveau du roman expérimental," in *Michel Houellebecq sous la loupe*, ed. Murielle Lucie Clément and Sabine van Wesemael (Amsterdam: Rodopi, 2007), 48.

73. Yann Moix describes it more playfully as a "recreational relief": "Le Minitel rose, avec ses petites promesses de soulagement récréatif et ses 36–15 poussifs et 'polissons,' a l'air d'une épicerie de quartier posée sur une autoroute." Yann Moix, "Années 80: La décennie où tout a basculé," *Paris Match*, August 22, 2016, http://www.parismatch.com/Actu/Societe/Annees-80-la-decennie-ou-tout-a-bascule-Par-Yann-Moix-1042588.

74. Periphrasis was linked inextricably with romanticism in the eyes of the nineteenth-century realists, who saw it as burdensome ornament. Léon Gautier writes, for

example, "Pendant plusieurs siècles, on s'est pudiquement efforcé de ne jamais écrire ou prononcer le mot propre." Léon Gautier, "M. Gustave Flaubert," in *Études littéraires pour la défense de l'Église* (Paris: Poussielgue et fils, 1865), 183. Noting with consternation the periphrastic tendency of his contemporaries, Henri Thulié wrote, "À remplacer tous les mots par des périphrases: quel langage alors!" Henri Thulié, "Le Roman. Le style," *Réalisme* 6 (April/May 1857): 86.

75. Poster argues that on the Minitel, "genderless anonymity undermines the Cartesian subject." Mark Poster, *The Mode of Information: Poststructuralism and Social Context* (Cambridge: Polity, 2007), 121.

76. Philippe, "Aurélien Bellanger, le nouveau Houellebecq?"

77. Bellanger, *Théorie*, 446.

78. Bellanger, *Houellebecq*, 203n1.

79. Nora and Minc, *The Computerization of Society*, 10. This wordplay was used by Benoît Duteurtre, whose novel *L'Ordinateur du paradis* (Paris: Gallimard, 2014) combines the thematics of the internet and the afterlife. In his fragmented text on terrorism, Yann Moix also takes up the play on "ordinateur" and "ordonnateur," this time regarding the Islamic State and its online reach: "État islamique de la terre, État islamique de la Toile: même combat. Bien malin qui pourrait dire lequel est l'avatar de l'autre. Dans une époque où l'ordinateur remplace l'ordonnateur, et le clavier la mosquée, nous serions naïfs de penser que la version territoriale de Daech l'emporte en légitimité, mais aussi en réalité, sur sa version portative." Moix, *Terreur*, 13.

80. Marc Augé, *The War of Dreams: Exercises in Ethno-Fiction*, trans. Liz Heron (London: Pluto, 1999), 116.

81. Émile Zola, *The Experimental Novel and Other Essays*, trans. Belle M. Sherman (New York: Haskell House, 1964), 53.

82. Honoré de Balzac, *Honoré de Balzac in Twenty-Five Volumes*, 25 vols. (New York: Peter Fenelon Collier, 1900), 21.

83. Emmanuel Buzay, "Le désir d'être écrit: Étude comparative de deux modèles d'écriture computationnels dans *La Possibilité d'une île* de Michel Houellebecq et *La Théorie de l'information* d'Aurélien Bellanger," in *Lectures croisées de l'œuvre de Michel Houellebecq*, ed. Antoine Jurga and Sabine van Wesemael (Paris: Classiques Garnier, 2017), 93.

84. The first chapter of Bellanger's *Houellebecq, écrivain romantique* begins, "Houellebecq became acquainted with the Jansenist heights of the art of fear at the discotheque" (15) and goes on to describe the myriad ways in which Blaise Pascal has marked Houellebecq's oeuvre.

85. Bellanger, *Théorie*, 421.

86. Pierre-André Taguieff has argued: "La pensée du complot présente certaines analogies avec la pensée mythique: comme celle-ci, elle peuple le monde d'intentions bonnes et mauvaises, de démons et de dieux, elle 'investit l'univers objectif de volontés subjectives,' imaginant ainsi expliquer l'origine et la persistance du mal." Pierre-André Taguieff, *La Foire aux Illuminés: Ésotérisme, théorie du complot, extrémisme* (Paris: Mille et une nuits, 2005), 22.

87. Rheingold, *The Virtual Community*, 228.

88. Fredric Jameson, *The Antinomies of Realism* (London: Verso, 2015), 4.

89. Fredric Jameson, "Beyond the Cave: Demystifying the Ideology of Modernism," in *The Ideologies of Theory: Essays 1971–1986*, vol. 2: *The Syntax of History* (Minneapolis: University of Minnesota Press, 1988), 128.
90. Stanislaw Lem, *The Futurological Congress: From the Memoirs of Ijon Tichy*, trans. Michael Kandel (New York: Harcourt, 1974), 126.
91. Feenberg, *Alternative Modernity*, 140.
92. "Un lien inédit y est fait entre le réseau et le secret, il s'agit de forger une nouvelle grammaire de l'homme public. Cela suppose des réorganisations spatiales: la sociabilité des catacombes, la vie dans les cavernes, dans les 'terriers', sont les déplacements necessaires pour faire tourner ces nouveaux régimes de lumière 'en lames d'aluminium anodisé.'" Auray, "Les plis," 149.
93. Houellebecq's first book was *H. P. Lovecraft: Contre le monde, contre la vie* (Monaco: Éditions du Rocher, 1991).
94. "The agent brought back loads of mega-octets of all kinds of info on the Noelite Church, its guru, and the Rosicrucian sect it issued from; info collected on esoteric websites flowering on the Internet." Maurice G. Dantec, *Babylon Babies*, trans. Noura Wedell (Los Angeles: Semiotext(e), 2005), 203.
95. Philippe Vasset, *La Conjuration* (Paris: Fayard, 2013), 10.
96. See Hakim Bey, *T.A.Z.: The Temporary Autonomous Zone, Ontological Anarchy, Poetic Terrorism* (Brooklyn: Autonomedia, 2003). As Dominic Pettman writes of the relation between Bey's concept and the Minitel, "By creating a network that eluded governmental regulation (for a time, at least) the Minitel anticipated Hakim Bey's notion of a Temporary Autonomous Zone: socialism with an interface." Dominic Pettman, *After the Orgy: Toward a Politics of Exhaustion* (Albany: State University of New York Press, 2002), 34.
97. The novelist Jean Rolin has expressed his fascination with Google Earth as a tool for the writerly imagination: "Je me passionne pour Google Earth. Je trouve extraordinaire de pouvoir survoler n'importe quel territoire et de pouvoir zoomer sur un détail. J'aime énormément la lecture des cartes et elle précède presque toujours ma démarche d'écriture." Jean Rolin, in Myriam Boucharenc and Pierre Hyppolite, "Questions à Jean Rolin," in *Roman et reportage XXe–XXIe siècles: Rencontres croisées*, ed. Myriam Boucharenc (Limoges: Presses universitaires de Limoges, 2015), 277.
98. On their homepage, they describe their mission this way: "La Miviludes observe et analyse le phénomène sectaire, coordonne l'action préventive et répressive des pouvoirs publics à l'encontre des dérives sectaires, et informe le public sur les risques et les dangers auxquels il est exposé." http://www.derives-sectes.gouv.fr/.
99. After the publication of his novel, the Raëliens made Houellebecq an honorary priest. He also mentions their founder, Claude Vorilhon, by name in *The Map and the Territory*.
100. Antoine Bello, *Les Éclaireurs* (Paris: Gallimard, 2009), 214.
101. Antoine Bello, *Les Falsificateurs* (Paris: Gallimard, 2007), 120.
102. Antoine Bello, *Les Producteurs* (Paris: Gallimard, 2015), 571.
103. Bello, *Les Éclaireurs*.
104. Bello, *Les Falsificateurs*, 434.
105. Bello, *Les Producteurs*, 36–37.
106. Jameson, "Beyond the Cave," 123.

## 3. REAL-TIME REALISM, PART 1: JOURNALISTIC IMMEDIACY

1. Richard Grusin, *Premediation: Affect and Mediality After 9/11* (London: Palgrave Macmillan, 2010), 3.

2. Frédéric Beigbeder, *Windows on the World*, trans. Frank Wynne (New York: Hyperion, 2004).

3. In his 1997 book *La Guerre des rêves: Exercices d'ethno-fiction*, Marc Augé wonders "how we know what happens to our relationship with the real when the conditions of symbolisation change." Marc Augé, *The War of Dreams: Exercises in Ethno-Fiction*, trans. Liz Heron (London: Pluto, 1999), 6. He argues that through the internet and other forms of mediatization, the real is being fictionalized and fiction is being "realized," thus blurring the differences that separate them. He calls this process a "fictionalisation of the present" (119).

4. Steve Bannon and *Breitbart* famously promoted *The Camp of the Saints* in 2015. In 2018, the Social Contract Press, an American anti-immigration press based in Michigan, ran its tenth printing of Norman Shapiro's translation of the novel. The press publishes rants against overpopulation, "taxpayer-funded illegal aliens," refugees, "the toxic threat of infected migrants," "illegal alien crimes," Islam, and the Southern Poverty Law Center.

5. Anonymous, "*The Camp of the Saints*: Where Literature and Life Collide," *Radix*, October 27, 2015, https://radixjournal.com/2015/10/2015-10-27-sea-changes/.

6. Jean Raspail, *The Camp of the Saints*, trans. Norman Shapiro (Petoskey, MI: Social Contract Press, 2018), 217.

7. Andreu Domingo, "'Demodystopias': Prospects of Demographic Hell," *Population and Development Review* 34, no. 4 (December 2008): 736.

8. These include the presence in the novel of a latter-day Indian Christopher (bearer of Christ) who carries on his shoulder a monster Christ-child, references to the Second Coming, a Last Supper of sorts, references to Judas, and the arrival of the refugees on Easter morning, just to name a few examples.

9. Raspail uses the verse (Revelation 20:7–9) as the first epigraph of the novel: "And when the thousand years are ended, Satan will be released from his prison, and will go forth and deceive the nations which are in the four corners of the earth, Gog and Magog, and will gather them together for the battle; the number of whom is as the sand of the sea. And they went up over the breadth of the earth and encompassed the camp of the saints, and the beloved city" (xvii).

10. Just in chapter 12, they are called "flailing savages" (47), "unbridled, menacing hordes" (47), "this new swarthy reign" (47), "human anthills" (48), "Ganges scum" (48), "some gigantic beast with a million legs and a hundred heads" (49), "mob of Martians" (50), and "the surging beast" (50).

11. Just one of many examples: "We're going to die slowly, eaten away from the inside by millions of microbes injected into our body. Little by little. Easily, quietly. No pain, no blood" (190).

12. A thematically interesting pairing of readings would be Raspail's *Camp of the Saints* alongside Jean-Christophe Rufin's *Check-point* (Paris: Gallimard, 2015), both of which treat the question of humanitarian engagement in a globalized world but in starkly different terms. Rufin, president of Action contre la faim, a former French ambassador to Senegal and Gambia, and one of the pioneers of Médecins sans

frontières, who has written extensively on humanitarian crises, could be seen as the embodiment of the compassion and philanthropy against which Raspail fulminates.

13. In his novel *Petit frère* (Paris: Denoël, 2008), Éric Zemmour lampoons leftist journalists in a similar fashion. The condescending media, with its feminine call for compassion and understanding, is mocked by Zemmour as he puts words into this journalist-character's mouth: "C'est ma responsabilité de journaliste que de leur faire comprendre tout cela. Moi, au *Parisien*, je garde toujours ça en tête. Après tout, qu'est-ce que c'est que notre public? Des concierges et des chauffeurs de taxi. Spontanément, ils sont franchouillards et racistes. Nous devons, nous journalistes, les amener à plus d'humanité, plus de compassion, plus de compréhension du monde qui les entoure, pour favoriser le vivre ensemble. Et franchement, il n'y a pas mieux qu'une femme pour jouer ce rôle-là" (293).

14. Here is Raspail's portrait of the character: "Citizen of France, North African by blood, with an elegant crop of kinky hair and swarthy skin—doubtless passed down from a certain black harem slavegirl, sold to a brothel for French officers in Rabat (as he learned from the bill of sale in his family papers)—married to a Eurasian woman officially declared Chinese and author of best-selling novels, Dio possessed a belligerent intellect that thrived on springs of racial hatred barely below the surface, and far more intense than anyone imagined" (68).

15. See Roland Barthes's excellent analysis of Poujadist propaganda in *Mythologies* (Paris: Seuil, 1957), particularly in the essays "Quelques paroles de M. Poujade" and "Poujade et les intellectuels." See also Christy Wampole, "Poujade's Infowars: On Barthes' Anti-Anti-Intellectualism," *Yearbook of Comparative Literature* 62, no. 2016 (Summer 2019): 73–103.

16. These include a moment when Australia refuses to allow the refugees to land on its shores, when a Greek ship captain capsizes a refugee boat by ramming it, when refugees throw away supplies offered to them, when a refugee ship intentionally tries to ram another ship, and an episode in which "some thirty thousand Pakistanis, Bengalis, and Indians, reinforced by Jamaicans, Guyanans, Nigerians, and such, swarmed into the Manchester railroad station, on their way to take part in the demonstration planned for the following morning in London" (197).

17. William R. Beer, in Pascal Bruckner, *The Tears of the White Man: Compassion as Contempt*, trans. William R. Beer (New York: The Free Press, 1986), ix.

18. Raspail, *The Camp of the Saints*, 25.

19. Benedict Anderson, *Imagined Communities: Reflections on the Origin and Spread of Nationalism* (London: Verso, 2006), 25.

20. Christy Wampole, "What Is the Future of Speculative Journalism?," *New York Times*, January 22, 2018, https://www.nytimes.com/2018/01/22/opinion/speculative -journalism-future.html.

21. Peter Brooks, *Realist Vision* (New Haven, CT: Yale University Press, 2008), 21.

22. Adam Gopnik, "The Next Thing," *New Yorker*, January 26, 2015, https://www .newyorker.com/magazine/2015/01/26/next-thing.

23. In his novel *La fin du monde n'aurait pas eu lieu* (Paris: Éditions Allia, 2017), Patrik Ourednik's protagonist explains how to create the effect of clairvoyance as a writer: "Je tricherai aussi avec les dates, je les repousserai de quelques années. . . . Ainsi mon livre restera d'actualité même après les événements" (31).

24. Michel Houellebecq, in Christophe Duchatelet et al., *Michel Houellebecq: Les grands entretiens d'artpress* (Paris: IMEC, 2012), 65.

25. Claude Pérez, "Houellebecq, le vingt-heures et l'art du roman: À propos de *Soumission*," *Revue Critique de Fixxion Française Contemporaine* 11 (2015): 113. "Le futur de *Soumission* est entièrement *nominal*. Le lieu temporel du récit, ce n'est pas demain: c'est maintenant. C'est 2015 rebaptisé 2022; un aujourd'hui au cou duquel est accrochée une pancarte sur laquelle est écrit *demain*. . . . *Soumission* n'est pas un roman d'anticipation; c'est un roman d'actualité, un roman sur 'l'actualité.' 2022 est un moyen de parler de 2017, au moment où la rumeur d'élection à venir commence à enfler." Translated by SE.

26. Gopnik, "The Next Thing."

27. Tom Wolfe, "Stalking the Billion-Footed Beast: A Literary Manifesto for the New Social Novel," *Harper's* 279, no. 1674 (November 1989): 55.

28. Tom Wolfe, *The New Journalism* (New York: Harper and Row, 1973), 14.

29. Claude Grimal, "Le 'new journalism' et le 'non fiction novel': Un débat littéraire et journalistique aux États-Unis," in *Roman et reportage XXe–XXIe siècles: Rencontres croisées*, ed. Myriam Boucharenc (Limoges: Presses universitaires de Limoges, 2015), 15. For more on the literary aspects of *reportage*, see Paul Aron, "Entre journalisme et littérature, l'institution du reportage," *Contextes* 11 (2012), https://journals.openedition.org/contextes/5355.

30. Wolfe, *The New Journalism*, 31.

31. Dwight Macdonald, "Parajournalism, or Tom Wolfe & His Magic Writing Machine," *New York Review of Books*, August 26, 1965, https://www.nybooks.com/articles/1965/08/26/parajournalism-or-tom-wolfe-his-magic-writing-mach/.

32. Wolfe, *The New Journalism*, 35.

33. For more on this debate, see Jonathan Franzen, "Perchance to Dream: In the Age of Images, a Reason to Write Novels," *Harper's* (April 1996): 35–54; and Madhu Dubey, "Post-Postmodern Realism?," *Twentieth-Century Literature* 57, no. 3–4 (Fall/Winter 2011): 364–71. The critic James Wood's comment on the potential deflation of the social novel in the wake of 9/11 has not stopped them from proliferating. James Wood, "Tell Me How Does It Feel?," *Guardian*, October 6, 2001, https://www.theguardian.com/books/2001/oct/06/fiction.

34. Isabelle Meuret, "Le Journalisme littéraire à l'aube du XXIe siècle: Regards croisés entre mondes anglophone et francophone," *Contextes* 11 (2012), https://journals.openedition.org/contextes/5376. Meuret specifically mentions Emmanuel Carrère, Régis Jauffret, Élisabeth Filhol, Philippe Vasset, Jean Rolin, Tristan Garcia, Laurent Mauvignier, and Jean Hatzfeld. Muhlmann has traced a genealogy between American New Journalism of the 1960s and the kind of writing to be found in *Libération* throughout the 1970s. See the chapter "Les difficultés du décentrement: Le mouvement du *New Journalism* et les premières années du quotidien *Libération*" (127–79) in Géraldine Muhlmann, *Une histoire politique du journalisme: XIXe–XXe siècle* (Paris: Presses universitaires de France, 2004).

35. Such books include Didier Goupil's *Le jour de mon retour sur Terre* (Paris: Le Serpent à Plumes, 2003), Luc Lang's *11 septembre mon amour* (Paris: Éditions Stock, 2003), Yann Moix's *Partouz* (Paris: Grasset, 2004), Jonathan Safran Foer's *Extremely Loud and Incredibly Close* (Boston: Houghton Mifflin, 2005), Claire Messud's *The Emperor's Children* (New York: Knopf, 2006), Don DeLillo's *Falling*

*Man* (New York: Scribner, 2007), Mohsin Hamid's *The Reluctant Fundamentalist* (Orlando: Harcourt, 2007), Amy Waldman's *The Submission* (New York: Farrar, Straus and Giroux, 2011), and Fanny Taillandier's *Par les écrans du monde* (Paris: Seuil, 2018).

36. Beigbeder, *Windows on the World*.

37. Guido Isekenmaier, "Visual Event Realism," in *Realisms in Contemporary Culture: Theories, Politics, and Medial Configurations*, ed. Dorothee Birke and Stella Butter (Berlin: De Gruyter, 2013), 221–22.

38. Maureen Ramsden has argued that the work of French writer-journalists such as Jean-Pierre Chabrol and André Malraux used the same techniques as American New Journalists like Tom Wolfe and Gay Talese. Her article "seeks to show both the way in which the 'twin poles' of journalism, and particularly *reportage*, and fiction are brought together by the interaction of fact and fiction. It also examines the ways in which fiction adapts elements of the journalistic paradigm to serve its own ends." Maureen Ramsden, "The Reporter as Artist: The Interrelation of Fact and Fiction in Reportage," *New Zealand Journal of French Studies* 33, no. 2 (November 2012): 24.

39. Philippe Vilain, *La Littérature sans idéal* (Paris: Grasset, 2016), 73.

40. Claude Grimal ("Le 'new journalism,'" 15) describes Truman Capote's famous book *In Cold Blood* (New York: Random House, 1966) as a "roman-enquête."

41. Philippe Vasset, *Journal intime d'un marchand de canons* (Paris: Fayard, 2009). "Marchand de canons, il est le héros fictif d'aventures réelles. Les transactions décrites, les armes vendues, le nom des fabricants et des acquéreurs, le détail des contrats: tout est vrai. Fort de son expérience de journaliste, Philippe Vasset dévoile un pan de l'économie mondialisée habituellement soustrait aux regards." Translated by SE.

42. Frédéric Beigbeder, *Un roman français* (Paris: Librairie Générale Française, 2010), 23.

43. Frédéric Beigbeder, *Une vie sans fin* (Paris: Grasset, 2018), 11.

44. "Un roman: c'est un miroir qu'on promène le long d'un chemin." Stendhal, *Le Rouge et le noir* (New York: Charles Scribner's Sons, 1931), 88.

45. Georges Sand, *Indiana*, trans. Sylvia Raphael (Oxford: Oxford University Press, 1994), 5.

46. Edmond de Goncourt and Jules de Goncourt, *Germinie Lacerteux*, trans. Leonard Tancock (Middlesex: Penguin, 1984), 15.

47. Truman Capote, in George Plimpton, "The Story Behind a Nonfiction Novel," in *Truman Capote: Conversations*, ed. M. Thomas Inge (Jackson: University Press of Mississippi, 1987), 47–48.

48. See, for example, Charles Cogan, "*Qui a tué Daniel Pearl?* (review)," *French Politics, Culture, and Society* 23, no. 1 (Spring 2005): 166–69.

49. "Ou encore, autofiction, patiemment onaniste, qui espère faire maintenant partager son plaisir." Serge Doubrovsky, *Fils* (Paris: Galilée, 1977).

50. See, for example, Claude Burgelin et al., eds., *Autofiction(s): Colloque de Cerisy 2008* (Lyon: Presses universitaires de Lyon, 2010); and Richard J. Golsan, "The Poetics and Perils of Faction: Contemporary French Fiction and the Memory of World War II," *The Romanic Review* 105, no. 1–2 (January 2014): 53–68.

51. Jean Rolin, in Myriam Boucharenc and Pierre Hyppolite, "Questions à Jean Rolin," in *Roman et reportage XXe–XXIe siècles: Rencontres croisées*, ed. Myriam

Boucharenc (Limoges: Presses universitaires de Limoges, 2015), 272. Regarding the relationship between *reportage* and the novel, Rolin explains, "Comme c'est plutôt le reportage qui nourrit le roman . . . que l'inverse, le reportage témoigne de l'importance du réel" (263).

52. Isabelle Rüf, "En sillonant à pied Los Angeles, Jean Rolin enchante le roman d'espionnage," *Le Temps*, September 9, 2011, https://www.letemps.ch/culture /sillonnant-pied-los-angeles-jean-rolin-enchante-roman-despionnage.

53. Grimal, "Le 'new journalism,'" 15–16. "Il permet au journalisme d'abandonner des habitudes d'écriture stéréotypées et, en l'incitant à emprunter des techniques romanesques, d'atteindre une dimension fictionnelle; il ramène le roman, égaré dans des formalismes vains et des sujets oiseux, vers des méthodes et des préoc-cupations qu'il a oubliées, c'est-à-dire le réalisme et les événements de l'actualité." Translated by SE.

54. Antoine Jurga, "Michel Houellebecq, auteur classique?," in *Lectures croisées de l'oeuvre de Michel Houellebecq*, ed. Antoine Jurga and Sabine van Wesemael (Paris: Classiques Garnier, 2017), 17n3.

55. In Yann Moix's *Partouz*, discussed at length in chapter 1, an imaginary journalist suddenly interrupts the narrative. The narrator responds, "Get out! I don't want a journalist in my novel. There are already too many journalists who write novels," to which the journalist responds, "Fascist! Homophobe! Le Pen follower!" (85).

56. See Myriam Boucharenc, "Nouvelles fictions du reporter au XXe siècle," *Inter-férences Littéraire 7* (November 2011): 115–25.

57. Grégoire Leménager, "La loi du marché," *BibliObs*, June 30, 2015, https://bibliobs .nouvelobs.com/romans/20150629.OBS1727/la-loi-du-marche-revue-par-alexis -jenni.html.

58. Nicolas Léger, "The Literature of Inequality," trans. Isabelle Chalze, *Eurozine*, October 18, 2018, https://www.eurozine.com/the-literature-of-inequality/. For a useful survey of thinkers whose focus is globalization and its discontents, see Philippe Fleury, *Désenchantement et mondialisation* (Paris: L'Harmattan, 2016).

59. Yannick Haenel, *Les Renards pâles* (Paris: Gallimard, 2013), 78.

60. "Et c'est bien de guerre qu'il s'agit: une guerre civile divise la France, comme tous les pays qui suspendent le droit de certaines personnes en criminalisant leur sim-ple existence. Elle oppose les étrangers 'indésirables' . . . et les forces de police. Le plus souvent, elle est dissimulée pour des raisons politiques: ainsi reste-t-elle en partie secrète; mais il arrive, pour les mêmes raisons, qu'on l'exhibe: elle dégénère en spectacle, et les médias, en présentant les sans-papiers comme des délinquants qui enfreignent une loi, maquillent alors cette guerre en lutte contre l'insécurité." Haenel, *Les Renards pâles*, 146. Translated by SE.

61. "*Soumission* (en cela très contemporain) est un roman médiatique autant et plus que politique. Parce que le geste d'*allumer la télévision* y revient constamment, et que le réel, les événements, ce qui se passe, parvient au narrateur et au lecteur con-stamment et presque uniquement par ce canal, ou celui des smartphones, ou iphones, ce qui revient au même. Le narrateur s'informe sans cesse non pas seule-ment de ce qui se passe, mais des commentaires des 'commentateurs' pour les commenter à son tour. Et roman médiatique aussi parce que ce qui s'appelle ici politique émane entièrement des médias: la politique de Houellebecq, qui est sans *expérience* politique, sort du poste de télévision comme le diable sort de sa

boîte. Elle doit tout aux écrans, aux journaux; la matière travaillée, ce n'est pas 'le réel,' c'est le brouhaha médiatique qui se fait fort de le décrire." Pérez, "Houellebecq," 115.

62. "La politique de *Soumission*, c'est la matière du vingt-heures formatée de telle sorte qu'on peut mettre *roman* sur la couverture." Pérez, "Houellebecq," 115.

63. "Ce que *Soumission* emprunte aux médias, ce n'est pas seulement son sujet, c'est son langage. Sa langue lui est prescrite par les journaux." Pérez, "Houellebecq," 116.

64. Michel Houellebecq, *Submission*, trans. Loren Stein (New York: Picador, 2015), 124.

65. In a description of Luc Lang's 9/11 novel *11 septembre mon amour*, Philippe Vilain argues that reality in the novel is a construction, what he calls "un réel médiatisé par les écrans de télévision diffusant en boucle, sur CNN, les images des deux tours en feux." Vilain, *La Littérature sans idéal*, 50.

66. Wolfe, "Stalking the Billion-Footed Beast," 50.

67. Vasset, *Journal intime d'un marchand de canons*.

68. Jean-François Duclos, "'Nous ne laissons rien du monde': Philippe Vasset et les zones blanches de la carte," *French Review* 87, no. 2 (December 2013): 62.

69. Églantine Colon, "Neither *Lieux de Mémoire*, nor *Non-Lieux*: Towards a Concept of Precarious Spaces in Philippe Vasset's *Un livre blanc*," *French Studies* 71, no. 1 (January 2017): 69.

70. Philippe Vasset, *Un Livre blanc* (Paris: Fayard, 2007), 129.

71. Filippo Zanghi has noted the tendency of contemporary French writers to focus on urban marginality in their stories, studying this phenomenon specifically in the novels of François Bon, François Maspero, Jacques Réda, Jean Rolin, Denis Tillinac, and Philippe Vasset. See his *Zone indécise: Périphéries urbaines et voyage de proximité dans la littérature contemporaine* (Villeneuve-d'Ascq: Presses universitaires du Septentrion, 2014). See also Olivier Adam's novel *Les Lisières* (Paris: Flammarion, 2012), whose central theme is social, political, and affective marginality.

72. Philippe Vasset and Olivia Rosenthal, "Entretien avec Philippe Vasset," *Littérature* 160 (December 2010): 34.

73. Writing of the ways in which Vasset refuses to fill the empty spaces of the Parisian periphery with meaning, Éric Trudel writes, "Dans une certaine mesure, c'est même par cette sorte d'échec ou de devenir-déchet que le texte, par un curieux mimétisme de la forme, garantit sa véracité." Éric Trudel, "Passions du réel (sur Philippe Vasset, Olivia Rosenthal et Thomas Clerc)," *Australian Journal of French Studies* 54, no. 2–3 (2017): 122.

74. Dominique Kalifa, "Usages du faux: Faits divers et romans criminels au 19e siècle," *Annales. Histoire, Sciences Sociales* 54, no. 6 (November–December 1999): 1348.

75. Jean Touzot, "Du fait divers au roman: L'exemple de Mauriac," in *Roman et reportage XXe-XXIe siècles: Rencontres croisées*, ed. Myriam Boucharenc (Limoges: Presses universitaires de Limoges, 2015), 150. " Des nombreux cas de suicide par pendaison, noyade, défenestration, recours aux barbituriques ou, plus souvent encore au revolver; on y rencontre des assassins crapuleux ou non, un crime sexuel perpétré sur une adolescente, des accidents de la route, bref tout ce qui relève de la rubrique dite, par métonymie de l'espèce pour le genre, rubrique des chiens écrasés." Translated by SE.

76. Kalifa defines the characteristics of this genre—"des récits d'aventures où la rupture criminelle donne lieu à une exploration plus ou moins méthodique du monde social"—and describes it as an umbrella term comprising other genres: "les grands cycles feuilletonesques du milieu du siècle (Sue, Dumas, Féval, Ponson du Terrail, etc.), le roman judiciaire (Gaboriau et ses suiveurs) et les prémisses du roman de détection." Kalifa, "Usages du faux," 1345n3.

77. Kalifa, "Usages du faux," 1345.

78. Kalifa describes the contradictory demands of the culture industry "qui poussent les 'fait-diversiers' à écrire de plus en plus vite (coller à l'événement, voir le devancer pour déjouer la concurrence, ce qui devient l'objectif majeur des journaux à compter de la décennie 1880), tout en déployant talent et savoir-faire 'littéraire' pour séduire un lectorat de plus en plus sollicité." Kalifa, "Usages du faux," 1350.

79. Félix Fénéon, *Novels in Three Lines*, trans. Luc Sante (New York: NYRB, 2007), 69.

80. Yann Moix's *Partouz* begins with the premise that 9/11 was caused because a woman refused the amorous advances of Mohammed Atta. Moix had more to say about the connection between terrorism and the *fait divers*. He wrote, "Le terrorisme terrorise à la fois par son exceptionnalité et par sa banalité. Banalisation de l'exception. Le fait divers est devenu le mode opératoire du terroriste: Larossi Abballa assassine à coups de couteau Jean-Baptiste Salvaing et sa compagne Jessica Schneider—tous deux policiers—à Magnanville. Djihad à domicile; terrorisme domestique." Yann Moix, *Terreur* (Paris: Grasset, 2017), 20. For more on *fait divers* and contemporary French fiction, see the chapter "Fiction et faits divers" in Dominique Viart and Bruno Vercier, *La Littérature française au présent: Héritage, modernité, mutations* (Paris: Bordas, 2005), 228–44.

81. Jean Rolin, *Les Événements* (Paris: P.O.L., 2015), 82.

82. "En temps de guerre, et même dans le contexte d'un couvre-feu globalement respecté—mais allez savoir jusqu'à quel point, et si c'est en tout lieu—, la plupart des informations recueillies à distance sur la situation particulière de telle ou telle route ou de telle ou telle localité s'avèrent inexactes, à l'usage, soit parce qu'elles vous ont été communiquées à la légère, ou de mauvaise foi, soit parce que la situation a évolué, dans un sens ou dans l'autre, entre le moment où ces informations ont été recueillies et celui où elles vous parviennent." Translated by SE.

83. "Quant à la raison pour laquelle le narrateur se retrouve sur la départementale 721, alors que nous l'avions laissé en bordure de la nationale 20, c'est apparemment qu'il a quitté celle-ci, au moment où elle s'engage dans la traversée d'Étampes, sur la foi d'informations discutables faisant état d'une reprise des combats dans le chef-lieu de l'Essonne, au confluent de la Chalouette et de la Juine." Translated by SE.

84. Sophie Ménard, "Frénésie patrimoniale et monumentale: *Les Événements* de Jean Rolin," *Spirale* 259 (Winter 2017): 36.

85. Jean Rolin, in Boucharenc and Hyppolite, "Questions à Jean Rolin," 264. "J'avais envie d'écrire un roman de légère anticipation, je veux dire par là, un livre dont l'action, l'intrigue aurait été située en France, mais dans un avenir indéterminé assez proche. Mais comment décrire les lieux tels qu'ils seront dans quelques années? Et si je décris les lieux tels qu'ils sont maintenant, ça n'est pas puisque l'intrigue se situe dans un avenir indéterminé. J'ai été paralysé par un obstacle apparemment peu élevé, une sorte de taupinière, qui m'a fait trébucher, parce

que l'exactitude, le rendu des choses vues dans leur exactitude, dans leur préci-
sion, me faisait défaut." Translated by SE.
86. Sophie Ménard has noted the subordination of the action to description in Roland's
book and writes that "le laminage événementiel a pour contrepartie une juxtaposition de morceaux descriptifs du terroir français." Ménard, "Frénésie patrimoniale et monumentale," 36.
87. "Avec ce minuscule râteau aux dents très écartées, j'espère arriver à ramasser suf-
fisamment de choses pour construire un livre." Rolin, in Boucharenc and Hyppolite, "Questions à Jean Rolin," 276. "À force de traîner son râteau, on finit par
accrocher quelque chose" (278).
88. "J'ai tendance à rechercher dans la vie réelle ce qui ressemble à la littérature et au
cinéma." Rolin, in Boucharenc and Hyppolite, "Questions à Jean Rolin," 274.
89. Ruth Cruickshank, *Fin de Millénaire French Fiction: The Aesthetics of Crisis*
(Oxford: Oxford University Press, 2009), 41.
90. Jean Baudrillard, "The Spirit of Terrorism," in *The Spirit of Terrorism and Requiem
for the Twin Towers*, trans. Chris Turner (London: Verso, 2002), 31.
91. Alain Duhamel, *Les Peurs françaises* (Paris: Flammarion, 1993), 14. "La peur de
l'information peut sembler plus anecdotique: il n'en est rien. En pleine période
dépressive, la tentation de l'irrationalité, de la sujectivité, de l'approximation ou
du sensationnalisme font des ravages. La télévision pèse de plus en plus lourd sur
le moral des Français. Elle exerce un effet d'amplification. Le culte de l'instantanéité,
le risque de la superficialité, contribuent à façonner une image de la société littéralement illisible et indéchiffrable." Translated by SE.
92. "Que les Français eux-mêmes cèdent plus volontiers à leurs idées reçues, à leurs
réflexes conditionnés et à leurs pulsions émotives qu'à l'austérité des faits et à
l'équilibre du jugement, les exemples en abondent, et dans tous les domaines. Les
Français croient ce qu'ils veulent croire et non pas ce qui est." Duhamel, *Les Peurs
françaises*, 191.
93. Michel Onfray, *Miroir du nihilisme: Houellebecq éducateur* (Paris: Galilée, 2017),
127–28.
94. See Violaine Morin, "L'insaisissable Frédéric Lordon de la Nuit debout,"
*Le Monde*, April 19, 2016, https://www.lemonde.fr/idees/article/2016/04/21/l
-insaisissable-frederic-lordon-maitre-a-penser-de-la-nuit-debout_4906449_3232
.html.
95. Frédéric Lordon, "Politique post-vérité ou journalisme post-politique?," *Le
Monde Diplomatique*, November 22, 2016, https://blog.mondediplo.net/2016-11
-22-Politique-post-verite-ou-journalisme-post.
96. "La frénésie du fact-checking est elle-même le produit dérivé tardif, mais au plus
haut point représentatif, du journalisme post-politique, qui règne en fait depuis
très longtemps, et dans lequel il n'y a plus *rien* à discuter, hormis des vérités fac-
tuelles. La philosophie spontanée du fact-checking, c'est que le monde n'est qu'une
collection de faits et que, non seulement, comme la terre, les faits ne mentent pas,
mais qu'ils épuisent tout ce qu'il y a à dire du monde. Le problème est que cette
vérité post-politique, opposée à la politique post-vérité, est entièrement fausse, que
des faits correctement établis ne seront jamais le terminus de la politique mais à
peine son commencement, car des faits *n'ont jamais rien dit d'eux-mêmes*, rien!

Des faits ne sont mis en ordre que par le travail de médiations qui ne leur appartiennent pas." Translated by SE.

97. See the article "Macron veut une loi contre les fausses informations en période électorale," *Le Monde* (January 3, 2018), https://www.lemonde.fr/actualite-medias/article/2018/01/03/emmanuel-macron-souhaite-une-loi-pour-lutter-contre-la-diffusion-de-fausses-informations-pendant-les-campagnes-electorales_5237279_3236.html; and the "Avis sur les propositions de loi relatives à la lutte contre les fausses informations," http://www.conseil-etat.fr/content/download/134123/1359552/version/1/file/avis%20394641-394642.pdf.

## 4. REAL-TIME REALISM, PART 2:
### *LE ROMAN POST-PAMPHLÉTAIRE*

1. Frédéric Saenen, *Dictionnaire du pamphlet: De la Révolution à Internet* (Gollion: Infolio, 2010), 9.
2. Susan Rubin Suleiman, *Authoritarian Fictions: The Ideological Novel as a Literary Genre* (New York: Columbia University Press, 1983), 69.
3. Michel Hastings et al., "Les mutations du pamphlet dans la France contemporaine," *Mots: Les Langages du Politique* 91 (November 2009): 6.
4. To offer just a few examples, see Jean Bothorel's *Chers imposteurs* (Paris: Fayard, 2008), a rant against contemporary public intellectuals, the death of literature and critique, and the deculturation of the presidency; Richard Millet's *Langue fantôme, suivi de Éloge littéraire d'Anders Breivik* (Paris: Roux, 2012), which bemoans the death of French literature and celebrates the "formal perfection" of the Norwegian terrorist Breivik's murder of seventy-seven people in 2011. Annie Ernaux declared this text a "fascist pamphlet." Annie Ernaux, "Le pamphlet fasciste de Richard Millet déshonore la littérature," *Le Monde*, September 10, 2012, http://www.lemonde.fr/idees/article/2012/09/10/le-pamphlet-de-richard-millet-deshonore-la-litterature_1758011_3232.html. Also see Zineb El Rhazoui's *Détruire le fascisme islamique* (Paris: Ring, 2016), written by a Charlie Hebdo journalist who happened to be out of town when the offices were attacked in January 2015. Contemporary *romans à thèse* include Éric Zemmour's *Petit frère* (Paris: Denoël, 2008) or Richard Millet's *Province* (Paris: Éditions Léo Scheer, 2016).
5. Jérôme Meizoz, "Le roman et l'inacceptable: Sociologie d'une polémique: Autour de *Plateforme* de Michel Houellebecq," in *L'œil sociologue et la littérature* (Geneva: Slatkine Érudition, 2004), 138.
6. Agathe Novak-Chevalier, *Houellebecq, l'art de la consolation* (Paris: Stock, 2018), 59.
7. Suleiman, *Authoritarian Fictions*, 10.
8. Meizoz, in "Le roman et l'inacceptable," notes "quatre procédés caractéristiques du roman à thèse" present in *Platform*: "toute l'intrigue s'oriente vers une seule thèse anti-islamique; celle-ci bénéficie de trois personnages adjuvants qui la répètent à intervalles réguliers, sans que des opposants (les terroristes demeurent muets) acquièrent une vraie consistance doxique; un 'intertexte doctrinal' (Voltaire, Schopenhauer) fonde la thèse; la fonction idéologique du narrateur appuie

systèmatiquement celle-ci" (137). However, Mezioz raises the question, "Mais s'il y a 'thèse,' faut-il la lire sérieusement? Plusieurs indices invitent à une lecture distanciée: la redondance ostentatoire des contenus critiques, l'allusion appuyée à des argumentaires ultra-classiques; enfin, les effets rhétoriques massifs du narrateur . . . en font plutôt un pastiche satirique du roman à thèse" (137–38).

9. Dominique Rabaté, "Extension ou liquidation de la lutte? Remarques sur le roman selon Houellebecq," in *Le Discours "néo-réactionnaire": Transgressions conservatrices*, ed. Pascal Durand and Sarah Sindaco (Paris: CNRS Éditions, 2015), 266.

10. Gavin Bowd, "The Anti-Sartre? Michel Houellebecq and Politics," *Australian Journal of French Studies* 56, no. 1 (2019): 23.

11. See Adam Gopnik, "The Next Thing: Michel Houellebecq's Francophobic Satire," *New Yorker*, January 26, 2015, https://www.newyorker.com/magazine/2015/01/26/next-thing.

12. See Karl Ove Knausgaard, "Michel Houellebecq's *Submission*" (review), *New York Times*, November 2, 2015, https://www.nytimes.com/2015/11/08/books/review/michel-houellebecqs-submission.html; the chapter "Sex, Tourism, and the Politics of Enjoyment in Michel Houellebecq's *Platform*," in Graham Matthews, *Ethics and Desire in the Wake of Postmodernism: Contemporary Satire* (London: Continuum, 2012); Guy Berger, "Un conte satirique: *Soumission*," *Commentaire* 149 (2015): 197–200; and Alex Preston, "*Submission* by Michel Houellebecq Review: Satire That's More Subtle Than It Seems," *Guardian*, September 8, 2015, https://www.theguardian.com/books/2015/sep/08/submission-michel-houellebecq-review-satire-islamic-france.

13. Bruno Viard, *La République insoumise: Réponse à Michel Houellebecq* (Paris: Éditions Mimésis, 2016), 10.

14. Marc Angenot, *La Parole pamphlétaire: Contribution à la typologie des discours modernes* (Paris: Payot, 1982), 9.

15. For more on the invective spirit in literature, see the special issue "Esthétiques de l'invective," ed. Marie-Hélène Larochelle, *Études Littéraires* 39, no. 2 (Winter 2008).

16. Yves Avril, "Le pamphlet: Essai de définition et analyse de quelques-uns de ses procédés," *Études Littéraires* 11, no. 2 (1978): 265.

17. Cédric Passard, *L'âge d'or du pamphlet* (Paris: CNRS Éditions, 2015), 6.

18. Hastings et al., "Les mutations du pamphlet dans la France contemporaine," 5.

19. For the distinctions between these three genres, see Angenot, *La Parole pamphlétaire*, 38.

20. To the *polémique* and *satire*, Passard adds several other genres deployed by the *discours pamphlétaire*, writing: "Libelle, brochure, tract, placard, chanson, journal, essai, voire roman, le discours pamphlétaire a connu bien des avatars." Passard, *L'âge d'or du pamphlet*, 6.

21. Passard, *L'âge d'or du pamphlet*, 117.

22. Pascale Tournier, *Le vieux monde est de retour: Enquête sur les nouveaux conservateurs* (Paris: Stock, 2018), back cover.

23. I was able to find only one novel whose author labeled it explicitly as a *roman pamphlétaire*, and that is Georges Anquetil's strange book *Satan conduit le bal: Roman pamphlétaire et philosophique des mœurs du temps* (Paris: Anquetil, 1925).

24. Suleiman, *Authoritarian Fictions*, 7.

25. A few articles have addressed the topic. See, for example, Sylvie Servoise, "Roman à thèse et roman engagé: Exemplarité diégétique et exemplarité narrative," in *Littérature et exemplarité*, ed. Alexandre Gefen et al. (Rennes: Presses universitaires de Rennes, 2016), 347–56; Sylvie Servoise, *Le Roman face à l'histoire: La littérature engagée en France et en Italie dans la seconde moitié du XXe siècle* (Rennes: Presses universitaires de Rennes, 2011), chap. 2, "Roman engagé et roman à thèse: Les frères ennemis," 41–75; Michel Villette, "Thèses de sociologie et romans à thèse," *Sociedad e Estado* 17, no. 2 (2002): 541–60; and Maryse Souchard, "Towards a Semiotics of the Ideological Novel," *Sociocriticism* 2, no. 1 (October 1986): 47–68.

26. Suleiman, *Authoritarian Fictions*, 22.

27. Laurent Binet et al., "Interview with Laurent Binet," *The Romanic Review* 105, no. 1–2 (January 2014): 88.

28. "Le roman idéologique est un roman où les idées et surtout l'émotion provoquée par le jeu des idées occupent une part plus importante que l'intrigue. Bien souvent d'ailleurs celle-ci retrace un parcours de découvertes intellectuelles et morales." Claire Bompaire-Evesque, "Roman balzacien, roman 'idéologique': Les choix de Barrès dans *La Colline inspirée*," *Revue d'Histoire Littéraire de la France* 98, no. 4 (1998): 584.

29. "Dans ce type de roman, les éléments réalistes sont peu développés." Bompaire-Evesque, "Roman balzacien," 584.

30. Barrès, qtd. in Bombaire-Evesque, "Roman balzacien," 584.

31. Dominique Viart, "De la littérature contemporaine à l'université: Une question critique," *Fabula.org*, March 20, 2008, http://www.fabula.org/atelier.php?De_la_litt%26eacute%3Brature_contemporaine_%26agrave%3B_l%27universit%26eacute%3B%3A_une_question_critique.

32. Michel Houellebecq, *Platform*, trans. Frank Wynne (London: Heinemann, 2002), 125.

33. Houellebecq, *Platform*, 251.

34. Frédéric Beigbeder, *Windows on the World*, trans. Frank Wynne (New York: Hyperion, 2004), 283.

35. Yann Moix, *Partouz* (Paris: Grasset, 2004), 24. My translation.

36. Michel Houellebecq, *The Possibility of an Island*, trans. Gavin Bowd (New York: Vintage, 2005), 56.

37. Alexis Jenni, *L'Art français de la guerre* (Paris: Gallimard, 2011), 457. My translation.

38. Bernard-Henri Lévy, *Hôtel Europe* (Paris: Grasset, 2014), 41–42.

39. Michel Houellebecq, *Sérotonine* (Paris: Flammarion, 2019), 159. "Voilà comment une civilisation meurt, sans tracas, sans dangers ni sans drames et avec très peu de carnage, une civilisation meurt juste par lassitude, par dégoût d'elle-même." Translated by SE.

40. John Attridge, "Houellebecq's Occidentalism," *Australian Humanities Review* 62 (November 2017): 65.

41. See Ben Jeffrey, *Anti-Matter: Michel Houellebecq and Depressive Realism* (Winchester: Zero, 2011).

42. Attridge, "Houellebecq's Occidentalism," 66.

43. Michel Houellebecq, *Interventions 2: Traces* (Paris: Flammarion, 2009), 165.

44. "La religion la plus con, c'est quand même l'islam." Didier Sénécal, "Michel Houellebecq," *Lire*, September 1, 2001, http://www.lexpress.fr/culture/livre/michel-houellebecq_804761.html.
45. Douglas Morrey, *Michel Houellebecq: Humanity and Its Aftermath* (Liverpool: Liverpool University Press, 2013), 40.
46. Robert Dion and Élisabeth Haghebaert, "Le cas de Michel Houellebecq et la dynamique des genres littéraires," *French Studies* 55, no. 4 (2001): 520.
47. Liesbeth Korthals Altes, "Persuasion et ambiguïté dans un roman à thèse postmoderne (*Les Particules élémentaires*)," in *Michel Houellebecq*, ed. Sabine van Wesemael (Amsterdam: Rodopi, 2004), 22.
48. Denis writes that the thesis "consiste à poser qu'entre tourisme culturel de masse et tourisme sexuel, il n'y a de différence que de degré, l'une et l'autre activités n'étant fondamentalement que le produit du droit que s'est arrogé l'homme blanc en régime libéral de consommer le monde." Benoît Denis, "Ironie et idéologie: Réflexions sur la 'responsabilité idéologique' du texte," *Contextes* 2 (2007), http://journals.openedition.org/contextes/180.
49. Gopnik, "The Next Thing."
50. "Une analyse textuelle rigoureuse se focalisant sur le caractère postmoderne de l'ouvrage nous apprend au final que les accusations d'islamophobie prononcées à l'encontre de Houellebecq se trouvent nécessairement—postmodernisme oblige—annihilées." David Spieser-Landes, "Soumission ou simulacre de soumission? Michel Houellebecq et la métaphysique (Baudrillardienne) du radiateur," *French Cultural Studies* 28, no. 1 (2016): 43.
51. Douglas Morrey, "The Banality of Monstrosity: On Michel Houellebecq's *Soumission*," *Australian Journal of French Studies* 55, no. 2 (2018): 216–17.
52. Novak-Lechevalier, *Houellebecq*, 59. "Si les romans de Houellebecq affichent souvent les caractéristiques formelles du roman à thèse, la thèse elle-même semble paradoxalement s'y évanouir: la juxtaposition de perspectives et de tonalités incompatibles, le travail de la parodie, les jeux constants sur l'ambivalence minent de l'intérieur toute univocité et interdisent de figer les différents énoncés du roman en une doctrine identifiable." Translated by SE.
53. Viard, *La République insoumise*, 47.
54. For example, Jerry Andrew Varsava writes of *The Elementary Particles*: "A powerful *roman à thèse*, Houellebecq's work mounts what is, finally, an ineffectual challenge to the defining and ennobling tenets of liberalism: free will, self-determination, property rights, the separation of the public and private spheres, tolerance, and *laissez-faire* morality." Jerry Andrew Varsava, "Utopian Yearnings, Dystopian Thoughts: Houellebecq's *The Elementary Particles* and the Problem of Scientific Communitarianism," *College Literature* 32, no. 4 (Fall 2005): 145–46. Liesbeth Korthals Altes offers a long list of other critics who labeled Houellebecq's novels as *romans à thèse*. See Korthals Altes, "Persuasion et ambiguïté," 29–30.
55. See Frédéric Deslauriers' book *Les Deux-cents jours de Marine le Pen* (Paris: Plon, 2011), a novel that imagines a world in which Le Pen becomes president in the 2012 elections and Éric Zemmour is appointed minister of culture and communication.
56. Michel Onfray, *Miroir du nihilisme: Houellebecq éducateur* (Paris: Galilée, 2017), 127.

57. Gopnik, "The Next Thing."
58. François explains, "That old queer Nietzsche had it right: Christianity was, at the end of the day, a feminine religion." Michel Houellebecq, *Submission*, trans. Loren Stein (New York: Picador, 2015), 179.
59. Novak-Chevalier, *Houellebecq*, 57.
60. Michel Houellebecq and Bernard-Henri Lévy, *Public Enemies*, trans. Miriam Frendo and Frank Wynne (New York: Random House, 2011), 111. In a speech given upon the occasion of his winning of the Schirrmacher Prize in 2016, he continued to parse the term "reactionary": "Un souverainiste, ou toute personne hostile à la dissolution de son pays dans un espace fédéral européen, est un réactionnaire. Quelqu'un qui défend l'utilisation de la langue française en France, ou de toute langue nationale dans son propre pays, qui s'oppose à l'utilisation universelle de l'anglais, est un réactionnaire. Quelqu'un qui se méfie de la démocratie parlementaire et du système des partis, qui ne considère pas ce système comme la fin ultime de l'organisation politique, qui aimerait qu'on donne davantage la parole à la population, est un réactionnaire." Michel Houellebecq, "Schirrmacher-Preis, Michel Houellebecq, 26.9.2016," http://schirrmacher-stiftung.de/wp-content /uploads/2016/10/Dankesrede_original_Houellebecq_26.9.16.pdf.
61. In Brooks Adams's 1895 book *The Law of Civilization and Decay: An Essay on History*, he applies the logic of entropy to civilizational development and decline. "The theory proposed is based upon the accepted scientific principle, that the law of force and energy is of universal application in nature, and that animal life is one of the outlets through which solar energy is dissipated. Starting from this fundamental proposition, the first deduction is, that, as human societies are forms of animal life, these societies must differ among themselves in energy, in proportion as nature has endowed them, more or less abundantly, with energetic material." Brooks Adams, *The Law of Civilizational Decay: An Essay on History* (London: Swan Sonnenschein & Co., 1895), v. His preface concludes: "The evidence seems to point to the conclusion, that, when a highly centralized society disintegrates, under the pressure of economic competition, it is because the energy of the race has been exhausted. Consequently, the survivors of such a race lack the power necessary for renewed concentration, and must probably remain inert, until supplied with fresh energetic material by the infusion of barbarian blood" (vi). For a review of Adams's theories, see Theodore Roosevelt, "The Law of Civilization and Decay," in *American Ideals and Other Essays, Social and Political* (New York: G. P. Putnam's Sons, 1897), 318–42.
62. On the connection between Houellebecq and decadence, see Ludivine Fustin, "Michel Houellebecq: Un décadent au XXIe siècle," in *States of Decadence*, ed. Guri Barstad and Karen P. Knutsen (Newcastle: Cambridge Scholars Publishing, 2016), 1:185–98.
63. Houellebecq, in Sylvain Bourmeau, "Scare Tactics: Michel Houellebecq Defends His Controversial New Book," *Paris Review*, January 2, 2015, https://www .theparisreview.org/blog/2015/01/02/scare-tactics-michel-houellebecq-on-his -new-book/.
64. David Jack and Benjamin Andréo describe "the standard Houellebecquian narrator" as "white, male, middle-aged, middle-class and seemingly suffering from some kind of midlife crisis, resulting in various acerbic observations about

contemporary society which emerge from a deep-seated sexual dissatisfaction and general ennui with all things occidental." David Jack and Benjamin Andréo, "Introduction," *Australian Journal of French Studies* 56, no. 1 (2019): 3.

65. Houellebecq, *Submission*, 64.

66. Houellebecq explored the relationship between economy and sex in his 1994 novel *Extension du domaine de la lutte* (titled *Whatever* in English), in which the protagonist draws the conclusion that "economic liberalism is an extension of the domain of the struggle, its extension to all ages and all classes of society. Sexual liberalism is likewise an extension of the domain of the struggle, its extension to all ages and all classes of society." Just as economic liberalism allows for the simultaneous existence of a small, extremely wealthy class and a large impoverished class, sexual liberalism results in *"absolute pauperization,"* in which just a few are having constant good sex while the rest remain celibate or undersexed. Michel Houellebecq, *Whatever*, trans. Paul Hammond (London: Serpent's Tail, 1998), 99.

67. For more on this influence, see Alain-Philippe Durand, "Pascal Bruckner et Michel Houellebecq: Deux transécrivains au milieu du monde," in *Michel Houellebecq sous la loupe*, ed. Murielle Lucie Clément and Sabine van Wesemael (Amsterdam: Rodopi, 2007), 157–67.

68. For example, a character named Robert from Houellebecq's 2001 novel *Platform* delivers a defense of the "benevolent, almost humanist racism" that was standard among Europeans before they began to consider Third World people as their equals. "The moment the white man began to consider blacks as *equals,* it was obvious that sooner or later they would come to consider them to be *superior"* (113).

69. The full title of Kipling's poem is "The White Man's Burden: The United States and the Philippine Islands."

70. Houellebecq and Lévy, *Public Enemies*, 213.

71. Bruno Viard notes the variety of thinkers who haunt Houellebecq's works: "Auguste Comte dans *Extension* et dans *Plateforme*, Saint-Simon et Pierre Leroux dans *La Carte*, Charles Péguy dans *Extension* et dans *Soumission*, Gilbert Chesterton dans *La Carte* et dans *Soumission*." Viard, *La République insoumise*, 9. See also Bernard Maris, *Houellebecq économiste* (Paris: Flammarion, 2014); and George Chabert, "Michel Houellebecq, lecteur d'Auguste Comte," *Revue Romane* 37, no. 2 (2002): 187–204.

72. David Nowell Smith, "In the Midst of the Suicide of the West, It Was Clear They Didn't Stand a Chance," *Critical Quarterly* 58, no. 3 (2016): 30.

73. For a Derridean reading of the complex relationship between Houellebecq, writing, and far-right politics, see Delphine Grass, "Ghosts in the Text: Writing Technologies, Authorial Strategy, and the Politics of Reactionary Autoimmunity in Houellebecq's Works," *Australian Journal of French Studies* 56, no. 1 (2019): 53–69.

74. Claude Pérez, "Houellebecq, le vingt-heures et l'art du roman: À propos de *Soumission*," *Revue Critique de Fixxion Française Contemporaine* 11 (2015): 112.

75. At one point, François remarks, "The idea that political history could play any part in my own life was still disconcerting, and slightly repellent." Houellebecq, *Submission*, 92.

76. For more on race in Houellebecq, see Ania Wroblewski, "Les seuls blancs à Châtelet-les-Halles: Richard Millet, Michel Houellebecq et les limites du

nationalisme français," in *Lectures croisées de l'oeuvre de Michel Houellebecq*, ed. Antoine Jurga and Sabine van Wesemael (Paris: Classiques Garnier, 2017), 63–78.

77. See Bruno Viard, "Houellebecq romancier catholique et socialiste," *Australian Journal of French Studies* 56, no. 1 (2019): 70–74.

78. For example, François observes: "Hidden all day in impenetrable black burkas, rich Saudi women transformed themselves by night into birds of paradise with their corsets, their see-through bras, their G-strings with multicolored lace and rhinestones. They were exactly the opposite of Western women, who spent their days dressed up and looking sexy to maintain their social status, then collapsed in exhaustion once they got home, abandoning all hope of seduction in favor of clothes that were loose and shapeless." Houellebecq, *Submission*, 72.

79. Agathe Novak-Chevalier, "*Soumission*: Littérature comme résistance," *Libération*, March 1, 2015, https://next.liberation.fr/culture/2015/03/01/soumission-la-litterature-comme-resistance_1212088. "Le narrateur ne se convertit pas à la fin de *Soumission*; il envisage la conversion et ses suites comme une (tentante) possibilité. De son titre, donc, à ses dernières pages, le roman restera suspensif et instable. Nul appui, nulle clôture n'offriront au lecteur la garantie d'un sens hors de portée d'une menace de réversibilité incessante. En quoi *Soumission* ne saurait en aucun cas être considéré comme un roman à thèse, ni rangé sous aucune bannière." Translated by SE. Seth Armus describes this as a "speculative, rather than factual, last chapter." Seth Armus, "Trying on the Veil: Sexual Autonomy and the End of the French Republic in Michel Houellebecq's *Submission*," *French Politics, Culture, and Society* 35, no. 1 (2017): 137.

80. Carole Sweeney, " 'And Yet Some Free Time Remains . . .': Post-Fordism and Writing in Michel Houellebecq's *Whatever*," *Journal of Modern Literature* 33, no. 4 (Summer 2010): 41.

81. "Dans *Les Particules élémentaires*, le sexe, la science et l'économie sont indissociables." Jean-François Chassay, "Les Corpuscules de Krause: À propos de *Particules élémentaires* de Michel Houellebecq," *Australian Journal of French Studies* 42, no. 1 (2005): 37.

82. Nathan Gardels, "Cloning: Central Planning of the 21st Century?," *New Perspectives Quarterly* 18, no. 1 (Winter 2001): 56. Of this novel, Philippe Muray wrote, "Le roman de Houellebecq est un livre né du *sentiment de la fin*, et tous ses personnages se débrouillent, d'une façon ou d'une autre, avec ce sentiment." Philippe Muray, "Et, en tout, apercevoir la fin . . . ," in *Michel Houellebecq*, ed. Agathe Novak-Lechevalier (Paris: L'Herne, 2017), 248.

83. Nurit Buchweiz and Elie Cohen-Gewerc, "Leisure and Posthumanism in Houellebecq's *Platform* and *Lanzarote*," *Comparative Literature and Culture* 17, no. 4 (2015), http://docs.lib.purdue.edu/clcweb/vol17/iss4/3.

84. Bülent Diken, "The Map, the Territory, and the Impossibility of Painting a Priest," *Critical Sociology* 42, no. 7–8 (2014): 1110.

85. Louis Betty, " 'F&#% Autonomy': Houellebecq, *Submission*, and Enlightenment's 'Last Dismaying Dregs,' " *Modern and Contemporary France*, January 7, 2019, 2.

86. Rachel Donadio, "A Novel Made for the 'Yellow Vest' Moment," *Atlantic*, January 13, 2019, https://www.theatlantic.com/entertainment/archive/2019/01/michel-houellebecqs-new-book-indictment-eu/580165/.

87. Louis Betty, *Without God: Michel Houellebecq and Materialist Horror* (University Park: Pennsylvania State University Press, 2016), 12.

88. In a discussion on the legacy of Comtean positivism and burgeoning forms of humanism, the characters Walcott and Djerzinski reflect on the nature of reality: "Man no longer needed God, nor even the idea of an underlying reality. 'There are human perceptions,' said Walcott, 'human testimonies, human experiences; reason links them, and emotion brings them alive. All of this happens without any metaphysical intervention, without any ontology at all. We don't need concepts of God or nature or reality anymore.'" Michel Houellebecq, *The Elementary Particles*, trans. Frank Wynne (New York: Vintage, 2000), 249.

89. Michel Houellebecq, in Christophe Duchatelet et al., *Michel Houellebecq: Les grands entretiens d'artpress* (Paris: IMEC, 2012), 25.

90. In a brief excursus, the narrator explains that the different conceptions of love as perceived by men and by women lead them to live in "deux réalités radicalement différentes." Michel Houellebecq, *Sérotonine* (Paris: Flammarion, 2019), 70.

91. After the suicide of a friend and the death of several farmers at the hands of the riot police, the narrator explains, "Je me réveillai très tard le lendemain matin, dans un état de nausée et d'incrédulité proche du spasme, rien de tout cela ne me paraissait possible ni réel." Houellebecq, *Sérotonine*, 264. In a moment of psychosis, he convinces himself that the only way to get a former girlfriend to come back to him is to assassinate her four-year-old son. His behavior becomes more and more erratic and less rational as his reality falls apart.

92. For an excellent analysis of this book and its influence, see Jan-Werner Müller, "Julien Benda's Anti-Passionate Europe," *European Journal of Political Theory* 5, no. 2 (2006): 125–37.

93. Jean Bothorel, *Chers imposteurs* (Paris: Fayard, 2008), 12.

## CONCLUSION: NOVEL AS NATION: FORMS OF PARALLEL DECAY

1. Richard Millet, *Désenchantement de la littérature* (Paris: Gallimard, 2007), 25.

2. Sébastien Ledoux, "Dans l'enseignement de l'histoire, pensons 'un récit national émancipateur et inclusif," *Le Monde*, September 3, 2016, https://www.lemonde.fr/idees/article/2016/09/03/dans-l-enseignement-de-l-histoire-pensons-un-recit-national-emancipateur-et-inclusif_4992126_3232.html.

3. Durand specifically quotes Jean-Luc Mélenchon (Front de gauche): "À partir du moment où l'on est français, on adopte le récit national." Anne-Aël Durand, "'Roman national,' 'récit national': De quoi parle-t-on?" *Le Monde*, September 28, 2016, https://www.lemonde.fr/les-decodeurs/article/2016/09/28/roman-national-recit-national-de-quoi-parle-t-on_5004994_4355770.html.

4. Ledoux, "Dans l'enseignement de l'histoire."

5. See Gérard Tautil, *Le Roman national français au défi de l'extrême droite* (Paris: L'Harmattan, 2016).

6. Michel Houellebecq and Bernard-Henri Lévy, *Public Enemies*, trans. Miriam Frendo and Frank Wynne (New York: Random House, 2011), 106.

7. His protagonist François in *Submission* states, "Nations were a murderous absurdity, and after 1870 anyone paying attention had probably figured this out." Michel Houellebecq, *Submission*, trans. Loren Stein (New York: Picador, 2015), 210.

8. Vilain argues that the postrealist aesthetic "ne consiste plus à questionner l'objectivité de son rapport au réel mais à penser l'être du réel, sa contingence et sa subjectivité." Philippe Vilain, *La Littérature sans idéal* (Paris: Grasset, 2016), 48.

9. Nicolas Léger, "The Literature of Inequality," trans. Isabelle Chalze, *Eurozine*, October 18, 2018, https://www.eurozine.com/the-literature-of-inequality/.

10. Stéphane Bikialo and Julien Rault, *Au nom du réalisme: usage(s) politique(s) d'un mot d'ordre* (Paris: Éditions Utopia, 2018), 48–49. "Dans certains contextes, l'usage du mot *crise* pourra être au service d'une idéologie plus réactionnaire, liée au déclin, à la décadence. Dans le domaine littéraire et linguistique, par exemple, le mot apparaît souvent à l'écume d'un discours régressif; les syntagmes (dramatisants) tels que 'la crise du français,' ou 'la crise du roman' n'interviennent la plupart du temps que sous forme de crispation puriste et réactionnaire, activant l'idée anxiogène d'une dégradation, en fonction d'un modèle en arrière-plan: le mot *crise* accompagne souvent chez ceux qui l'emploient une idéologie passéiste, un regard rétrospectif, nostalgique, avec érection d'une norme implicite antérieure permettant de mieux juger les écarts et les déviances. On l'aura compris, la 'crise' est un adjuvant fondamental voire fondateur de l'injonction réaliste. Sans elle, le réalisme perd une partie de son caractère d'évidence." Translated by SE.

11. Patrik Ourednik, *La fin du monde n'aurait pas eu lieu* (Paris: Éditions Allia, 2017), 17.

# BIBLIOGRAPHY

Achille, Étienne. "En marge du discours 'néo-réactionnaire': Le rap identitaire." *French Cultural Studies* 29, no. 3 (2018): 218–27.

——. "Fiction 'néo-réactionnaire' avec Richard Millet." *Modern and Contemporary France* 26, no. 4 (2018): 370–79.

Adam, Olivier. *Les Lisières*. Paris: Flammarion, 2012.

Adams, Brooks. *The Law of Civilizational Decay: An Essay on History*. London: Swan Sonnenschein & Co., 1895.

Agee, James, and Walker Evans. *Let Us Now Praise Famous Men*. New York: Houghton Mifflin, 2001.

Ajavon, François-Xavier. "Michel Houellebecq et la notion de 'sélection sexuelle.'" *Le Philosophoire* 18 (2002–3): 167–73.

Albertini, Dominique, and David Doucet. *La Fachosphère: Comment l'extrême droite remporte la bataille du net*. Paris: Flammarion, 2016.

Alduy, Cécile. "What a 1973 French Novel Tells Us About Marine Le Pen, Steve Bannon, and the Rise of the Populist Right." *Politico*, April 23, 2017. http://www.politico.com/magazine/story/2017/04/23/what-a-1973-french-novel-tells-us-about-marine-le-pen-steve-bannon-and-the-rise-of-the-populist-right-215064.

Alduy, Cécile, and Stéphane Wahnich. *Marine Le Pen prise aux mots: Décryptage du nouveau discours frontiste*. Paris: Seuil, 2015.

Amraoui, Abdelaziz, and Marie-Rose Abomo-Maurin, eds. *Littérature et réalité: Regards croisés*. Paris: L'Harmattan, 2018.

Anderson, Benedict. *Imagined Communities: Reflections on the Origin and Spread of Nationalism*. London: Verso, 2006.

Angenot, Marc. *La Parole pamphlétaire: Contribution à la typologie des discours modernes*. Paris: Payot, 1982.

Anonymous. "*The Camp of the Saints:* Where Literature and Life Collide." *Radix,* October 27, 2015. https://radixjournal.com/2015/10/2015-10-27-sea-changes/.

Anquetil, Georges. *Satan conduit le bal: Roman pamphlétaire et philosophique des mœurs du temps.* Paris: Anquetil, 1925.

Armstrong, Joshua. "Empiritexts: Mapping Attention and Invention in Post-1980 French Literature." *French Forum* 40, no. 1 (Winter 2015): 93–108.

Armstrong, Nancy. *How Novels Think: The Limits of British Individualism from 1719–1900.* New York: Columbia University Press, 2005.

Armstrong, Nancy, and Leonard Tennenhouse. "The Problem of Population and the Form of the American Novel." *American Literary History* 20, no. 4 (Winter 2008): 667–85.

Armus, Seth. "Trying on the Veil: Sexual Autonomy and the End of the French Republic in Michel Houellebecq's *Submission.*" *French Politics, Culture, and Society* 35, no. 1 (2017): 126–45.

Ascott, Roy. *Telematic Embrace: Visionary Theories of Art, Technology, and Consciousness.* Berkeley: University of California Press, 2007.

Attridge, John. "Houellebecq's Occidentalism." *Australian Humanities Review* 62 (November 2017): 65–78.

Audet, René, and Nicolas Xanthos. "Le roman contemporain au détriment du personnage: Introduction." *L'Esprit Créateur* 54, no. 1 (Spring 2013): 1–7.

Auerbach, Erich. *Mimesis: The Presentation of Reality in Western Literature.* Trans. Willard R. Trask. Princeton, NJ: Princeton University Press, 2003.

Augé, Marc. *No Fixed Abode: Ethnofiction.* Trans. Chris Turner. London: Seagull, 2013.

——. *The War of Dreams: Exercises in Ethno-Fiction.* Trans. Liz Heron. London: Pluto, 1999.

Auray, Nicolas. "Les plis du capitalisme cognitif." *Multitudes* 52 (2013): 147–54.

Avril, Yves. "Le pamphlet: Essai de définition et analyse de quelques-uns de ses procédés." *Études Littéraires* 11, no. 2 (1978): 265–82.

Bachelay, Guillaume. *La Politique sauvée par les livres.* Paris: Stock, 2016.

Badiou, Alain. *À la recherche du réel perdu.* Paris: Fayard, 2015.

Badiou, Alain, and Alain Finkielkraut. *Confrontation.* Trans. Susan Spitzer. Cambridge: Polity, 2014.

Baju, Anatole. "Aux lecteurs!" *Le Décadent* 1 (April 10, 1886): 1.

Balzac, Honoré de. *Honoré de Balzac in Twenty-Five Volumes.* 25 vols. New York: Peter Fenelon Collier, 1900.

——. *Lost Illusions.* Trans. Kathleen Raine. New York: Modern Library, 1997.

Barnhart, Robert, ed. *The Barnhart Concise Dictionary of Etymology.* New York: HarperCollins, 1995.

Barth, John. *The Friday Book.* Baltimore, MD: Johns Hopkins University Press, 1997.

Barthes, Roland. *Mythologies.* Paris: Seuil, 1957.

Baudorre, Philippe, et al., eds. *Littérature et sociologie.* Bordeaux: Presses universitaires de Bordeaux, 2007.

Baudrillard, Jean. *The Gulf War Did Not Take Place.* Trans. Paul Patton. Bloomington: Indiana University Press, 1995.

——. "The Spirit of Terrorism." In *The Spirit of Terrorism and Requiem for the Twin Towers,* trans. Chris Turner, 3–34. London: Verso, 2002.

——. *The Transparency of Evil: Essays on Extreme Phenomena*. Trans. James Benedict. London: Verso, 2002.

Baumier, Matthieu. *La Démocratie totalitaire: Penser la modernité post-démocratique*. Paris: Presses de la Renaissance, 2007.

——. "Penser la modernité post-démocratique." *Controverses* 5 (June 2007): 139–44.

Bavarez, Nicholas. *La France qui tombe*. Paris: Perrin, 2003.

Becker, George J. *Realism in Modern Literature*. New York: Frederick Ungar, 1980.

Beigbeder, Frédéric. *£9.99*. Trans. Adriana Hunter. London: Picador, 2002.

——. *Holiday in a Coma and Love Lasts Three Years: Two Novels*. Trans. Frank Wynne. London: Fourth Estate, 2007.

——. *Un roman français*. Paris: Librairie Générale Française, 2010.

——. *Une vie sans fin*. Paris: Grasset, 2018.

——. *Windows on the World*. Trans. Frank Wynne. New York: Hyperion, 2004.

Bélit, Marc. *Le Malaise de la culture: Essai sur la crise du modèle culturel français*. Biarritz: Séguier, 2006.

Bellanger, Aurélien. *Houellebecq, écrivain romantique*. Paris: Éditions Léo Scheer, 2010.

——. *La Théorie de l'information*. Paris: Gallimard, 2012.

Bello, Antoine. *Les Éclaireurs*. Paris: Gallimard, 2009.

——. *Les Falsificateurs*. Paris: Gallimard, 2007.

——. *Les Producteurs*. Paris: Gallimard, 2015.

Berger, Guy. "Un conte satirique: *Soumission*." *Commentaire* 149 (2015): 197–200.

Berl, Emmanuel. *La France irréelle*. Paris: Grasset, 1957.

Bernat, Harold. *Vieux réac! Faut-il s'adapter à tout?* Paris: Flammarion, 2012.

Bernheimer, Charles. *Decadent Subjects*. Baltimore, MD: Johns Hopkins University Press, 2002.

Betty, Louis. "'F&#% Autonomy': Houellebecq, *Submission*, and Enlightenment's 'Last Dismaying Dregs.'" *Modern and Contemporary France*, January 7, 2019.

——. *Without God: Michel Houellebecq and Materialist Horror*. University Park: Pennsylvania State University Press, 2016.

Bey, Hakim. *T.A.Z.: The Temporary Autonomous Zone, Ontological Anarchy, Poetic Terrorism*. Brooklyn: Autonomedia, 2003.

Bikialo, Stéphane, and Julien Rault. *Au nom du réalisme: Usage(s) politique(s) d'un mot d'ordre*. Paris: Éditions Utopia, 2018.

Binet, Laurent, et al. "Interview with Laurent Binet." *The Romanic Review* 105, no. 1–2 (January 2014): 87–90.

Bloy, Léon. *Les Funérailles du naturalisme*. Paris: Les Belles Lettres, 2001.

Blumenthal, Paul, and J. M. Rieger. "This Stunningly Racist French Novel Is How Steve Bannon Explains the World." *Huffington Post*, March 3, 2017. https://www.huffingtonpost.com/entry/steve-bannon-camp-of-the-saints-immigration _us_58b75206e4b0284854b3dc03.

Bompaire-Evesque, Claire. "Roman balzacien, roman 'idéologique': Les choix de Barrès dans *La Colline inspirée*." *Revue d'Histoire Littéraire de la France* 98, no. 4 (1998): 583–616.

Bothorel, Jean. *Chers imposteurs*. Paris: Fayard, 2008.

Boucharenc, Myriam. "Nouvelles fictions du reporter au XXe siècle." *Interférences Littéraire* 7 (November 2011): 115–25.

Boucharenc, Myriam, and Pierre Hyppolite. "Questions à Jean Rolin." In *Roman et reportage XXe–XXIe siècles: Rencontres croisées*, ed. Myriam Boucharenc, 263–81. Limoges: Presses universitaires de Limoges, 2015.

Boulle, Pierre. *La Planète des singes*. Paris: Julliard, 1963.

Bourget, Paul. *Essais de psychologie contemporaine*. Vol. 1. Paris: Plon, 1901.

Bourmeau, Sylvain. "*La Théorie de l'information*, un puissant avatar de l'époque." *Libération*, August 22, 2012. http://next.liberation.fr/livres/2012/08/22/la-theorie -de-l-information-un-puissant-avatar-de-l-epoque_841306.

——. "Scare Tactics: Michel Houellebecq Defends His Controversial New Book." *Paris Review*, January 2, 2015. https://www.theparisreview.org/blog/2015/01/02/scare -tactics-michel-houellebecq-on-his-new-book/.

Bowd, Gavin. "The Anti-Sartre? Michel Houellebecq and Politics." *Australian Journal of French Studies* 56, no. 1 (2019): 8–23.

Brandt, Jenn. "9/11, Hyperreality, and the Global Body Politic: Frédéric Beigbeder's *Windows on the World*." *Studies in Twentieth- and Twenty-First-Century Literature* 39, no. 1 (2015): article 4.

Brinkmann, Svend. "Literature as Qualitative Inquiry: The Novelist as Researcher." *Qualitative Inquiry* 15, no. 8 (2009): 1376–94.

Brooks, Peter. *Reading for the Plot: Design and Intention in Narratives*. Cambridge, MA: Harvard University Press, 1992.

——. *Realist Vision*. New Haven, CT: Yale University Press, 2008.

Bruckner, Pascal. *The Tears of the White Man: Compassion as Contempt*. Trans. William R. Beer. New York: Free Press, 1986.

——. *The Tyranny of Guilt: An Essay on Western Masochism*. Trans. Steven Rendall. Princeton, NJ: Princeton University Press, 2010.

Brunet, Éric. *Sauve qui peut!* Paris: Albin Michel, 2013.

Bry, Dominique. "*La Théorie de l'information*, c'est wiki qui dit qu'y est." *Mediapart*, August 27, 2012. https://blogs.mediapart.fr/edition/bookclub/article/270812/la -theorie-de-l-information-c-est-wiki-qui-dit-qu-y-est.

Buchweiz, Nurit, and Elie Cohen-Gewerc. "Leisure and Posthumanism in Houellebecq's *Platform* and *Lanzarote*." *Comparative Literature and Culture* 17, no. 4 (2015). http://docs.lib.purdue.edu/clcweb/vol17/iss4/3.

Bureaud, Annick. "Art and Minitel in France in the 1980s." In *Social Media Archaeology and Poetics*, ed. Judy Malloy, 139–46. Cambridge, MA: MIT Press, 2016.

Burgelin, Claude, et al., eds. *Autofiction(s): Colloque de Cerisy 2008*. Lyon: Presses universitaires de Lyon, 2010.

Burn, Stephen J. "Neuroscience and Modern Fiction." *Modern Fiction Studies* 61, no. 2 (Summer 2015): 209–25.

Buzay, Emmanuel. "Le désir d'être écrit: Étude comparative de deux modèles d'écriture computationnels dans *La Possibilité d'une île* de Michel Houellebecq et *La Théorie de l'information* d'Aurélien Bellanger." In *Lectures croisées de l'œuvre de Michel Houellebecq*, ed. Antoine Jurga and Sabine van Wesemael, 93–104. Paris: Classiques Garnier, 2017.

Campe, Rüdiger. *The Game of Probability: Literature and Calculation from Pascal to Kleist*. Trans. Ellwood H. Wiggins Jr. Stanford, CA: Stanford University Press, 2012.

Camus, Renaud. *France: Suicide d'une nation*. Paris: Éditions Mordicus, 2014.

——. *Le Grand Remplacement*. Paris: David Reinharc, 2011.

Capote, Truman. *In Cold Blood*. New York: Random House, 1966.

Capuana, Luigi. *Gli 'ismi' contemporanei*. Catania: Giannotta, 1898.

Caro, Elme-Marie. "Études morales sur le XIXe siècle." *Revue Contemporaine* 13 (April 1854): 427–62.

Carroll, David. *French Literary Fascism: Nationalism, Anti-Semitism, and the Ideology of Culture*. Princeton, NJ: Princeton University Press, 1995.

Cervulle, Maxime. "The Uses of Universalism: 'Diversity Statistics' and the Race Issue in Contemporary France." *European Journal of Cultural Studies* 17, no. 2 (2014): 118–33.

Chabert, George. "Michel Houellebecq, lecteur d'Auguste Comte." *Revue Romane* 37, no. 2 (2002): 187–204.

Chafer, Tony, and Emmanuel Godin, eds. *The End of the French Exception? Decline and Revival of the "French Model."* New York: Palgrave Macmillan, 2010.

Champfleury. "Encore quelques mots à propos de *M. de Boisdhyver*." *Figaro*, August 7, 1856.

Chaplin, Tamara. "Lesbians Online: Queer Identity and Community Formation on the French Minitel." *Journal of the History of Sexuality* 23, no. 3 (2014): 451–72.

Chassay, Jean-François. "Les Corpuscules de Krause: À propos de *Particules élémentaires* de Michel Houellebecq." *Australian Journal of French Studies* 42, no. 1 (2005): 36–49.

Chesnais, Jean-Claude. *Le Crépuscule de l'Occident: Démographie et politique*. Paris: Robert Laffont, 1995.

Chevrel, Yves. *Le Naturalisme*. Paris: Presses universitaires de France, 1982.

Chollet, Mona. "Twitter jusqu'au vertige." *Le Monde Diplomatique*, October 2011. https://www.monde-diplomatique.fr/2011/10/CHOLLET/21103.

Cioran, E. M. *A Short History of Decay*. Trans. Richard Howard. New York: Arcade, 2012.

Cirio, Paulo, ed. *Evidentiary Realism: Investigative, Forensic, and Documentary Art*. Berlin: Nome, 2017.

Cixous, Hélène. "The Towers: *Les tours*." *Signs* 28, no. 1 (Autumn 2002): 431–33.

Clavaron, Yves. *Francophonie, postcolonialisme et mondialisation*. Paris: Classiques Garnier, 2018.

Clément de Ris, Comte Louis. *Critiques d'art et de littérature*. Paris: Didier, 1862.

Clerc, Thomas. *Paris, musée du XXIe siècle*. Paris: Gallimard, 2007.

Clermont, Philippe. *Darwinisme et littérature de science-fiction*. Paris: L'Harmattan, 2011.

Cogan, Charles. "*Qui a tué Daniel Pearl?* (review)." *French Politics, Culture, and Society* 23, no. 1 (Spring 2005): 166–69.

Colon, Églantine. "Neither *Lieux de Mémoire*, nor *Non-Lieux*: Towards a Concept of Precarious Spaces in Philippe Vasset's *Un livre blanc*." *French Studies* 71, no. 1 (January 2017): 66–83.

Connelly, Matthew, and Paul Kennedy. "Must It Be the West Against the Rest?" *Atlantic Monthly* 274, no. 6 (December 1994): 61–84.

Cooper, Brian P. *Family Fictions and Family Facts: Harriet Martineau, Adolphe Quetelet, and the Population Question in England, 1798–1859*. London: Routledge, 2007.

Counter, Andrew J. "Zola's *Fin-de-Siècle* Reproductive Politics." *French Studies* 68, no. 2 (April 2014): 193–208.

Crowley, Martin. "Houellebecq's France." *Australian Journal of French Studies* 56, no. 1 (2019): 24–36.

Cruickshank, Ruth. *Fin de Millénaire French Fiction: The Aesthetics of Crisis.* Oxford: Oxford University Press, 2009.

Cusset, François. *French Theory: How Foucault, Derrida, Deleuze, and Co. Transformed the Intellectual Life of the United States.* Trans. Jeff Fort. Minneapolis: University of Minnesota Press, 2008.

d'Agata, John, and Jim Fingal. *The Lifespan of a Fact.* New York: Norton, 2012.

Dantec, Maurice G. *Babylon Babies.* Trans. Noura Wedell. Los Angeles: Semiotext(e), 2005.

Daoud, Kamel. "Sexual Misery of the Arab World." *New York Times*, February 12, 2016. https://www.nytimes.com/2016/02/14/opinion/sunday/the-sexual-misery-of -the-arab-world.html.

De Gans, Henk. "Vision, Future, Forecaster: On Demons and Soothers in Long-Range Demographic Prediction." In *The Joy of Demography . . . and Other Disciplines*, ed. Anton Kuijsten, Henk De Gans, and Henk De Feijter, 103–15. Amsterdam: Thela Thesis, 1999.

DeLillo, Don. *Falling Man.* New York: Scribner, 2007.

Denis, Benoît. "Ironie et idéologie: Réflexions sur la 'responsabilité idéologique' du texte." *Contextes* 2 (2007). http://journals.openedition.org/contextes/180.

Deslauriers, Frédéric. *Les Deux-cents jours de Marine le Pen.* Paris: Plon, 2011.

Despentes, Virginie. *King Kong Theory.* Trans. Stéphanie Benson. London: Serpent's Tail, 2009.

Devecchio, Alexandre. *Les Nouveaux enfants du siècle.* Paris: Éditions du Cerf, 2016.

——. "*Sérotonine* de Houellebecq, un roman qui fait écho à la France des 'gilets jaunes'?" *Le Figaro*, December 27, 2018. http://www.lefigaro.fr/vox/culture/2018/12 /27/31006-20181227ARTFIG00008--serotonine-de-houellebecq-un-roman-qui-fait -echo-a-la-france-des-gilets-jaunes.php.

Diken, Bülent. "The Map, the Territory, and the Impossibility of Painting a Priest." *Critical Sociology* 42, no. 7–8 (2014): 1109–24.

Dion, Robert. *Des fictions sans fiction ou le partage du réel.* Montreal: Les Presses de l'Université de Montréal, 2018.

Dion, Robert, and Élisabeth Haghebaert. "Le cas de Michel Houellebecq et la dynamique des genres littéraires." *French Studies* 55, no. 4 (2001): 509–24.

Domingo, Andreu. "'Demodystopias': Prospects of Demographic Hell." *Population and Development Review* 34, no. 4 (December 2008): 725–45.

Donadio, Rachel. "A Novel Made for the 'Yellow Vest' Moment." *Atlantic*, January 13, 2019. https://www.theatlantic.com/entertainment/archive/2019/01/michel -houellebecqs-new-book-indictment-eu/580165/.

Doubrovsky, Serge. *Fils.* Paris: Galilée, 1977.

Drieu la Rochelle, Pierre. "Le Capitalisme, le Communisme et l'Esprit." *Les Derniers Jours* 1 (February 1, 1927): 1–4.

Dubey, Madhu. "Post-Postmodern Realism?" *Twentieth-Century Literature* 57, no. 3–4 (Fall/Winter 2011): 364–71.

Duchatelet, Christophe, et al. *Michel Houellebecq: Les grands entretiens d'artpress.* Paris: IMEC, 2012.

Duclos, Jean-François. "'Nous ne laissons rien du monde': Philippe Vasset et les zones blanches de la carte." *French Review* 87, no. 2 (December 2013): 61–71.

Duhamel, Alain. *Le Désarroi français*. Paris: Plon, 2003.

——. *Les Peurs françaises*. Paris: Flammarion, 1993.

Dupuis, Jérôme. "Aurélien Bellanger, ennuyeux comme un annuaire électronique." *L'Express*, August 23, 2012. http://www.lexpress.fr/culture/livre/la-theorie-de-l -information_1151599.html.

Dupuis-Déri, Francis. "Le 'masculinisme': Une histoire politique du mot (en anglais et en français)." *Recherches Féministes* 22, no. 2 (2009): 97–123.

Dupuy, Jean-Pierre. *Pour un catastrophisme éclairé: Quand l'impossible est certain*. Paris: Seuil, 2002.

Durand, Alain-Philippe. "Pascal Bruckner et Michel Houellebecq: Deux transécriv- ains au milieu du monde." In *Michel Houellebecq sous la loupe*, ed. Murielle Lucie Clément and Sabine van Wesemael, 157–67. Amsterdam: Rodopi, 2007.

Durand, Anne-Aël. "'Roman national,' 'récit national': De quoi parle-t-on?" *Le Monde*, September 28, 2016. https://www.lemonde.fr/les-decodeurs/article/2016 /09/28/roman-national-recit-national-de-quoi-parle-t-on_5004994_4355770.html.

Durand, Pascal, and Sarah Sindaco, eds. *Le Discours "néo-réactionnaire": Transgres- sions conservatrices*. Paris: CNRS Éditions, 2015.

Duteurtre, Benoît. *L'Ordinateur du paradis*. Paris: Gallimard, 2014.

Duvall, John C., and Robert P. Marzec, eds. *Narrating 9/11: Fantasies of State, Security, and Terrorism*. Baltimore, MD: Johns Hopkins University Press, 2015.

Du Valdor, Jean. *Les Signes de la fin d'un monde*. 2nd ed. Saint Amand: Société ano- nyme de l'imprimerie Saint-Joseph, 1893.

Eko, Lyombe. *American Exceptionalism, the French Exception, and Digital Media Law*. Plymouth: Lexington, 2013.

——. "New Technologies, Old Mentalities: The Internet, Minitel, and Exceptionalist Infor- mation and Communication Technology Policy." In *New Media, Old Regimes: Case Studies in Comparative Communication Law and Policy*. Plymouth: Lexington, 2012.

El Rhazoui, Zineb. *Détruire le fascisme islamique*. Paris: Ring, 2016.

Ercolino, Stefano. *The Maximalist Novel: From Thomas Pynchon's Gravity's Rainbow to Roberto Bolaño's 2666*. Trans. Albert Sbragia. New York: Bloomsbury, 2014.

Ernaux, Annie. "Le pamphlet fasciste de Richard Millet déshonore la littérature." *Le Monde*, September 10, 2012. http://www.lemonde.fr/idees/article/2012/09/10/le -pamphlet-de-richard-millet-deshonore-la-litterature_1758011_3232.html.

Fabre, Daniel, and Marie Scarpa. *Le Moment réaliste: Un tournant de l'ethnologie*. Nancy: Presses universitaires de Nancy, 2017.

Faerber, Johan. "Contre la Zemmourisation de la critique littéraire." *Diakritik*, October 15, 2018. https://diacritik.com/2018/10/15/contre-la-zemmourisation-de-la -critique-litteraire/.

Feenberg, Andrew. *Alternative Modernity: The Technical Turn in Philosophy and Social Theory*. Berkeley: University of California Press, 1995.

Fénéon, Félix. *Novels in Three Lines*. Trans. Luc Sante. New York: NYRB, 2007.

Ferguson, Frances. "Malthus, Godwin, Wordsworth, and the Spirit of Solitude." In *Literature and the Body: Essays on Populations and Persons*, ed. Elaine Scarry, 106–24. Baltimore, MD: Johns Hopkins University Press, 1988.

Fisher, Mark. *Capitalist Realism: Is There No Alternative?* Winchester: Zero, 2010.

Fleming, Paul. *Exemplarity and Mediocrity: The Art of the Average from Bourgeois Tragedy to Realism.* Stanford, CA: Stanford University Press, 2009.

Fleury, Philippe. *Désenchantement et mondialisation.* Paris: L'Harmattan, 2016.

Flourens, Émile. *La France conquise.* Paris: Garnier Frères, 1906.

Foer, Jonathan Safran. *Extremely Loud and Incredibly Close.* Boston: Houghton Mifflin, 2005.

Fore, Devin. *Realism After Modernism: The Rehumanization of Art and Literature.* Cambridge, MA: MIT Press, 2012.

Forest, Philippe. *Le Roman, le réel, et autres essais.* Paris: Éditions Cécile Defaut, 2007.

Foster, Hal. "Real Fictions: Alternatives to Alternative Facts." *Artforum International* 55, no. 8 (April 2017). https://www.artforum.com/print/201704/real-fictions-alternatives-to-alternative-facts-67192.

——. *The Return of the Real: The Avant-Garde at the End of the Century.* Cambridge, MA: MIT Press, 1996.

Frank, Robert. *La Hantise du déclin: La France de 1914 à 2014.* Paris: Belin, 2014.

Franzen, Jonathan. "Perchance to Dream: In the Age of Images, a Reason to Write Novels." *Harper's*, April 1996, 35–54.

Freund, Julien. *La Décadence: Histoire sociologique et philosophique d'une catégorie de l'expérience humaine.* Paris: Éditions Sirey, 1984.

Frey, Hugo, and Benjamin Noys. "Introduction: More Reactionary Times: Culture." *Journal of European Studies* 3, no. 4 (2007): 341–47.

Fustin, Ludivine. "Michel Houellebecq: Un décadent au XXIe siècle." In *States of Decadence*, ed. Guri Barstad and Karen P. Knutsen, 1:185–98. Newcastle: Cambridge Scholars Publishing, 2016.

Gagnier, Regenia. "The Decadence of the West in Huysmans and Houellebecq: Decadence in the Longue Durée." *English Literature in Translation, 1880–1920* 60, no. 4 (2017): 419–30.

Galanopoulos, Philippe. "L'Étranger: Une figure de la décadence? Les discours scientifiques et politiques sur les races, en France, dans la seconde moitié du XIXe siècle." In *La Décadence dans la culture et la pensée politique. Espagne, France et Italie (XVIIIe–XXe siècle)*, ed. Jean-Yves Frétigné and François Jankowiak, 321–38. Rome: École française de Rome, 2008.

Gardels, Nathan. "Cloning: Central Planning of the 21st Century?" *New Perspectives Quarterly* 18, no. 1 (Winter 2001): 56.

Gauthier, Tim. "French Fiction, Empathy, and the Utopian Potential of 9/11." *Studies in Twentieth- and Twenty-First-Century Literature* 37, no. 1 (2013): 113–42.

Gautier, Léon. "M. Gustave Flaubert." In *Études littéraires pour la défense de l'Église*, 183–95. Paris: Poussielgue et fils, 1865.

Gefen, Alexandre. "'La Muse est morte, ou la faveur pour elle': Brève histoire des discours sur la mort de la littérature." In *Fins de la littérature: Esthétiques et discours de la fin*, ed. Laurent Demanze and Dominique Viart, 1:37–49. Paris: Armand Colin, 2011.

Gefen, Alexandre, Oana Panaïté, and Cornelia Ruhe. "Savoir lire: Un droit de réponse." *Diakritik*, October 16, 2018. https://diacritik.com/2018/10/16/savoir-lire-un-droit-de-reponse/.

Gefen, Alexandre, and René Audet, eds. *Frontières de la fiction*. Quebec: Éditions Nota Bene, 2002.

Genette, Gérard, and Tzvetan Todorov. *Littérature et réalité*. Paris: Seuil, 1982.

Glad, Vincent. "Houellebecq, la possibilité d'un plagiat." *Slate*, February 9, 2010. http://www.slate.fr/story/26745/wikipedia-plagiat-michel-houellebecq-carte -territoire.

——. "La théorie du déclin français." *Slate*, September 18, 2012. http://www.slate.fr /story/61857/aurelien-bellanger-la-theorie-de-linformation.

Glaudes, Pierre, and Jean-François Louette, eds. *Cynismes littéraires*. Paris: Classiques Garnier, 2018.

Glucksmann, Raphaël. *Génération gueule de bois: Manuel de lutte contre les réacs*. Paris: Allary Éditions, 2015.

——. "Tout reste à écrire." *Le Nouveau Magazine Littéraire*, December 16, 2017. https:// www.nouveau-magazine-litteraire.com/manifesto.

Gobineau, Arthur de. *Essai sur l'inégalité des races humaines*. Vol. 1. 2nd ed. Paris: Firmin-Didot, 1884.

Golsan, Richard J. "The Poetics and Perils of Faction: Contemporary French Fiction and the Memory of World War II." *The Romanic Review* 105, no. 1–2 (January 2014): 53–68.

Gopnik, Adam. "The Next Thing." *New Yorker*, January 26, 2015. https://www .newyorker.com/magazine/2015/01/26/next-thing.

——. "The Second Coming of the French Far-Right Tradition." *New Yorker*, March 31, 2017. https://www.newyorker.com/news/daily-comment/franco-american.

de Goncourt, Edmond, and Jules de Goncourt. *Germinie Lacerteux*. Trans. Leonard Tancock. Middlesex: Penguin, 1984.

Gonzalez, Antonio. "Minitel: Histoire du réseau télématique français." *Flux* 47, no. 1 (2002): 84–89.

Goupil, Didier. *Le Jour de mon retour sur Terre*. Paris: Le Serpent à Plumes, 2003.

Grass, Delphine. "Domesticating Hierarchies, Eugenic Hygiene, and Exclusion Zones: The Dogs and Clones of Houellebecq's *La Possibilité d'une île*." *L'Esprit Créateur* 52, no. 2 (Summer 2012): 127–40.

——. "Ghosts in the Text: Writing Technologies, Authorial Strategy, and the Politics of Reactionary Autoimmunity in Houellebecq's Works." *Australian Journal of French Studies* 56, no. 1 (2019): 53–69.

Gratton, Peter. *Speculative Realism: Problems and Prospects*. London: Bloomsbury, 2014.

Gregorio, Laurence A. *Maupassant's Fiction and the Darwinian View of Life*. New York: Peter Lang, 2005.

Greenslade, William. *Degeneration, Culture, and the Novel, 1880–1940*. Cambridge: Cambridge University Press, 1994.

Grimal, Claude. "Le 'new journalism' et le 'non fiction novel': Un débat littéraire et journalistique aux États-Unis." In *Roman et reportage XXe–XXIe siècles: Rencontres croisées*, ed. Myriam Boucharenc, 15–27. Limoges: Presses universitaires de Limoges, 2015.

Grusin, Richard. *Premediation: Affect and Mediality After 9/11*. London: Palgrave Macmillan, 2010.

Guénolé, Thomas. *Islamopsychose: Pourquoi la France diabolise les musulmans*. Paris: Fayard, 2017.

Guillard, Achille. *Éléments de statistique humaine, ou démographie comparée*. Paris: Guillaumin, 1855.

Haenel, Yannick. *Les Renards pâles*. Paris: Gallimard, 2013.

Hamid, Mohsin. *The Reluctant Fundamentalist*. Orlando, FL: Harcourt, 2007.

Hamon, Philippe. *Puisque réalisme il y a*. Geneva: Éditions La Baconnière, 2015.

Harkness, Nigel, et al., eds. *Birth and Death in Nineteenth-Century French Culture*. Amsterdam: Rodopi, 2007.

Harman, Graham. *Speculative Realism: An Introduction*. Cambridge: Polity, 2018.

Hastings, Michel, et al. "Les mutations du pamphlet dans la France contemporaine." *Mots: Les Langages du Politique* 91 (November 2009): 5–17.

Herman, Luc. *Concepts of Realism*. Columbia, SC: Camden House, 1996.

Hewitt, Nicholas. *Literature and the Right in Postwar France*. Oxford: Berg, 1996.

Hippolyte, Jean-Louis. *Fuzzy Fiction*. Lincoln: University of Nebraska Press, 2006.

Hochmann, Jacques. *Théories de la dégénerescence: D'un mythe psychiatrique au déclinisme contemporain*. Paris: Odile Jacob, 2018.

Hoffleit, Gerald. "Progress and Decadence—Poststructuralism as Progressivism." In *Decadence in Literature and Intellectual Debate Since 1945*, ed. Diemo Landgraf, 67–81. New York: Palgrave Macmillan, 2014.

Houellebecq, Michel. *The Elementary Particles*. Trans. Frank Wynne. New York: Vintage, 2000.

——. *H. P. Lovecraft: Contre le monde, contre la vie*. Monaco: Éditions du Rocher, 1991.

——. *Interventions 2: Traces*. Paris: Flammarion, 2009.

——. *The Map and the Territory*. Trans. Gavin Bowd. New York: Vintage International, 2011.

——. *Platform*. Trans. Frank Wynne. London: Heinemann, 2002.

——. *The Possibility of an Island*. Trans. Gavin Bowd. New York: Vintage, 2005.

——. "Schirrmacher-Preis, Michel Houellebecq, 26.9.2016." http://schirrmacher -stiftung.de/wp-content/uploads/2016/10/Dankesrede_original_Houellebecq_ 26.9.16.pdf.

——. *Sérotonine*. Paris: Flammarion, 2019.

——. *Submission*. Trans. Loren Stein. New York: Picador, 2015.

——. *Whatever*. Trans. Paul Hammond. London: Serpent's Tail, 1998.

Houellebecq, Michel, and Bernard-Henry Lévy. *Public Enemies*. Trans. Miriam Frendo and Frank Wynne. New York: Random House, 2011.

Hu, Tung-Hui. *A Prehistory of the Cloud*. Cambridge, MA: MIT Press, 2016.

Hugo, Victor. *Les Misérables*. Trans. William Walton. New York: George H. Richmond & Co., 1893.

Huntington, Samuel. *The Clash of Civilizations and the Remaking of World Order*. New York: Simon and Schuster, 1996.

Huret, Jules. *Enquête sur l'évolution littéraire*. Paris: Charpentier, 1891.

Isekenmaier, Guido. "Visual Event Realism." In *Realisms in Contemporary Culture: Theories, Politics, and Medial Configurations*, ed. Dorothee Birke and Stella Butter, 214–26. Berlin: De Gruyter, 2013.

Jack, David, and Benjamin Andréo. "Introduction." *Australian Journal of French Studies* 56, no. 1 (2019): 3–7.

James, Alison, and Christophe Reig, eds. *Frontières de la non-fiction: Littérature, cinéma, arts.* Rennes: Presses universitaires de Rennes, 2013.

Jameson, Fredric. *The Antinomies of Realism.* London: Verso, 2015.

——. "Beyond the Cave: Demystifying the Ideology of Modernism." In *The Ideologies of Theory: Essays 1971–1986,* vol. 2: *The Syntax of History,* 115–32. Minneapolis: University of Minnesota Press, 1988.

Jeffrey, Ben. *Anti-Matter: Michel Houellebecq and Depressive Realism.* Winchester: Zero, 2011.

Jenni, Alexis. *L'Art français de la guerre.* Paris: Gallimard, 2011.

Joignot, Frédéric. "Le fantasme du 'grand remplacement' démographique." *Le Monde,* January 23, 2014. http://www.lemonde.fr/politique/article/2014/01/23/le-grand -boniment_4353499_823448.html.

Jourde, Pierre. *La Littérature sans estomac.* Paris: L'Esprit des péninsules, 2002.

Jurga, Antoine. "Michel Houellebecq, auteur classique?" In *Lectures croisées de l'oeuvre de Michel Houellebecq,* ed. Antoine Jurga and Sabine van Wesemael, 15–30. Paris: Classiques Garnier, 2017.

Kahn, Jean-François. "Le réalisme est un pétainisme." *BibliObs,* January 7, 2011. https://bibliobs.nouvelobs.com/essais/20110531.OBS4250/jean-francois-kahn-le -realisme-est-un-petainisme.html.

——. *Philosophie de la réalité: Critique du réalisme.* Paris: Fayard, 2011.

Kalifa, Dominique. "Usages du faux: Faits divers et romans criminels au 19e siècle." *Annales. Histoire, Sciences Sociales* 54, no. 6 (November/December 1999): 1345–62.

Kaprièlan, Nelly. "*Sérotonine* de Michel Houellebecq, premières impressions avant la suite . . ." *Les Inrockuptibles,* December 15, 2018. https://www.lesinrocks.com/2018 /12/15/livres/serotonine-de-michel-houellebecq-premieres-impressions-avant-la -suite-111152153/.

Kelleter, Frank. "A Tale of Two Natures: Worried Reflections on the Study of Literature and Culture in an Age of Neuroscience and Neo-Darwinism." *Journal of Literary Theory* 1, no. 1 (2007): 153–89.

Kim, Annabel L. *Unbecoming Language: Anti-Identitarian French Feminist Fictions.* Columbus: Ohio State University Press, 2018.

Knausgaard, Karl Ove. "Michel Houellebecq's *Submission* (review)." *New York Times,* November 2, 2015. https://www.nytimes.com/2015/11/08/books/review/michel -houellebecqs-submission.html.

Korthals Altes, Liesbeth. "Persuasion et ambiguïté dans un roman à thèse postmoderne (*Les Particules élémentaires*)." In *Michel Houellebecq,* ed. Sabine van Wesemael, 29–45. Amsterdam: Rodopi, 2004.

Kramer, Richard. "The Politics of Information: A Study of the French Minitel System." In *Between Communication and Information,* vol. 4: *Information and Behavior,* ed. Jorge R. Schement and Brent D. Ruben, 453–86. New Brunswick, NJ: Transaction, 1993.

Kröner, Tonio, et al., eds. *Post-Apocalyptic Realism.* Cologne: Walther König, 2018.

Kuijsten, Anton. "Demografiction." In *The Joy of Demography . . . and Other Disciplines,* ed. Anton Kuijsten, Henk De Gans, and Henk de Feijter, 83–102. Amsterdam: Thela Thesis, 1999.

Labadie, Aurore. *Le Roman d'entreprise français au tournant du XXIe siècle.* Paris: Presses Sorbonne Nouvelle, 2016.

Lageira, Jacinto. *La Déréalisation du monde: Réalité et fiction en conflit*. Nîmes: Éditions Jacqueline Chambon, 2010.

Lang, Luc. *11 septembre mon amour*. Paris: Éditions Stock, 2003.

——. *Au commencement du septième jour*. Paris: Stock, 2016.

Lanzmann, Claude. "*Jan Karski* de Yannick Haenel: Un faux roman." *Les Temps Modernes* 657 (2010): 1–10.

Lavocat, Françoise. *Fait et fiction: Pour une frontière*. Paris: Seuil, 2016.

Le Bras, Hervé. *Naissance de la mortalité: L'origine politique de la statistique et de la démographie*. Paris: Hautes Études, 2000.

——. *The Nature of Demography*. Princeton, NJ: Princeton University Press, 2008.

Ledoux, Sébastien. "Dans l'enseignement de l'histoire, pensons 'un récit national émancipateur et inclusif.'" *Le Monde*, September 3, 2016. https://www.lemonde.fr/idees/article/2016/09/03/dans-l-enseignement-de-l-histoire-pensons-un-recit-national-emancipateur-et-inclusif_4992126_3232.html.

Lee-Potter, Charlie. *Writing the 9/11 Decade: Reportage and the Evolution of the Novel*. New York: Bloomsbury, 2017.

Léger, Nicolas. "The Literature of Inequality." Trans. Isabelle Chalze. *Eurozine*, October 18, 2018. https://www.eurozine.com/the-literature-of-inequality/.

Lehmann, Albrecht. "Homo narrans—Individuelle und kollektive Dimensionen des Erzählens." In *Erzählkultur: Beiträge zur kulturwissenschaftlichen Erzählforschung*, ed. Rolf Wilhelm Brednich, 59–70. Berlin: Walter de Gruyter, 2009.

Lejeune, Geoffrey. "Nous avons lu *Sérotonine*, le nouveau roman de Houellebecq sur la France des gilets jaunes." *Valeurs Actuelles*, December 27, 2018. https://www.valeursactuelles.com/culture/nous-avons-lu-serotonine-le-nouveau-roman-de-houellebecq-sur-la-france-des-gilets-jaunes-102110.

Lem, Stanislaw. *The Futurological Congress: From the Memoirs of Ijon Tichy*. Trans. Michael Kandel. New York: Harcourt, 1974.

Lemaître, Jules. *Opinions à répandre*. 4th ed. Paris: Société française d'imprimerie et de librairie, 1901.

Leménager, Grégoire. "La loi du marché." *BibliObs*, June 30, 2015. https://bibliobs.nouvelobs.com/romans/20150629.OBS1727/la-loi-du-marche-revue-par-alexis-jenni.html.

Lemos, André. "The Labyrinth of the Minitel." In *Cultures of Internet: Virtual Spaces, Real Histories, Living Bodies*, ed. Rob Shields, 33–48. London: Sage, 1996.

Leucate, Aristide. *Dictionnaire du grand épuisement français et européen*. Paris: Dualpha, 2018.

Levet, Bérénice. *Le Crépuscule des idoles progressistes*. Paris: Stock, 2017.

Levinson, Paul. *Digital McLuhan: A Guide to the Information Millennium*. London: Routledge, 1999.

Lévy, Bernard-Henri. *Hôtel Europe*. Paris: Grasset, 2014.

Lewis, Pericles. *Modernism, Nationalism, and the Novel*. Cambridge: Cambridge University Press, 2000.

Likhachev, D. S. *The Poetics of Early Russian Literature*. Trans. Christopher M. Arden-Close. Plymouth: Lexington, 2014.

Lilla, Mark. "Our Reactionary Age." *New York Times*, November 6, 2016. https://www.nytimes.com/2016/11/07/opinion/our-reactionary-age.html.

——. "Republicans for Revolution." *New York Review of Books*, January 12, 2012. https://www.nybooks.com/articles/2012/01/12/republicans-revolution/.

Lindenberg, Daniel. *Le Rappel à l'ordre: Enquête sur les nouveaux réactionnaires.* Paris: Seuil, 2002.

Livia, Anna. "Public and Clandestine: Gay Men's Pseudonyms on the French Minitel." *Sexualities* 5, no. 2 (2002): 201–17.

Lordon, Frédéric. "Politique post-vérité ou journalisme post-politique?" *Le Monde Diplomatique*, November 22, 2016. https://blog.mondediplo.net/2016-11-22-Politique -post-verite-ou-journalisme-post.

Lundquist, Jennifer Hickes, Douglas L. Anderton, and David Yaukey. *Demography: The Study of Human Population.* 4th ed. Long Grove, IL: Waveland, 2015.

Lyle, Louise. "*Le Struggleforlife*: Contesting Balzac Through Darwin in Zola, Bourget, and Barrès." *Nineteenth-Century French Studies* 36, no. 3–4 (Spring-Summer 2008): 305–19.

Lyon-Caen, Judith. "Enquêtes, littérature et savoir sur le monde social en France dans les année 1840." In *Le Moment réaliste: Un tournant de l'ethnologie*, ed. Daniel Fabre and Marie Scarpa, 31–58. Nancy: Presses universitaires de Nancy, 2017.

Lyotard, Jean-François. *The Inhuman.* Trans. Geoffrey Bennington and Rachel Bowlby. Cambridge: Polity, 1991.

——. *Postmodern Fables.* Trans. Georges Van Den Abbeele. Minneapolis: University of Minnesota Press, 1997.

Macdonald, Dwight. "Parajournalism, or Tom Wolfe & His Magic Writing Machine." *New York Review of Books*, August 26, 1965. https://www.nybooks.com/articles /1965/08/26/parajournalism-or-tom-wolfe-his-magic-writing-mach/.

Mack, Mehammed Amadeus. *Sexagon: Muslims, France, and the Sexualization of National Culture.* New York: Fordham University Press, 2017.

Mack, Michael. *Philosophy and Literature in Times of Crisis: Challenging Our Infatuation with Numbers.* New York: Bloomsbury, 2014.

Mailland, Julien. "Minitel." In *Paid: Tales of Dongles, Checks, and Other Money Stuff*, ed. Bill Maurer and Lana Swartz, 167–84. Cambridge, MA: MIT Press, 2017.

Mailland, Julien, and Kevin Driscoll. *Minitel: Welcome to the Internet.* Cambridge, MA: MIT Press, 2017.

Manaugh, Geoff. "Concrete-Printing Bees and Other Living 3D Printers." *Gizmodo*, December 6, 2013. https://gizmodo.com/concrete-printing-bees-and-other-living -3d-printers-1477853742.

Marchand, Marie. *Minitel.* Paris: Larousse, 1987.

Maris, Bernard. *Et si on aimait la France.* Paris: Grasset, 2015.

——. *Houellebecq économiste.* Paris: Flammarion, 2014.

Marshall, Colin. *Compassionate Moral Realism.* Oxford: Oxford University Press, 2018.

Mathis-Lilley, Ben. "Bannon, Adviser Behind Travel Ban, Is Fan of Novel About Feces-Eating, Dark-Skinned Immigrants Destroying White Society." *Slate*, March 6, 2017. http://www.slate.com/blogs/the_slatest/2017/03/06/steve_bannon _and_the_camp_of_the_saints.html.

Mathy, Jean-Philippe. "Seeing Is Disbelieving: The Contested Visibility of 9/11 in France." In *9/11 in European Literature*, ed. Svenja Frank, 105–29. Cham: Palgrave Macmillan, 2017.

Mattéi, Jean-François. *Le Regard vide: Essai sur l'épuisement de la culture européenne.* Paris: Flammarion, 2007.

Matthews, Graham. *Ethics and Desire in the Wake of Postmodernism: Contemporary Satire.* London: Continuum, 2012.

Maudsley, Henry. *Body and Will.* New York: Appleton, 1884.

Maupassant, Guy de. *Pierre et Jean.* Trans. Julie Mead. Oxford: Oxford University Press, 2001.

McLane, Maureen N. *Romanticism and the Human Sciences: Poetry, Population, and the Discourse of the Species.* Cambridge: Cambridge University Press, 2000.

Meillassoux, Quentin. *Après la finitude: Essai sur la nécessité de la contingence.* Paris: Seuil, 2006.

Meizoz, Jérôme. "Le roman et l'inacceptable: Sociologie d'une polémique: Autour de *Plateforme* de Michel Houellebecq." In *L'œil sociologue et la littérature,* 181–209. Geneva: Slatkine Érudition, 2004.

Mélet, Xavier. "*Fécondité.*" *Le Temps,* October 13, 1899.

Ménard, Sophie. "Frénésie patrimoniale et monumentale: *Les Événements* de Jean Rolin." *Spirale* 259 (Winter 2017): 36–38.

Merlio, Gilbert. *Le Début de la fin? Penser la décadence avec Oswald Spengler.* Paris: Presses universitaires de France, 2019.

Messud, Claire. *The Emperor's Children.* New York: Knopf, 2006.

Meuret, Isabelle. "Le Journalisme littéraire à l'aube du XXIe siècle: Regards croisés entre mondes anglophone et francophone." *Contextes* 11 (2012). https://journals .openedition.org/contextes/5376.

Michallat, Wendy. "Modern Life Is Still Rubbish: Houellebecq and the Refiguring of 'Reactionary' Retro." *Journal of European Studies* 37, no. 3 (2007): 313–31.

Millet, Richard. *Désenchantement de la littérature.* Paris: Gallimard, 2007.

——. *Langue fantôme, suivi de Éloge littéraire d'Anders Breivik.* Paris: Roux, 2012.

——. *L'Enfer du roman: Réflexions sur la postlittérature.* Paris: Gallimard, 2010.

——. *L'Opprobre.* Paris: Gallimard, 2008.

——. *Province.* Paris: Éditions Léo Scheer, 2016.

Moix, Yann. "Années 80: La décennie où tout a basculé." *Paris Match,* August 22, 2016. http://www.parismatch.com/Actu/Societe/Annees-80-la-decennie-ou-tout-a -bascule-Par-Yann-Moix-1042588.

——. *Partouz.* Paris: Grasset, 2004.

——. *Terreur.* Paris: Grasset, 2017.

Morin, Violaine. "L'insaissisable Frédéric Lordon de la Nuit debout." *Le Monde,* April 19, 2016. https://www.lemonde.fr/idees/article/2016/04/21/l-insaisissable -frederic-lordon-maitre-a-penser-de-la-nuit-debout_4906449_3232.html.

Morrey, Douglas. "The Banality of Monstrosity: On Michel Houellebecq's *Soumission.*" *Australian Journal of French Studies* 55, no. 2 (2018): 202–17.

——. *Michel Houellebecq: Humanity and Its Aftermath.* Liverpool: Liverpool University Press, 2013.

——. "Natural and Anti-natural Evolution: Genetics and Schizophrenia in Maurice G. Dantec's *Babylon Babies.*" *L'Esprit Créateur* 52, no. 2 (Summer 2013): 114–26.

Moulaison, H. L. "The Minitel and France's Legacy of Democratic Information Access." *Government Information Quarterly* 21 (2004): 99–107.

Muhlmann, Géraldine. *Une histoire politique du journalisme: XIXe–XXe siècle*. Paris: Presses universitaires de France, 2004.

Müller, Jan-Werner. "Julien Benda's Anti-Passionate Europe." *European Journal of Political Theory* 5, no. 2 (2006): 125–37.

Muray, Philippe. *Chers djihadistes*. Paris: Mille et une nuits, 2002.

——. "Et, en tout, apercevoir la fin..." In *Michel Houellebecq*, ed. Agathe Novak-Lechevalier, 247–51. Paris: L'Herne, 2017.

Narjoux, Cécile, and Claire Stolz, eds. *Fictions narratives du XXIe siècle: Approches rhétoriques, stylistiques et sémiotiques*. Rennes: La Licorne, 2014.

Nora, Simon, and Alain Minc. *The Computerization of Society: A Report to the President of France*. Cambridge, MA: MIT Press, 1981.

Nordau, Max. *Degeneration*. Lincoln: University of Nebraska Press, 1993.

——. *Entartung*. Berlin: De Gruyter, 2013.

Novak-Chevalier, Agathe. *Houellebecq, l'art de la consolation*. Paris: Stock, 2018.

——. "*Soumission*: Littérature comme résistance." *Libération*, March 1, 2015. https://next.liberation.fr/culture/2015/03/01/soumission-la-litterature-comme-resistance_1212088.

Onfray, Michel. *Miroir du nihilisme: Houellebecq éducateur*. Paris: Galilée, 2017.

O'Sullivan, Michael. *Weakness: A Literary and Philosophical History*. London: Continuum, 2012.

Oualid, William. "La France deviendra-t-elle un pays de minorités nationales?" *Le Musée Social* 5–6 (1927): 160–84.

Ourednik, Patrik. *La Fin du monde n'aurait pas eu lieu*. Paris: Éditions Allia, 2017.

Palacio, Jean de. *La Décadence: Le mot et la chose*. Paris: Les Belles lettres, 2011.

Passard, Cédric. *L'âge d'or du pamphlet*. Paris: CNRS Éditions, 2015.

Passmore, Kevin. *The Right in France from the Third Republic to Vichy*. Oxford: Oxford University Press, 2013.

Peck, Henry Thurston. *Studies in Several Literatures*. Freeport, NY: Books for Libraries Press, 1968.

Peltier, Elian, and Nicholas Kulish. "A Racist Book's Malign and Lingering Influence." *New York Times*, November 22, 2019. https://www.nytimes.com/2019/11/22/books/stephen-miller-camp-saints.html.

Pérez, Claude. "Houellebecq, le vingt-heures et l'art du roman: À propos de *Soumission*." *Revue Critique de Fixxion Française Contemporaine* 11 (2015): 112–20.

Périer, Denis. *Le Dossier noir du Minitel rose*. Paris: Albin Michel, 1988.

Perreau, Bruno. *Queer Theory: The French Response*. Stanford, CA: Stanford University Press, 2016.

Perret, Pierre. "Interview." *Le Progrès*, November 16, 2018. https://www.leprogres.fr/france-monde/2018/11/16/pierre-perret-je-soutiens-les-gilets-jaunes-il-y-a-un-ras-le-bol-general.

Pettman, Dominic. *After the Orgy: Toward a Politics of Exhaustion*. Albany: SUNY Press, 2002.

Peytel, A. "Le Roman réaliste en Amérique." *Gazette littéraire*, June 25, 1864, 97–100.

Philippe, Elisabeth. "Aurélien Bellanger, le nouveau Houellebecq?" *Les Inrockuptibles*, August 20, 2012. http://www.lesinrocks.com/2012/08/20/livres/aurelien-bellanger-le-nouveau-houellebecq-11287237/.

——. "Aurélien Bellanger remporte le prix de Flore." *Les Inrockuptibles*, November 13, 2014. http://www.lesinrocks.com/2014/11/13/livres/aurelien-bellanger-remporte -prix-flore-11535357/.

——."La Critique littéraire est-elle en voie de 'zemmourisation'?" *BibliObs*, October 16, 2018. https://bibliobs.nouvelobs.com/idees/20181015.OBS3953/la-critique-litteraire -est-elle-en-voie-de-zemmourisation.html.

Plimpton, George. "The Story Behind a Nonfiction Novel." In *Truman Capote: Conversations*, ed. M. Thomas Inge, 47–68. Jackson: University Press of Mississippi, 1987.

Poirier, Agnès. "Is There No End to Books on the 'End of France'?" *Spectator*, April 21, 2018. https://www.spectator.co.uk/2018/04/is-there-no-end-to-books-on-the-end -of-france/.

Pool, Ithiel de Sola. "*The Computerization of Society* by Simon Nora and Alain Minc (Review)." *Technology and Culture* 22, no. 2 (April 1981): 352–54.

Poster, Mark. *Information Please: Culture and Politics in the Age of Digital Machines*. Durham, NC: Duke University Press, 2006.

——. *The Mode of Information: Poststructuralism and Social Context*. Cambridge: Polity, 2007.

Posthumus, Stephanie. "Les Enjeux animaux (humains) chez Michel Houellebecq, du darwinisme au post-humanisme." *French Studies* 68, no. 3 (July 2014): 359–76.

Potolsky, Matthew. *The Decadent Republic of Letters: Taste, Politics, and Cosmopolitan Community from Baudelaire to Beardsley*. Philadelphia: University of Pennsylvania Press, 2013.

Preciado, Paul B. *Testo Junkie*. Trans. Bruce Benderson. New York: Feminist Press, 2013.

Preston, Alex. "*Submission* by Michel Houellebecq Review: Satire That's More Subtle Than It Seems." *Guardian*, September 8, 2015. https://www.theguardian.com /books/2015/sep/08/submission-michel-houellebecq-review-satire-islamic-france.

Provost, Lauren. "Dans *Sérotonine* de Michel Houellebecq, voici ce qu'il y a de 'gilets jaunes.'" *Huffington Post*, January 3, 2019. https://www.huffingtonpost.fr/2019/01 /03/dans-serotonine-de-michel-houellebecq-voici-ce-quil-y-a-de-gilets-jaunes _a_23632459/.

Quetelet, Adolphe. *A Treatise on Man and the Development of His Faculties*. English translation. Edinburgh: W. and R. Chambers, 1842.

Rabaté, Dominique. "Extension ou liquidation de la lutte? Remarques sur le roman selon Houellebecq." In *Le Discours "néo-réactionnaire": Transgressions conservatrices*, ed. Pascal Durand and Sarah Sindaco, 265–79. Paris: CNRS Éditions, 2015.

Rabinowicz, Léon. *Le Problème de la population en France*. Paris: Marcel Rivière, 1929.

Rabosseau, Sandrine. "Houellebecq ou le renouveau du roman expérimental." In *Michel Houellebecq sous la loupe*, ed. Murielle Lucie Clément and Sabine van Wesemael, 43–51. Amsterdam: Rodopi, 2007.

Rachilde. "Les Romans. Émile Zola, *Fécondité*." *Le Mercure de France* 119 (November 1899): 485–93.

Ramsden, Maureen. "The Reporter as Artist: The Interrelation of Fact and Fiction in Reportage." *New Zealand Journal of French Studies* 33, no. 2 (November 2012): 23–49.

Raspail, Jean. *The Camp of the Saints.* Trans. Norman Shapiro. Petoskey, MI: Social Contract Press, 2018.

Raymond, Dominique. "Trois instances et un roman: *La Théorie de l'information* d'Aurélien Bellanger." *L'Esprit Créateur* 54, no. 1 (Spring 2014): 115–25.

Read, Max. "Does Even Mark Zuckerberg Know What Facebook Is?" *New York Magazine*, October 1, 2017. http://nymag.com/selectall/2017/10/does-even-mark -zuckerberg-know-what-facebook-is.html.

Renan, Ernest. *What Is a Nation?* Trans. Wanda Romer Taylor. Toronto: Tapir, 1996.

Rheingold, Howard. "Daily Life in Cyberspace: How the Computerized Counterculture Built a New Kind of Place." In *Social Media Archeology and Poetics*, ed. Judy Malloy, 61–85. Cambridge, MA: MIT Press, 2016.

——. *The Virtual Community: Homesteading on the Electronic Frontier.* Boston: Addison-Wesley, 1993.

Robinson, Charles. *Dans les cités.* Paris: Seuil, 2011.

——. *Fabrication de la guerre civile.* Paris: Seuil, 2016.

——. *Génie du proxénétisme, ou beautés de la religion péripatéticienne.* Paris: Seuil, 2008.

Roche, Jules. "La Révision de la constitution." *Le Figaro* 162 (June 11, 1897): 1.

Roger, Philippe. *L'Ennemi américain: Généalogie de l'antiaméricanisme français.* Paris: Seuil, 2002.

Roldan, Sébastian. "Victimes d'eux-mêmes ou de l'espèce? Darwin et les suicidés du roman naturaliste." In *Les voies de l'évolution: De la pertinence du darwinisme en littérature*, ed. Jean-François Chassay, Daniel Grenier, and William S. Messier, 75–100. Montreal: Presses de l'Université de Québec, 2013.

Rolin, Jean. *Les Événements.* Paris: POL, 2015.

Romains, Jules. *Men of Good Will.* Trans. Warre B. Wells. New York: Knopf, 1933.

Roosevelt, Theodore. "The Law of Civilization and Decay." In *American Ideals and Other Essays, Social and Political*, 318–42. New York: G. P. Putnam's Sons, 1897.

Rosenthal, Olivia. *Viande froide: Reportages.* Paris: Centquatre, 2008.

Roth, Marco. "The Rise of the Neuronovel." *N+1*, Fall 2009. https://nplusonemag.com /issue-8/essays/the-rise-of-the-neuronovel/.

Rouart, Jean-Marie. *Adieu à la France qui s'en va.* Paris: Grasset, 2003.

Roxburgh, Natalie, Anton Kirchhofer, and Anna Auguscik. "Universal Narrativity and the Anxious Scientist of the Contemporary Neuronovel." *Mosaic* 49, no. 4 (December 2016): 71–87.

Rubino, Gianfranco, and Dominique Viart, eds. *Le Roman français contemporain face à l'Histoire.* Macerata: Quodlibet, 2016.

Rüf, Isabelle. "En sillonant à pied Los Angeles, Jean Rolin enchante le roman d'espionnage." *Le Temps*, September 9, 2011. https://www.letemps.ch/culture /sillonnant-pied-los-angeles-jean-rolin-enchante-roman-despionnage.

Ruffel, Lionel. "Un réalisme contemporain: Les narrations documentaires." *Littératures* 166 (2012): 13–25.

Rufin, Jean-Christophe. *Check-point.* Paris: Gallimard, 2015.

Saenen, Frédéric. *Dictionnaire du pamphlet: De la Révolution à Internet.* Gollion: Infolio, 2010.

Sand, Georges. *Indiana.* Trans. Sylvia Raphael. Oxford: Oxford University Press, 1994.

Sand, Schlomo. *The End of the French Intellectual: From Zola to Houellebecq* (London: Verso, 2018).

Sapiro, Gisèle. "Notables, esthètes et polémistes: Manières d'être un écrivain 'réactionnaire' des années 30 à nos jours." In *Le Discours "néo-réactionnaire": Transgressions conservatrices*, ed. Pascal Durand and Sarah Sindaco, 23–46. Paris: CNRS Éditions, 2015.

Sayre, Robert. *La Sociologie de la littérature: Histoire, problématique, synthèse critique*. Paris: L'Harmattan, 2011.

Scarry, Elaine, ed. *Literature and the Body: Essays on Populations and Persons*. Baltimore, MD: Johns Hopkins University Press, 1988.

Schehr, Lawrence. "Effondrements: Frédéric Beigbeder's *Windows on the World*." *French Cultural Studies* 21, no. 2 (2010): 131–41.

——. *French Post-Modern Masculinities: From Neuromatrices to Seropositivity*. Liverpool: Liverpool University Press, 2009.

Schober, Rita. "Vision du monde et théorie du roman, concepts opératoires des romans de Michel Houellebecq." In *Le Roman français au tournant du XXe siècle*, ed. Bruno Blanckeman, Aline Mura-Brunel, and Marc Dambre, 505–15. Paris: Presses Sorbonne nouvelle, 2004.

Sénécal, Didier. "Michel Houellebecq." *Lire*, September 1, 2001, http://www.lexpress.fr /culture/livre/michel-houellebecq_804761.html.

Servigne, Pablo, and Raphaël Stevens. *Comment tout peut s'effondrer: Petit manuel de collapsologie à l'usage des générations présentes*. Paris: Seuil, 2015.

Servoise, Sylvie. "Roman à thèse et roman engagé: Exemplarité diégétique et exemplarité narrative." In *Littérature et exemplarité*, ed. Alexandre Gefen et al., 347–56. Rennes: Presses universitaires de Rennes, 2016.

——. "Roman engagé et roman à thèse: Les frères ennemis." In *Le Roman face à l'histoire: La littérature engagée en France et en Italie dans la seconde moitié du XXe siècle*, 41–75. Rennes: Presses universitaires de Rennes, 2011.

Sherry, Vincent. *Modernism and the Reinvention of Decadence*. Cambridge: Cambridge University Press, 2015.

Shonkwiler, Alison. *The Financial Imaginary: Economic Mystification and the Limits of Realist Fiction*. Minneapolis: University of Minnesota Press, 2018.

Shonkwiler, Alison, and Leigh Claire La Berge, eds. *Reading Capitalist Realism*. Iowa City: University of Iowa Press, 2014.

Shriver, Lionel. "Population in Literature." *Population and Development Review* 29, no. 2 (June 2013): 153–62.

Smith, David Nowell. "In the Midst of the Suicide of the West, It Was Clear They Didn't Stand a Chance." *Critical Quarterly* 58, no. 3 (2016): 27–46.

Sontag, Susan. "9.11.01." In *Susan Sontag: Later Essays*, ed. David Rieff, 709–10. New York: Library of America, 2017.

——. *Illness as Metaphor and AIDS and Its Metaphors*. New York: Farrar, Straus and Giroux, 1990.

Souchard, Maryse. "Towards a Semiotics of the Ideological Novel." *Sociocriticism* 2, no. 1 (October 1986): 47–68.

Spackman, Barbara. *Decadent Genealogies: The Rhetoric of Sickness from Baudelaire to D'Annunzio*. Ithaca, NY: Cornell University Press, 1989.

Spengler, Oswald. *The Decline of the West.* 2 vols. Trans. Charles Francis Atkinson. New York: Knopf, 1950.

Spieser-Landes, David. "Soumission ou simulacre de soumission? Michel Houelle-becq et la métaphysique (Baudrillardienne) du radiateur." *French Cultural Studies* 28, no. 1 (2016): 42–53.

Stendhal. *Le Rouge et le noir.* New York: Charles Scribner's Sons, 1931.

Suleiman, Susan Rubin. *Authoritarian Fictions: The Ideological Novel as a Literary Genre.* New York: Columbia University Press, 1983.

Sweeney, Carole. "'And Yet Some Free Time Remains . . .': Post-Fordism and Writing in Michel Houellebecq's *Whatever." Journal of Modern Literature* 33, no. 4 (Summer 2010): 41–56.

——. *Michel Houellebecq and the Literature of Despair.* London: Bloomsbury, 2013.

Taguieff, Pierre-André. *Les Contre-Réactionnaires: Le progressisme entre illusion et imposture.* Paris: Denoël, 2007.

——. *La Foire aux Illuminés: Ésotérisme, théorie du complot, extrémisme.* Paris: Mille et une nuits, 2005.

Taillandier, Fanny. *Par les écrans du monde.* Paris: Seuil, 2018.

Taine, Hippolyte. *History of English Literature.* Trans. H. van Laun. New York: Holt & Williams, 1871.

Tattersall, Mason. "Thermal Degeneration: Thermodynamics and the Heat-Death of the Universe in Victorian Science, Philosophy, and Culture." In *Decadence, Degeneration, and the End: Studies in the European Fin de Siècle,* ed. Marja Härmänmaa and Christopher Nissen, 17–34. New York: Palgrave Macmillan, 2014.

Tautil, Gérard. *Le Roman national français au défi de l'extrême droite.* Paris: L'Harmattan, 2016.

Thulié, Henri. "Le Roman. Le style." *Réalisme* 6 (April/May 1857): 86–87.

Tillinac, Denis. *Du bonheur d'être réac.* Sainte-Marguerite-sur-Mer: Équateurs, 2014.

Tiqqun. *Preliminary Materials for a Theory of the Young-Girl.* Trans. Ariana Reines. Los Angeles: Semiotext(e), 2012.

——. *Premiers matériaux pour une théorie de la Jeune-Fille.* Paris: Éditions Mille et une nuits, 2001.

Tournier, Pascale. *Le vieux monde est de retour: Enquête sur les nouveaux conservateurs.* Paris: Stock, 2018.

Touzot, Jean. "Du fait divers au roman: L'exemple de Mauriac." In *Roman et reportage XXe–XXIe siècles: Rencontres croisées,* ed. Myriam Boucharenc, 149–57. Limoges: Presses universitaires de Limoges, 2015.

Trudel, Éric. "Passions du réel (sur Philippe Vasset, Olivia Rosenthal et Thomas Clerc)." *Australian Journal of French Studies* 54, no. 2–3 (2017): 113–28.

Trumbull, Gunnar. *Silicon and the State: French Innovation Policy in the Internet Age.* Washington, DC: Brookings Institution Press, 2004.

Truong, Nicolas, ed. *Le Crépuscule des intellectuels français?* La Tour d'Aigues: Éditions de l'aube, 2016.

van Wesemael, Sabine. "Michel Houellebecq, figure de roman." In *Lectures croisées de l'œuvre de Michel Houellebecq,* ed. Antoine Jurga and Sabine van Wesemael, 31–47. Paris: Classiques Garnier, 2017.

Vantses, Martine. *Sexe et mensonge: Enquête sur la sexualité féminine auprès d'utilisatrices du minitel, des petites annonces et agences matrimoniales.* Paris: Éditions Joëlle Losfeld, 1993.

Varsava, Jerry Andrew. "Utopian Yearnings, Dystopian Thoughts: Houellebecq's *The Elementary Particles* and the Problem of Scientific Communitarianism." *College Literature* 32, no. 4 (Fall 2005): 145–67.

Vasset, Philippe. *La Conjuration.* Paris: Fayard, 2013.

——. *Journal intime d'un marchand de canons.* Paris: Fayard, 2009.

——. *Un Livre blanc.* Paris: Fayard, 2007.

Vasset, Philippe, and Olivia Rosenthal. "Entretien avec Philippe Vasset." *Littérature* 160 (December 2010): 30–36.

Vattimo, Gianni. *Of Reality: The Purposes of Philosophy.* New York: Columbia University Press, 2016.

Vercors. *Les Animaux dénaturés.* Paris: Albin Michel, 1952.

Viard, Bruno. *Houellebecq au scanner: La faute à Mai 68.* Nice: Éditions Ovadia, 2008.

——. "Houellebecq romancier catholique et socialiste." *Australian Journal of French Studies* 56, no. 1 (2019): 70–74.

——. *La République insoumise: Réponse à Michel Houellebecq.* Paris: Éditions Mimésis, 2016.

Viart, Dominique. "De la littérature contemporaine à l'université: une question critique." *Fabula.org*, March 20, 2008. http://www.fabula.org/atelier.php?De_la_litt%26eacute%3Brature_contemporaine_%26agrave%3B_l%27universit%26eacute%3B%3A_une_question_critique.

——. *Le Roman français au XXe siècle.* Paris: Armand Colin, 2011.

Viart, Dominique, and Bruno Vercier. *La Littérature française au présent: Héritage, modernité, mutations.* Paris: Bordas, 2005.

Vilain, Philippe. *La Littérature sans idéal.* Paris: Grasset, 2016.

Villette, Michel. "Thèses de sociologie et romans à thèse." *Sociedade e Estado* 17, no. 2 (2002): 541–60.

Virilio, Paul. *A Landscape of Events.* Trans. Julie Rose. Cambridge, MA: MIT Press, 2000.

Waldman, Amy. *The Submission.* New York: Farrar, Straus and Giroux, 2011.

Walter, Richard D. "What Became of the Degenerate? A Brief History of a Concept." *Journal of the History of Medicine and Allied Sciences* 11, no. 4 (1956): 422–29.

Wampole, Christy. "Poujade's Infowars: On Barthes' Anti-Anti-Intellectualism." *Yearbook of Comparative Literature* 62, no. 2016 (Summer 2019): 73–103.

——. *Rootedness: The Ramifications of a Metaphor.* Chicago: University of Chicago Press, 2016.

——. "What Is the Future of Speculative Journalism?" *New York Times*, January 22, 2018. https://www.nytimes.com/2018/01/22/opinion/speculative-journalism-future.html.

Weigel, Moira, and Mal Ahern. "Further Materials Toward a Theory of the Man-Child." *New Inquiry*, July 9, 2013. https://thenewinquiry.com/further-materials-toward-a-theory-of-the-man-child/.

Weinberg, Bernard. *French Realism: The Critical Reaction, 1830–1870.* Oxford: Oxford University Press, 1937.

Weinstein, Jay, and Vijayan K. Pillai. *Demography: The Science of Population.* 2nd ed. Lanham, MD: Rowman & Littlefield, 2016.

Williams, Thomas Chatterton. "'The French Origins of 'You Will Not Replace Us.'" *New Yorker,* December 4, 2017. https://www.newyorker.com/magazine/2017/12/04 /the-french-origins-of-you-will-not-replace-us.

Winock, Michel. *Décadence fin de siècle.* Paris: Gallimard, 2017.

Wolf, Nelly. *Le Roman de la démocratie.* Saint-Denis: Presses universitaires de Vincennes, 2003.

Wolfe, Tom. *The New Journalism.* New York: Harper and Row, 1973.

——. "Stalking the Billion-Footed Beast: A Literary Manifesto for the New Social Novel." *Harper's* 279, no. 1674 (November 1989): 45–56.

Wood, James. "Tell Me How Does It Feel?" *Guardian,* October 6, 2001. https://www .theguardian.com/books/2001/oct/06/fiction.

Wroblewski, Ania. "Les seuls blancs à Châtelet-les-Halles: Richard Millet, Michel Houellebecq et les limites du nationalisme français." In *Lectures croisées de l'oeuvre de Michel Houellebecq,* ed. Antoine Jurga and Sabine van Wesemael, 63–78. Paris: Classiques Garnier, 2017.

Yee, Jennifer. *The Colonial Comedy: Imperialism in the French Realist Novel.* Oxford: Oxford University Press, 2016.

Zanghi, Filippo. *Zone indécise: Périphéries urbaines et voyage de proximité dans la littérature contemporaine.* Villeneuve-d'Ascq: Presses universitaires du Septentrion, 2014.

Zeller, Florian. *La Fascination du pire.* Paris: Flammarion, 2004.

Zemmour, Éric. *Petit frère.* Paris: Denoël, 2008.

——. *Le Suicide français.* Paris: Albin Michel, 2014.

Zenetti, Marie-Jeanne. *Factographies: L'enregistrement littéraire à l'époque contemporaine.* Paris: Classiques Garnier, 2014.

Zerofsky, Elisabeth. "France's Frenzy Over the Discourse of Decline." *New Yorker,* December 17, 2014. https://www.newyorker.com/news/news-desk/frances-frenzy -discourse-decline-zemmour.

Zola, Émile. "Dépopulation." *Le Figaro,* no. 144 (May 23, 1896): 1.

——. *The Experimental Novel and Other Essays.* Trans. Belle M. Sherman. New York: Haskell House, 1964.

——. *The Fortune of the Rougons.* Trans. Brian Nelson. Oxford: Oxford University Press, 2012.

# INDEX

Scott, Walter, 21
*semence*, 57
Sénécal, Didier, 233n44
*sens du combat, Le* (Houellebecq), 167
sentimentalism, 68–69, 236n82
*Sérotonine* (Houellebecq), 26, 166, 179,
    212n117, 232n39, 237nn90, 91
sex: 9/11 as castration, 56–72; as economic
    solution, 56–60; kept mental, 102–3;
    literary excesses, 57–58; maximalism
    and overstatedness of, 34; *Minitel rose*
    and, 101–4; prostitution and sexual
    tourism, 42, 57–60, 101–2, 210n86,
    233n48; recreational versus
    reproductive, 28, 33, 35, 56–72;
    stalemate, 56–72; swingers, 66, 70;
    textual and sexual production related,
    34–35, 79; virtualization of, 29, 101–4
*sexagon*, 75–76
*Sexagon: Muslims, France, and the*
    *Sexualization of National Culture*
    (Mack), 75–76
sexism, benevolent, 72–73
sexual determinism, 103
sexual economy, 74, 172, 235n66
"sexual imperialism," 76–77
sexual liberalism, 210n85, 235n66
"Sexual Misery of the Arab World"
    (Daoud), 71
Shannon, Claude, 95
*Short History of Decay, The* (Cioran), 45
Shriver, Lionel, 40
silence, fear of, 34
Silicon Valley, 29, 218n45; as cult object,
    105, 114; French, 93, 100
Sindaco, Sarah, 15
Smith, David Nowell, 174–75
social body, deterioration of, 1–2
Social Contract Press, 133, 222n4
social Darwinism, 35, 52–56;
    *struggleforlifeurs*, 39, 204n25. *See also*
    Darwinism
socialism, 58
social media, 2, 5, 16, 42, 81–82, 123, 136.
    *See also* Facebook; internet; Minitel;
    Twitter
social multiplicity, 41

social sciences, 2, 18, 185, 204n18;
    parasitism of, 22. *See also*
    demography
*société du spectacle*, American, 63
sociologie-fiction, 56, 201n91
*soixante-huitards*, 145
Sola Pool, Ithiel de, 87
Sontag, Susan, 60, 102–3
space and place, theories of, 148
species, death of, 34–35
spectacularization, 68
speculative journalism, 136–37
Speiser-Landes, David, 168, 233n50
Spencer, Richard, 125
Spengler, Oswald, 4, 191n5, 205n41
Stendhal, 23, 24, 32, 86, 141
Stille, Alexander, 52
Stolz, Claire, 10, 194n28
*Story of O, The* (Aury/Réage/Desclos),
    169–70
*struggleforlifeurs*, 39, 204n25
subjective realism, 24, 26, 78
*Submission* (film), 170
*Submission* (Houellebecq), 7, 31, 46, 137,
    206n46, 224n25, 260n61; ambiguity
    of, 167, 178; characters, multiplicity
    of, 175–76; citations in, 174–75;
    collaboration in, 169; final chapter,
    236n79; François (character), 41–42,
    169–78, 234n58, 235n75, 236n78,
    238n7; *Grand Remplacement* in, 55;
    listening tour in, 175–78; as mediatic,
    144–45; plot, 168–69; as postmodern,
    167–68; religion in, 176–77; as *roman*
    *à thèse*, 166–79
Suffert, Georges, 52
suicide: Islamization as, 52, 55; national,
    1, 28, 33, 35, 36, 44, 51–52
*Suicide* (Durkheim), 51
*Suicide* (Levé), 51–52
*Suicide français, Le* (Zemmour), 11, 52,
    208n69
Suleiman, Susan Rubin, 2, 31, 158–60,
    163–65, 167
sun, extinguishment of, 94, 218n47
*surproduction*, 34
surrealism, 23, 66–67